Translating Rumi into the West

Focusing on Rumi, the best-selling Persian mystical poet of the 13th century, this book investigates the reception of his work and thought in North America and Europe – and the phenomenon of 'Rumimania' – to elucidate the complexities of intercultural communication between the West and the Iranian and Islamic worlds.

Presenting tens of examples from the original and translated texts, the book is a critical analysis of various dimensions of this reception, outlining the difficulties of translating the text, but also exploring how translators of various times and languages have performed, and explaining why the quality of reception varies. Topics analyzed include the linguistic and pragmatic issues of translation, comparative stylistics and poetics, and nontextual factors like the translator's beliefs and the political and ideological aspects of translation. Using a broad theoretical framework, the author highlights the difficulties of intercultural communication from linguistic, semiotic, stylistic, poetic, ethical, and sociocultural perspectives. Ultimately, the author shares his reflections on the semiotic specificities of Rumi's mystical discourse and the ethics of translation generally.

The book will be valuable to scholars and students of Islamic philosophy, Iranian studies, and translation studies but will appeal to anyone interested in the cultural dichotomies of the West and Islam.

Amir Sedaghat holds a PhD in translation studies and transcultural communication from the Université Sorbonne Nouvelle, Paris 3. He teaches translation at the University of Toronto, Canada. Specializing in semiotics, he focuses his research on intercultural and interreligious relations between the West and the Islamic World.

Iranian Studies

Series editors: Homa Katouzian
University of Oxford
Mohamad Tavakoli-Targhi
University of Toronto

Since 1967 the International Society for Iranian Studies (ISIS) has been a leading learned society for the advancement of new approaches in the study of Iranian society, history, culture, and literature. The new ISIS Iranian Studies series published by Routledge will provide a venue for the publication of original and innovative scholarly works in all areas of Iranian and Persianate Studies.

Judeo-Persian Writings
A Manifestation of Intellectual and Literary Life
Edited and Compiled by Nahid Pirnazar

Foreign Policy of the Islamic Republic of Iran
Between Ideology and Pragmatism
Przemyslaw Osiewicz

Secularization of Islam in Post-Revolutionary Iran
Mahmoud Pargoo

Iran's Green Movement
Everyday Resistance, Political Contestation and Social Mobilization
Navid Pourmokhtari

Poetry and Revolution
The Poets and Poetry of the Constitutional Era of Iran
Edited by Homa Katouzian and Alireza Korangy

Translating Rumi into the West
A Linguistic Conundrum and Beyond
Amir Sedaghat

Evidentiality in Sa'dī's Poetry and Prose
A Corpus Stylistic Study
Behrooz Mahmoodi-Bakhtiari and Masoumeh Mehrabi

For more information about this series, please visit: www.routledge.com/middle eaststudies/series/IRST

Translating Rumi into the West
A Linguistic Conundrum and Beyond

Amir Sedaghat

LONDON AND NEW YORK

First published 2023
by Routledge
4 Park Square, Milton Park, Abingdon, Oxon OX14 4RN

and by Routledge
605 Third Avenue, New York, NY 10158

Routledge is an imprint of the Taylor & Francis Group, an informa business

© 2023 Amir Sedaghat

The right of Amir Sedaghat to be identified as author of this work has been asserted in accordance with sections 77 and 78 of the Copyright, Designs and Patents Act 1988.

All rights reserved. No part of this book may be reprinted or reproduced or utilised in any form or by any electronic, mechanical, or other means, now known or hereafter invented, including photocopying and recording, or in any information storage or retrieval system, without permission in writing from the publishers.

Trademark notice: Product or corporate names may be trademarks or registered trademarks, and are used only for identification and explanation without intent to infringe.

British Library Cataloguing-in-Publication Data
A catalogue record for this book is available from the British Library

Library of Congress Cataloging-in-Publication Data
Names: Sedaghat, Amir, author.
Title: Translating Rumi into the west : a linguistic conundrum and beyond / Amir Sedaghat.
Description: Abingdon, Oxon ; New York, NY : Routledge, 2023. | Series: Iranian studies | Includes bibliographical references and index
Identifiers: LCCN 2022040547 (print) | LCCN 2022040548 (ebook) | ISBN 9780367744526 (hardback) | ISBN 9780367744533 (paperback) | ISBN 9781003157960 (ebook)
Subjects: LCSH: Jalāl al-Dīn Rūmī, Maulana, 1207-1273—Translations—History and criticism. | Jalāl al-Dīn Rūmī, Maulana, 1207-1273—Appreciation. | East and West. | LCGFT: Literary criticism.
Classification: LCC PK6482 .S43 2023 (print) | LCC PK6482 (ebook) | DDC 891/.5511—dc23/eng/20220916
LC record available at https://lccn.loc.gov/2022040547
LC ebook record available at https://lccn.loc.gov/2022040548

ISBN: 978-0-367-74452-6 (hbk)
ISBN: 978-0-367-74453-3 (pbk)
ISBN: 978-1-003-15796-0 (ebk)

DOI: 10.4324/9781003157960

Typeset in Times New Roman
by Apex CoVantage, LLC

À mes parents, Fatemeh et Sohrab

Et à ma fleur florissante

Contents

List of Figures — ix
List of Examples — x
List of Tables — xii
Foreword — xiii
Acknowledgements — xv
List of Abbreviations — xvi

Introduction — 1

1 First Order Linguistic Difficulties — 29

  1 Translatability as a Linguistic Principle 29
  2 Grammatical and Syntactic Problems 32
  3 Lexicological Difficulties 47
  4 Graphic Aspects of Translation 54

2 Translation or the Retrieval of the Discoursive Form — 62

  1 For a Theory of the Discoursive Form in Translation 62
  2 Connotative Semantics and Translation 89
  3 Linguistic Variations and Discoursive Heterogeneity 107

3 Recreating the Poetics of Rumi — 123

  1 The Music of Persian Poetry 124
  2 Music and Poetry in the Persianate World 132
  3 Hybrid Semiotic Systems 136
  4 Translating Rumi's Hybrid Discourse 142

4 Translating Rumi's Rhetoric — 153

  1 Comparative Rhetoric: An Elusive Classification 153

    2 Lexical Figures of Speech 155
    3 Figures of Syntagmatic Construction 164

5 Hermeneutics of Translating Rumi   177

    1 Translating as Understanding 177
    2 Mystical Discoursive (In-)Coherence 183
    3 Translating Figures of Thought 191
    4 The Hermeneutic Conundrum of Mystical Imagery 195

6 On the Politics of Reception   215

    1 Beyond Language and Discourse 215
    2 Sociocultural Aspects of Reception 216
    3 Ideological and Political Dimensions of Translation 230

7 Translation as an Ethical Locus   242

    1 The Aim of Translation 242
    2 Target-Oriented Positions 247
    3 The Analytics of Rumi Translations 253
    4 For an Ethics of Translating Rumi 260

Conclusion   270

Bibliography   279
Appendices   297
Index   309

Figures

2.1	The Saussurean sign	63
2.2	The Peircean sign	64
2.3	Hjelmslev's sign model	67
2.4	Connotative sign	70
2.5	Generative trajectory of discoursivization	72
2.6	Barbara Folkart's model of discoursivization	79
2.7	Factors of verbal communication	82
2.8	Jakobson's linguistic functions	82
3.1	Rhyme structure of *masnavi*	126
3.2	Rhyme structure of *robā'i*	126
3.3	Rhyme structure of ghazal and *qaside*	127
3.4	The meter of *Masnavi MI) l.1*	129
3.5	Graphic indication of a *Baḥr-e Sari'* used in D) G.37	129
3.6	The semiotic structure of Persian classical verse	140
3.7	The semiotic structure of *āvāzi* composition	140
5.1	Fields of indication and interpretation	182
5.2	Fields of indication and interpretation in translation	200
6.1	Constituents of the polysystem	217
6.2	Chronology of Rumi's reception in the Anglosphere	222
6.3	Chronology of Rumi's reception in other polysystems	222

Examples

1.1	M.I) l.1	35
1.2	M.I) l.8	36
1.3	M.I) l.30	39
1.4	M.II) l.130/135–136	40
1.5	D) G.2131, l.12	42
1.6	D) G. 522, l.1–2	43
1.7	D) G. 636, l.6–7	46
1.8	D) R. 90, l.1	48
1.9	M.I) l.12	48
1.10	M.II) l.132–133	49
1.11	D) Q.95, l.4	53
1.12	D) G. 464, l.5	54
1.13	D) G. 1462, l.6	55
1.14	D) G. 1145, l.15	56
2.1	M.III) 1751–1752	91
2.2	M.II) 116	93
2.3	M.I) 1207	94
2.4	M.I) 1207	94
2.5	M.III) l.1814–1815	101
2.6	M. II) l.105	102
2.7	D) G. 464, l.6–8, 11	103
2.8	D) G2131, l.11	108
2.9	D) G 441, l. 2, 14	108
2.10	D) G. 1521, l.1, 9	110
2.11	MIII) l. 1723–1725, 1790	113
2.12	M.IV) l.1334, 1336–13382	115
2.13	M.V) l.511	116
3.1	D) R. 1891	131
3.2	D) G37, l.1–2, 5	131
3.3	D) G. 95, l.1–3	145
3.4	D) R. 447	146
4.1	M.I) l.11 and 15	157
4.2	G. 527, l.8	159

4.3	Q. VII) l.8	160
4.4	D) G. 436, l.8	163
4.5	D) G. 2039, l.5	165
4.6	MII) l.1741–1742	165
4.7	D) R. 846	168
4.8	MIII) l.1754	170
4.9	D) R. 1104, l.2	171
4.10	D) R. 1104, l.2	172
4.11	D) G) R. 1315	173
5.1	MI) l.1758	192
5.2	MI) l.1735	192
5.3	MI) l.1751	194
5.4	D) G. 464, l.2	195
5.5	D) G. 1759, l.1,4	198
5.6	MIII) l.1766–1768	201
5.7	D) G. 527, l.7	203
5.8	MII) l.125	204

Tables

Appendix I Rumi's Life		299
I	Rumi's Life	299
Appendix II Rumi Translations		300
I	Chronology of English Translations	300
II	Chronology of Translations: French	305
III	Chronology of Translations: German	306
IV	Chronology of Translations: Italian	307
V	Chronology of Translations: Spanish	307
VI	Chronology of Translations: Russian	308

Foreword

The present monograph is primarily based on seven years of research work conducted in the framework of a Université Sorbonne Nouvelle doctorate dissertation (Sedaghat 2015) on a corpus of over 72,000 words comprised of passages from *Masnavi-ye Ma'navi* and *Divān-e Shams-e Tabrizi*, along with the totality of their existing translations in English and French, and an analysis of the reception of Rumi's work and thought in the West. A large array of contrastive textual analyses was presented, juxtaposing Rumi's source text with all its existing French and English translations. In the present book, however, a more concise goal is set: only English-language translations of Rumi, in a limited number of the most relevant ones, will be the object of a contrastive analysis. This strategy was adopted for various simple reasons. The extent of the translations of Rumi in various European languages as well as the sheer volume of his original works do not allow for a multilingual textual analysis in the framework of this research monography. Moreover, the importance of the reception of Rumi's work in the English-speaking world through translation, retranslation, and adaptation overshadows its reception in any other European linguistic and cultural sphere, including in the French-, German-, and Russian-speaking worlds – despite the latter world's long-lasting tradition of Iranian Studies. In any case, as will be shown, a large number of translations in European languages other than English, including the French translation of *Masnavi* by Eva de Vitray-Meyerovitch, are in fact *retranslations* of an earlier English version. This phenomenon also occurs in most Spanish versions of Rumi's work that are based on American versions, themselves often retranslations of the *classical* versions presented by English scholars Nicholson and Arberry. Nevertheless, the reception of Rumi's work in other major cultural spheres of the "Western world" will not be neglected. Comparisons will be made with the translation of Rumi's work in other languages in an attempt to understand the scope of the unique American cultural phenomenon of Rumi cult known as *Rumimania*. As the title of the present monography indicates, the question of translation is tackled not only from a linguistic standpoint but also by adopting a diverse theoretical approach in order to go *beyond* the text, the author, and the translator to look at a multifaceted cultural phenomenon from a higher altitude.

As for the corpus of this study, it is comprised of *all* published English translations of Rumi's poetic works by well-known and respected international editors and excludes numerous attempts to translate Rumi's poetry proliferating on the Internet, in blogs, and on social media. Translations in other languages are recorded in the Bibliography but are not analyzed in the examples and are technically not part of the corpus.

Due to the large number of references and in an effort to keep notes to a minimum, I have adopted the system of abbreviations to refer to original works and their English translations most commonly used in excerpts and comparative analyses. For the same reason, only the English transliteration of the original Persian text appears in the examples, unless graphic aspects of the Persian script are the specific focus of the discussion. As for the transliteration systems of Persian script, none seems to be satisfying. Among commonly used romanization systems, some have a rather misleading choice of symbols as they represent Persian alphabets in the light of their Arabic phonological characters. For instance, ALA-LC and IJMES both use symbols "i" and "u" to indicate Persian short vowels /e/ and /o/. Others, like the *Journal of Iranian Studies*, use a simplified system that fails to indicate the graphic distinction between various graphemes of Arabic origin that correspond to the same phonemes in Persian, that is indicating ص ث س by one symbol *s*. The most accurate transliteration system seems to belong to the *Encyclopedia Iranica*. Nevertheless, it uses special symbols š, č, and ž instead of *sh*, *ch*, and *zh* for ش چ ژ. This may make reading the Persian transliteration somewhat counterintuitive for English speakers. Consequently, I opted for a modified version of the Library of Congress ALA-LC Romanization Table[1] to preserve the graphic accuracy of the first group and the phonetic authenticity of the second group while avoiding the complexity of the third group of these transliteration systems. The only modification concerns the use of short vowels: *e* instead of *i* for the short vowel /e/ indicated by *kasreh* and *o* instead of *u* for the short vowel /o/ indicated by *zammeh* in the Persian alphabet. As a result, there is no need to use ū for the long /u/ and ī for the long /i/ as they are represented respectively by *u* and *i*. As for the transliteration of Arabic, ALA-LC Romanization rules are followed with no modification.

Note

1 *Cf.* www.loc.gov/catdir/cpso/roman.html

Acknowledgements

I am indebted to my colleague and dear friend Mireille Truong, without whose astute advice and generous assistance the accomplishment of this work would have never been possible.

I am grateful to my spiritual father, the French philosopher and author Pierre Dortiguer, who was a great teacher and a true source of inspiration for many, including me.

I also thank my supervisors and the members of my panel in my PhD thesis: Professor Christine Raguet, Professor Yann Richard, and Professor Mohammad Ali Amir-Moezzi, for their comments and advice, which helped me in the preparation of the original research that preceded this monograph by seven years.

I express my gratitude towards Professor Mohammad Tavakoli-Targhi from the University of Toronto, whose suggestions and advice helped improve the relevance of certain pedagogical points and the clarity of this book.

Abbreviations

1 General References

D.:	*Divān-e Shams-e Tabrizi* Foruzānfar's edition
Ex :	English translation number *x*
Fx :	French translation number *x*
G.:	Ghazal number according to Foruzānfar's edition
L.:	Line (or verse) number in the original text
M.:	*Masnavi-ye Ma'navi*, Nicholson's Edition, followed by book number
R.:	*Robā'i* (quatrain) number according to Foruzānfar's edition
SL:	Source language
ST:	Source text
TL:	Target language
TN:	Translator's note
TT:	Target text
13xx [xxxx]:	Iranian Solar Hejri year [Gregorian equivalent]

2 Translations

Ac:	Arberry 1956
Am:	Arberry 1968/1972
Ap:	Arberry 1964
Ar:	Arberry 1949
At:	Arberry 1961/1963
Bb:	Barks 2007
Be:	Barks 1995
Bo:	Barks and Moyne 1999
Bs:	Barks 2002
Bt:	Barks 1988
Bu:	Barks 2001
Chi:	Chittick 1984
Cow:	Cowan 1997
Erc:	Ergin 1992
Erf:	Ergin and Johnson 2006

Erj:	Ergin and Johnson 2007
Erm:	Ergin 1993
GaFa:	Gamard and Farhadi 2008
Hal:	Harvey 1988
Hel:	Helminski 2000
Helr:	Helminski 2010
Her:	Helminski, 2000
Hom:	Homayounfar 2007
Jam:	Jambet 1998
Khd:	Khalili 2001
Khf:	Khalili 1994
Lel:	Anvar 2011
Lr:	Franklin Lewis 2007
Ls:	Franklin Lewis 2008
Mag:	Mafi 2004
Maw:	Mafi 2000
Moj:	Mojaddedi 2004/2007
Nid:	Nicholson 1898
Nim:	Nicholson 1900–1921
Nir:	Nicholson 1950
Red:	Redhouse 1881
Sab:	Saberi 2000
Sch:	Schimmel 1996
Shg:	Shiva and Star 1992
Shh:	Shiva 1999
Shr:	Shiva 1995
Sta:	Star 2008
SWJ:	Sir William Jones 1791
Taj:	Tajadod 1993
Tch:	Tchelebi 1950
Vm:	Vitray-Meyerovitch 1990
Vo:	Vitray-Meyerovitch 1973
Vr:	Vitray-Meyerovitch 1987
Whi:	Whinfield 1887
Wil:	Wilson 1910
Will:	Williams 2006

Introduction

Translation as Revelation

The question of language is a crucial one, as it is at the heart of all human intellectual activities. The semiotic system par excellence, language is not only a means of expression, that is, a tool of communication but, most importantly, the generator of meaning. If linguistic semiosis (the genesis of meaning) is likely not the only source of meaning, it is at least the main way of understanding, since it is the interpreter of all other semiotic systems: human language is the only system that interprets all other systems of meaning.[1] In this capacity, language is what translates the world to the mind and, here, I use "translation" in the broader sense of the term, coming from the Latin *translatio* [transfer]. Translation is at the core of the linguistic operation since to transfer is what language is supposed to accomplish: the transfer of meaning – from a person to another, from a semiotic system to another, from a source of knowledge to a recipient – or, perhaps, more importantly, the transfer of reality from the experienced *sensible* world to the understood *intelligible* world. That is probably why German idealists from Schleiermacher and Hölderlin to Antoine Berman to Walter Benjamin saw in translation a salutary shortcut to *pure language* and a pivotal linguistic activity in which the problems of language are manifested like nowhere else (Benjamin [1913] 2004). George Steiner, the British polymath, goes far enough in his *After Babel* (1975) to consider the very act of understanding as translation. He considers any understanding as an act of translating the sensible world into the intelligible realm of the mind. By its nature and in its end, ontologically and pragmatically, translation is the revelation of *hidden* aspects, not only of the source text or language, nor only of the target language (TL), but also of language itself. Translation can reveal the reality of language and thus the epistemology of culture. Revelation here is taken in a Heideggerian sense, that is ἀλήθεια, *Unverborgenheit* [unconcealment], a recurring theme also in the works of mystic authors like Rumi. The translational operation can tear apart the veil of the reality of the text, translator, and the very fundamental functioning of language.

Studying translation in all three senses attributed to it by Roman Jakobson[2] – intralingual, interlingual, and intersemiotic – can therefore be of utmost value when it comes to the reception of a major figure of Islamic mysticism in the Western world[3] through the translation of his major works. It can potentially reveal

DOI: 10.4324/9781003157960-1

2 *Introduction*

numerous otherwise hidden facts about this quintessential instance of intercultural communication, ongoing since the late 18th century to the present day at various linguistic, hermeneutic, ethical, and even sociopolitical levels. Understanding and interpretation of the mystical poetry of Rumi already constitutes a remarkable case of interlingual translation. The way Rumi used various semiotic platforms such as language, music, and *samā'* to create a unique hybrid medium to generate and convey meaning can be studied as an attempt to reach, through intersemiotic translation, not only a pure language but a pure semiotic system. In a more restrictive and commonplace definition, interlingual translation is the main means of communication between various cultural spheres bound by specific languages. Translation seems to be the main tool in bridging the gap between two fundamentally remote if not opposing cultures: a 13th-century Persian poet becomes for many years the top best-selling foreign-language author in the United States of America.

This curious phenomenon can raise a plethora of questions. How can the incredible success of Rumi's poetry in North America and, to a lesser extent, in the West, sometimes called *Rumimania*, be explained? (Lewis 2007, 1–5). To what extent have English translations and adaptations of Rumi poetry done justice to the original work? What have been the motivations and intentions of the translators and editors engaged in this somewhat lucrative business of transcultural communication? What are the fundamental difficulties of translating Persian classical poetry on the one hand, and the complex if not hermetic thought of a mystical Sufi like Rumi on the other hand? Are these difficulties mainly of a linguistic nature or are there other more hidden obstacles of other natures, such as rhetorical, hermeneutic, and even sociopolitical? What are the nature and intensity of these difficulties and what are the strategies adopted by various translators belonging to different epochs and countries to render an adequate if not accurate version to their consecutive readers? What can be learned from their strategic choices or adherence to certain translation norms?

On an epistemological level, one can use the case of the translation of Rumi to reflect upon more basic problems of translation as a fundamental act of linguistic communication. Is translation of poetry possible at all, especially of the kind of poetry that tries to surpass the limits of verbal communication in its attempt to integrate other semiotic systems?[4] How is the interlingual translation of mystical poetic works a function of their intralingual translation within the source language, that is the exegetical commentaries destined to help understand the text? Translation of formally elaborate poetry like that of Rumi also raises questions on an ethical level. How should the translator proceed to preserve the most from the semantic content while recreating the formal structure? What difficult choices are to be made, what is to be sacrificed in a frustrating operation that is substantially associated with loss? These are only some of the major questions discussed in this book.

An Interdisciplinary Effort

To tackle the various aspects of the question, this essay adopts a multidisciplinary approach that relies on theoretical devices borrowed from linguistics, textual analysis, literary criticism, hermeneutics, poetics, cultural studies, Islamic philosophy, and above all, semiotics. This large array of disciplines meeting at the junction of the problematic of translation are indispensable to help understand a surprising example of transcultural communication, the modalities of which are to be observed, described, and explained. This multidisciplinary approach is in fact in line with the interdisciplinary nature of translation studies[5] to which the present study at least partially adheres. Born as an independent discipline in the second half of the 20th century, translation studies has the theory and the practice of translation as its subject.[6] In recent decades, translation studies has established itself both as a privileged multidisciplinary field of research in humanities, touching upon theories generated in linguistics, sociology, philosophy, and psychoanalysis, and as a discipline in its own right within the language sciences.[7] This growing popularity, on both sides of the Atlantic, is due to the fact that translation is at the heart of language problems,[8] not to mention the growing number of texts, literary or not, translated between languages and cultures increasingly distant from each other, a trend that is gaining momentum with technological advances in the field of telecommunications.

If the question of translation occupied a central place in the work of philosophers and thinkers dating as early back as Cicero (106–43 BC) and Saint Jerome (AD 347–420), the debates concentrated on the dialectic relation of two opposed poles: sense-for-sense or word-for-word translation. One can see a sheer preference for free content-based translation with little attention to the formal aspects of the source text in the Western Christian world[9] since Cicero, who famously boasted that he translated Greek to Latin "not as an interpreter, but as an orator" (Cicero [46 BC]1960, 364). The priority has always been to preserve the meaning and the spirit of the text with less regard for the particularities of the source text. The imperative was clarity and conformity to the TL practices. The only exception was made for the Holy Scriptures, as indicated by Saint Jerome in his historic letter to Pammachius (Letter LVII) about his translation of the Bible:

> For I myself not only admit but freely proclaim that in translating from the Greek I render sense for sense and not word for word, except in the case of the Holy Scriptures, where even the order of the words is a mystery.
> (Jerome 1989, 286)

Saint Jerome originated the idea of "dynamic equivalence" in translation, that is the recreation of an equivalent sense in TL that imitates the effect of the source text without preserving the exact words. However, while he adheres to the general paradigm of semantic content prevailing over discoursive form in interlingual transfers, he recognizes the mystery hidden in the form of the text, albeit exclusively in the context of the sacred. This recognition leads to an epistemological dimension in the theory of translation, which will be one of the fundamental arguments of this book in terms of translatability and translation ethics. The problematic is to determine if "the mystery of the syntax" can exist in profane texts.

Despite the frenzy around this perennial epistemological debate on translation, attitudes remained practically in favor of clarity sacrificing ST (source text) formal features on the altar of readability and elegance of the TS (target text) throughout the Renaissance when, liberated from the monopoly of Latin, classic texts were translated into vernacular languages. The move started with daring efforts of such Protestant reformist theologians as William Tyndale, Étienne Dolet, and Martin Luther, who translated the Holy Book into English, French, and German respectively. Luther, for instance, was criticized by the Church for taking great liberties in adapting the text of the Scripture to the taste and norms of his German dialect, hence altering its content when necessary. This attitude deviates even from the explicit exception made by Saint Jerome in the translation of sacred texts.[10] One can observe similar preoccupations with style and clarity at the expense of form in the translation of profane texts throughout the classic era, when classical Greek and Latin literature were translated into European languages. It is in this era that notions like *fidelity*, *spirit*, and *truth* were debated among translators and variably conceptualized according to contexts. The global understanding then was that while the translator needs to be the *fidus interpres* [faithful interpreter] of the ST, word-by-word translation was deemed awkward and weak since the *truth*, that is the content of the text since Saint Jerome, and the *spirit*, that is the inspiration or creative energy of the text, were intertwined, and the commitment was to be to the *spirit* of the text and not its form. In other words, a truly faithful translation had to be faithful to the sense and not the form of the ST. Moreover, the classical norms of writing were dictated, since ancient Rome, by grammatical principles of correctness, purity, and clarity, as well as rhetorical (stylistic) values of elegance and dignity. John Dryden, in his translation of Ovid, recognized three categories of translation as *metaphrase* (literal), *paraphrase* (translation with latitude following the sense), and *imitation* (equivalent of today's adaptation), fostering the second and rejecting the others. A translator was expected to recreate the genius, force, and spirit of the original text in the target text and do as if the author had created the text in the TL to begin with. Dryden boasts, "I have endeavored to make Virgil speak such English as he would himself have spoken, if he had been born in England, and in this present age" (quoted in Munday (2012, 44). The translator's job was, therefore, to *naturalize* the text within the target culture.

It is with German Romantics like Herder, Humbolt, Goethe, and especially Schleiermacher that this translation paradigm began to change. Translation became a central activity of cultural enrichment, making the foreignness of the translated text not a weakness but a source of wealth. Schleiermacher moves the debate beyond the word-for-word, literal, versus sense-for sense, free translation. He places the concept of faithfulness on a binary spectrum consisting in the choice between bringing the author to the foreign reader or the reader to the foreign author. Differentiating between *Dolmetscher* [technical translation] and *Übersetzer* [literary translation], Schleiermacher advocates for an *alienating* (foreignizing as Venuti puts it) rather than a *naturalizing* (domesticating) process in literary translation in order to educate the reader and move toward a pure ideal language (Venuti [1995] 2008). These revolutionary ideas continued to impact reflections on translation to the modern time through thinkers such as George Steiner and Walter Benjamin. In the mid-20th century, though, translation studies started off as a branch of Applied Linguistics with first theorists among linguists who used linguistics to propose prescriptive theories[11] for equivalence in translation (Nida's theory of dynamic and formal equivalence). Later, the cultural turn regarded translation not as a purely linguistic product but also as a social and cultural phenomenon. Descriptive theories of translation took the lead over prescriptive ones with the School of Tel Aviv under the influence of Jakobson's structural model of communication functions. Also, functional theories of translation in Germany and the English-speaking world dominated the scientific examination of translation. With Antoine Berman and Henri Meschonnic in France, and their counterpart Lawrence Venuti in North America, translation studies revived the philosophical debates initiated by German Romantics by introducing an ethical aspect to the transfer of texts between languages and cultures.

Translation studies is a reflexive discipline, affirms French scholar Jean-René Ladmiral,[12] in the sense that it constantly questions its own purpose, asking for instance, "what is the use of translation studies?" to which one can answer, to remedy "the difficulties of translation." Now the more complex the difficulties, the more effective the remedies must be. Nonetheless, this relatively young discipline, born in Europe, has been so far more concerned with translations within European languages. More recently its methods have been applied to study of more distant understudied regions like Hebrew, Arabic, Turkish, and Persian, but this trend must continue and be given impetus since the difficulties of transferring the message between more remote linguistic and cultural zones require deeper descriptions and more ingenious solutions. Applying the various theories of translation, in particular descriptive theories, to literary texts translated from Persian into European languages represents a solid research potential that can contribute to the enrichment of the discipline. This is the objective of this research. The need to broaden the research field of translation studies by addressing the problems of literary translation from Persian is felt all the more since there have been very few serious studies in this field since the beginning of the emergence of the discipline, despite a long tradition of studies of the Iranian world, "Iranology," which has occupied an important place in European universities since the end of the 18th century and, more recently, in North America.

Translation of Rumi in the English-speaking world in particular, and in the Western Christian world in a broader view, can be analyzed on two main levels: the linguistic and stylistic difficulties of transferring the discourse on the one hand and the extra- or nonlinguistic issues of the translation of mystical texts on the other, namely hermeneutic problems, questions of ethics of translation, and sociocultural circumstances of the reception. In other words, difficulties are initially examined at the level of language, then at the level of text or discourse, before stepping up beyond the level of language to analyze the phenomenon from ethical and sociocultural standpoints. Thoroughness will be ensured by contrastive analysis of examples from the source and target texts to demonstrate different translators' strategies to overcome the obstacles in question. The problems of translation are investigated from three main perspectives: linguistic – syntactic and lexical aspects of the medieval text; stylistic – the poetic and rhetoric particularities of

Persian classical poetry; and pragmatic – taking account of the specific ways in which the author made use of his language and its devices to create his unique discourse. What follows the first level of linguistic analysis is a critical account of the hermeneutic challenges of the translation of Rumi's text and the ethical questions the translation of such discourse can raise. My analysis is both descriptive and prescriptive insofar as it stands to explain how and why certain target texts have deviated from the source text on the one hand, and to suggest what can be done in order to raise the quality of the translation of mystical poetic works on the other.

The book is also a sociolinguistic probe into the various main target cultural spheres in the West, in Europe and North America. Evaluating the modalities of the reception of Rumi through the translation of mystical poetic work in Western societies, I apply the polysystem theory to account for the frequency, quality, popularity, and reach of various waves of translation in different TLs and cultures from late 19th century to the present day. Furthermore, the book shows how ideological and political considerations have played a central role in determining the norms of translation and consequentially shaped the representation of Rumi's mystical work in the target cultural spheres. The present monography is, in short, a multidisciplinary effort to study the translation of one of the most emblematic figures of Persian literature, Islamic mysticism, and Iranian philosophy into the Western Christian world. By "translation" I mean more than just the common sense of the term as in interlingual transfer of a text. Here the term can be thought of in a much broader sense, in close relation to its etymology and to Christianity: the *translatio* [transfer] of the relics of Rumi, his thought and his work from their cultural Oriental homeland to their Occidental resting place of pilgrimage. What is lost of these relics in this perilous odyssey? How and why? To answer these questions, I will utilize translation as a moment of revelation, *dévoilement*, since it is the best window into the underlying hidden intricacies of language, of the *logos*.

Mystical Thought in the Islamic World

To refer to mysticism in the cultural zone known as the Islamic world[13] poses the first linguistic hurdle insofar as it seems difficult to find a perfect terminological equivalent in European languages for terms such as *taṣavvof* or *'erfān*, not to mention the difficulty of describing spiritual thought in Islam that, unlike in Christianity, cannot by any means be reduced to a religious phenomenon. "Philosophy" cannot be an appropriate term to refer to mystical thought in Islam either, given its lack of a unified systematic logic and epistemology. Even the polysemy of terms like *Sufism*, *mysticism*, and *gnosis*[14] with large connotational values varying with historical and geographical contexts poses an obstacle to the transposition of a concept from one linguistic system to another. While "Sufism" has been established as the English version of *taṣavvof*,[15] "mysticism" is more commonly used as an equivalent to the hypernym *'erfān*. The semantic conflict between source and target utterances starts here: "mysticism," from *mystical*, denotes "of or related to mystery,"[16] and evokes the unknown and the secret, a mysterious operation that takes place in the soul of the mystic, or the state of silence corresponding to the experience of standing in awe of a sublime phenomenon. In contrast, the Arabic term *'erfān* from the verb *'arafa* [to know][17] means the acquisition of supreme knowledge. As such, it is more closely related to the concept of *gnosis*. In other words, while the central notion in Iranian and Islamic *'erfān* is the quest for enlightenment, for direct and immediate ontological knowledge, the common idiomatic use of the term "mysticism" assimilates this practice and philosophy with the Western Judeo-Christian tradition of mystery and secret in esoteric spirituality. Moreover, the term *'erfān* is more common in modern Persian and almost interchangeable with its synonym, *taṣavvof* [Sufism], while *'āref* is preferred to *Sufi*, which has acquired over time a rather negative connotation as Henry Corbin points out (Corbin 1974, 1076). Historical reasons at the origin of the rather negative connotation of *taṣavvof* or *ṣufi-gari* [Sufi's attitude] among the Iranians are apparently both political and epistemological: the desire, after the advent of the Safavids, to break with the sociopolitical influence of the Sufi brotherhoods, which were an obstacle to the centralization of the ideological and clerical power of Shiism on the one hand, and the social stigma of the passive ascetic lifestyle or esoteric communitarianism, even secretive conspiration, associated with Sufi sects on the other. This semantic shift means that today, in the Iranian world, the term "Sufism" can have an ambivalent connotation: depending on whether it refers to ascetic practices, to the traditions and rituals of the Sufi brotherhoods, or whether it evokes mystical theosophy, it can have a negative or neutral connotation. In the second case, namely that of Sufism as thought, the terms *'erfān* and *'orafā* [mystics] (instead of "Sufis") are often privileged; hence Corbin's preference for the word *'erfān*. Throughout this research paper, the terms (Islamic) mystic and Sufi will be used interchangeably in conformity with the common uses in Western languages.

The use of the term "mystic" to refer to *'orafā* [gnostic/knower] in the West may be related to the fact that the occultist behavior of mystics seems to have overshadowed the gnostic character of the initial beliefs of mystical metaphysics, favoring a quest for personal spiritual knowledge over conformity with literalist religious doxa. The occultism of mystics can also be explained at different levels: on the one hand, the nature of Divine Truth is such that no word can be sufficient to describe it, that is to say the divine nature is ineffable. On the other hand, the spiritual quest for the Ultimate Truth can by all means be a great source of danger for mystics in different epochs and places because of their nonconformity with the religious dogma, hence their tendency to live on the margin of societies ruled by institutionalized religions. This danger led to some sort of a proclivity to live in brotherhoods and confreries of mystics, manifested in the monastic lifestyle of various Christian orders in the Western world and the Sufi orders in the Islamic world.

There is also a misconception about Sufism within the Western world given its restrictive association with the spiritual dimension of Islam. According to *Encyclopedia Britannica*, "Islamic mysticism is called *taṣawwuf* (literally, "to dress in wool") in Arabic, but it has been called Sufism in Western languages since the early 19th century" (Schimmel, Sufism n.d.). The epistemological impoverishment that can be seen in this rather reductionist definition of mysticism can have two negative effects: on the one hand, other forms of mystical thought in the Islamic world risk being excluded. On the other hand, the association of Sufism with certain sectarian occultist practices followed by organized brotherhoods and secret societies undermines the spiritual and most importantly metaphysical aspects of *'erfān*. In fact, what distinguishes Islamic mystic thought from the mainstream body of Islamic theology, both in its jurisprudence (*fiqh*) and its scholastic tradition (*kalām*), is rooted in a much broader epistemological and theological foundation that cannot be reduced to a lifestyle assimilated with asceticism or a social organization associated with Sufi brotherhoods. At the epistemological level, Islamic mysticism distances itself from what is known as *falsafe*, or Hellenic philosophy, and *hekmat*, or Islamic metaphysics in general. The core distinction lies in the concept of *hikmat-i ilāhi*, which Henry Corbin translates as "divine philosophy" or *theosophy* that corresponds to the thinker's rigorous intellectual process spurred by and guided by divine light. This mystical philosophical method, according to Corbin, is neither limited to one branch of Islam nor constitutes a separate branch from it, as has been misconceived and misrepresented by some modern depictions of the Islamic world, juxtaposing Sufism, Sunnism, and Shiism as independent schools. As Henry Corbin stresses, the mystical dimension of Islam is by no means limited to the "metaphysics of Sufism"; it manifests itself in the "oriental" theosophy of Sohravardi, known as the philosophy of *eshrāq* [illumination], in *hikmat-e yamāni* or *imāni* [of Yemen or of faith] theosophy, and especially, in the purest forms of Shiite theosophy (Corbin 1974, 1067–1077). When it comes to the knowledge of God and his/her word, for Corbin, the most fundamental characteristic of *'erfān* – in all its forms and not only Sufism – is its approach to the question of knowledge and its hierarchy:

> Between *Kalām*, on the one hand, and what is designated, on the other hand, as *hikmat-i ilāhī* (metaphysics, literally "divine philosophy", etymologically *theosophia*), *'irfān* (mystical theosophy), *hikmat-i ishrāqīya* ("oriental" theosophy), *hikmat-i yamānya* ("Yemeni" theosophy, by interference between the word Yemen and the word *īmān*, faith), there is all the distance which separates the certainty of theoretical knowledge (*'ilm al-yaqīn*) and the certainty of personally realized and lived knowledge (*haqq al-yaqīn*).
> (1974, 1071)[18]

The keyword here is "lived knowledge." To understand the full dimensions of its meaning, one needs to be familiar with the fundamentals of *'erfān* in its various forms. In short, the common denominator between all these forms of mystical metaphysics consists of a set of ontological, phenomenological, and epistemological fundamental principles. It is, above all, the ontological core of the system that can be observed in its subsequent phenomenological and epistemological ramifications. Firstly, the unity of existence or the idea that *being* is only one and the One Being, which could be understood as the transcendent unique God in a simplified argument, is the source of all sorts of beings in existence. This idea, widely elaborated and theorized by Molla Sadra Shirazi, is known as *vahdat-e vojud* [the unity of existence]. There is a crucial distinction to be made here between *vahdat-e vojud*, which postulates the unity of *existence*, and the idea of the unity of *existent* that is the basis of Vedic cosmogony and ontology, also found in Western philosophy in the *pantheism* of thinkers like Spinoza. While pantheism considers the unity of being in one existent that is God and corresponds to the whole of universe and nature, *vahdat-e vojud* postulates the unity of existence in God in whom the universe and all existents exist and of whom all existence emanates. As such, the unity of existence in its Islamic mystical sense should be understood more as a form of *panentheism*. This seminal differentiation is reflected in the two mystical statements *lā mawjud illā allāh* [there is no existent but God] and *lā wojud illā allāh* [there is no existence but God].[19] It is in this sense that the mystic can become one with God once he takes full account of the illusion of his self. Thus, antinomic statements made by a Sufi like Hallaj, deemed even by his Sufi contemporaries as *gholov* [exaggerations], when he affirmed "*ana al-haq*" [I am the Truth], can be perfectly explained in the light of this worldview.

Secondly, the separation of the *zāher* [apparent], the exoteric aspect of being, and the *bāten* [hidden interior], the esoteric dimension of being, is at the core of mystical phenomenology. This duality may seem at first sight in contrast to the strict unity of existence in God, but one needs to distinguish the ontological nature of the former from the phenomenological essence of the latter. The hidden reality of phenomena can be different or even radically opposed to its apparent aspect and, in this dichotomy, it is always the hidden or esoteric truth that is taken into account. The exoteric and esoteric understandings of reality, applicable to all entities, become of remarkable importance in the context of exegesis of the Holy Scripture. Mystical exegesis or *ta'wil* [ascending] constantly seeks to surpass the surface of the text by ascending to the higher exoteric layers of the word of God. In fact, the sacred text can by no means be fully understood at the literal level; it has multiple layers of which the deepest are only known to the figure of the *imam* – for the Shias for instance. It goes without saying that in the very likely event of a contradiction between the esoteric and exoteric meaning of the text, it is the deep esoteric spiritual meaning that prevails. The annulation or abandon of the exoteric, the surface reality, in favor of the esoteric or deeper reality is, in fact, ubiquitous not only vis-à-vis the exegesis of sacred texts, but in all aspects of life. The omnipresence of the notion of *secret* in Islamic gnosis (*'erfān*) is a direct consequence of its esoterism. The heart of the mystic saint must be a safe chest of secrets to which initiated disciples gain access only after spiritual growth and once they obtain the capacity to absorb higher levels of the manifestation of esoteric truth. It is of utmost importance that secrets, or esoteric realities, remain concealed and not be revealed to the lay. Otherwise, the fate of the imprudent mystic would that of Hallaj,[20] as Hafez puts it:

> He said: "that companion whose head was exalted on the gallows;
> His crime was that he revealed the secrets."
>
> (*Divan*, Q.143, V.8)

10 *Introduction*

By the same token, there are numerous allusions to the secrets of creation. The following ṣalavāt or benedictional prayer, dedicated to Fatemeh, clearly alludes to her as the bearer of a mystery as the mother of the twelve Saint Imams:

> Oh God, praise Fatemeh and her father, her husband, and her children, and the secret concealed in her, to the extent to which your knowledge reaches.

According to some interpretations, this secret is the holy existence of the Hidden Imam. It also shows the importance of the feminine character of Fatemeh, whose epithet is *zahrā* or the most illuminated.[21]

Thirdly, on the epistemological level, appears the question of divine knowledge, that is, how God can be known by the knower. Perhaps the most radical revolution of Islamic mysticism can be found in this dimension insofar as the basic intellectual process consisting in the knower knowing the known is revered. It is not the knower that is the *subject* of the act of knowing, that *knows* the *known*, that is the *object* of the act of knowing: God, as the source of all being, is not the object of the knowledge; s/he can only be the *subject* of the knowledge. In other words, it is the Divine Truth that is the *subject* of the act of knowing in a process of manifestation whereby God reveals her/himself to humans who become the *objects* of this act of epiphany. This is what breaks the dialectic of the knowing *subject* and the known *object* – a fundamental notion for *kalām*. It is the *object* of knowledge that becomes the *absolute subject*, which, "absolved from all objectivity," must manifest itself to the primitive *subject*: "It is the Divine subject who is in fact the active subject of all knowledge of God" (Corbin 1974, 1076). In this process the receiving and active organ of knowledge ceases to be the intellect – or brain in a modern sense – but is the heart. It is the notion of *theophany* that is the ultimate goal in mystical theosophy as well as in Christian *speculative theology* according to which Divine Truth appears to the mystic's heart as in a mirror (*speculum*).[22]

There are evidently several subsequent metaphysical principles that are subsumed in this mystical worldview, some of which are common to non-Islamic or nonmystical doctrines, like Hellenic, Mazdean, and medieval philosophies. Some of these concepts will be brought up in subsequent chapters, namely those of the hierarchy of existence at the cosmic level, the concept of the division of the cosmos in different realms, the microcosm–macrocosm analogy or the relations between macrocosmic and microcosmic bodies, the idea of *ensān-e kāmel* or the accomplished human. Among these common concepts, the division of the cosmic realms into three hierarchical domains is of particular importance in Sufism: *'alam-e jabarut* [the world of power] or *'alam-e 'oqul* [the intelligible world] corresponds to the spiritual realm, which is the highest level of existence; *'alam-e malakut* [the world of dominion] assimilated to *'alam-e meṣāli* [the world of images], whose equivalent in European medieval philosophy *mondus imaginalis* is the intermediary realm of being where spiritual bodies are manifested; and finally *'alam-e nāsut* or *'alam-e nāsut* [the sensible world], which consists in the material and physical dimension of being (Corbin 1990). The projection of the intelligible realm is on the imaginal realm which, itself, influences the material realm. *Jabarut* is the platonic realm of pure forms, whereas the imaginal realm is that of immaterial beings like angels who represent bridges between the highest plane and the lowest, that of the sensible world. The imaginal world is perhaps the most important plane of existence insofar as it is the place of epiphany. Mystics strive to purify their soul to access this realm hoping for a reunion with the source of being. A purified mystic's heart then becomes the mirror (*speculum*) in which is reflected the divine light, or what Mazdeans called *khwarne* or the light of glory. Such humans are the manifestations of God's nature; God shows his/her face by an act of theophany. Such a person is the paragon that is followed by all mystics who aspire to reach his/her rank in the hierarchy of existence, far higher than that of even angels. The concept of *ensān-e kāmel* is central to both Shiism and Sufism; however, whereas it corresponds to the figure of *morshed* or spiritual leaders in Sufi metaphysics, very much comparable to Vedic gurus, in Shia esoterism, especially the Twelver branch, it remains more abstract, restricted to the status of Saint Imams: Ali, the most accomplished of all accomplished men, and his progeny with Fatemeh, Mohammad's daughter and the figure of accomplished woman.[23]

Mystics' lives are then entirely focused on their progression on a path towards ultimate illumination motivated by love. The concept of love, the subject of a particularly elaborated theory by Ruzbahan Baqli, becomes almost the single central notion of mystics like Rumi. Love is at the same time the reason for creation by the emanation of divine light, what holds the universe together and what pushes every creature to desire to reunite with its source of being. Love is also what motivates mystics to undertake the long and painstaking mystical odyssey. That is because mystical praxis consists of a journey, divided into stages, that raises humans from a lower earthly existence to higher spiritual levels and, ultimately, to the beatitude of union with the *Beloved*.[24] The metaphors of spiritual journey and pathfinding are best shown in the Sufi term of *tariqat* [path], which means the journey of the Sufi as a spiritual *rahrow* [wayfarer]. In this quest for enlightenment, the mystic is no longer satisfied with knowing *Ḥaq* [Truth] but seeks to become one with it, as a parcel of its being. This union implies the denial of self to the point of entire self-annihilation. Here lies this heterogeneous character of the mystical experience, akin to an extreme erotic drive, a passionate pulsion dissolving the created in its Creator, its source of light, its source of being. Moreover, the Divine Truth is associated with feminine desirability in the symbolism of mystic poetry. This vision has given rise to an exquisite abundance of antimonial bacchanalian language in the mystical literature as well as the prose work of the Andalusian mystic Ibn Arabi. Persian poetry is teeming with erotic imagery, passionate descriptions of a lover's chagrin, his suffering caused by the estrangement of his beloved, his longing for reunion, the fire of love consuming him from within, a state of intoxication by the wine of love, the moments of intimacy between lovers, even erotic descriptions of sensual encounters with the beloved. This *ad hoc* poetic language has developed over several centuries and has deeply marked Persian literature to this day. Mystical poetry has created a paradigm from which it is difficult to escape even in modern times, a paradigm to which various poets have contributed, in varied styles, from Sanāyi to Attār, Bābā Ṭāher, Neẓāmi, Rumi, Saʻdi, Hafez, and Jāmi, among others. As it is explained in Chapter 5, contrary to a common orthodox exegetic tradition, the antinomian language of mystic poetry should not be interpreted as mere metaphors, that is, second-degree statements of which the literal meaning must be rejected in favor of a second deeper meaning. These are symbols where both semantic levels of the statement must be kept for a complete interpretation. For the mystic, the duality of body and spirit or the dichotomy of earthly and divine love is well surpassed in a state of ecstasy.

If the terminology and the ideas evoked here resonate, it is because Islamic mysticism was not born in a vacuum. The key concepts of mystical thought, such as the unity of being, the dichotomy of noumena (*bāṭen*) and phenomenon (*ẓāher*), or Sufi/Shia cosmological model, bear close resemblances to ideas present in non- or pre-Islamic philosophies: Hellenic Neoplatonism, Iranian Mithraism and Mazdeism, or Vedic Buddhism. The syncretic nature of mysticism in Islam is actually a serious point of contest among Muslims as well as Islamic scholars. The origins of Sufism and its epistemological compatibility with an Islamic orthodoxy founded upon a literalist exegesis of the Koran and Muhammad's tradition (*sunna*) have given rise to an interminable controversy. The fundamental epistemological and pragmatic differences between the literalist character of orthodox Islam and mystical metaphysics have spurred long debates and controversies about the origins of the mystical thought. In his four-volume opus magnus, *Literary History of Persia*, Edward Browne offers a synthesis of the origins of mysticism in Islam. He examines four hypotheses (Browne [1906–1908] 1997, 416–422). The first is the official version of most Sufis, and supported by many Western Islamic scholars today, but refuted by Browne and the vast majority of his contemporaries, according to whom the mystical component of Islam has its roots in the Koran and the prophet's life. The final goal of Sufi teachings embodied in various *tariqats* is parallel to, and in perfect harmony with, the dominant thought of Islamic orthodoxy embodied by *kalām, fiqh* (Islamic jurisprudence). Mystical thought proposes a spiritual interpretation of the sacred text deeper than the literalist perspective, accompanied by an ascetic lifestyle reminiscent of the prophet or other saints. The main argument of these thinkers is that *tariqat* and *sharia* are two faces of the same coin and have the same end goal.

The second hypothesis, quite popular in the 19th century, is radically opposed to the first one. It considers Sufism as the Aryan reaction of the Iranian and Indian peoples to a Semitic religious and ideological invasion. This is especially the idea defended by Palmer (Palmer 1867, ix–xii),[25] regarded unfavorably by Browne, who does not see enough points of contact between Indian civilization and the Muslim world to support this hypothesis. Although such statements as Edward Browne's may be dismissed today as residues of orientalism[26] given the present zeitgeist of political correctness, one cannot deny that early Western Islamic scholars had a certain sincerity as external observers and that their points of view can only be corroborated by the antimonial nature of some Sufi practices. Although the attribution of mysticism to anti-Islamic reaction and non-Semitic ethnic resistance may sound somewhat reductionist, the theory of the decisive influence of Iranian and Indian religions on Islamic gnosis has also drawn attention since late 20th century among several Iranian and Indian thinkers. Iranian philosopher Daryush Shayegan, in his thesis on Hinduism and Sufism (Shayegan 1979), points to the work of Indian mystic and Mughal prince Dārā Shokuh (d. 1659), who presented a strong case for the profound influences of Vedic philosophies on Sufism. More recently, Mostafa Vaziri published a monography on what he calls the rebellion of Rumi and Shams (Vaziri 2015, 137–154) and the Vedic origins of their mystical thought, highlighting concepts like *Brahman*, *maya*, *samsara*, and *atman* resurfacing in Rumi's thought in the form of the unity of being, the hierarchy of existence, the sorrow of separation, and the self.

The third thesis, supported by Raymond Nicholson, perhaps the most renowned translator and specialist of Rumi, is that of the influence of Neoplatonism (Nicholson [1898] 2001, xxv–xxxv). This view is to some extent shared by Henry Corbin, who calls Sohravardi and his disciples the "Neoplatonists of Iran." Unlike Nicholson, who finds in Neoplatonism the source and inspiration of Sufism, Corbin argues in favor of the common origins of Hellenic and Islamic Neoplantonic thought in Mazdean angelology (Corbin 1974). This is perhaps due to the fact that Corbin had a more profound understanding of other forms of *'erfān*, in Islamic thought as well as a deeper understanding of Iranian pre-Islamic monotheism, finding the nexus between the two traditions in a theosophy of illumination (*eshrāq*). Browne, himself, hypothesizes an independent albeit eclectic source of Sufism, attributing its emergence to the spiritual quest "common to mystics of various times, beliefs, and countries" (Browne [1906–1908] 1997, 421). Abdolhossein Zarrinkub, the Iranian historian, recognizes an even higher degree of syncretism in Islamic mysticism. He presents various events and worldviews as the contributing factors to the emergence of Sufism, such as Mazdeism, through the figure of Salman of Persia's influence, Manichaeism – itself a 3rd-century syncretistic religious reform of Mazdeism by incorporating Christian and Buddhist elements to Mazdean dualism, Buddhism, Mandaean Gnosticism, and Neoplatonism, among others. Nonetheless, Zarrinkub does not single out one philosophy as the main source of Sufism (Zarrinkub, *Josteju dar Taṣavvof-e Iran* [Searching in Iranian Sufism] 1369 [1990], 4–28).

Whatever the origins of mystical thought in Islam, certain facts are undeniable about the metaphysics and praxis of Islamic gnosis. Firstly, mystical ideas have had a very uneasy relation with the orthodox proponents of an essentially legalist religion. Even some of the Western advocates of the Islamic nature of Sufism, mostly Sufis, spiritualists, or traditionalists, admit the depth of the gap that separates orthodoxy and spirituality in Islam, a religion dominated by a rigid jurisprudential framework and an obsessive application of sharia.[27] René Guénon, the French traditionalist philosopher, recognizes that "of all traditional doctrines, the Islamic doctrine is the most clearly marked by the distinction . . . between exoterism and esotericism" (Guénon 1973, 13). Another example is Annemarie Schimmel, the German scholar of Rumi, herself a Sufi, who examines the theories about the origin of mysticism, admitting its syncretic nature (Schimmel 2011, 3–22). She evokes several hypotheses highlighting the influence of Christian and

Vedic thoughts in the mystical cosmogony of Islam. Another aspect of Islam's gnostic phenomenon is that most manifestations of mystical metaphysics in the Islamic world either originated and/or thrived in the Iranian land or the Persianate world. Edward Granville Browne, one of the forefathers of modern Islamic Studies, says about Sufism: "its chief home, if not the centre and well-spring, [is] in Persia" (Browne [1906–1908] 1997, 418–419). These manifestations of mysticism often stand in sharp contrast and opposition to the core dogma of Islam. If mystical Islam and institutional Islam have more or less successfully cohabited throughout centuries, from time to time, the contrast between them, their opposition have given rise to major, deep conflicts in the context of which an orthodox legalist interpretation of religion based on an exoteric literal interpretation of the Koran has not been able to tolerate doctrinal dissent and has led to excommunications and accusations of heresy even to our days.[28] Nicholson explains this by reiterating Austrian orientalist Alfred von Kremer's observation:

> Although on the surface Islam is not directly assailed, it sustains many indirect attacks, [by the Sufi thought] that all religions and revelations are only the rays of a single eternal Sun; that all Prophets have only delivered and proclaimed . . . the same principles of eternal goodness and eternal truth.
> (Nicholson [1898] 2001, xxvi)

Islam is not a monolith. Like other religions it has multiple faces in both theory and praxis. Any discussion on the origins of spiritual mysticism as well as its place in relation to the core dogma of Islam cannot be without serious consequences at both epistemological and pragmatic levels, within and without the Islamic world. Likewise, various views on Rumi's place and role in the wider Islamic mystical doctrine can only have major repercussions on the minds and decisions of those who were the point of entry of his thought and works in the West. Choices made by Rumi's Western translators and commentators can then be examined and interpreted as indicators of underlying ideological tendencies at all levels of the transcultural communication.

Rumi: An Eastern Mystic in the West

Rumi is an Oriental mystic in the Occident, in both the literal and the figurative sense of the term: geographically and epistemologically. On the one hand, he was born on the eastern boundaries of the Persianate world[29] in a region situated today at the border of Afghanistan and Tajikistan while he lived his entire life in the westernmost part of the Islamic Empire in western Anatolia; on the other hand, his thought was deeply influenced by the Vedic philosophy well established in his native Bactria thanks to the long-standing presence of Buddhists since the Parthian Empire, while remaining a Muslim mystic, with striking resemblances, like his peers, to a Napoleonian paradigm of gnostic metaphysics. It should not come as a surprise then his works and thought do not cease to appeal in the modern heartland of Western civilization, North America, given his dual belonging to two diagonally opposed geographic zones and the remarkable capacity of his system of thought to bridge the deepest ideological gaps of all times. His principle of nonbelonging is well reflected in a famous ghazal attributed to him:[30]

> What solution is there, o Muslims? As I don't know myself
> I am no Christian, nor am I Jewish, nor Zoroastrian, nor Muslim.
> Neither am I of the East, nor the West, neither am I of the Earth nor the sea;
> Neither am I of natural elements, nor am I of the rotating skies.

Jalāleddin Mohammad-e Balkhi or Rumi, better known in the Persianate world as Mowlānā [our master][31] or Mowlavi, was born in 1208 in Vakhsh near Balkh (the ancient region of Bactria, an Achaemenid satrapy) in the eastern part of the Persianate world corresponding to present-day Central Asia. His father, Bahā'oddin Valad, a notable theologian and mystical himself, decided to leave the family's homeland under the Khwarazm shahs, most probably following a dispute with a local overlord or, according to a less likely popular myth, in anticipation of the Mongolian invasion.[32] Rumi's father set out on a long journey that included a pilgrimage to Mecca, finally settling in Konya [Iconium] in western Anatolia, invited by the local ruler to move to these newly conquered territories of Islam under the sultanate of Rum. In Konya, in a heterogeneous society – made up of Greek, Turkish, and migrant populations – Bahā'oddin obtained the chair and dean of the madrasa of the city. Rumi himself, meanwhile, after several years of studies in Islamic philosophy and theology (jurisprudence, *kalām*, Koranic exegesis) under the supervisions of his master, Borhānoddin Mohaqqeq, and Sufism under his father, eventually succeeded the latter after his death as a theologian and preacher, in Syria in particular. Rumi assumed the responsibilities of his father ensuring the management and teaching of various courses at the madrasa until his legendary meeting with Shamsoddin Mohammad Tabrizi (aka Shams of Tabriz), a wandering dervish, a cynical qalandar[33] with a fiery attitude.[34] This encounter turned Rumi's life upside down. A sober intellectual on a conventional Sufi course became a singing and dancing ecstatic mystic ready to sacrifice his name and fame for a short moment of Shams's presence. Shams is the first theophany for Rumi, the incarnation of the Absolute Truth.

This meeting, amply recounted, crystalized, and mystified in different versions by various hagiographers of Rumi,[35] will forever mark his life and thought, as well as Persian mystical literature. Rumi finds Shams to be a true theophany, an incarnation of God. He then falls madly in love with Shams, with a burning passion whose qualities and peculiarities have few examples in the literature and history of Iranian mysticism. It is after this encounter that Rumi begins to compose lyrical poetry. This relationship is even more dramatic in its sequel: a few years later, after a passing eclipse and a short reunion, Shams (whose name "Shams" literally means "the sun") disappears for good (probably murdered by Rumi's jealous entourage who cannot stand the profound metamorphosis of their teacher). During these years spent together, and after his beloved's disappearance,

16 *Introduction*

Rumi composes one of the most abundant works in Persian literature (and perhaps in world literary history). This passion transforms this sober preacher into a perplexed dervish, an Islamic jurist into a wine drinker, a man of reason into a fearless gamer of the love bet:

> An ascetic I was; you turned me into a singer.
> The troublemaker of the circle, the relentless wineseeker.
> Nobly dwelling in my prayer rug I was,
> You turned me into the laughingstock of the street kids.
> *(Divan* Q. 1891)

The profound influence of Shams on Rumi was judged intoxicating and scandalous by Rumi's circle of disciples and family, who could hardly stand an obscure wandering dervish spending hours, if not days, alone behind closed doors with their master. Shams's cynicism and aggressive nonconformist behavior did not help alleviate the situation either. He is forced to leave Konya under the pressure and fearing reprisal. His sudden disappearance leaves Rumi in despair. He longs for the vanishing beloved and keeps composing lyrical odes and quatrains. Rumi sent his son for Shams, who was found in Aleppo and brought back to Konya. Rumi's jubilation would not last long as Shams disappears for a second time and, this time, forever.[36] The devastation is total for Rumi who would burn in Shams's fire until the end of his life. Nevertheless, his love chagrin proved to be a source of matchless wealth for Persian literature. Rumi's lyrical and mystical *Divan* is amongst the finest and largest in the history of world literature. Although not leading to the same level of revolutionary intensity, Rumi would have two more epiphanic encounters of this type like that of Salāḥeddin Zarkūb. Towards the end of his life, on his students' advice, he undertakes the redaction of his Sufi didactic work *Masnavi*. After Rumi's passing in 1273, his disciples and descendants founded a Sufi order called *Mevleviyya* (the Turkish pronunciation of *Mowlavieh*) specially known in Europe since the 19th century as the whirling dervishes because of the widespread practice of the spiritual musical and dance concerts of *samā'*.[37]

Regarding Rumi's place in the constellation of Islamic thought, particularly in Islamic mysticism, two major elements in his biography must be noted: his education, realized thanks to his father, Bahā'oddin Valad, and to Borhānoddin Moḥaqqeq, his main teacher, and his encounter with Shams, his spiritual master. The origin of Rumi's thought is, in reality, to be found in the teachings of his father, Bahā'oddin Valad, theologian, preacher, notable jurist of his native region (Khorasan), but also a mystic himself, whose speeches and epigraphs collected in a volume entitled *Ma'āref* [the knowledge/the teachings] by Foruzānfar (Bahā'e Valad 1352 [1973]) constitute a mystical (esoteric) interpretation of passages of the Koran and hadith (prophetic tradition). If Rumi was already predisposed to Sufism from being Bahā'e Valad's son and successor as a notable and teacher of Islamic jurisprudence with an important mystical vocation,[38] it was his encounter with Shams that raised him to a whole new level of quest for divine love. This turning point in Rumi's life turned him from what is commonly called a sober mystic to an ecstatic one. The contrast between these two faces of the author is reflected in the general themes and tone in his two major poetic works. Rumi, on his own, incarnates the conflict that opposes the orthodox dogma of Islam and the heterodoxy of gnostic spirituality, which can be seen among other mystic poets such as Hafez, Sa'di, and Neẓāmi. It is hard to determine his adherence to or rejection of the exoteric legalist aspect of religion based on textual evidence insofar as contradictory statements and paradoxical positions in his poetry and discourses do not point to a clear conclusion. If antimonial declarations are abundant in his poetry, enough for any orthodox Muslim legalist to dismiss him as a heretic or for any secular reader to praise him as an anti-Islamic resistant, his official adherence to the Islamic religious institution and belonging to the Muslim community is beyond contest. His *Masnavi* is in fact a spiritual *exegesis* of the Koran. References to the Koran and hadith are omnipresent in his work. This kind of paradox and ambiguity is typical of Iranian mystics. That is why they chose poetry, the language of metaphor and symbolism par excellence to express their thoughts. Rumi expressed his stance on exoteric and esoteric aspects of religion, perhaps most explicitly in the preface of Book IV of *Masnavi*. He breaks down the three aspects of faith as *shariat* [law], *tariqat* [path], and *ḥaqiqat* [truth]. He recognizes the authenticity of the three notions, considering that they pursue the same goal. Nonetheless, he puts them in the order of importance, with Truth being the ultimate goal.

Rumi's Work and Its Western Adventure

Rumi's work can be classified according to its content and literary form: poetry and prose. His poetic work is comprised of a lyric divan [poetic collection] of some 35,000 *beyts* [lines/verses][39] by the name of *Divān-e Shams-e Tabrizi* (named after Shams of Tabriz to whom it is dedicated), also known as the *Divān-e Kabir* [the great *divan*], a collection of over 3,200 ghazals [odes] and 800 *robā'i* [quatrains] edited for the first time by Badi'ozzamān Forūzūnfar in the middle of the previous century from the Konya codex. Towards the end of his life and on the advice of his disciples, Rumi undertook the composition of a major didactic work consisting of six books of some 25,688 mystical couplets narrating various stories and parables, named *Maṣnavi-e Ma'navi* [Spiritual Couplets], edited for the first time by Reynold Alley Nicholson, who was also its first English translator.[40] There are also two texts in prose: *Fihi mā fih*, whose Arabic title means "Is inside what is inside" and corresponds to Rumi's discourses, and *Maktūbāt*, which is the collection of his correspondences. Adopting a thematic approach, we can divide this body of creations into two categories, that of didactic works on the one hand, namely *Masnavi*, *Fihi mā fih*, and *Maktūbāt*, and that of lyrical texts on the other, collected in his *Divan*.

These divisions can only be approximate. There are, in fact, many verses and passages of a lyrical character in the *Masnavi* and verses with a didactic undertone in the *Divan* especially among the quatrains. The qualifiers "lyric" and "didactic" are also far from doing justice to the spirit of Rumi's mystical work: if indeed the thematic structure of *Masnavi* makes it a book of mystic teachings, much as Shabestari's *Golshan-e rāz* intended for disciples of *tariqat*, it is, nonetheless, a narrative work with philosophical content on subjects as varied as life, marriage, love, justice, free will, religion, food, and customs, among others. Concerning structure, *Masnavi* consists of six books that contain mostly disparate narratives, in addition to the preludes, including that of *Book I*, entitled *Neynâme* [The Book of the Reed Flute], one the best-known passages in Persian literature. These stories can be organized into one or more subchapters that follow one other without necessarily following a specific thematic or chronological order. It is very common to see in the middle of a story subchapters telling parallel stories or giving educational speeches, mystic lessons, or the narrator's analytical comments. This peculiar structure, as discussed in Chapter 5, is reminiscent of that of Holy Books such as the Old Testament or the Koran and carries many hermeneutic consequences. The poetic genre of *Masnavi*, as its title suggests, is *maṣnavi* [couplet] where the two *meṣra'* [verses] of each *beyt* [line] rhyme, giving each line its autonomous rhyme. In Persian prosody, *maṣnavi* plays the role of the Alexandrian in French poetry, both being used for very long poems, thanks to their prosodic maneuverability in terms of meter and rhyme. Before Rumi, Ferdowsi used the same structure in his opus magnus *Shāhnāme*, Nezāmi in his *Panj Ganj* [The Five Treasures], and Attār in his *Manṭeq-o al-ṭṭayr*. There are three poetic forms in the *Divan*: ghazal, a genre comparable to odes or sonnets, accounting for over 85% of the content, *robā'i* or quatrain,[41] and *tarji'band*, a similar form to the ghazal with some thematic nuances. Rumi's poetic work is immense by all standards, in excess of 60,000 lines. Given that every *beyt* equals on average two verses in English in terms of the number of syllables, this poetic work exceeds some 120,000 verses. As pointed out by Lewis (2007, 314), Rumi composed more verses than did Homer, Milton, Dante, or Shakespeare. These staggering numbers suggest spontaneity on the part of the poet. Rumi hagiographers, such as Aflāki (Manāqeb alārefin [1318] 1362 [1983]) or Sepahsalār (1328), talk about Rumi's extemporaneous composition of some ghazals while dancing around a column in his madrasa in a state of ecstasy.

The sheer length of Rumi's poetic work is probably one of the reasons why he has been one of the best-known and most frequently translated Iranian poets in the West. No other Persian-speaking author and no other Persian work is even nearly subject of as many translated titles published in the English language, and this includes Omar Khayyam, Hafez, Sa'di, and Ferdowsi. Rumi's immense work has been entirely translated into English at least once, if not directly from Persian then at least from Gölpinarli's Turkish version (Dîvân-i Kebîr: [Yazan] Mevlānā Celāleddin 1957–1960). All of *Masnavi* has been translated more than once into English and many ghazals and quatrains several times. This is true to a much lesser extent in French and German. Translations into other Western languages are mostly retranslations from English or French. It is particularly in more recent times, i.e., the end of the 20th century to present, that translations and adaptations of Rumi's poetry have tremendously proliferated, leading to a phenomenon known as *Rumimania*.[42] Rumi's first translations were carried out at the end of the 18th century, in the Romantic era, when the taste for exoticism gave birth to a craze for the literature and culture of the East, attested also by the arrival of translations of Iranian poets like Hafez into German, French, and English.[43] The first contacts with Rumi's thought would have been made through observations of the practices of the Mevlevi dervishes,[44] known as whirling dervishes, and their ritual dance of *samā'* during the travels of diplomats and orientalists in the Ottoman Empire. That is the case, for example, of Clément Huart and his account, *Konia, la ville des derviches tourneurs: souvenirs d'un voyage en Asie mineure* (Huart 1897).

The first textual contacts with Rumi were made in the German-speaking world and by German-speaking people. Jacques van Wallenbourg, an Austrian diplomat in Istanbul in the 1790s, collected the manuscripts of the *Masnavi* and edited them in Persian. This should be considered the first modern edition of *Masnavi* and of Rumi's work. First German translations appeared in the 19th century with Valentin Freiherr von Hussard's translations in *Fundgruben des Orients*, a journal published by the Austrian diplomat, Joseph von Hammer-Purgstall. Later on, Freidrich Rückert (1822) made a success out of his adaptation of a few ghazals. Certain excerpts of the *Divan* and *Masnavi* appeared in Hammer-Purgstall's anthology entitled *Geschichte der schönen Redekünste Persiens* in 1818. August Graf von Platen in 1821 in Leibniz and Vincenz von Rosenzweig in 1838 in Vienna each published an anthology of Rumi's ghazals that have been republished numerous times. If the German reception of Rumi outdates that of all other European languages, it has not been nearly as consistent and successful as in English or even French. This may be explained by a number of factors, for instance, the fact that Hafez had already taken a very important place in German culture thanks to Goethe's interest in the latter's poetry and his relative disinterest for Rumi (Lewis 2007, 565). Also, as discussed in Chapter 7 in the light of the polysystems theory, the predominantly lyrical tone of Hafez's poetry may have appealed more to the aesthetic canon of German Romanticism than the didactic verses of *Masnavi*, whose Book I had been translated by Georg Rosen in 1849. The interest in Rumi was reborn in the Germanic world in the mid-20th century thanks to one of the most prominent Rumiologists of all time, Annemarie Schimmel (1922–2003), who published several monographies about Rumi and translations of his works in German as well as in English. After Schimmel's success, several translations and retranslations of Rumi have appeared in German, mostly from Persian and some from classical versions. More recently, the North American waves of Rumi's success have apparently spread to the German-speaking world, where not fewer than ten titles have appeared in the 21st century, half of which since 2015.[45]

There is a sad irony about the reception of Rumi in Francophonie. Jacques van Wallenbourg translated the *Masnavi* into French and if his translation had not been lost in a fire, French would have been the first European language welcoming the entire *Masnavi*. Subsequent French translations lagged considerably behind those published in German and English. Although French Rumi scholarship dates back to the late 19th century, it was not until 1949 that Henri Massé, in an *Anthologie Persane*, presented the first French translations of Rumi's poems in the *Divan* and *Masnavi*, along with *Roubâ'yat*, a selection of 276 quatrains published by a Turkish surrealist poet, Assâf Hâlet Tchélébi, in 1950.[46] The large wave of translations of Rumi into French are credited to Rumi's French translator, Eva de Vitray-Meyerovitch, who, in the 1970s, not only translated the entire *Masnavi*, a few hundred ghazals, and a collection of quatrains, but also the prosaic work of Rumi (including his letters). A member of the Centre national de la recherche scientifique devoting a lifetime to Mowlavi and Sufism, Vitray is also the author of several books on Sufism and Rumi. Most French translations of Rumi carry her name and a "Persian Speaker" by the name of Djamchid Mortazavi; nonetheless, her work has been criticized by certain French Iranian scholars for lack of transparency in terms of her source texts. It has already been demonstrated (Sedaghat 2015) how Vitray-Meyerovitch's translation of *Masnavi* is almost entirely based on Nicholson's English version. This evidence, along with her dependence on collaboration with Persian speakers in all other translations, sheds doubt on Vitray's actual command of the Persian language.

Later on, two other major attempts at translating ghazals were made: one by Persian speakers Mahin and Nahal Tajadod, in collaboration with Jean Claude Carrière (1993) and (2020), and the other by French scholar Christian Jambet (1999). More recently, another French scholar, Leili Anvar, specialist in Sufi literature, has devoted herself to Rumi's studies. Her *Rûmî, La Religion de l'amour* (2011) includes translations of excerpts of both the *Masnavi* and the *Divan*. There are also other French prose adaptions appearing in the 2000s.

As our tables and references[47] in this book demonstrate, in no other language, Indo-European or not, have Rumi's works been received nearly as well. The volume and frequency of Rumi translations in English even largely surpasses those in Arabic, Turkish, or Hindi, which are languages more closely related to Persian. Interest in Rumi began very early in Britain, with the publication of a first English translation of the prelude to *Book I* of *Masnavi* in *Asiatic Society* in 1791. This interest has continued to grow until today, taking various forms, from literal translation, in verse or prose, to freestyle versions, adaptations, and imitations. After that first attempt, English-speaking readers waited a while before getting access to Rumi's poetry in a published volume, although Emerson in Boston published a few retranslations from Hammer-Purgstall's German version. Despite their initial intention, neither Cowell nor FitzGerald was ever able to devote themselves to the business of translating Rumi (Lewis 2007, 570–572). It was Sir James William Redhouse who published a rhymed translation of *Book I* in 1881, along with a long introduction with numerous references to Aflāki's biography of Rumi. Edward Henry Whinfield provided a 3,500-line prose anthology of the six books of *Masnavi* in 1887, followed by a second volume of commentaries. Charles Edward Wilson, professor of Persian at Cambridge and the University of London, continued Redhouse's enterprise by publishing *Book II* in prose in 1910. Whinfield's and Wilson's translations respected the graphic aspect of the original poem, while remaining in prose, with each line corresponding either to a couplet (*beyt*) or to a verse. This model was followed by subsequent translators such as Nicholson and Arberry.

If there were a discipline called *Rumiology*, Reynold Alleyne Nicholson of Cambridge University would be its founding father. Edward Browne's student, Nicholson dedicated a lifetime's work to studying, translating, and commenting on Rumi. Nicholson even published the first Persian edition of Rumi based on the *Konia* manuscript. His complete translation of *Masnavi* (1926) and his selection of ghazals (1898), all in prose, as well as his attempts to versify these same translations are, still today, a reference for any researcher and translator of Rumi. Albeit to a lesser extent, that is also the case of Nicholson's successor at Cambridge, Arthur John Arberry, whose translations of ghazals and quatrains, as I shall demonstrate in this book, are still unsurmountable in terms of quality, elegance, and accuracy. Arberry's and Nicholson's translations are at the roots of a unique sociocultural phenomenon called *Rumimania* manifested in a myriad of translations, retranslations, and adaptations published in the United States since the second half of the 20th century up to now. A second popularizing wave of Rumi translations saw the light of day thanks to the emergence of a new generation of (re)translators who, Persian speakers and scholars aside, had no or little knowledge of Persian. They actually based their free versions on the translations of Nicholson and Arberry, which they judged too dry to be read by a large audience. Colman Barks and Kabir Edmund Helminski are the most successful and prolific of these popularizers – with more than 30 translation titles each – although there are also other major actors: Persian speakers such as Nader Khalili, Shahram Shiva, Maryam Mafi, Reza Saberi, and Houshmand; English speakers such as Thackston, Gupta, Star, and Bly; and Sufis such as the scholar William Chittick, Ibrahim Gamard, Nevit Ergin, and Turkmen. Annemarie Schimmel, the German Rumi scholar, has also published several works in English. In fact, a third wave of translations has emerged in recent years that can be referred to as the *return to the academic circle* and whose protagonists are specialists in Persian language and literature, such as Franklin D. Lewis, the prominent Chicago-based reference in Rumi Studies, and British scholars Alan Williams and Jawid Mojaddedi, who each has been publishing his new complete translation of *Masnavi*.

Rumi has been translated in other European languages as well, directly from Persian to Russian, Italian, Spanish, and Polish. There are also indirect translations based on English, French, or German versions into Swedish, Norwegian, Romanian, and Hungarian, among others. In Russia, for instance, where Iranian Studies is well rooted, Rumi scholarship dates back only to the 20th century with collective translations of Persian anthologies by state-sponsored institutions as early as the 1970s. In addition to some translations of William Chittick's English version in 1995, there have been a few direct translations of the *Divan*. A scholarly collective translation of the entire *Masnavi* has been offered between 2007 and 2012. Swedish translator Axel Eric Hermelin translated Nicholson's English version into Swedish in 1933, paving the way for further translations much later in the 2000s, almost all based on English. Władysław Dulęba first translated anthologies of Persian poetry to Polish where Rumi was well represented. There have been more attempts in recent years, albeit mostly based on English translations. The first Italian translations date back to 1980 with Alessandro Bausani's *Poesie mistiche* and to the 1990s with Sergio Foti's translation of *Fihe mā fih*. Most other translations are based either on the French versions, including Mandel's complete translation of *Masnavi* (2006), or on English versions, like Fiorentini's translations that are retranslations of Kabir Helminski. Given that both these versions are themselves retranslations offered by non-Persian speakers (Vitray-Meyerovitch and Helminski), one could be forgiven for doubting their Italian accuracy. A similar situation can be observed in the Spanish-speaking world, although most translations began to appear only in the 2000s, except Alberto Menzano's *Poema Sufíes* (1997). Most Spanish translations are based on English retranslations as well, namely Jonathan Star's. Clara Janés and Ahmad Taheri's translation of certain ghazals and quatrains from *Divan* (2006 and 2015), as well as Mahmud Piruz and José María Bermejo's *Luz del Alma: Selección de poemas de Rumi* (2010), should be considered direct translations given that they are collaborative work between Persian and Spanish speakers. No complete translation of *Masnavi* exists in Spanish. The common denominator of the reception in all these European languages is that Rumi has been mostly represented either in anthologies of Persian classical poetry alongside Hafez, Sa'di, Nezāmi, Khayyām, and Attār or by retranslations of existing English, German, and French versions. More recently and in the 21st century, thanks to the Persian-speaking diaspora, more translations have been published either by members of this diaspora or in collaboration with native speakers of the TL. One can also observe an influence of the American Rumi trend in Europe with more popularizing translations and musical adaptations available.

In the East, the first translations of Rumi date back to the 18th century, especially into Ottoman Turkish and Arabic. Sheikh Mohammad Al-Qaṭifi's Arabic partial translation of *Masnavi* appeared in 1757. It was not until 1812 that Yūsof Ben Moḥammad translated the entire work into Arabic. Turks have made multiple attempts to translate *Masnavi* to poetry, namely with Soleymān Nahifi's translation of *Masnavi*. However, scholarly translations in Turkish are relatively recent: no complete Turkish version of *Masnavi* was available until Gölpinarli's translation. This may sound rather surprising to a Western reader given that Rumi's work has been very influential in the non-Arab Islamic world. One may explain this shortage of transcultural effort a number of ways. Historically, Sufis and scholars in the non-Arab Muslim world did not ever need translations to have access to Rumi's works since they had full command of the Persian language, themselves living in societies that either belonged to the Persianate world or were profoundly influenced by it. Sufis living in the Ottoman or Mughal Empires, from Anatolia to the Indian subcontinent, were presumably fluent enough in Persian to read *Masnavi* or enjoy poems of the *Divan*, in their *samā'* ceremonies, for instance. Furthermore, intercultural communication within the Islamic world through translation is a relatively modern phenomenon dating back to the post-colonial era when new Muslim nations including Turkey were actually born. The idea of translating mystical poetry was far from appealing to readers in this part of the world in the premodern era. For a Sufi reader, the nature of poetry in general and mystical poetry in particular is such that the form and the spirit of the text are inseparable and thus any translation of Rumi's work would have seemed impossible.[48]

Notes

1 It is the French linguist, one of the forefathers of semiotics Émile Benveniste, who calls language the interpreter of all semiotics in his seminal theory of intersemiotic relations (1974, 53–54). As he argues, the meaning of a musical partition or painting can be explained by a commentary, that is a linguistic utterance, but not vice versa.
2 See Jakobson's article "On Linguistic Aspects of Translation" (1971, 260–267).
3 I try to avoid the common cliché but semantically vague terms as West, East (and *a fortiori* Middle East), except in a figurative manner. The scientific rigor of a research work necessitates a clear and precise definition of notions and historic and geographic entities. In this case, the use of the West could be problematic as its semantic content cannot be precisely delineated except in a specific context. In our study, if I were to refer pertinently to our object of study as the West, I would need to include all (Judeo-) Christian civilizations including the Orthodox Eastern Europe, Catholic Latin America, and even Jewish Israel in that cultural unit. However, this definition does not correspond to the commonplace understanding of the West, hence the heuristic and local use of the term Christian world as an alternative, although it admittedly has its own inaccuracy problems: should I include Christian Africa or the Philippines in that cultural sphere?
4 See Sedaghat (2020) on how Rumi uses other semiotic systems such as music to create hybrid multimedia utterances. This question is briefly broached in Chapter 3.
5 According to Edwin Gentzler (2001, 93), the term "Translation Studies" and the distinction of the discipline dates back to in the early 1970s and in James Holmes's paper named "The Name and Nature of Translation Studies" ([1988] 2004).
6 For a concise but comprehensive overview of the discipline, see *Introducing Translation Studies* (Munday 2012). Some of the founding texts of the discipline have been collected by Lawrence Venuti in *The Translation Studies Reader* ([2000] 2012). Also, Mona Baker's *Routledge Encyclopedia of Translation Studies* ([1998] 2009) is an indispensable reference. See also Snell-Hornby (1998), Gentzler (2001), S. Bassnett (2002), and Anthony Pym's work detailed account of translation theories (2014).
7 In French *les sciences du langage* is the denomination of an umbrella discipline encompassing all branches of general and applied linguistics, semiotics, translation and language acquisition, while posing questions about the epistemology of language and communication.
8 Walter Benjamin in his essay *The Translator's Task* (Benjamin [1913] 2004) and Roman Jakobson in his text entitled "Linguistic Aspects of Translation" (1971, 260–266) both put the object of translation on an equal footing with the central problem of language: "Equivalence in difference is the cardinal problem of language, and the main object of linguistics" (*Ibid.*, 262). Translation in its different types seeks to establish equivalence in the message by means of different words, belonging either to the same language or to different ones.
9 The primacy of sense for sense has also existed in the Chinese tradition at least after Dào'ān (AD 312–385) and his organized translation program of Buddhist sutras from Sanskrit (Huang and Pollard 2009). In Islamic tradition, the theological position is interestingly unique: while the translation of profane texts to Arabic is rather target oriented, translations from Arabic must be as literal as possible. Translation is considered only an exegetical tool for the Koran and has no other value. No prayer can be said in any other language than Arabic. Even in Shiism, where a myriad of prayers originated by imams are used in daily liturgy, texts are recited in Arabic, accompanied by their literal translations, as a comprehension aid for Persian speakers, for instance.

24 *Introduction*

10 A striking example is Luther's translation of Paul's words in Romans 3:28 in Greek, where he added *allein* [only] in his German translation: "Therefore, I hold that man is justified without the works of the law, only through faith." Luther defended himself by saying that he was supposed to translate into "pure, clear German" (cited in Munday 2012, 39). This only shows how seminal the impact of a minor addition for the sake of TL could be, as attested by Luther's example whereby Protestant theology was shaped in contrast with Catholicism based on a simple linguistic addition: salvation by faith rather than by actions.
11 See Vinay and Darbelnet (1995).
12 Speaking of conceptual and psychological reflexivity: the translating practice constantly asks itself questions in order to objectify the problems facing the translator in order to solve them (Ladmiral 2014, XX).
13 To be semantically precise, I use "Islamic world" rather than Muslim world because the latter implies a cultural sphere in which at least the majority of people are necessarily Muslim, whereas the epithet "Islamic" refers to a historic and geographic reality, that is the part of the world where the dominant political power was associated with a religion based on the teachings of Mohammad and the Holy book of Koran.
14 In the literal sense of the term (supreme knowledge of the mysteries of religion) and not gnosis as a Christian doctrine of Gnosticism, referring to the formula of Saint Paul: γνῶσις τοῦ θεοῦ, knowledge of God by illumination.
15 There are two hypotheses as to the root of the term. The first and more common theory is the Arabic *ṣuf* [woolen coat] in reference to the coarse fabric of the woolen coat worn by ascetic mystics of Islam. Corbin refutes this theory as being part of a frequent annexationist Arabization process of loanwords in Arabic, citing Abu Reyḥān Biruni, the tenth Iranian polymath, who attributes the etymology of the term to the Greek σοφία [wisdom].
16 Derived from the Greek *μυστικός* [secretive, silent], of the verb μύω [to conceal], like a silent spectacle of reality so high that no word could express it, like the mystery of the Christian mass or the mysteries of Mithra in the Roman Empire.
17 It is curiously of a close phonetic resemblance to the German *erfahren* [to learn by experience], although no evidence is available at the moment for any etymological relation. The expression *Gott zu erfahren* [to know God by experience] was ubiquitous in the teaching of Rhine mystics like Meister Eckhart.
18 All translations from Persian, French, Italian, and German are mine unless otherwise specified.
19 This fundamental distinction has been neglected by many Western orientalists and commentators who, perhaps too hastily, assimilated Sufism with pantheism and attributed its origins to Plotinus, the central figure of the Neoplatonists or to the Vedic pantheistic notions of *Brahman* [Ultimate Reality], *Atman* [self], and *Maya* [illusion of existence].
20 The symbolic charge of the figure of Hallaj is far more important than the anecdote of his sacrifice for revealing the esoteric secrets. Hallaj represents the mystical figure of *zabih* [the sacrificed], recycled in many forms as Ismail/Isaac in Judaism and Islam, Jesus in Christianity, and Hossain Ibn Ali, the third Imam of Shiism. See Massignon ([1975] 2010).
21 The femininity of the Divine Being in Islamic and Iranian mysticism is a central theme, demonstrated in the Sufi poetic symbolism where the ultimate Beloved is usually depicted with feminine features.
22 The opening verse of Rumi's famous ghazal 441 describes the mystic's aspiration for this particular moment:

> Show your face, as the garden of flowers is my desire.
> Open your mouth, as sweetness in abundance is my desire.
> O Sun of beauty! Come out of the clouds, for a moment,
> As that radiant illuminating face is my desire.

23 See Corbin, En Islam iranien. Aspects spirituels et philosophiques 1991, vol. I, Chapter II, "Notion du shî'isme des Douze Imâms," 39–73. Also: Amir-Moezzi 2009, Part II, "On the Nature of the Imam: Initiation and Dualism," 103–306.
24 This transcendent movement from a lower state of being towards enlightenment cannot be better symbolized than in Faridoddin Aṭṭār Neishāburi's allegorical account *Manṭeq aṭ-ṭayr* [Speech of the Birds] (1177), translated as *The Conference of the Birds* (1954). Birds set off on a journey to join the Simorgh going through various stages, at each of which some birds abandon the group due to hardships. The metaphor of "seven realms of love" used by Aṭṭār describes the stages of a spiritual journey made by the mystic to reach enlightenment: *ṭalab* [desire], *eshq* [love], *ma'refat* [knowledge], *esteqnā* [magnanimity], *towḥid* [uniqueness], *ḥeyrat* [perplexity], and *faqr o fanā* [poverty and annihilation].
25 The British orientalist, translator of the Koran and writer of an Arabic grammar, also translated an anthology of Rumi (1877).
26 In terms defined by Edward Said (*Orientalism* 1979).
27 Among these scholars and thinkers, one finds such names as René Guénon, William Chittick, Leonard Lewisohn, and Annemarie Schimmel, Eva de Vitray-Meyerovitch, and Leili Anvar.
28 One should not forget that the first victims of Islamic extreme legalism, represented today by movements like Salafism or Wahabism, are members of the Islamic community themselves, mostly adepts of nonorthodox affiliations such as Shias or Sufis.
29 The term "Persianate Society" (*le monde iranien*) was coined by orientalist Marshall G. S. Hodgson (*The Venture of Islam, Volume 2: The Expansion of Islam in the Middle Periods* 1977). He defines the term with historical reference to societies that have been either entirely founded upon or directly under the influence of the Persian language and literature and/or Iranian art and culture, especially during the Middle Ages. This phenomenon could be witnessed in various geographic zones under Turkified rulers in Central Asia, Mesopotamia, South Asia, and Caucasus. Some examples were territories under Seljuqs, Timurids, Mughals, and earlier the Ottoman Empire.
30 The problem of "attributed but not verified poems" by renowned classical Persian poets is a common and multidimensional one. Many poems have been composed by disciples or less-known poets and attributed to their masters and included in old manuscripts. It is at the editor's discretion to verify the authenticity of each text in a manuscript, while basing his judgment on stylistic and thematic traits of the text as well as the historical context and the source of the manuscript. This particularly famous ghazal is an epitome of this issue. While it has not been recognized in Foruzānfar's edition of the *Divan*, it is included in Nicholson's *Selected Poems From the Dīvāni Shamsi Tabrīz* (2001).
31 The use of "our master" to refer to Rumi allegedly comes from an honorific title in use in the hierarchy of the esoteric order of Ismailis. According to some sources, Sham, the mysterious qalandar who turned Rumi's life upside down, was previously a member of this order.
32 It should be noted that the long-favored hypothesis of Rumi's family's escape from the Mongol invasion has since been rejected by several experts, including Lewis, due to chronological issues.
33 A wandering dervish who goes from one city to another without real earthly attachment, engaged in an ascetic life dedicated to spiritual activities and education of the population. Shams could have belonged to a group of dervishes called *Malamatian* (Lewisohn), a similar group of ascetics with a similar demeanor to the cynics of the Hellenic era.
34 It remains a collection of discourses from Shams, named *Maqālāt* [the Essays].
35 Rumi's biography has been the subject of discussion and even controversy because of legends mixed with reality, which is typical of the hagiography of this epoch. The first biographer of Rumi, one of the disciples of the circle created by his descendants,

26 *Introduction*

Shamsoddin Moḥammad Aflāki (d. 1292), the author of the *Manāqeb ol-'ārefin*, did not hesitate to add his imaginations to dramatize the mystical twists and turns of Mowlānā [our master's] life.
36 It may have been Shams who decided to flee for fear of his life, or he might have been murdered by Rumi's entourage. The second hypothesis has been favored by most hagiographers, albeit with no tangible evidence.
37 See Appendix I, Table I, for a brief chronological synopsis. Works on Rumi's life are numerous in English. The most recent and perhaps best organized is that of Franklin D. Lewis (2007, 271–326).
38 The mystical aspects of Bahā'oddin's work and his profound influence on Rumi's thought have been demonstrated by Fritz von Meier (1989).
39 *Beyt* is taken by most orientalists as the equivalent of a verse and *meṣra'* that of a hemistich in classical Persian (or Arabic) poetry. However, this definition is inaccurate. For instance, the number of syllables in a typical *meṣra'* is comparable to that in an English verse of the iambic meter. See Chapter 3.
40 For the ease of use, I shall henceforth use the short form the *Divan* and the *Masnavi* throughout this paper. The Persian term *divān* in this context means "collection of poetry."
41 A genre known to English readers introduced to the English literature by Fitzgerald's translation of Omar Khayyam's quatrains in the 19th century.
42 For a precise census of Rumi's important translations in major European languages as well as Rumi scholarship in the West, see Lewis (2007, ch 12–14, 499–616).
43 Whereas Rumi maybe the most cited poet in Greater Iran, Hafez is arguably the most popular poet in Iran. Hafez's divan is considered to be the apogee of Persian classical poetry by all standards: mystical themes, exquisite images, prosodic perfection. Goethe was so profoundly marked by Hafez's work, translated in 1814 by Austrian orientalist Joseph von Hammer-Purgstall, that he composed and dedicated his *West – östlicher Divan* to Hafez. That was one of the crucial literary encounters between Persian and Western cultures (Tafazoli 2001).
44 The disciples of Mowlānā [our master], pronounced Mevlānā in Turkish, hence the term *mevlevi*.
45 For the history of Rumi translation in German, see Lewis (2007, 566–569).
46 To be chronologically precise, Baudry's prose adaptation of a tale in *Masnavi*, "Moïse et le chevrier," published text in *Magasin Pittoresque* (1857), was the very first French translation.
47 See "Primary Sources' in Bibliography for the full list of the published translations of Rumi's poetic work in various European languages and the respective tables in Appendix II for their chronological order.
48 One should never forget that even the idea of translating the Koran has never received canonization by any Islamic school. There is no equivalent for the Septuagint in the Islamic world. Translations of the Koran are only used for nonliturgical purposes, for example in pedagogical contexts, to give an approximate understanding of the Holy Text.

References

Aflāki, Shamsoddin Ahmad. [1318] 1362 [1983]. *Manāqeb alārefin*. Edited by Tahsin Yaziji. Tehrān: Donyāye ketāb.
Amir-Moezzi, Mohammad Ali. 2009. *The Spirituality of Shi'i Islam: Beliefs and Practices*. London: I. B. Tauris.
Bahā'e Valad, Mohammad ebn Hosein. 1352 [1973]. *Ma'āref*. Edited by Badi'ozzamān Foruzānfar. Tehrān: Ṭahuri.

Baker, Mona et al. [1998] 2009. *Routledge Encyclopedia of Translation Studies*. London: Routledge.
Bassnett, Susan. 2002. *Translation Studies*. London and New York: Routledge.
Benjamin, Walter. [1913] 2004. "The Task of the Translator." In *Walter Benjamin: Selected Writings, Volume 1: 1913–1926*, by Walter Benjamin, edited by Marcus Bullock and Michael Jennings. Boston: Harvard University Press.
Benveniste, Émile. 1974. *Problèmes de linguistique générale*. Vol. 2. Paris: Gallimard.
Browne, Edward Granville. [1906–1908] 1997. *A Literary History of Persia*. 4 vols. Cambridge: Ibex Pub.
Cicero, Marcus Tullius. [46 BC]1960. *De inventione. De optimo genere oratorum. Topica*. Translated by Harry Mortimer Hubbell. Cambridge, MA: Harvard University Press.
Corbin, Henry. 1974. "La philosophie islamique depuis la mort d'Averroës jusqu'à nos jours." In *Histoire de la philosophie, tome III*, edited by Yvon Belaval, 1065–1188. Paris: Gallimard.
Corbin, Henry. 1990. *Corps spirituel et terre céleste: De l'Iran mazdéen à l'Iran shï'ite*. Paris: Buchet-Chastel.
Corbin, Henry. 1991. *En Islam iranien. Aspects spirituels et philosophiques*. 4 vols. Paris: Gallimard.
Gentzler, Edwin. 2001. *Contemporary Translation Theories*. Clevedon, UK: Multilingual Matters.
Gölpinarli, Abdĭbāki. 1957–1960. *Dîvān-i Kebîr: [Yazan] Mevlānā Celāleddin*. Istanbul: Remzi Kitabevi.
Guénon, René. 1973. *Aperçus sur l'ésotérisme islamique et le taoïsme*. Paris: Gallimard.
Hodgson, Marshall G. S. 1977. *The Venture of Islam, Volume 2: The Expansion of Islam in the Middle Periods*. Chicago: University of Chicago Press.
Holmes, James Stratton. [1988] 2004. "The Name and Nature of Translation Studies." In *The Translation Studies Reader*, edited by Lawrence Venuti, 180–192. London: Routledge.
Huang, Eva, and David Pollard. 2009. "The Chinese Tradition." In *Routledge Encyclopedia of Translation Studies*, edited by Mona Baker et al., 369–378. London: Routledge.
Huart, Clément. 1897. *Konia, la ville des derviches tourneurs: souvenirs d'un voyage en Asie mineure*. Paris: Ernest Leroux.
Jakobson, Roman. 1971. *Selected Writings II. Word and Language*. The Hague: Mouton.
Jerome, Saint. 1989. *St. Jerome: Letters and Select Works*. Edited by William Henry Fremantle, George Lewis, and William Gibson Martley. Grand Rapids, MI: Eerdmans Pub. Co.
Ladmiral, Jean René. 2014. *Sourcier ou cibliste*. Paris: Les Belles Lettres.
Lewis, Frankin D. 2007. *Rumi Past and Present, East and West: The Life, Teachings, and Poetry of Jalal al-Din Rumi*. Oxford: Oneworld.
Massignon, Louis. [1975] 2010. *La passion de Husayn ibn Mansûr Hallâj*. 4 vols. Paris: Gallimard.
Meier, Fritz von. 1989. *Bahā'-i Walad: Grundzüge seines Lebens und seiner Mystik*. Leiden: E.J. Brill.
Munday, Jeremy. 2012. *Introducing Translation Studies*. 4th ed. London: Routledge.
Nicholson, Reynold Alleyne. [1898] 2001. *Selected Poems From the Dīvāni Shamsi Tabrīz*. Bethesda, MD: Ibex Publishers.
Palmer, Edward Henry. 1867. *Oriental Mysticism. A Treatise on the Sufiistic and Unitarian Theosophy of the Persians*. London: Bell and Daldy.
Pym, Anthony. 2014. *Exploring Translation Theories*. New York: Routledge.
Said, Edward W. 1979. *Orientalism*. New York: Vintage Books Random House.

Schimmel, Annemarie. 2011. *Mystical Dimensions of Islam*. Chapel Hill: University of North Carolina Press.

Schimmel, Annemarie. n.d. "Sufism." *Encyclopedia Britannica*. Accessed July 31, 2022. www.britannica.com/topic/Sufism.

Sedaghat, Amir. 2015. *Le soufisme de Roumi reçu et perçu dans les mondes anglophone et francophone: étude des traductions anglaises et françaises*. Paris: Université Sorbonne Paris Cité. https://tel.archives-ouvertes.fr/tel-01579400.

Shayegan, Daryush. 1979. *Les relations de l'hindouisme et du soufisme: d'après le Majmaʻ al-Bahrayn de Dārā Shokûh*. Paris: Éditions de la différence.

Snell-Hornby, Mary. 1998. *Translation Studies: An Integrated Approach*. Amsterdam: John Benjamins.

Steiner, George. 1975. *After Babel, Aspects of Language and Translation*. London: Oxford University Press.

Tafazoli, Hamid. 2001. "Goethe, Johann Wolfgang von." *Encylopedia Iranica* XI, Fasc. 1: 40–43.

Vaziri, Mostafa. 2015. *Rumi and Shams' Silent Rebellion: Parallels with Vedanta, Buddhism and Shaivism*. London: Palgrave Macmillan.

Venuti, Lawrence. [1995] 2008. *The Translator's Invisibility: A History of Translation*. Edited by Lawrence Venuti. London: Routledge.

Venuti, Lawrence. [2000] 2012. *The Translation Studies Reader*. Edited by Lawrence Venuti. London: Routledge.

Vinay, Jean-Paul, and Jean Darbelnet. 1995. *Comparative Stylistics of French and English. A Methodology for Translation*. Translated by Juan C. Sager and M.-J. Hamel. Amsterdam and Philadelphia: John Benjamins.

Zarrinkub, ʻAbdolḥoseyn. 1369 [1990]. *Josteju dar Taṣavvof-e Iran* [Searching in Iranian Sufism]. Tehrān: Amir Kabir.

1 First Order Linguistic Difficulties

1 Translatability as a Linguistic Principle

Language is a system of signs. Verbal communication is based on the formation of a chain of individual signs regulated by a set of syntactic rules. The chain of any given length also forms a sign. A sign is defined as *aliquid stat pro aliquo* [something that stands for something else]. There are two prominent sign models: the triadic model proposed by the American figure of semiotics, Charles Sanders Peirce, and the famous dyadic model of the Swiss father of linguistics, Ferdinand de Saussure.[1] According to the Saussurean definition, a sign consists of the union of two realities: a conceptual reality called the signified (*signifié*) and the physical reality called signifier (*signifiant*). The acoustic or visual reality of the linguistic sign constitutes its signifier and the mental image it corresponds to, i.e., its meaning, is its signified. Unlike Saussure, Peirce identifies three features in the sign: the sign-vehicle or *representamen* is the physical reality of the sign, the *object* is what the sign refers to, and the *interpretant* is the meaning of the sign, its signification or interpretation in the mind. Pierce also defines the triadic action of the sign consisting in representing an object while creating a cognitive trace in its interpreter as *semiosis*. Both Saussurean and Peircean sign models are influential and relevant to linguistics and semiotics to date. Nonetheless, it is not an overstatement to say that Saussure's explanation of semiosis established itself more solidly in the Human Sciences than did Peirce's, in part thanks to its systematic development into the new disciplines of linguistics and semiology (see Chapter 2).

The relationship between the two planes of the sign in the Saussurean model is arbitrary nature. In other words, any sound can be the signifier of any meaning: *arbor*, *Baum*, *derakht*, or *shajar* are different signifiers belonging to different sign systems, for which the signified is tree. In consequence, the process of interlingual translation in the context of verbal communication, simply put, consists in finding a sign or chain of signs in any given target language (TL) for which the signified is equal to that of the signs or chain of signs in a given source language. In principle, then, translation is a simple matter of the transposition of signs between various sign systems with the aim of recreating an equivalent content. There is always a way of saying the same thing in any given language system, however dissimilar they may be. This has been the long-standing position of linguists on both sides

DOI: 10.4324/9781003157960-2

of the Atlantic, be it of Americans such as Eugene Nida or of Europeans such as Émile Benveniste, Georges Mounin (1976), and Roman Jakobson.

The strongest argument in favor of actual translatability despite potential structural differences between languages is made by Jakobson in a seminal text for translation studies, entitled "On Linguistic Aspects of Translation" (1971, 260–266). According to Jakobson, any meaning can be communicated by any language regardless of the speaker's first-hand direct experience of the extralinguistic reference. In other words, any language can communicate the meaning of a unicorn even if nobody has ever seen one. Jakobson uses Peirce's idea that any sign interpretant can be further interpreted as a sign object itself, to affirm that language signs can always be further interpreted when "converted into a more explicit designation." Jakobson then defines this process by claiming, "interlingual translation rewording is an interpretation of verbal signs by means of other signs of the same language" (*Ibid.*, 261). This view was later restated by George Steiner (Steiner 1975, 1–50) when he asserts that any act of understanding is primarily an act of translation, as words can and should be further interpreted in more explicit terms in order to be understood. Anyone can relate to this phenomenon in the everyday use of language for verbal communication: one can rephrase an utterance by using more or less synonymous words or resort to a circumlocution to be understood or to make sure one understands one's interlocutor.

Intralingual translation is all the more relevant to Persian classical literature since paraphrasing constitutes the core of classical and modern commentaries and is a very common practice, especially in the case of mystical poetry. Rephrasing classical poetry in modern Persian using simpler syntax and contemporary lexicon is even a common exercise at all school levels. In the liturgical context as well, exegetic commentaries of sacred texts (Koran and hadith) involve primarily rephrasing the text in more explicit terms using synonyms before adding extra information. Yet synonymy, as Jakobson argues, is not "complete equivalence." Even in the case of individual signs – or lexical items – no two units within the same language can be considered semantically equivalent. This is true in the case of denotation, i.e., of signification *per se*, as well as in the case of connotation, i.e., signification in relation to other units. In other words, paraphrasing an utterance keeps the content more or less intact but inevitably changes the arrangement of the content. Given the difference in the semantic field of various words, paraphrasing also alters the tone, the rhythm, the tenor, and especially the connotative value of the signs. Jakobson explains:

> Likewise, on the level of interlingual translation, there is ordinarily no full equivalence between code units while messages may serve as adequate interpretations of alien code-units or messages.
>
> (1971, 261)

If full formal equivalence is impossible even in the process of rephrasing and reinterpreting the text in the same language, *a fortiori* no equivalence can be expected in the process of rephrasing utterances in a different linguistic sign system. Jakobson gives the example of the word "cheese" compared to its Russian equivalent *сыр*, pointing out that they cannot be identified since the English word has a wider semantic field. The English term *cheese* is a hypernym that includes cottage cheese, for example, whereas the Russian term is restricted to fermented dairy products.[2] Due to their arbitrary character, languages have different approaches to the *segmentation of reality*. Language, being a system of *semiotization*, i.e., representation of reality by signs, can have different ways of categorizing reality that may be both the cause and the consequence of fundamentally dissimilar experiences of the world (umwelt).[3] The common popular example given by linguists is the difference of code-units or words to refer to colors in different languages.[4]

However, as Jakobson indicates, in both intralingual and interlingual translation, it is often the equivalence in the message rather than in individual code-units that is sought. Utterances to be rephrased in reported speech or in translation are rarely single lexical items but entire expressions, phrases, clauses, or sentences. While single lexicological units (individual words) may have no equivalent, denotatively and connotatively, entire utterances are often easily transferred between languages because their content can be reuttered using other, nonequivalent, words. Words may not be equivalent, but their semantic sum can. Even individual allegedly "untranslatable" words or expressions, such as the German word *Dasein* that remains as such in most translations of Heidegger's work, can be interpreted, rephrased, or replaced by alternative explanatory utterances, certainly not equivalent in number of words, syntax, or style, but equivalent in semantic content. Likewise, a term like *cottage cheese*, which corresponds to two code-units in English, may have an equivalent in Russian which contains a single code-unit (творогу) or no equivalent at all in Persian, in which case it can be explained by an entire sentence. In either case, translation is possible between languages or within the same language even if the number and style of the source and target utterances are not identical. This is what Jakobson calls "equivalence in difference" and considers the "cardinal problem of language" and linguistics. There are countless differences that occur at the level of the lexicon and the noncompatibility of semantic fields (e.g., there is no equivalent in French or Persian for the term *sibling*), grammar (e.g., gender or absence thereof, determination), or syntax (e.g., verbal aspects in Russian). Grammatical and lexical rules determine what a given language conveys, what aspects of the reality are expressed in a given utterance, but they don't prevent the same information from being expressed in other ways. The idea expressed by the French (or Persian) subjunctive mode can be expressed by an English modal verb, for instance. Such differences may make *literal* translation impossible, but the lost information can always be retrieved by other means in the target language. In other words, "languages differ essentially in what they must convey and not in what they may convey" (Jakobson 1971, 265).

Jakobson's analysis rejects the common idea about untranslatability based on linguistic relativism.[5] "Equivalence in difference" shapes the founding principle of interlingual translation, whereby translatability becomes a question of degree and adequacy. A systematic descriptive method is then necessary to determine the level of difficulty in creating equivalence in the transfer of the utterance between languages and the extent to which differences in linguistic codes impose dissimilarity between source and target utterances. Eugene Nida describes two basic orientations in creating equivalence between source and target languages: *formal equivalence* where the focus is on both form and content of the transferred message and *dynamic equivalence* or *correspondence* where the content is transferred with the aim of creating an *equivalent effect* on the target receptor of the message, similar to the effect of the original text on the receptor in the source language (Jakobson [1960] 1964, 159–160). This effect is not only determined by the formal aspects of the utterance but also by the connotative value of the message as well as the cultural aspects of translation. On a more technical level, comparative stylistics provides a more tangible method to determine how linguistic differences have implications for the *equivalent effect*. Introduced by Vinay and Darbelnet in their *Stylistique compareé* (1958), this comparative approach was further developed into deeper studies of the linguistic and syntactic problems of translation in the English/French language group (see Guillemin-Flescher 1981; Chuquet et Paillard 1987). Vinay and Darbelnet use *text segmentation* to extract *units of translation* and determine suitable strategies and procedures to transfer them from the source to the target language. These *units of thought* – which may or may not correspond to lexicological units – are defined as "the smallest segment of the utterance in which the cohesion of signs is such that they must not be translated separately" (Vinay and Darbelnet 1995, 16 & 36–43). They can be transferred using *direct* (mostly literal) or *oblique* (transposition or modulation) methods.

The need for a thorough comparative stylistic study between Persian and major European languages is long due. However, in this chapter, I will limit myself to applying a comparative linguistic approach to describe some of the most obvious linguistic problems of interlingual translation from Persian to English in Rumi's texts. Some of these linguistic problems, as shown in following chapters, are a source of major hermeneutic complications with ethical and ideological repercussions. Following the examination of the corpus of Rumi's texts, linguistic difficulties appeared at various levels: grammatical categories (tense, aspect, and number), syntactic construction, and structure of utterance, lexicon, and lexical morphology.

2 Grammatical and Syntactic Problems

2.1 *Persian Grammar*

Persian, also called Farsi, Dari, or Tajik, is an Indo-European language, belonging to the Eastern *satem* family and, more specifically, to its Indo-Iranian branch. Its syntax bears striking similarities to both Romance and German languages while it shares certain grammatical features such as determination with other members of the *satem* family like Slavic languages. This is all the more fascinating that modern Persian, one of the oldest languages in the world,[6] has preserved its main Indo-European morphological and syntactic characteristics despite hundreds of years of close interaction on the one hand with Semitic languages whose fundamentally different morphology is due to the triliteral lexical structure and, on the other, with Altaic languages and their agglutinative features. The graphic aspect of Persian evokes that of Arabic for the average Western reader because Persian and Arabic share an alphabet derived from Syriac, a descendant of the Imperial Aramaic of the Sassanid era. In spite of Persian's massive lexicological borrowings from Semitic languages (Imperial Aramaic, Syriac, and especially classical Arabic) as well as Turkic languages (Oghuz, Chagatai, Uzbek, and Kipchak), in its grammatical heart, modern Persian remains entirely Indo-European.[7] There are, however, enough fundamental syntactic differences between Persian and English to push the translator to resort to *oblique* translation methods, quite often in order to compensate for a loss. After all, as Vinay and Darbelnet mention, even apparently related languages such as French and English can prove to be quite distant in syntax and stylistics.

> The relationships between languages can be classified according to the frequency with which oblique translation methods have to be used. In this respect, and despite Nida's position, we assert here that English and French are as far apart as, if not further, than English and some Amerindian languages. If some ethnolinguists believe that they have to go to the extremities of the earth to discover new cultures and modes of thinking, we suggest that a simple Channel crossing will provide them with the same amount of metalinguistic evidence of linguistic divergence.
> (Vinay and Darbelnet 1995, 279)

While there are few systematic studies in comparative stylistics of Persian and European counterparts, Persian grammar has been well studied since as early as the 18th century with Sir William Jones's *A Grammar of the Persian Language* ([1771] 1993). Meerza Mohammad Ibraheem's *Grammar* (1841) was the first modern grammar of Persian. More recently, we can mention Lambton's (1953) and Mace's (2003) grammars in English as well as Gilbert Lazard's works (2006) in French as some of the references on Persian grammar in European languages. What is common in Persian grammars, whether they are published in European languages or in Persian, is that their approach is that of modern grammars of European languages rather than that of the classical Latin grammar. For instance, only Sir William Jones (1828, 24–26) and Ibraheem (1841, 22) discuss Persian grammatical cases, whereas modern authors only speak of the *rā* direct object marker. In my analysis of Rumi's texts and their translation in various European languages (Sedaghat 2015), I tried to adopt a comparative grammatical approach. The structural proximity of Persian to certain European languages made the formal equivalence in translation easier compared to translation in other languages. For instance, certain utterances seem more easily transferrable into English using a direct method

34 *First Order Linguistic Difficulties*

than into a Romance language, whereas other utterances proved the opposite. The examples that follow in this chapter are limited to the Persian-English pair, albeit with rare comparative hints at the problems of transfer to other languages such as French.

2.2 *Determination and Actualization*

The first important problem of equivalence arises at the level of noun phrases and determiners in Persian and their transfer to English and other Western Indo-European languages. In a nominal group, the determiner is the term or affix that accompanies a noun and expresses the reference of the noun or of the noun phrase in the context of communication. Determiners indicate whether the noun refers to a definite or indefinite object or to its number, gender, possession, and grammatical case. Articles (definite or indefinite), demonstratives (this, that), possessives (my, his, their), interrogatives (which, what), and quantifiers (some, all, no) are determiners in modern English. Determination serves three basic functions: *generic referencing*, usually marked by zero article in English, is the qualitative reference to a generic concept or a class of objects such as *cats* in "**cats** are cute," or such as *life* in "**life** is beautiful." *Extraction* consists in picking an element out of many to place it in a particular situation with or without a quantitative determination, as in "she drinks **coffee**," "there is **a cat** here," and "**some people** think." Finally, *pinpointing* is the operation of identifying an already extracted object, i.e., referring *back* to a first determination. Pinpointing can be situational, as in "give me **the salt**," or contextual, as in "**the car** I bought is stolen."[8] Determination has important semantic consequences on the speech act, as it is the main *actualizer* of a nominal phrase. *Actualization* is a complex linguistic notion that, in simple terms, consists in the semantic passage of a term from the *generic* status – the term taken in general, as a notion or a class or category of things or *processes*[9] – to the *actual* status – the term indicating an individual entity taken in a concrete expression (Vinay and Darbelnet 1995, 338). In the sentence "the contact between acids and bases results in salt formation," the terms *acid, base,* and *salt* are referred to in their generic properties, whereas the same terms are actual in the following expressions: *the sulfuric acid, some bases, too much salt.*

Various modalities of determination in different languages can be a source of difficulty in translation. This is all the more obvious in Persian where, like in Slavic languages, no concept of article exists. In Persian, there is no definite article in literary language. A bare noun can designate a specific object if the context (or the "situational context") so indicates (Lazard 2006, 62). In other words, Persian nouns are definite by default until they are made indefinite by means of a suffix or prefix (Jones [1771] 1826, 25). The problem of determination in Persian is imposed on translators from the very first words of the *Masnavi, Neynāme,* or the famous prelude of *Ney* [flute]. The first verse, translated numerous times into English, constitutes the first discrepancy between Nicholson's edition and the later editions.

Example 1.1 M.I) l.1[10]

a) Nicholson's edition: Beshnow **az ney** chon ḥekāyat mikonad		
b) Latter editions: Beshnow **in ney** chon ḥekāyat mikonad		
a) Hear **of** *Ney* as it recounts		
b) Hear **this** *Ney* as it recounts		
E1) SWJ in Ap: p. 118–119: Hear, how **yon** reed in sadly pleasing tales	E2) Red: p. 1–3: **FROM** reed-flute hear what tale it tells;	E3) Whi: p. 3–5: HEARKEN **to the** reed-flute, how it complains,
E4) Nim: p. 5–6: Listen **to the** reed how it tells a tale	E5) Nir: p.31: Hearken **to this** Reed forlorn,	E6) At: p. 21–22: Listen **to this** reed, how it makes complaint
E7) Be: p. 17–19: Listen **to** the story told by **the** reed,	E8) Her: p. 146–147: Listen **to the** reed and the tale it tells,	E9) Lr: p. 362–364: Listen as **this** reed . . .
E10) Moj: p. 4–6: Now listen **to this** reed-flute's deep lament	E11) Will: p. 7–9: Listen **to this** reed as it is grieving;	

In this example, we are faced with two problems. First, the discrepancy between old and new versions of the source text means that it is not clear what version a translation is based on. In the old version as reference, the determination of *ney* presents a problem insofar as it is an archaic form of the Persian genitive: *az ney* [from *ney*]. The lack of a definite article in Persian leads to vague situations in the absence of a clear reference in the context. It is unclear if *ney* is definite or indefinite: hear the *ney* or hear any *ney*? In recent editions, the problem is solved by replacing the preposition *az* [from] with the demonstrative adjective *in* [this]. The fact that Nicholson replaces "the" by "this" in his second translation may stem from his uncertainty as the first editor of the *Masnavi* regarding the choice of the determinant in the original text. This choice is also repeated in the most recent English translations (E9, E10, E11) evidently based on the latest editions of the *Masnavi*. The choice of certain modern translators (E7, E8) also suggests their reliance on the English version of Nicholson rather than the newer Persian editions.

In fact, the use of demonstrative adjectives (in and ān) in determination is a common actualizing process in Persian in the absence of definite articles, strengthening the deictic character of the utterance without concretizing the discourse, whereas the same choice in English or French can make the object less abstract.[11] The real problem of determination is posed by the old edition. In the absence of a definite or zero article in Persian, *ney* can be understood both in its generic aspect, in reference to a notion (a class of objects), and in an actualized sense, as an object identified in a situation (the specific *ney* known to the reader). The preposition *az* functions as a marker of the ablative case (hear something **from someone**) or, as Lazard (2006, 49) suggests, it can be taken for a partitive article, as in an *extraction* operation: listen to *some ney* [music]. In either case, *ney* is not actualized in the Persian text, whereas in most English translations it is actualized and clarifies the vague status of the determination in Persian. All translation choices, including the use of demonstrative (*this ney*), have semantic and connotative consequences on the discourse. The vague status of *ney* in the source text will lead in English to the *explicitation* of the utterance by the translator in the target text, whatever his choice may be. This explicitation is all the more problematic as *ney* has also been interpreted in various lights by many Rumi commentators who have considered it the personification of the author himself.

As Example 1.2 shows, the lack of markers distinguishing generic referencing from pinpointing in Persian indeed poses problems of explicitation right through English translations, English being a TL with strong and unmistakable determining markers.

Example 1.2 M.I) l.8

Tan ze **jān** o **jān** ze **tan** mastur nist	Lik kas rā did-e **jān** dastur nist

The body of the soul and the soul of the body is not hidden.
But seeing the **soul** is not in order for anyone.

E1) SWJ in Ap: p. 118–119:	E2) Red: p. 1–3:	E3) Whi: p. 3–5:
Free through **each mortal form the spirits** roll, But sight avails not. Can we see **the soul**?	Though **soul** and **body** be as one, Sight of **his soul** hath no man won.	**Body** is not veiled from **soul**, neither soul from body, Yet no man hath ever seen **a soul**.
E4) Nim: p. 5–6:	E5) At: p. 21–22:	E6) Be: p. 17–19:
Body is not veiled from **soul**, nor **soul** from **body**, yet none is permitted to see **the soul**.	**Body** is not veiled from **soul**, nor **soul** from **body**, yet to no man is leave given to see **the soul**.	**spirit** up from **body**: no concealing / that mixing. But it's not given us to *see* **the soul**.
E7) Her: p. 146–147:	E8) Lr: p. 362–364:	E9) Moj: p. 4–6:
The body is not hidden from **the soul**, nor is **the soul** hidden from **the body**, and yet **the soul** is not for everyone to see.	Not **soul** from **flesh** not **flesh** from **soul** are veiled, yet none is granted leave to see **the soul**.	**Body** and **soul** are joined to form one whole But no one is allowed to see **the soul**.
E10) Will: p. 7–9:		
There's no concealment of the **soul** and **body**, yet no one has the power to see **the soul**.		

The lack of determiners in the ST means that the status of the nouns should be determined by the context. All nouns occur in the utterance as generic concepts in the ST: *body* and *soul* in general. However, the status of *soul* in the second verse is slightly modified by a *pinpointing* determiner in all translations but T3, in which a definite known soul is referred to. This pinpointing could have been avoided by pluralizing the noun or, as Whinfield (T3) did, *a soul*. Helminsky's version (T8) modifies the lexical aspect of all nouns in the first verse, whereas Redhouse (T2), the translator of the *Masnavi* in verse, takes more liberties by adding a possessive adjective. This could be problematic since in Persian generic referencing has a higher frequency in poetic text where contextualization is more rare and challenging. Among all translations for instance, Arberry's (T6) seems to be syntactically the closest to ST insofar as, on top of its lexical aspects, he even preserves the *valency*[12] of the verb in the second verse, albeit resorting to a passive voice. On the contrary, Williams's translation appears the furthest (Sir Jones's free adaptation apart) from the structure of ST. The definite article for all nouns reinforces the pinpointing character of determination, as if there were a specific soul and a specific body in question.

While it may be difficult for Romance languages to keep the determination intact, English has a closer determination logic for nominal groups to Persian, thanks to its zero article. The choice of the determinant leading to the actualization of generic notions is tantamount to the concretization of the abstract, which is unfortunate. This process of actualization can in fact undermine the characteristic *unsaid* (*non-dit*) component of discourse in Persian, which authors exploit freely in their poetic texts, alternatively revealing or dissimulating as they please. As we will see in numerous examples of this phenomenon in the following sections, the most frequent translation shifts in the poetic discourse of Rumi occur in the form of *explicitation*. Ironically, explicitation is caused above all by the syntagmatic character of the utterance, that is the inevitable linguistic choices rather than translator's preference. Barbara Folkart justly points out in her pivotal work, *Le conflit des énonciations: traduction et discours rapporté*, taking translated text as reported speech, that among all instances of the potential alteration of discourse, "the most salient events, the most significant differences, are ultimately situated at the level of the syntagm" (Folkart 1991, 220).

2.3 Grammatical Gender and the Absence Thereof

Perhaps the most perilous feature of Persian for the translation of mystical poetry is its agender character, with consequences going from simple *amplification*[13] to disruptive explicitation and sheer semantic shift. In Persian, despite the presence of a few lexemes borrowed from Arabic, gender can only be indicated directly by semantic markers, qualificative epithets, or naturally gendered terms (e.g., girl, woman) or indirectly by the referential context. In mystical and lyrical poetry, the referential function of verbal communication being of minimum importance compared to its poetic function (see chapter 3), the question of gender becomes the hallmark of the Persian *unsaid*, especially when it comes to the gender of the object of love. This simple syntactic difference creates a huge conundrum for translation, the limits of which go well beyond language to touch on hermeneutic and ethical issues, since translators' choices in determining the *unsaid* can be indicative of their ideological and subjective tendencies as well as of the set of values governing their target languages and cultures.

Although English is also partially agender, and as such less prone to this problem than Romance or other Germanic languages, grammatical gender does exist in third person singular pronouns and adjectives: he/she, him/her, his/her, etc. It goes without saying that English is much less explicit than those examples, hence a better receiving terrain for the poetic *unsaid* of Persian. Whatever the choice of the translator, however, there is no escaping at least some degree of *clarification* of a vague discourse translated from Persian.[14] This deformation is all the more serious that it affects not only the formal aspect of the linguistic sign but the very meaning of the utterance, either by arbitrarily attributing an added meaning or by altering the original meaning. While this distorting explicitation is inevitable, the question of how to keep it to a minimum remains. A translator's choice could be justified in two distinct situations identified by Vinay and Darbelnet as *option* and *servitude*. According to their definitions:

> *Servitude*: the situation of language production where the choice, form, and order of words are imposed by the nature of the language. In principle, servitude is relevant to this book only where it confirms certain already underlying principles.
>
> (1995, 349) *Option*: The process of choosing between several structures with the same meaning. There is option when a language has a choice between two different structures with the same meaning.
>
> (1995, 347)

It is therefore within the framework of the *servitude/option* binomial that the translator can act in order to avoid alterations in the discourse according to linguists. However, the effect of these linguistic constraints on the interlingual transfer of the text is not equal in all situations. The following examples show how gender neutrality, a central feature in the mystical discourse of Rumi, can be preserved or undermined by translation. Compared to Arabic Sufi poetry like Ibn Arabi's texts where the beloved is always feminine, gender ambiguity in Persian fosters ambivalence in the creation of romantic imagery in mystical-lyrical poetry. In fact, while, as per Jakobson, languages can rephrase in their own way anything that is said in another language, they are sometimes incapable of not saying what is not said in another language.

Example 1.3 brings to light the proximity of Persian and English due to the absence of grammatical gender and syntagmatic agreement in these languages as opposed to the distance of Persian to Romance languages represented by French translations in these respects.

Example 1.3 M.I) l.30

Jomle **ma'shuq** ast o 'āsheq pardeyi		Zende **ma'shuq** ast o 'āsheq mordeyi
All is the beloved and the lover just a veil.		
Alive is the beloved and the lover just a dead.		
E1) Red, p. 1–3: **His** love was all; **himself**, a note. **His** love, alive; **himself**, dead mote.	E2) Whi: p. 3–5: The **BELOVED** is all in all, the lover only veils **Him**;[15] The **BELOVED** is all that lives, the **lover** a dead thing.	E3) Nim, p. 5–6: The **Beloved** is all and the **lover** (but) a veil; the **Beloved** is living and the **lover** a dead thing.
E4) Her: p. 146–147: The **Beloved** is all; the **lover** just a veil. The Beloved is living; the **lover** a dead thing.	E5) Lr: p. 362–364: The **Beloved** is everything – the lover a veil The **Beloved's** alive – the **lover** carrion.	E5) Moj: p. 4–6: The **loved** one's all, the **lover's** lust a screen, A dead thing, while the **loved** one lives, unseen.
E6) Will: p. 7–9: The **lover** is a veil, All is **Beloved**, **Beloved** lives, the **lover** is a corpse.	F1) Vm: p. 53–55: Le **Bien-Aimé** est tout, l'**amant** n'est qu'un voile; le **Bien-Aimé** est vivant, et l'**amant** chose morte.	F2) Lel: p. 59–61: Le **Bien-Aimé** est tout et l'**amant** n'est qu'un voile Le **Vivant**, c'est l'**Aimé** et l'amant n'est qu'un mort

Apart from the first two free translations, all English translations and versions can conceal the gender, hence nature, of the beloved in the ST. In French translations, however, the translator's choice governed by *servitude* attributes the masculine gender to the *untold* gender of the mystical discourse. While this choice is inevitable in French, the hermeneutic consequences are quite heavy. The French-speaking readers or those in the Victorian era who do not have access to the original Persian are destined to have a limited understanding determined by the choice of translators who opt not to indicate the linguistic conditions of the transfer by means of a *meta-translative* footnote (see Chapter 5). Indeed, one may also wonder why the imposed choice of gender has always been in favor of the masculine. One explanation is that masculine is the gender by default, often associated with the so-called neutral gender, even morphologically in languages with three grammatical genders, such as German and Latin.

Nonetheless, there is other evidence suggesting that this grammatical choice in the silence of translation, that is, in the absence of informative translator's notes or comments, is not an entirely anodyne one. The hermeneutic position of translators, many more examples of which will be presented, actually has roots in the dominant dogma in the exegesis of Islamic mysticism according to which God is the object of love in the antinomic bacchanalian language, only it is a God disguised in pure metaphoric descriptions.[16] In short, there is God, obviously masculine in the long-lasting Abrahamic tradition of the male mystic. This interpretation is an erasure of the feminine gender in a source text which is devoid of any discriminatory character, at least at the linguistic level if not at the extralinguistic level,[17] which could not go unnoticed for translation scholars like Sherry Simon (1996) or the Canadian Luise von Flotow (2000), pioneer scholars introducing gender issues in translation studies. As in Example 1.4, this ideological tendency can even affect neutral substantives whose contextual reference should be construed as feminine.

40 *First Order Linguistic Difficulties*

Example 1.4 M.II) l.130/135–136

Man che guyam yek ragam hoshyār nist ... Goftamash pushide behtar serr-e **yār** Khoshtar ān bāshad ke serr-e **delbarān** What can I say – not a single vein of mine is sober – The description of that friend for whom there is no friend? ... I tell him/her: the friend's secret is best when veiled You, yourself keep an ear on it in the course of the story. It is better that the secret of heart-robbers (seducers) Be said in the story of the others.		sharḥ-e ān **yāri** ke u rā **yār** nist khod to dar ẓemn-e ḥekāyat gush dār gofte āyad dar ḥadiṣe digarān
E1) Red: I. p. 8–11: Bid me describe, whose every nerve is seared, A **lover's** woe, whom **mistress** never cheered. ... **Love's** sweetest favours are conferred by stealth; Its darksome hints are treasured mines of wealth. The tale's most pleasant to a **lover's** ears, That tells of joys he's tasted, ills he fears.	E2) Whi: p. 7–12: What can I say when not a nerve of mine is sensible? Can I explain **'The Friend'** to one to whom **He** is no **Friend**? ... I said, "Tis best to veil the secrets of **'The Friend.'** So give good heed to the morals of these stories. That is better than that the secrets of **'The Friend'** Should be noised abroad in the talk of strangers."	E3) Nim: p. 9–11: How should I – not a vein of mine is sensible – describe that **Friend** who hath no **peer**? ... I said to **him**: "It is better that the secret of the **Friend** should be disguised: do thou hearken (to it as implied) in the contents of the tale. It is better that the **lovers'** secret should be told in the talk of others."
E4) Nir: p. 175–176 from Man: 123–143: How should I – not a vein of mine is sensible – describe that **Friend** Who hath no **peer**? ... I said to **her**: "Better that the secret of the **Friend** should be disguised: do thou hearken to it as implied in contents of the tale. Better that the **lovers'** secret should be told (allegorically) in the talk of others."[18]	E5) Moj: Book One: p. 10–13: Since all my veins now pulse with drunkenness[19] How can I represent **his** loftiness? ... **'The loved one's** secret's best kept veiled,' I said. 'Listen to it in ecstasy instead. The **lover's** secret that's been kept concealed Is best through tales of other loves revealed.'	E6) Will: p. 16–19: What can I say – no vein of mine is sober – to explain that **Friend** who is beyond a **friend**? ... I told **him**, 'Best to hide **God's** mysteries, and pay attention to what's in the tale! It is to be preferred that **lovers'** secrets are spoken of in tales of other folk.'
F1) Vm: p. 59–61: "Comment pourrais-je, alors qu'aucune parcelle de mon être n'est lucide, décrire cet **Ami** qui n'a point son **pareil**? ... Je lui dis : "Mieux vaut que le secret de l'**Ami** soit dissimulé : prends-en connaissance grâce à cette histoire. "Mieux vaut que le secret **des amants** soit conté par autrui."		

A few points strike in this example: the inevitable choice of gender in English due to the existence of anaphoric functions (object pronouns), the choice of two different genders in each of Nicholson's versions (E3 and E4), and the quasi unanimity of translators in their erroneous translation of *delbarān* [seductresses]. The passage is from the tale of a slave girl who was destined to marry a king while she was deeply in love elsewhere, resulting in her falling ill. This excerpt is part of one of those famous pivotal digressions in Rumi's apparently incoherent storytelling (see Chapter 5). It is a long discussion between the narrator and an imaginary interlocutor who keeps asking him for the revelation of more secrets about love. Nicholson's change of position in his choice of gender for this interlocutor seems as enigmatic as the identity of the interlocutor him/herself.[20] With the exception of Nicholson and Williams (E6), English translators avoided the gender markers by not translating any reference to the interlocutor. One can believe that this omission is deliberate given that other references to gender-neutral lovers and beloveds can be preserved as such in English. If French cannot generally afford this luxury, in this particular case, the gender-neutral indirect object pronoun *lui* allows for formal equivalence.

Vitray-Meyerovitch employs, nonetheless, the masculine gender consistently to translate all the Persian neutrals substantives, even if circumstantial elements, such as the diegetic descriptions of the protagonists, suggest visibly feminine features. For instance, *delbar*, literally "heart-robber," and *yār* [friend/companion] both have feminine connotations, despite the lack of grammatical gender, evocative of a female seducer in Persian lyrical poetry. The meaning of *delbarān* has been shifted in all translations. It has been impoverished by the choice of the term *friends*, the same translation as *yār* or by the term *lovers*. The tendency to consider God as the sole object of love in mystical poetry is obvious both in the French translation, with the capitalization and masculinization of *Ami* [friend], and in Williams's choice of the term *God*. Indeed, Williams does not even leave a shred of doubt as to the true nature of Rumi's *yār*, totally effacing the lyrical component of the poetic discourse in favor of its religiosity. This distorting reductionism is all the more disturbing as the ambiguity created around the dichotomy of terrestrial and celestial love, the eroticism and spiritualism of sensual metaphors, is the hallmark of Persian mystical poetry.

On the other hand, there is the case of Redhouse and his deliberate choice of explicating the gender by *option*, i.e., with no grammatical obligation imposed by the target language. In his Victorian-era version, also the oldest translation of this passage, it is not only the gender that is explicated; the entire semantic content is altered to give the message of an exotic, romantic, or even dramatic feeling.[21] Similarly, Mojaddedi's choice of the possessive *his* in his rather free translation exemplifies *option* in a situation of avoidable gender clarification. There are, however, numerous examples of *servitude* in English resulting in explicitation or even distortion of Persian gender neutrality.

Explicitation is inevitable in the case of anaphoric functions like third person singular pronouns and possessives. What makes the question of gender all the more interesting is that unlike in Romance or other Germanic languages, where

42 First Order Linguistic Difficulties

gender is fundamentally a linguistic category before being based on *extralinguistic* criteria, in English, gender is fundamentally based on an extralinguistic reality.[22] In English, the distinction between *he*, *she*, and *it* is based on human traits determining gender and neutrality attributed to objects and concepts with an intermediary zone of nonhuman personified *animates* (*dog, ship, Britain*). In Romance languages or German, this distinction is strictly based on grammatical criteria (Chuquet and Paillard 1987, 65). In fact, English gender, just as gender in Persian, does not correspond to a grammatical category but to an extralinguistic reality, thus a masculine choice is justified by some cultural data, whereas in French the masculine gender also plays the role of the neutral gender and is used when referring to a class comprising both feminine and masculine components. Yet, as Example 1.5 shows, in most cases of translative *option*, the English translator does not hesitate to masculinize Persian markers of pronominal gender.

Example 1.5 D) G.2131, l.12

Gar chehre benmāyad **ṣanam**, por sho az **u** chun āyene var zolf bogshāyad **ṣanam** row shāne show row shāne show		
If the idol shows her/his face, fill up with her like [a] mirror. And if the idol opens up her/his hair, go become [a] comb, go become [a] comb!		
E1) Shg: p. 134: If the **Sweetheart** reveals **Her** beauty, become a mirror. If **She** lets down **Her** hair, become a comb, become a comb.	E2) Erm: p. 87 Omitted	E3) Ls: p. 121–123: If **that** gorgeous **idol** shows her face fill up with **her** like a mirror if **she lets** her silky hair down become **her** comb and brush **her**
F1) Taj: p. 180–184: Si **l'amant** montre son visage, Sois plein de **lui**, comme un miroir, Et **s'il** ouvre **sa** chevelure Peigne deviens, peigne deviens		

This excerpt is taken from an ode in the *Divan*. Unlike most of the passages in the *Masnavi*, of a narrative and didactic nature, hence with a relatively higher focus on the extralinguistic referential function of verbal communication, the lyrical character of the *Divan* means that utterances have quintessentially a poetic and expressive function (see Chapter 2). What strikes here is that in contrast to older English translations, more modern translators have opted for the feminine gender, in any anaphoric reference to the agentive argument[23] *ṣanam* [idol] of the first proposition. However, once again, the French-speaking translator has opted for the masculine gender for both the substantive and all its pronominal references, despite the clearly feminine semantic load shown by the image of the *idol*'s hair. The Example 1.6 will be even more revealing of this semantic conflict generated by the translation of another Persian synonym for idol: *bot*.[24]

Example 1.6 D) G. 522, l.1–2

Boti ku zohre o mah rā hame shab shive āmuzad
Do chashm-e u be jāduyi do chashm-e charkh barduzad
Shomā delhā negahdarid mosalmānān ke man bāri
Chonān āmikhtam bā u ke del bā man nayāmizad
Nakhost az 'eshq-e u zādam, be ākhar del be u dādam
cho mive zāyad az shākhi az ān shākh andar āvizad

That idol who teaches tricks to Venus and the Moon every night
Her/his two eyes, by a stroke of magic, sews up the eyes of the firmament.
You, o Muslims, keep your hearts, as I, anyways,
Mingled with her/him in such a way that no heart mingles with me.
First, I was born from her/his love; in the end, I gave her/his my heart,
When/As a fruit is born to a branch, it clings onto it.

E1) Nid: XXI, p. 84–85:	E2) Am: tome I, n°69, p. 62:	E3) Sta: p. 112:
A beauty that all night long teaches love-tricks to Venus and the moon, Whose two eyes by their witchery seal up the two eyes of heaven. Look to your hearts! I, whate'er betide, O Moslems, Am so mingled with **him** that no heart is mingled with me. I was born of **his** love at the first, leave **him** my heart at the last; When the fruit springs from the bough, on that bough it hangs.	A fair **idol** that all the night teaches tricks to Venus and the moon, **his** two eyes by witchery sew up the two eyes of heaven. Look out for your hearts, Moslems, for I at all events am so commingled with **Him** that no heart is commingled with me. First I was born of **His** love, finally I gave my heart to **Him**; when fruit is born of a branch, from that branch it hangs.	Who is this Beautiful **One**, **This One** who stays up all night teaching love tricks to Venus and the Moon? This One whose enchanting gaze seals up the two eyes of heaven? O seekers, it is your own heart! Day and night, I am so taken by **Him** that no one else can be taken by me. At the beginning I was born of **His** love, In the end I gave Him my heart. A fruit which falls from a branch must first cling to that same branch.
E4) Bb: p. 128:	F1) Vo: p. 268–269:	F2) Jam: n° 38, p. 122–123:
There is **one** who teaches the moon and the evening star their beauty. Muslims, I am so mingled with **that** that no one can mingle with me. I was born of **this** love, so now I hang from this branch	C'est **une beauté** qui toute la nuit enseigne des artifices d'amour à Vénus et à la lune, Et dont les deux yeux, par leur magie, aveuglent les yeux du ciel. O Musulmans, gardez bien vos cœurs! Quant à moi, Je suis si mêlé à **Lui** qu'aucun cœur ne demeure plus en moi. Je suis si mêlé à Lui qu'aucun cœur ne demeure plus en moi. Je suis d'abord né de son amour, à la fin je lui ai donné mon cœur;	**Une idole** qui la nuit entière enseigne des ruses à Vénus et à la lune : Ses deux yeux, par leur magie, ferment les deux yeux du firmament. Veillez sur vos cœurs, ô vous les musulmans, car pour moi Je suis à **lui** ainsi mêlé que de mon cœur je me suis défait. Je suis né de son amour et pour finir je **lui** ai donné mon cœur. Quand le fruit naît du rameau, à ce rameau il pendra.

Just as in English where there is an intermediary zone where nonhuman inanimate objects can be personified and be attributed a gender, in Persian certain objects and concepts are associated with a metaphoric gender. That is the case of celestial objects, often symbols of female beauty in the Iranian aesthetic canon: the moon, Venus, etc. Adding the imagery of the magical eyes enchanting the firmament (the entire universe) to the verb *āmikhtan* [to mingle with, to mate with], there remains no doubt as to the feminine nature of the described protagonist. In the third verse, the poet/narrator completes the eroticism of this sensual picture by describing how he, himself, is the fruit of this copulation as he is born to the same tree. The situation between English and French in terms of *option* and *servitude* can be inverted in this example, if the French translator opts for the epicene indirect object pronouns *lui* or *y* rather than disjunct pronoun *lui* in its anaphoric references whereas in English the gender is imposed by *him* and *his*. That is the case in Jambet's (F2) second choice but not the first one. The coincidental fact that the French grammatical gender of *idole* with extralinguistic contextual information is feminine gives the translator's choice an edge over English in creating a formal equivalence without explicitation. Unfortunately, Vitray-Meyerovitch, bound to use the disjunct masculine pronoun *lui*, insists on distorting the ST by capitalizing *Lui* (the divine marker) in accordance with her traditionalist Sufi interpretation, which dictates that "the object of love" in mystical literature is unequivocally the male Abrahamic God. No linguistic constraint would otherwise have disturbed the mystical aura around the *untold* of the Persian utterance in the French translations. The situation of English translations is more desperate here. Apart from Bark's free adaptation, where he skillfully circumvents the association of any gender at the expense of personifying the *idol*, all English translators unequivocally divinized the object of love both by their choice of the masculine gender and the capitalization of terms, eliminating the erotic component of Rumi's imagery.

Beyond the merely linguistic problem we have described, a further question undoubtedly arises. One can wonder why there is such an unabashed will to masculinize the mystical poet's object of love to the point of destroying the *underlying networks of signification*[25] and reducing a multilayered and exquisite mystical poetic discourse to a bland religious one. As per the earlier examples, the main French translator and the vast majority of English translators, with the exception of a few at the end of the 20th century (Lewis and Shiva), tend to masculinize all syntactic occurrences of the neutral gender in Persian. Their choice is justified by the idea that the object of love in mystical poetry is indeed God, automatically associated with the male gender in all Abrahamic traditions, in the Arabic Koran, and in all versions of the Bible. The same explains the capitalization of all primary and secondary references to God, indicating the uniqueness of the referent of the term. Yet even if we accept that the beloved of mystical poetry is indeed God, it is still curious that the gender assigned to God is masculine, despite all textual and contextual evidence to the contrary in the ST. Whereas the Persian *khodā* [God][26] is neutral and never associated with any gender, the Koranic term *Allāh* and the Arabic pronouns referring to *Allāh* are all masculine. However, in mystical and lyrical Persian literature, the image of God is associated with a female object of desire, in radical contrast to the Abrahamic tradition where the masculinity of God is undeniable both textually and extralinguistically. Luise von Flotow broaches this tradition that consists of feminizing God citing Joan Haugerud, the translator of the Bible, entitled *The Word for Us: The Gospels of John and Mark, Epistles to the Romans and the Galatians* on this hotly debated topic:

> Earlier versions of the Bible are full of male-biased language, male imagery, and metaphors couched in such language "that people can scarcely avoid thinking of God as a male person" (Haugerud 1977, i). The effect of the "ponderous weight of masculine pronouns" (Haugerud, iii) and the metaphorical language that casts both the history of the Jews and the teachings of Christ in male terms has been to exclude women from full participation in Christian belief.
> (Von Flotow 1997, 52–53)

The linguistic choices made by the majority of Rumi translators in the West can then be explained by their conscious or unconscious ideological proclivity, shaped by the phallocentric construction of the divine in the Judeo-Christian tradition. Von Flotow evokes the notion of *positionality* to explain this deforming tendency:

> In translation, the translator's "positionality" is undeniable. The translator writes from a specific moment, from within a specific culture and usually sub-culture, and often in dialogue with the social and political culture of the moment. Inevitably, there is an ideological slant on the texts.
> (Von Flotow 2000, 18)

It is perhaps a truism to state that translation is inevitably affected by the dominant ideology and culture of the translating language at the moment of translation. The systematic masculinization of Rumi's deliberately ambiguous mystical discourse illustrates this phenomenon to perfection. Our understanding of the sensual imagery of mystical poetry is undeniably more nuanced now thanks to Western scholars such as Annemarie Schimmel who explains how the erotic Sufi discourse can be strictly interpreted as a plain coded language of Sufi symbolism (Schimmel 2011, 287–343).[27] Interestingly, the shift of ideological paradigm is visible in the change of linguistic choices made by more recent translators like Franklin Lewis.

2.4 Problems of Grammatical Number

While Persian does not mark gender at the level of inflections, number manifests itself at the level of the actualization of substantives and process (the conjugation of verbs). Whereas this poses no constraint to translation into Romance languages and German, where conjugation is the main marker of the actualization of the process, in English, the transposition of number becomes difficult. The difficulty this time manifests itself in the opposite direction to that we saw in the case of genre. Instead of tending towards explicitation or over-translation, *servitude* results in

46   *First Order Linguistic Difficulties*

the loss of semantic content. This is the case with the distinction between the singular and the plural of the second person imperative of the verb.

As will be discussed in the next chapter, Rumi's narrative style in the *Masnavi* is characterized among other things by his polyphony. The change of voice is often marked by the change of address in the utterance, whereby the author calls on his reader or some imaginary character addressed as him/her *delā*, [o heart] or *ey pesar* [o son], utilizing a vocative case. The call upon the audience can be made concrete by conjugating the imperative verb in the second person singular or plural. In the ghazals as well, it is not uncommon for the poet to address the speech to a character or a diegetic interlocutor in an imaginary dialogue. The constant change of voice, tone, and addressee, as well as the high frequency of dialogism, is far from accidental in Rumi's rhetoric. This pedagogical style imitates the Holy Scriptures, namely the Koran, with its frequent direct addresses to believers, for instance. Example 1.7 shows how linguistic constraints and the disappearance of number can cause lack of consistency in the discourse.

Example 1.7 D) G. 636, l.6–7

Bemirid, bemirid, vaz in abr barāyid	cho zin abr barāyid hame badr-e monirid
Khamushid, khamushid, khamushi dame marg ast	ham az zendegiast inke ze **khāmush** nafirid
Die! Die! And get out of this cloud! When you step out of this cloud, you will all be radiant full moons. You are silent; you are silent. Silence is near death. It is because of life that you hate silence.	
E1) Am: tome I, n°80, p. 70: Die now, die now, and come forth from this cloud; when you come forth from this cloud, you will all be radiant full **moons**. Be silent, be silent; silence is the sign of death; it is because of life that you are fleeing from the **silent** one.	E2) Be: p. 22: You're covered with thick cloud. Slide out the side. Die, and be quiet. Quietness is the surest sign that you've died. Your old life was a frantic running from **silence**. The speechless full moon comes out now.

E3) Sta: p. 150:
 Lose **yourself**,
 Lose **yourself**.
 Escape from the black cloud
   that surrounds you.
 Then you will see your own light
   as radiant as the full moon.
 Now enter that silence.
 This is the surest way
   to lose **yourself**. . . .
 What is your life about, anyway? –
   Nothing but a struggle to be someone,
   Nothing but a running from your own **silence**.	

The entire ghazal here is organized around the operative function of the imperative *bemired* [die] in the second person plural. Coupled with the rhythmical effect of the repetition of the term, the use of the plural creates an epic tone throughout the ghazal. In the absence of a conjugation difference in English, the plural can only be indicated marginally by adjuncts and deictic references in the TT. In Arberry's translation, the most literal of all, plural attributes after copulas like *moons* are one of these indicators. There are four occurrences of such indicators in the entire ghazal (seven lines), a far cry from no less than 32 anaphoric occurrences of plural imperatives and other markings of plurality, such as the adverb *hame* [all] in the original text. This mystical invitation to dying to the material earthly life to reach a higher level of existence, formulated in a multitude of interpellations addressed to the entire humanity, loses its rhetoric power in the TT despite all translators' efforts.

To make things worse, the stylistic effect as well as the semantic content are completely distorted in modern versions. Star opts for the singular whereas he could have used the plural "yourselves" instead of "yourself" in his reflexive construction to compensate for the lack of the number distinction for the second person in English. Bark's version is a distant adaptation of the original, having gone through an intermediate English translation. An adaptation that recreated a dynamic equivalence to the spirit of the original text would have been conceivable by adopting plural markers. However, lacking knowledge of Persian, retranslators were probably not aware of the stylistic effect of the anaphoric use of plural imperative in the ST.

3 Lexicological Difficulties

3.1 Similarities and Dissimilarities

It is in the lexical domain, even more so than in that of syntax and stylistics, that translation difficulties appear most obviously. The problem of linguistic relativism and the arbitrariness of the segmentation of reality by different languages are best demonstrated by the incompatibility of semantics fields, on the one hand, and the noncorrespondence of the lexical fields between different languages on the other. While Persian as an Indo-European language shares more lexical elements with target languages like English than the average person may imagine, thousands of years mark its evolution. The tremendous number of loanwords, particularly from Semitic languages, have made the Persian lexicon a more daunting challenge to translate into English than most European languages characterized by a common lexical pool rooted in Latin and classical Greek. Nonetheless, some rare etymological proximities with Persian can sometimes help reconstruct original prosodic and rhetoric forms in target languages. In English, for instance, this can happen thanks to the etymological and phonological identity between the Persian *māh/mah* and the English word *moon*:

48 First Order Linguistic Difficulties

Example 1.8 D) R. 90, l.1

Ey **māh**-jabin shabi to **mah**vār makhosb Dar dowr darā cho **charkh-e davvār** makhosb		
O moon-brow, one night, like the moon, sleep not. Enter the circle, like the turning wheel, sleep not.		
E1) Ar: p. 54: Radiant is the **moon thy brow**; Night is fallen; sleep not now, But like **heaven's turning sphere** Wheel into our circle here.	E2) Bs: p. 126: Don't sleep now. Let the turning night wheel through this circle. Your **brow**, the **moon**, this lantern we sit with.	E3) Sab: n°23, p. 230: One night, O **moon-browed**, like the moon, sleep not Start whirling, and like the turning sky, sleep not.
E4) Khd: p. 58: My beautiful friend for one night **like the moon** don't go to sleep like the universe begin dancing in orbital round don't go to sleep	E5) GaFa: n°374, p. 118: O **Moon**, on such a night as this, be **moonlike** and don't sleep. Begin whirling, like the rotating heavens, and don't sleep.	F1) Vr: p. 198: Ô toi **pareil à la lune**! À **l'instar de la lune**, ne dors pas en une telle nuit Comme la roue céleste qui tourne, tourne, et ne dort pas Notre éveil est le flambeau qui illumine le monde

In Romance languages, a surprising similarity exists between their interrogative pronouns and the ones in Persian *ke/ki* or *che/chi*:

Example 1.9 M.I) l.12

Hamcho ney zahri o taryāqi **ke did**   Hamcho ney damsāz o moshtāqi **ke did**
Such *ney*, who ever saw a poison and an antidote? Such *ney*, who ever saw a companion (maker of moments) and a passionate lover?
F1) Vm: p. 53–55: Qui vit jamais un poison et un antidote comme la flûte? Qui vit jamais un consolateur et un amoureux comme la flûte?

However, such propitious occurrences are few and far between in the translation of Rumi and mostly remain helpful only at the prosodic level. What is commonplace is that cultural specificity of lexical items used in an ST result in sheer untranslatability of certain Sufi technical terms that belong to a radically different era and geography and give rise to borrowings or calques by certain translators. A borrowing – lexical or structural (calque) – is usually justified by what we call *lacunae* in technical terms (Vinay and Darbelnet 1995, 65–67). Lacunae may exist because the signified does not exist or is not recognized in the target language. That is the case of *Sufi* and *son of time* as shown in Example 1.10, further analyzed in section 3.3.

Example 1.10 M.II) l.132–133

Qāla eṭ'emni fa enni jā'e'on **Sufi ebnolvaqt** bāshad ey rafiq	va 'tajel f-alvaqto ṣayfun qāte'on Nist fardā goftan az sharṭ-e ṭariq
He said: "feed me I'm hungry. And hurry up because time is a sharp sword. Sufi is the son of time (opportunist) o friend! It is not the rule of the *path* to say 'tomorrow.'		
E1) Red: I. p. 8–11: He cries: "O succour me; I faint, I pant; And quickly; lest delay the dagger plant!" The **Mystic**[28] true **relieves each moment's need**; "To-morrow"'s not a point in his pure creed.	E2) Whi: p. 7–12: He said, "Feed me, for I am an hungered, And at once, for 'the time is a sharp sword.'" O comrade, the **Sufi** is **'the son of time present.'**[29] It is not the rule of his canon to say, 'To-morrow.'	E3) Nim: p. 9–11: He said: "Feed me, for I am hungry, and make haste, for Time is a cutting sword. The **Súfí** is **the son of the (present) time**, O comrade: it is not the rule of the Way to say 'To-morrow.'
E4) Nir: p. 175–176 from Man: 123–143: She answered: "Feed me, for I am hungry, and make haste, for the 'moment' (*waqt*) is a cutting sword.[30] The **Sufi** is **the son of the 'moment'** (*ibnu 'l-waqt*), O comrade: 'tis not the rule of the Way to say 'To-morrow.[31]	E5) Moj: Book One: p. 10–13: He said, '*I'm hungry and must now be fed!* "*Time is a cutting sword*" the Prophet said, The **sufi** is **the present moment's son**. Talk of "tomorrow" sufis learn to shun –	E6) Will: p. 16–19: *He said, 'Give me to eat, for I am hungry, and quick! Time is indeed a cutting sword.* The **Sufi** is **the son of Time**, my friend; tomorrow's no condition of the Way

Ebnolvaqt (*Ibn ul-waqt* in Arabic) is a loanword in the ST that turns into a calque in English, *son of time*, except in Redhouse's free version. He also stops short of borrowing the term *Sufi* and only offers an explanatory note on its origins. It should be noted that unlike Nicholson and Whinfield, who translated primarily for academic audiences, Redhouse's versified translation is intended for a general albeit well-cultured audience. Whinfield is the first to introduce the term *Sufi* into English.[32] The capitalization of the word, except in Mojaddedi's version, is also noteworthy since it removes its generic character. The strategy used by these translators, borrowing words and justifying this action by translator's notes, is a good example of what Berman describes as foreignizing translation.

The differences and the similarities in terms of lexical composition between Persian and the translating languages can provide abundant material that surpasses the scope of the present research monography. I therefore restrict myself to the analysis of these few examples showcasing lexical syntax and lexical semantics.

3.2 Problems of Lexical Units

While a comparative linguistic study can focus on the morphological aspects of studied languages, it is above all at the level of the syntax of lexical constructions that the problems of translation are revealed more clearly than on the morphological level. Émile Benveniste notes an over-concentration on morphology and what he calls the abandonment of the syntactic structures of lexical compositions by linguistics (Benveniste 1974, 181). He looks specifically into compound nouns and noun phrases, i.e., individual signifieds represented by multiple signifiers, considering them no longer as morphological classes but as micro-syntaxes. The divergence and convergence between lexical syntax in Persian and translating languages constitute a major issue in the linguistic transfer.

The shift from morphology to lexical syntax to analyze lexicological problems of translation is justified by the focus on the fundamental concept of the translation unit, i.e., "lexicological units within which lexical elements are grouped together to form a single element of thought" (Vinay and Darbelnet 1995, 21). Although criticized by linguists as a vague notion, a unit of translation can be useful in contrastive analyses of ST and TT as it constitutes the smallest segment of the utterance that is transferred to the TL separately. It can be a *functional unit* (serving a syntactic function) or a *semantic unit* and often does not correspond to lexicological units or *lexemes*.[33] In this sense, compound lexicological units, such as verbal, nominal, adverbial, and adjectival locutions, idiomatic expressions, and even collocations, should be considered as single semantic units, hence individual units of translation. For instance, *kick the bucket* should be translated as one word: *die*. However, this can only be true at the linguistic and stylistic levels of analysis, not at the discursive level, where the interlingual transfer alters the discursive form of the utterance. As discussed in the next chapter, the pragmatic effect of verbal communication does not only depend on its referent, i.e., the extralinguistic reality it refers to, but the discursive form of the utterance, i.e., the way this reality is semiotized.

The problem is not caused by the structure of noun phrases of determination,[34] possession, or attribution, which are structured on a free syntactic basis, but by the structure of nominal, adjectival, verbal, or adverbial groups that are semantically bound to constitute single lexicological units. Compound lexicological units are different from simple noun phrases that are linked syntactically on a punctual basis, such as *car door* or *Ministry of Agriculture*. In a compound noun, the elements are semantically linked in a way that the meaning of the group is not equal to the sum of individual constituents: *doormat, to score a goal*. Benveniste recognizes two main classes of compound units in Indo-European languages with multiple subcategories: Noun-Noun, where the elements are related by *determination* (like *Justice of the Peace, editor-in-chief*), and Noun-Verb classical units (like *bottle opener, icebreaker*) (Benveniste 1974, 146–160).

In Persian, noun phrases of determination, derivation, and possession, called *ezāfe*, are generally formed by adding an enclitic particle (*-e, -ye*) added to a first noun, the determined, followed by a second noun, the determiner. This is true both in epithetic N + Adj phrases (*xāne-ye bozorg* [the big house]) and in N + N phrases (*dar-e xāne* [door of house]) (Lazard 2006, 55–60). The enclitic particle can also be considered as a case inflection marker indicating the genitive case. Compound nouns usually follow the same format, although they can have several different forms. A compound *lexia* can take a form similar to that found in Romance languages: N + Adj determined-determiner (*del-e khosh* [joyful heart]) or N + Preposition + N (*dar be dar* [errant]); or to that typical of Germanic languages: N + Adj determiner-determined (*khosh-del* [happy-heart]) or N + N (*sardard* [headache]). Moreover, Persian, especially in its more archaic and literary forms, acts very liberally in creating new N + N and N + V compounds, adopting certain agglutinative characteristics like German.

The absence of lexicological compounds following the same micro-syntax as well as the rigidity of compound constructions in the TT are the main source of problems in translating Rumi's 13th-century Persian. Example 1.8, cited earlier, demonstrates the difficulty of translating two of these compounds: *māh-jabin* [moon browed], *mah-vār* [moon-like] and *charkh-e gardun* [the whirling wheel]. *Māh-jabin* is a periphrasis for a pretty face, moon being the canonic symbol of beauty. It is a N + N compound forming a single lexeme. Different choices to translate it are quite revealing of translators' tendency ranging from target oriented (E4) to source oriented (E3), where the translator invents a neologism in English: *moon-browed*. In either case, the TT shows a higher degree of linguistic novelty due to the incongruence of the metaphor in the target culture. At the same time, the recycling of *mah* as part of a fixed or dead metaphor and its use in a larger poetic image around the moon is lost in the TT.

Mahvār is another brazen attempt to challenge the rigidity of the TT in E5. These literalist foreignizing efforts naturally reduce the fluidity and elegance of the TT compared to Arberry's translation, which tries to hold an uneasy balance between ST forms and English poetic elegance. *Charkh-e gardun* is a metonymical term designating the firmament/heavens and follows an N + Adj model of determination. The only loss here is the metonymical content of the compound that has been compensated by *heaven* (E1 and E5) or *universe* and *sky*. In the French translation, on the other hand, none of the compensatory measures could be conceivable because of the extreme rigidity of nominal composition in Romance languages, solely based on the N + Prep + N model: *pareil à la lune*.

3.3 Lexicological Lacuna

The problem of lexical semantics has different dimensions: a different conceptual segmentation of reality in the ST and TT, metasemia – that is metaphorical and metonymic shifts – stylistic factors like register or archaism, and sociolinguistic aspects of secondary meaning and connotation (Chuquet and Paillard 1987, 209–221). Here my focus is on the semantic analysis of *lexia*, leaving other aspects for the following chapters. Julien Greimas's structural semantics offers a deep insight into the elementary structure of signification, which seems useful in our analysis

(1966, 18–29). In fact, semantic lacuna is the result of differing ways of representing the reality in languages. Extralinguistic reality preexists human language. Languages seek through independent, arbitrary, and *discontinuous* signs to designate reality, which is a *continuous* continuum. For instance, between a fully closed and a fully open window, there are an *infinity* of positions, yet in English, there are only a few terms to designate these positions: *wide open, open, half open*, and *shut*. In fact, there are a myriad of realities that are not represented by language. As mentioned earlier, languages have an arbitrary way of segmenting the *continuum* of reality. Hence, this division of the continuum cannot be identical among natural languages, a fact that is most conspicuous in a confrontation of languages, namely in translation. Whether we defend linguistic relativism or universalism, and whether we believe that these differences are rooted in various conceptualizations of the world or share common deep structures manifested differently only on the surface, does not change anything in the end result: different conceptual representations of the world give rise to different worldviews, and these differences cannot be entirely reflected in interlingual translation. Representation of the *continuous* by disjunct signs necessarily gives rise to inequivalent *lexemes* within the same language and *a fortiori* among different languages. *Synonymy* is hardly possible even within a language because of the *polysemous* nature of each lexeme and the noncorrespondence of their semantic field, the *extension* of its significations.[35]

The semantic value of a lexeme, as Greimas explains in his concept of *semic* analysis, consists in one or several *sememes*. A sememe is formed by a combination of signification units called *seme*, the core distinctive semantic units. A word like "table" can be *polysemous*, that is associated with various sememes: "a piece of furniture to place objects upon, a list of facts set up in order, a tablet, etc." In logical terms, the sum of all sememes belonging to a lexeme constitutes its semantic *extension*. Semantic extension explains that lexemes usually do not have one meaning but different meanings. Polysemy in particular poses a problem insofar as a lexeme in the ST can have a semantic field more or less *extensive* than the perceived equivalent in the TT or vice versa. Also, the distribution of semes within similar sememes can be unequal, for instance the lexeme *room* has a large extension that corresponds to several French lexemes: *pièce, chambre, bureau*. The uneven *semic* distribution in a particular lexical field can also exist within the same language, namely in the form of *hyponyms* and *hypernyms* – specific words grouped under the umbrella of a general term designating a class. The term *assets* for instance englobes a wide range of financial instruments: stocks, government bonds, futures, options, etc.

I have already mentioned some examples of structural semic disparity between certain lexicological elements in Persian and European languages, namely *taṣavvof* and *'erfān* and their English counterparts *Sufism, mysticism*, and *gnosis*. The cultural difference in these cases means not only that the denotative signification has dissimilar semic structure, but also that the connotative meaning is affected by contextual circumstances. The Example 1.11, however, focuses solely on semantic dissimilarities in terms of denotation. It brings to light the full extent of the problem of lexical semantics since some simple lexemes prove to be extremely challenging to transcode in English supposed equivalents.

Example 1.11 D) Q.95, l.4

Zahi **shur** zahi **shur** ke *angikhte 'ālam*	zahi **kār** zahi **bār** ke ānjāst khodāyā
O what passion/fermentation! O what passion/fermentation that the world has stimulated! O what works, o what results that exists there! O God!	
E1) Ls: p. 139: What **ferment**, what **exquisite ferment** the *world **stirs up*** What **exquisite works**, what **exquisite fruits** they have there O God!	

The problematic lexicological items here contain abstract and concrete sememes. A lexeme with multiple sememes and base of several homonyms, *shur* is the foremost source of difficulty. It has several meanings referring to concrete notions and abstract concepts. Its semantic field extends from concrete to abstract, *shur* meaning at the same time effervescence, tumult, revolt, elation, passion, fervor, ardor, zeal, etc. *Ferment* in its figurative sense creates only an approximative equivalence as its semantic extension is more limited in English. *Passion* is another possible option, as in French translations (not shown here), although this choice leads to over-abstraction of meaning, making it incompatible with the use of *angikhte* [to stimulate]. In fact, *shur angikhtan* is a strong collocation in Persian (with compound adjectival derivatives like *shurangiz*) with a more abstract connotation in its metaphorical sense than in its original literal concrete sense.

Kār [task, work, action, occupation] and *bār* [load, result, fruit, harvest] contain mainly concrete sememes. At first glance, there is not a large extension gap between these words and their English equivalents. As Chuquet and Paillard argue (1987, 210), whereas difference in extension is a common phenomenon in the case of abstract notions – the typical example being philosophical concepts, often borrowed from one language to another – such gaps are less spontaneously admitted in the case of concrete objects where we tend to favor one-to-one correspondences. However, the homophonic *kār* and *bār* form a collocation, affected by a metasemy (metonymic displacement), and denote an abstract notion: *business*. Two concrete sememes gives rise on the syntagmatic axis to an abstract figurative sememe. The contextualization of these signs makes their interpretation somewhat difficult insofar as the referential context is very limited in a ghazal, unlike in the narrative the *Masnavi*. The translator has been forced to switch to an epithetic determiner (exquisite) to add to the abstractness of the noun phrase.

The adverb *zahi*, with no semantic equivalent in English, the verb *angikhtan* [to excite, stimulate, spur] and even *ālam* [universe] present serious challenges for the translator as well. Whereas the semantic charge of *zahi* is partially compensated contextually and by other syntagms, *world* does not have the same semantic field as *ālam*, a lexeme of Arabic origin that has multiple connotations especially in the Sufi jargon. Be that as it may, any loss of the semantic content of the ST can always be explained in a metalinguistic translation note.

4 Graphic Aspects of Translation

4.1 The Persian Script: A Source of Confusion

Graphic aspects of Persian classical poetry can, quite unexpectedly, be a major source of problem for translation. This is of course because of the old age of manuscripts and the fact that they needed to be regrouped and edited into a modern version. Multiple editions of the *Masnavi* and a few editions of the *Divan* may sometimes show minor but decisive variations in graphemes resulting in lexicological or syntactic variations. This was the case in Example 1.1, for instance, or hereafter.

Example 1.12 D) G. 464, l.5

a) Forūzānfar: *Dar sar-e khod **pich** lik hast shomā rā do sar in sar-e khāk az zamin, vān sar-e pāk az samāst* b) Nicholson: *Dar sar-e khod **hich** lik hast shomā rā do sar in sar-e khāk az zamin, vān sar-e pāk az samāst*		
LT: a) **Turn** in your head, nonetheless, you have two heads: This clay head is from the earth, and that pure head is from heaven. b) In your head, **nothing**. Nonetheless, you have two heads . . .		
E1) Nid: IX, p. 32–37: In the head itself is **nought**, **but** ye have two heads; This head of clay is from earth, and that pure head from **heaven**.	E2) Ls: p. 149: You **writhe** for it in your head **but** you are all of two minds an earthly head of clay and one **celestial**, pure	F1) Vo: p. 250–251: **Occupe-toi** de ta tête – **mais**, en réalité tu en as deux : Cette tête d'argile vient de la terre, et cette tête pure vient du **ciel**.

In their respective editions, Foruzānfar and Nicholson have two different readings of the third term of the first verse: پیچ (*pich*) [turn/whirl] and هیچ (*hich*) [nothing]. This is because the first grapheme must have been hard to decipher in the original manuscript to which they had access. It is easy to confuse *P* and *H* in the *shekaste*[36] script due to the similarity of their diacritical marks. The difference of readings drastically affects the meaning of the whole verse as demonstrated by the difference between Nicholson's translation and the more recent translation by Lewis based on Foruzānfar's interpretation. Foruzānfar's choice seems more accurate as the word *pich* fits better in the second clause in this verse. In fact, there is a wordplay,[37] in the second verse, based on the paronymy between *samā'* [firmament] and *samā'* [musical audition/mystical whirling dance], which would be an allusive response to *pich* in the first verse. As for the French translation, which precedes Lewis's version but antecedes Foruzānfar's edition, it seems somewhat strange, most probably due to Vitray-Meyerovitch's lack of knowledge of Persian, which prevented her from direct access to the ST.

However, the discrepancies between various editions can have no semantic impact whatsoever on the utterance, as Example 1.13 shows where the two editors disagree on the marker of the vocative case for *jān* [soul] in Persian. The vocative case has two morphological forms: it is either marked by inflection (*jānā*) with the affix *ā*, or by the disjunct preposed lexical morpheme *ey* [o].

Example 1.13 D) G. 1462, l.6

a) Foruzānfar: *Yā khāne dara **jānā** yā khāne bepardāzam* b) Nid: p.135: *Yā khāne dara **ey jān** yā khāne bepardāzam*
LT a and b: Either come in the house, **o soul**, or I abandon the house

A more important feature of Persian script that can cause difficulties in reading the ST is the absence of markers for short vowels. The Persian alphabet, like Arabic or Hebrew alphabets, is an abjad, i.e., it has no letter to stand for the short vowels *o*, *a*, and *e*. While these phonemes can be indicated by diacritical marks placed over or under consonants, they are usually omitted in manuscripts. This absence of marks in the ST causes confusion and errors of interpretation for readers and naturally also for translators. Another way of looking at this absence of marks causing confusion and "errors" of reading is that, on the contrary, it opens up a wealth of interpretations. For is not poetry the language of ambivalence and double meaning? Does Rumi not take advantage of all linguistic and rhetoric tools in his language to create a discourse full of mystery? Just as the absence of grammatical gender is utilized intentionally by the author to increase ambiguity in enunciation, graphic features such as graphemic markers and punctuation are a valuable tool in the hands of the poet to reduce the transparency of his text. As discussed in Chapter 4, a number of frequently used formal figures of speech in Persian classical poetry are indeed based on homophony and homography. A translator's best strategy in these situations seems to be, once again, metalinguistic notes whereby the inevitable loss of the discoursive form can be explained.

The creative use of graphic proximity to create wordplays and double meanings is best exemplified by the emblematic protagonist of Rumi's famous prelude of *ney* in the *Masnavi*. The polysemy of *ney* (نی) – meaning both *reed* and the Iranian musical instrument made of reed – is accompanied by its graphic resemblance with the adverb of negation *ni* (نی). With no diacritical mark, these two lexemes are written in the same way. This association of ideas can hardly be deemed accidental. The symbolic value of *ney* has been repeatedly emphasized by various commentators of Rumi.[38] *Ney* symbolizes the mystic seeker of truth, who can only reach the Beloved by abnegation of his *self*. Rumi's personified lamenting musical instrument incarnates in itself the mystical wayfarer – the negator of self since it is hollow – the lover longing for reunion with his/her beloved – since it generates a highly melancholic sound – and the tragic condition of human being, separated from its celestial origins and doomed to live in the material world. The multiple semantic layers of this sign are matched at the graphic level in the written form of the verse.

4.2 Punctuation and (Un)wanted Ambiguity

As previously mentioned, another grand absentee in classical Persian texts are punctuation signs. Older editors like Nicholson and Foruzānfar also refrained, as per the editing norms, from adding them in order to preserve the original form of the poems, although more recent editions have abandoned this practice. It goes without saying that this phenomenon is a crucial source of both ambiguity and confusion as we ignore the original intent of the author. The conundrum is that whatever choice translators make in their rendering of an ambiguous utterance admitting multiple possible readings, the integrity of the ST is inevitably undermined. The translated text fixes the semantic content of an utterance that has multiple significations. It is as if we translated multiple utterances by one, omitting the others. In the absence of punctuation, translators had to speculate about Rumi's intention and translate accordingly.

Example 1.14 D) G. 1145, l.15

a) Frouzānfar: *Be shahr-e mā to **che** ghammāz-xāne bogshādi* *Dahān-e baste to qammāz bāsh hamchon nur* b) Nicholson: *Be shahr-e mā to **cho** ghammāz-xāne bogshādi . . .*		
a) In our city, what an ogling-house you have opened!/what (sort of) ogling-house have you opened? With mouth shut, be an ogler, like light. b) In our city, since you have opened an ogling-house, . . .		
E1) Nid: XXV, p. 99–103: Since Thou hast opened house in our city as dealer in amorous glances, Deal out glances, like light, with closed lips.	E2) Am: Vol. I, 147: What sort of ogling-house have you opened in our city! Mouth shut, shoot out glances, like light.	E3) Chi: p. 347–348: Why have you opened a tale bearer's house in our city? Be a shut-mouth tale bearer, like light!
E4) Cow: p. 101–102: Since you have opened a shop in our city as a dealer in amorous glances, Then bike light, deal out glances with closed lips.	E5) Be: p. 138–139: Now what shall we call this new sort of gazing-house that has opened in our town where people sit quietly and pour out their glancing like light, like answering?	E6) Sta: p. 171: What kind of gossip-house have you opened in our city? Close your lips and shine on the world like loving sunlight.

Four readings are possible of the first verse of this line given that there are two sources of ambiguity. First, different readings of the second grapheme in Persian *cho/che* (چه/چو) in the original manuscripts have resulted in two completely different sentences. If Nicholson's reading is correct, as *cho* is an archaic conjunctive adverb meaning *when* and *since*, then the first line is an adverbial subordinate clause expressing cause. However, based on Foruzānfar's edition, supposedly the most reliable, the situation is even more complicated. *Che* [what] being an interrogative adverb, the first line becomes and independent clause, yet with no punctuation mark indicating the nature of the clause, it can be understood both as an interrogative sentence and an exclamative one. In its archaic meaning, *che*, as the short form of *ze che* [for what], could also mean *why*. Interestingly, the four readings of the text are reflected in translations. E1 and E4 – probably based on E1 – interpret the utterance as a subordinate clause, giving the whole proposition an argumentative tone. Arberry – whose innovative translation of *ghamaz* also presents by far the best lexical choice – prefers the exclamative tone that fits the general context of the ghazal. The rest of the translators have preferred the interrogative function.

Notes

1 See Nöth (1990, 42–44 and 59–61).
2 The same parallel can be drawn between the Persian *panir* and French *fromage*, where Persian has a much more restricted use of the term than does the French. For instance, the French *fromage blanc* corresponds more to Persian *māst* [yogurt].
3 The cause, according to the hypothesis of linguistic relativism or determinism, is defended by American linguists such as Edward Sapir and Benjamin Lee Whorf (quoted in Munday (2012, 60)), who claim that these differences shape the conceptualization of the world in different linguistic communities. On the contrary, linguistic universalism, enjoying a stronger consensus among structuralists, including Chomsky, considers that languages may differ on the surface manifestation but have a universal root. Differences are the consequence of different human experiences in various environments: Arabs have several words for "dates" and Native Canadians several terms for "snow."
4 See, among other authors, André Martinet ([1960] 1980, 11–12 & 63–64) on the segmentation of reality. He also evokes the example of Welsh term *glas* to refer to both *blue* and *green* in English (Martinet 1962, 22–23, and Martinet 1965, 40).
5 The exception Jakobson makes is in the case of poetic texts. In poetry, equivalence among constitutive elements of the utterance is a constructive principle of the text. Loss of this formal equivalence by translation damages the semiotic aspect of the discourse. See Chapters 2 and 3.
6 The earliest texts in modern Persian, for instance poetry composed by Rudaki (d. 940), dating back to the late 9th and early 10th centuries, are still perfectly intelligible for average modern Persian speakers. For a history of Persian language, see the classics like Edward Browne's *A Literary History of Persia* ([1906–1908] 1997), Arthur Christensen (1970), Gilbert Lazard (*La formation de la langue persane*, 1995), and Ẓabihollah Ṣafā (2535/1355 [1976]). For an insight into Persian etymology, see Asatrian (2010).
7 There are few examples of grammatical influence from Arabic such as the construction of certain adverbials in Persian phrases using the suffix *-an*, or the use of Arabic *ism-i fā'il* [the active present participle] and the verb *budan/hastan* [to be].
8 See Chuquet et Paillard (1987, 42–63) on a contrastive analysis of determination in English and French.
9 Process (*procès*) is a technical term used in regard to the aspectual properties (*Aktionsarten*) of words. As opposed to state predicates, which indicate events that last for a time with no change, *process predicates* indicate the unfolding of an action in time, i.e., the passage from one state to another (Crystal 2003, 388 & 451).
10 In all examples, the first section corresponds to the transliteration of the Persian source text, the second section, underneath, contains my strictly literal translation in English and following sections, English (or French) translation appearing in chronological order of publication. Bolded or italicized terms are the immediate focus of the discussion.

58 *First Order Linguistic Difficulties*

11 *Deictic* elements: "by contrast with anaphoras* (or cataphoras*) which, within the discourse, refer to given units or segments, deictics are linguistic elements which refer to the domain of the enunciation and to its spatiotemporal coordinates: I, here, now" (Greimas and Courtes [1979] 1982, 71). As opposed to *anaphora* that is a reference to other terms within the utterance (third person pronouns), *deictic* markers are terms that refer to the spatiotemporal context of the enunciation outside the utterance (first and second person pronouns, demonstratives, etc.) *Deictic* terms *point at* objects present in the context of communication, without which they have no meaning. See also Vinay and Darbelnet (1995, 7).
12 *Valency* corresponds to the capacity of a verb (or other lexical classes like nouns, adjectives, or prepositions) to take a number or type of *arguments*, that is syntactic constituents of a predicate attached to it. A verb like *to go* is univalent and agentive, having one agent as argument, whereas *to kill* is bivalent: it has an agent and a patient (Crystal 2003, 509). See also Lazard (1994) in French and Allerton (1982) in English on *valency*.
13 "Amplification: The translation technique whereby a TL unit requires more words than the source language to express the same idea" (Vinay and Darbelnet 1995, 339).
14 Clarification and explicitation are considered as deforming tendencies in the ethical theory of Antoine Berman, for instance.
15 TN: *All phenomenal existences (man included) are but "veils" obscuring the face of the Divine Noumenon, the only real existence, and the moment His sustaining presence is with-drawn they at once relapse into their original nothingness.* See Gulshan i Raz, *I. 165.*
16 See Chapter 5.
17 See Crystal (2003, 182) for the definition of *extralinguistic situation*:

> In its most general sense, this term refers to anything in the world (other than language) in relation to which language is used – the extralinguistic situation. The term extralinguistic features is used both generally, to refer to any properties of such situations, and also specifically, to refer to properties of communication which are not clearly analysable in linguistic terms, e.g., gestures, tones of voice. Some linguists refer to the former class of features as metalinguistic; others refer to the latter class as paralinguistic.

18 TN: *Even to the elect, the mysteries of gnosis can only be communicated – for "he who knows God is dumb" – through a screen of symbolism; and elsewhere Rumi shows that he, like every Sufi Shaykh, is aware of the danger of any attempt to divulge them to outsiders.*
19 *Drunkenness*: this term is used in Sufi literature to mean intoxication due to love.
20 I have broached this topic in an article (Sedaghat 2020a, 91):

> Who is Rūmī's interlocutor here? According to most Rūmī scholars, including Nicholson and Furūzānfar, the conversation is between the poet and his disciple Ḥusām al-Dīn Chalabī, who would write down the verses of *Mathnawī* as Rūmī dictated them. It is possible, however, to challenge this interpretation which is solely based on biographic information about the author and the circumstances of the work's genesis. Adopting a more modern hermeneutic stance, one may propose other explanations for such rhetorical uses of dialogue. We might also think that Rūmī's interlocutor here may actually be himself, resorting to a soliloquy to recount this internal conflict with his own inner self as to how to express the experience of love.

21 His translation is somewhat evocative of what Berman calls exoticization of the vernacular network (Berman 1999, 63–64).
22 Gender in Romance languages, for instance, is above all a linguistic class determined historically (i.e., in classical Latin) by morphological properties, namely the ending of the substantive. That is why the reality of grammatical gender seems physiologically counterintuitive, for instance in the case of sexual organs or biological gender-related

human features: the word for beard or mustache [*la moustache/la barbe*] are both feminine in French whereas breast [*le sein*] is masculine. This can incidentally constitute a strong counterargument against the partisans of *inclusive language* in all languages, attempting to feminize all titles or doubling up references to a population of both female and male individuals, since their view seems to be trapped in a fundamentally "English" way of considering gender.

23 *Argument* in the grammatical sense of the term. In generative grammar and valency grammar, the construction of the proposition relies on three components: the predicate (best represented by the verbal phrase/process), *arguments* (or *actants* in the valency grammar) that are the primary terms of the proposition linked to the predicate, the number of which varies according to the valency of the verbal phrase (e.g., subject, first/direct object, second/indirect object), and *adjuncts*, the secondary or optional elements of the construction, e.g., *adverbials* (Crystal 2003, 9, 12, 33).

24 Persian noun etymologically related to Buddha, probably referring to the historical ubiquity of Buddha's statues and the cult around them in the Eastern territories of the Persianate world.

25 Antoine Berman's eighth deforming tendency (Berman 1999, 61). See Chapter 7.

26 Etymologically akin to Germanic *gott, goth, guth*.

27 See Chapter 5 for a broader discussion on mystical symbolic mode of expression and Chapter 6 on the ideological factors of translation.

28 TN: *The word "sūfī," used in the original, is probably the Greek σοφόι but is explained as meaning, literally; "clad in woollen," from "sūf," wool. Metaphorically, in common use, it means: "a pious man."*

29 TN: *The Sufi is the "son of the time present," because he is an Energumen, or passive instrument moved by the divine impulse of the moment. "The time present is a sharp sword," because the divine impulse of the moment dominates the Energumen and executes its decrees sharply. See Sohrawardi quoted in Notices et Extraits des MSS., xii. 371 note.*

30 TN: *Waqt, a technical term for the "moment" of immediate mystical experience, is compared to a sharp sword, because "it cuts the root of the future and the past."*

31 TN: *The son of the moment should live only in the present, whether he be an adept, whose "moment" is "the eternal Now," or a novice who must learn that nothing good will come of him if he looks beyond his actual state and hopes to provide for the morrow.*

32 *Sofism* had already appeared in the work of German philosopher Arthur Schopenhauer, *Die Welt als Wille und Vorstellung* (1819).

33 To clarify the rather vague notion of "words" in a language, we need to differentiate *monemes, morphemes*, and *lexemes. Monemes* are the smallest elements of the speech that have either meaning or a grammatical function. Monemes can be divided into semantic (*sememe*), grammatical (*morpheme*), and lexical (*lexeme*) classes.

   Morpheme is a grammatical *moneme*, i.e., the "minimal distinctive unit of grammar," which has a function but not necessarily an individual meaning. Morphemes can be *free*, occurring as separate words, or *bound*, like affixes.

   Lexeme is a lexical moneme, the "minimal distinctive unit in the semantic system of a language" corresponding to individual words in the syntactic chain of utterance. Lexemes can be monomorphemic, being comprised of one morpheme (*apple*), or polymorphic, having several morphemes (*unscrupulous* = un + scrupul + ous). Certain lexicological units may contain multiple lexemes, like idiomatic expressions: *as the crow flies*. Certain linguists call the whole group as a *lexemic unit* or a *lexia* (from French *lexie*) (Crystal 2003, 276 & 313).

34 To be distinguished from grammatical determination of the noun in the sentence by means of determiners (articles, quantifiers, etc.).

35 *Signification* and not *meaning*. According to Greimas (inspired by Louis Hjelmslev's notion of *mening* [matter/purport]), meaning is different from signification insofar as it

precedes *semiosis* (semiotic production), whereas the latter is the result of semiotization. Signification is the *articulated meaning*, i.e., the *manifestation* of form in a process of semiotic articulation (Greimas and Courtes [1979] 1982, 187 & 298). See also chapter 2.
36 Along with the *nasta'liq* script, *shekaste* (literally broken, given the broken aspect of certain letters) is a popular calligraphic and writing style used in medieval manuscripts. Lazard finds it "tightly linked and often difficult to read" (2006, 37).
37 An occurrence of the Persian figure of speech called *ihām*. See Chapter 4.
38 See, among other titles, Zarrinkub (1368 [1989]).

References

Allerton, D. J. 1982. *Valency and the English Verb*. London: Academic Press.
Asatrian, Garnik. 2010. *Etymological Dictionary of Persian*. Leiden Indo-European Etymological Dictionary Series. Leiden: Brill Academic Publishers.
Benveniste, Émile. 1974. *Problèmes de linguistique générale*. Vol. 2. Paris: Gallimard.
Berman, Antoine. 1999. *La traduction et la lettre ou l'auberge du lointain*. Paris: Seuil.
Browne, Edward Granville. [1906–1908] 1997. *A Literary History of Persia*. 4 vols. Cambridge: Ibex Pub.
Christensen, Arthur Emanuel. 1970. *Études sur le persan contemporain*. Copenhague: Munksgaard.
Chuquet, Hélène, and Michel Paillard. 1987. *Approche linguistique des problèmes de traduction. Anglais-français*. Gap/Paris: Ophrys.
Crystal, David. 2003. *A Dictionary of Linguistics and Phonetics*. 5th ed. Oxford: Blackwell.
Folkart, Barbara. 1991. *Le conflit des énonciations: traduction et discours rapporté*. Montréal: Balzac.
Greimas, Julien Algirdas. 1966. *Sémantique structurale: recherche de méthode*. Paris: Larousse.
Greimas, Julien Algirdas, and Joseph Courtes. [1979] 1982. *Semiotics and Language: An Analytical Dictionary*. Translated by Larry Crist et al. Bloomington: Indiana University Press.
Guillemin-Flescher, Jacqueline. 1981. *Syntaxe comparée du français et de l'anglais. Problèmes de traduction*. Paris: Ophrys.
Ibraheem, Meerza Mohammad. 1841. *A Grammar of the Persian Language, to Which Are Subjoined Several Dialogues: With an Alphabetical List of the English and Persian Terms of Grammar: And an Appendix, on the Use of Arabic Words*. London: W.H. Allen.
Jakobson, Roman. [1960] 1964. "Linguistics and Poetics." In *Style in Language*, edited by Thomas Sebeok, 350–377. Cambridge, MA: M.I.T. Press.
Jakobson, Roman. 1971. *Selected Writings II. Word and Language*. The Hague: Mouton.
Jones, Sir William. [1771] 1993. *The Collected Works of Sir William Jones*. Edited by Garland Cannon. Vol. 4. New York: New York University Press.
Lambton, Ann Katharine Swynford. 1953. *Persian Grammar*. Cambridge: Cambridge University Press.
Lazard, Gilbert. 1994. *L'actance*. Paris: Presses universitaires de France.
Lazard, Gilbert. 1995. *La formation de la langue persane*. Paris: Peeters.
Lazard, Gilbert. 2006. *Grammaire du persan contemporain*. Téhéran: Institut français de recherche en Iran.
Mace, John. 2003. *Persian Grammar: For Reference and Revision*. London: Routledge.

Martinet, André. [1960] 1980. *Éléments de linguistique générale*. Paris: Armand Colin.
Martinet, André. 1962. *A Functional View of Language*. Oxford: Clarendon Press.
Martinet, André. 1965. *La linguistique synchronique*. Paris: Presses universitaires de France.
Mounin, Georges. 1976. *Les problèmes théoriques de la traduction*. Paris: Gallimard.
Munday, Jeremy. 2012. *Introducing Translation Studies*. 4th ed. London: Routledge.
Ṣafā, Ẓabiḥollah. 2535/1355 [1976]. *Seyri dar tārix-e zabānhā va adab-e irāni* [A Review of Iranian Languages and Literatures]. Tehrān: Showrā-ye Farhang va Honar, Markaz-e Moṭāle'āt va hamāhangi-e Farhangi.
Schimmel, Annemarie. 2011. *Mystical Dimensions of Islam*. Chapel Hill: University of North Carolina Press.
Schopenhauer, Arthur. 1819. *Die Welt als Wille und Vorstellung*. Leipzig: F. M. Brodhaus.
Sedaghat, Amir. 2015. *Le soufisme de Roumi reçu et perçu dans les mondes anglophone et francophone: étude des traductions anglaises et françaises*. Paris: Université Sorbonne Paris Cité. https://tel.archives-ouvertes.fr/tel-01579400.
Sedaghat, Amir. 2020a. "Rūmī's Verse at the Crossroads of Language and Music." *Mawlana Rumi Review* 9, no. 1–2 (2018): 91–128.
Sherry, Simon. 1996. *Gender in Translation: Cultural Identity and the Politics of Transmission*. New York: Routledge.
Steiner, George. 1975. *After Babel, Aspects of Language and Translation*. London: Oxford University Press.
Vinay, Jean-Paul, and Jean Darbelnet. 1995. *Comparative Stylistics of French and English. A Methodology for Translation*. Translated by Juan C. Sager and M.-J. Hamel. Amsterdam and Philadelphia: John Benjamins.
Von Flotow, Luise. 1997. *Translation and Gender: Translating in the "Era of Feminism"*. Manchester: St. Jerome.
Von Flotow, Luise. 2000. "Women, Bibles, Ideologies." *TTR: traduction, terminologie, rédaction* 13, n° 1: 9–20.
Zarrinkub, 'Abdolḥoseyn. 1368 [1989]. *Serr-e ney: Naqd va sharḥ-e taḥlili va taṭbiqi-e Maṣnavi*. [The Secret of Ney: A Comparative and Analytical Commentary of Masnavi]. Tehrān: 'Elmi.

2 Translation or the Retrieval of the Discoursive Form

1 For a Theory of the Discoursive Form in Translation

It is common to think that the translation of poetry is difficult or even impossible. It is harder to analyze, qualify, and quantify the degree and nature of these difficulties in a systematic manner: this will be my aim here and in the two following chapters. I will bring to bear on our analysis various linguistic theories and focus in particular on the concepts of *discourse, form,* and *function,* concepts I consider particularly useful for our purposes. So far, we have seen how differences between natural languages as systems of sign and their methods of representation of reality make the interlingual transfer of content challenging. Dissimilar methods of segmenting the continuum of reality by means of discontinuous individual signs mean that achieving formal equivalence in the TT is often impeded. Translation seems only possible by deploying oblique strategies that recreate the utterance by way of what Eugene Nida called "dynamic correspondence," i.e., by creating the equivalent effect rather than the equivalent form. Due to difference of segmentation of realities in various languages, individual *semes* in the ST are, by necessity, rearranged in the TT, creating a different sequence of semes in the target chain, whose sum of semantic value is expected to be equivalent to that of the source chain of utterance.

The *arrangement* of semes on the chain of utterance can itself be of a signifying nature that "dynamic equivalence" doesn't capture. Indeed, the way meaning is generated and communicated has an impact on meaning itself to various degrees, depending on the *function* of the text (see later). Moreover, the arrangement of the units of meaning in the chain of utterance can create specific effects on the recipient (the interlocutor or the reader). In other words, if languages are all capable of communicating the same semantic package in their own manner, as Jakobson claims, the way they are *utilized* to utter the same semantic package sometimes differs fundamentally. These differences in the structure of the *text*, or *discourse*, constitute in our analysis the central obstacle to translation. The more these differences are significant, either because of their effect or because of their semantic value, the more challenging the re-enunciation of the utterance becomes. A theory of translation rooted in *structural discoursive semiotics* seems more pertinent to the analysis of the translation of poetry than does applied linguistics or

DOI: 10.4324/9781003157960-3

Translation or the Retrieval of the Discoursive Form 63

comparative grammar, lexicology, and stylistics. While the latter all deal with the fundamental differences and similarities between the ST and the TT as *systems*, discoursive semiotics focuses on the genetic circumstances of *discoursivization* in the original text and the implications for the rediscoursivization of target texts.

Therefore, I shall turn my attention from *language* to the *use* of language, from what Saussure calls *langue* to what he calls *parole*, from language as a *code system* to *text* as the product and manifestation of the code. I will show how this specific *use* can raise the stakes of translating Persian poetry to a completely different level. My demonstration henceforth is based on three crucial concepts: *form* (or *structure*, as it is referred to in linguistics), the fundamental difference between linguistic form and discoursive form, and linguistic *function*. I therefore initially dedicate a large portion of this chapter to explaining some of the basic notions of semiotics and structural linguistics, such as sign, sign function, discourse, and connotative semiotics, in order to set the theoretical foundation of my future discussion in subsequent chapters organized focused on three domains of stylistics, poetics, and rhetoric. My theoretical literature review is followed by the application of these theories to analyzing the difficulties of translating Rumi's poetry, such as his use of archaism, *ad hoc* mystical jargon, his narratology and rhetoric, and the place of rhythm in his text. Again, as will become clear, these difficulties are not solely related to the constraints imposed by language *per se* but to the discoursivization of the text, i.e., the way Rumi uses language.

1.1 Form and Structure

1.1.1 Semiotic Models and Structural Linguistics

Semiotics is the theory of signs, meaning, and signification. Since human natural language is a system of signs among others, semiotics as the fundamental theory of signification should be considered the root science that encompasses linguistics. However, language is by far the most systematic of all semiotic systems.[1] Saussure calls language the *patron general* of all semiology (Saussure [1916] 1995, 11), one of the dictums that has been reiterated in different forms by other linguists such as Émile Benveniste, who recognizes language as the interpreter of all semiotic systems in his article on intersemiotic relationships (1974, 43–66). As previously noted, there are two major paradigms in the description of sign, signification, representation, and semiotic systems. In Saussure's dyadic model, the sign is compared to a sheet of paper and the signifier and signified are the two sides or planes of this sheet. Signifier and signified are inextricably and *arbitrarily* connected to each other like the two sides of a sheet of paper.

Signifier	**Signified**
Sound-Image	Concept

Figure 2.1 The Saussurean sign

Peirce's triadic model – consisting in object-representamen-interpretant – is more complex: in addition to the physical reality of the sign (its auditive or visual reality) and to its meaning, what the sign refers to, the referent, is a constitutive part of the relation. Peirce explains:

> A sign, or *representamen*, is something which stands to somebody for something in some respect or capacity. It addresses somebody, that is, creates in the mind of that person an equivalent sign, or perhaps a more developed sign. That sign which it creates I call the *interpretant* of the first sign. The sign stands for something, its *object*. It stands for that object, not in all respects, but in reference to a sort of idea, which I have sometimes called the *ground* of the representamen.
> (Peirce 1931–1958, §2.228, emphasis in original)

Object	Representamen	Interpretant
Referent	Perceptible Sign	Signification

Figure 2.2 The Peircean sign

What strikes in Peirce's definition is that the *interpretant* of the sign is itself also a sign. This creates an interminable chain of interrelated signs. Every sign has an interpretant that is also a sign, and this latter sign itself has an interpretant, and so forth. This *infinite semiosis* ultimately constitutes, in Peircean phenomenology, the foundation of human cognition. Peirce's model only had a late reception, as it is Saussure's model that dominated linguistics and, subsequently, other human sciences.

Whereas Saussure focuses on natural language as the main subject of his semiotic research, Peirce has a holistic, pan-semiotic view of the world, describing it as a sequence of signs of which language is only a variant. Saussure's theoretical system, on the other hand, is a mentalistic description of the human representation of the world based on an old philosophical tradition of idealism. As François Rastier argues in his essay (2017) on Cassirer's role in the creation of Structuralism, Saussure's thought finds its source in a phenomenological tradition that goes back to Kantian idealism, particularly to Kant's theory of schemes, bridging the gap between the *sensible* and the *intelligible*, the *perceptible* and the *abstract*. Peirce's semiotics, on the other hand, has its own phenomenological system of universal categories (§1.300, §8.328). As opposed to Aristotle's ten ontological categories or Kant's 12 categories of understanding, Peirce's phenomenology is based on three categories: *firstness* "is the mode of being of that which is such as it is, positively and without reference to anything else" (§8.328); *secondness* involves the *relation* between a first entity to a second, as in comparison, action, or experience of time and space; finally, *thirdness* is the category of mediation, establishing the relation between a first and a third. Representation, communication, and *semiosis* belong to this category of being. On the basis of this triadic phenomenology, Peirce presents an elaborate classification of sign. Trichotomy applied to the *representamen* results in the distinction of *qualisign* (belonging to the category of *firstness*, a quality that is a sign), *sinsign* or *token* (as *secondness*, when the qualisign is embodied in an actual thing or event), and *legisign* or *type* (a law that is a sign, not a single object but a general type that has been agreed to be significant) (§2.243–246). The same principle applied to the nature of interpretant classifies signs into *rheme*, *dicent*, and *argument* (equivalent of the traditional logical division of term, proposition, and argument) (§8.337). But most importantly, the fundamental classification of sign is based on the relation between representamen and object. Sign is an *icon* when representamen is a sign of object by virtue of resemblance (an image or a diagram), an *index* by virtue of inference (smoke for fire), and a *symbol* when this relation is arbitrary and conventional, like linguistic signs (§2.227). "A *Symbol* is a sign which refers to the Object that it denotes by virtue of a law, usually an association of general ideas" (§2.449).

Peirce's sign model is very useful, among other things, in communication theory and the theory of metaphors in Linguistics. However, its influence in semiotics and structural linguistics only became apparent with Jakobson's introduction of Peirce's theory in structural linguistics (1971, 345–359), specifically in his categorization of linguistic functions. Peirce became even more prominent in structural semiotics thanks to Umberto Eco's *La struttura assente* (1968). The essential value of Peirce's model is the fundamental differentiation he establishes between signification and reference. The question of reference, which had long been somewhat neglected in Saussure's structural theory because he never explicitly developed it in his *Cours de linguistique générale*, eventually took a central place in functional theories of linguistics and communication.

Inspired by the Saussurean dyadic model of sign and signification, as opposed to the Peircean triadic one, several major schools developed the semiology of language into a very influential discipline that revolutionized all human sciences: the School of Prague, with Roman Jakobson, and the School of Copenhagen, shaped around Louis Hjelmslev, followed by the School of Paris, with figures like Algirdas Julien Greimas and more recently, François Rastier.[2] The functionalist works of the School of Prague on Saussure's original theory shaped a major part of the modern understanding of language, elaborating on the inherent *binary oppositions* in language: *langue-parole*, signifier-signified, syntagmatic-paradigmatic axes, syntactic-semantic analyses, metaphor-metonymy, etc. Functionalists also developed the social aspects of verbal communication with Jakobson's theory of verbal functions. Meanwhile, Russian formalists of the School of Moscow further expanded the functionalist method of linguistics to such domains as Textual Analysis and Narratology, as hallmarked by the seminal work of Vladimir Propp *Morphology of the Folktale* ([1926] 1968). In the United States, contrary to Europe, Saussure's teachings were used in an anti-mentalist approach by behaviorists like Bloomfield, concentrating on the analysis of speech acts at the expense of semantics. This trend of "distributionalism" that American structuralists were associated with was reversed with Chomsky's generative grammar that shifted the focus on the deep structures of language rather than the surface manifestation of speech acts.

The application of linguistic methodology, originally concerned with linguistic *structures*, to the study of nonverbal systems is at the origin of an epistemological shift not only in textual analysis or literary theory (Roland Barthes) but also in the social sciences (Louis Althusser), anthropology (Claude Lévy-Strauss), psychoanalysis (Jacques Lacan), and philosophy (Michel Foucault). The label of "Structuralist" was soon rejected as reflecting a positivistic attitude in the human sciences and the "death" of structuralism hastily declared and replaced by "text semiotics." However, what was then called "post-structuralism" in continental philosophy was not any less influenced by the same methods.[3] The structuralist paradigm is characterized by the recognition of *formal relations* called *structures* that constitute and run systems. Since in language it is the formal relations that create individual objects and interrelate them, the structuralist method focuses on the structures that are at the basis of all systems that relate to human life: perception, thought, and action. It is in fact the fundamental abstract structures of the system that are *manifested* on the surface level as local phenomena, in the same way as in a language deep underlying semantic and syntactic structures are manifested at the surface level of *discourse*. The common denominator of all structuralist methods is the application of a set of rules that were originally used to analyze linguistic phenomena, in particular, phonology: rules of *immanence, pertinence, commutation, compatibility, integration, diachronic change*, and *the rule of function*. Although not all structuralists and post-structuralists systematically made use of this methodology, sign, systemic dichotomies, and binary oppositions have been the hallmark of their preoccupations, comparisons, and theoretical modeling of their object of studies: human culture for Lévi-Strauss, human psyche for Lacan, and the history of knowledge for Foucault.[4]

1.1.2 Form in Glossematics

While the School of Prague and Russian formalists are at the origin of linguistic structuralism and its subsequent influence on other human sciences, the School of Copenhagen pursued a rather different path on the development of Saussure's semiotic theory, one that was less functionalist and more focused on the question of *form* and *formal relation*. Louis Hjelmslev's glossematics concentrates on Saussure's consideration of language as a system of values rather than on the reality of language as a social institution and on the social dimensions of language and discourse. Glossematics remains, nonetheless, very influential in semiotics and general linguistics as demonstrated by the later works of the School of Paris and even generative and transformational grammar in North America. This is thanks to the glossematics project's complete theory of *semiosis*, its remarkably elaborate and pertinent sign model, as well as its classification of sign systems (see Chapter 3).

Hjelmslev's theory relies on the *functional* value of *form*, elaborating one of Saussure's pivotal postulates at the conclusion of a chapter on "valeurs linguistiques": *la langue est une forme, non une substance* ([1916] 1995, 169). For Saussure, the essence of language is in the *relations* between sounds that create a form, which is then associated with a meaning. In other words, what is important are the relations or structures and not their individuation in specific words or meanings. Hjelmslev then complements Saussure's dyadic *signifier-signified* sign model by recognizing form and substance in both the signifier and signified components of the sign, which he calls respectively the *expression* and *content* planes. He considers the two sides of the "Janus-like" sign as two planes, the *expression plane* and *content plane*, both containing a form and a substance carved out of an extralinguistic – or presemiotic – amorphic space, called *purport* (or *matter*).[5] By distinguishing these components on each plane of the sign, he establishes a dual articulation, between expression and content on the one hand, and form and substance on the other. In effect, there exists a solidarity or mutual dependence between the form and substance on each plane, between *expression-form* and *content-form*, and between *expression-substance* and *content-substance*.

As for the nature of form and substance, Hjelmslev explains that form is *relation* on the contiguous space of *matter*, structuring the substance once projected upon the presemiotic "amorphous thought-mass" of matter. *Form* consists of the *imminent* pre-existing structures *manifested* by and in the *substance* on the surface of *matter*. Form is the "necessary presupposition of substance" insofar as the expression-substance and the content-substance are both created by a "form's being projected on to the purport, just as an open net casts its shadows on an undivided surface." Therefore, form is an abstract structure (idea) while substance is "but a reflex of pure form." The projection of the form on the matter creating the substance on both expression and content planes constitutes the process of *semiotization* (Hjelmslev [1943] 1961, 50–52). To understand how these components of a sign can be pinpointed to a simple linguistic sign, we can take the example of the lexeme *apple*. The relation between the three phonemes /a/, /p/, and /l/ in the particular control space of sounds in the English language constitutes the *expression-form* of the sign. What is seen graphically or heard phonetically is the *expression-substance* of "apple." Another set of relations between various *semes* (smallest unit of meaning), such as the concepts of "fruit, round, red/green, growing on trees, sweet etc.," constitute the *content-form* of this sign, and the image of apple shaped in the mind and the message that is understood with reference to this fruit is considered the *content-substance*.

Expression-plane	Content-plane
Expression-form	**Content-form**
▼	▼
Expression-substance	Content-substance
Expression-purport	Content-purport

Figure 2.3 Hjelmslev's sign model

Hjelmslev's terminological choice is inspired by the ancient Hellenic notions of form (εἶδος), substance (οὐσία), and matter (ὕλη) (Nöth 1990, 67). The concept of form in particular may be strongly suggestive of Plato's archetypal forms; however, these concepts must not be understood in their original sense but redefined in a logico-semiotic context. The concept of form in structural linguistics has been subject to multiple interpretations and perhaps some misunderstandings. The distinction of form and substance with form being the active *a priori* agent of the creation of substance does evoke Plato's notion of unchanging celestial pure forms of which all phenomena are only a reflection. By way of association, this model can be compared to the notion of *ṣurat* [apparent form] and *ma'nā* [archetypal meaning] central to Iranian and Islamic Neoplatonic mysticism found with such thinkers as Sohravardi or Rumi.

1.1.3 Form as Relation

The association of semiotic form and the Neoplatonic concept of archetypal forms is, nonetheless, as hasty as it is simplistic. Hjelmslev uses the term "form" in a semiotic context, in a sense close to the logico-mathematic sense of form, i.e., as a *relationship* between given terms. The raw datum of analysis for glossematics is the *text*, defined as *process* as opposed to *system*. Taking the text as *class*, the point of the analysis is to discern its components, then to take the components as *class* and to distinguish in turn their components, and so on. However, "the important is not the division of object to parts, but the conduct of analysis so that it conforms to the mutual dependences between these parts." The description of the *relationships* or *dependences*[6] between parts of the *text* constitutes the main purpose of the analysis since "both the object under examination and its parts have existence only by virtue of these dependences" (Hjelmslev [1943] 1961, 22–23). Hjelmslev calls "a dependence that fulfills the conditions for an analysis" a *function*[7] and its terminals, i.e., the terms of the dependence, *functive* (*Ibid.*, 33). He also uses the term "sign function" to refer to a sign, considering its *expression* and *content* as sign functives which stand in *solidarity*.

Later on, two French mathematicians, René Thom and Jean Petitot, inspired by Greimas and his work on structural semantics and narrative schemes, worked extensively on a mathematical theory of meaning. Petitot uses the theory of singularity in Rahmanian geometry and René Thom's theory of catastrophes to propose a morphodynamical model of signification.[8] The starting point was the notion of *form*, pivotal to sign, as a geometric concept, and the aim is a mathematical modelling of the morphogenesis of meaning. Petitot considers form to be generated at a point of singularity – or in Thom's term, a catastrophe – in the *control space*, namely where the control spaces cease to be homogeneous by taking a sudden and abrupt change.[9] On a three-dimensional object like the cone, the apex constitutes a singularity. Petitot defines structure as a form when the space control is not the geometrical *space* but any other contiguous set, for instance, the set of figures corresponding to the measures of pressure in a thermodynamic system or the continuum of frequencies on an electromagnetic spectrum (Petitot 1985, 24–29).

It goes without saying that forms are easier to discern in the geometrical space thanks to the human's perceptive and cognitive capacities: the shape of a red apple on a brown table constitutes a form because it constitutes a rupture, a catastrophic point, in relation to the continuum. In a nongeometrical space, the phonetic combination of sounds /a/, /p/, and /l/ constitute an immanent structure by marking a rupture of the sound continuum corresponding to an *expression-form*. The particularity of the English language as a semiotic system is that this expression-form is in a relation of interdependence with the content-form or "apple," hence the existence of the sign-function *apple* in the system of English.

1.1.4 Denotative, Connotative, Metasemiotic

In addition to the structure of a basic sign, Hjelmslev mentions the existence of complex signs whose expression-plane or content-plane are comprised of an entire sign. In fact, the discussed model is that of a *denotative* sign while there exist *metasigns* whose content plane consists of an entire sign. A metasign is, for example, a metalinguistic utterance, like one in a grammar book, where the content of the utterance concerns another utterance in its entirety: expression and content. More common are the connotative signs, those whose expression is an entire denotative sign.

In his initial analysis, Hjelmslev proceeds "on the tacit assumption that the datum is a text composed in one definite semiotic, not a mixture of two or more semiotics. . . . This premise, however, does not hold good in practice. On the contrary, any text . . . contains derivates that rest on different systems" (1961, 115). Thus these derivates are subjected to the same analysis as the main *denotative* semiotic and, as such, are secondary systems called *connotative semiotics*. These *connotative signs* include, but are not restricted to, "stylistic forms, style, value-style, medium, vernacular, national language, regional language, and physiognomy" (1961, 116). They are in fact sign functions whose expression-plane is a sign itself, consisting of a (simple) *denotative* sign, and whose content-plane is the *connotator* (1961, 119). Roland Barthes (*Mythologies* 1957 and *Système de la mode* 1967) was particularly inspired by Hjelmslev's concept of connotators in his semiotic analysis of cultural phenomena and literature. Whereas Barthes's model relies only on a basic concept of connotative semiotics, the less-known works of Hjelmslev's disciples – such as Svend Johansen (1949) and Sørensen, with an essay on Baudelaire's poetry (Sørensen 1955) – propose an elaborate literary theory based on connotative signs as aesthetic principles. They distinguish namely between *simple aesthetic connotators* – which Hjelmslev calls *signals* (1961, 118) – and *complex connotators*. Simple aesthetic connotators are connotative signs that have only part of a denotative semiotic (only one of its four strata) in their expression-plane. Complex connotators are those whose *expression-plane* consists of the entire denotative sign (Johansen 1949, 296–302). In the latter case, the denotator constitutes the *expression-substance* of the connotative sign (literary work) while the connotative *expression-form* corresponds to its verbal structure or what Sørensen (1955) calls *style*. Hjelmslev also postulates the potential existence

70   *Translation or the Retrieval of the Discoursive Form*

of a *hybrid connotative sign* whose expression-plane contains elements not just of language but of other semiotic systems as well. Firstly, he suggests, "By combination of a member of one category arise hybrids, which often have, or can easily be provided with, special designations" (1961, 116), and elsewhere, while speaking of "translatability" (here convertibility) of connotators (1961, 117), he recognizes that other semiotics than language could exist in the expression-plane of a connotative sign. I will argue here that Persian classical poetry, as a result of its highly rhythmic character, can be considered as an example of these *hybrid connotators*.

Connotative Sign (Sign 2)	
Expression-plane 2: denotator	**Content-plane 2: connotator**
Expression-form 2	Content-form 2
Expression-substance 2	Content-substance 2
Denotative Sign (Sign 1)	
Expression-plane 1	**Content-plane 1**
E-form 1	C-form 1
E-substance 1	C-substance 1

Figure 2.4 Connotative sign

1.2   Discourse and Discoursivization

1.2.1   Discourse as a Dynamic Process

Saussure's central conceptual dichotomy between *langue* and *parole* ([1916] 1995, 129–131) has been revisited many times by successive thinkers. In Hjelmslev's glossematics the main distinction is between *system* and *process*, whereas in Jakobson's functional theory of communication the differentiation is between *code* and *message*. In Chomsky's *generative grammar*, the distinction is set between *competence* and *performance* ([1965] 1969, 3–15), whereas a similar differentiation exists in Greimas's *generative trajectory* between *semio-narrative structures* and *discoursive structures*. The bottom line of all these theories is more or less the fundamental distinction that exists between the *a priori* set of structures existing in the language and the incidental use of these structures at specific points of time and space to generate a linguistic chain called *text* or *discourse*.[10] Hjelmslev underlines how a set of finite abstract structures comprise a constant *system* that underlies the infinitely variable *process*:

> It is the aim of linguistic theory to test, on what seems a particularly inviting object, the thesis that a process has an underlying system – a fluctuation an underlying constancy.
>
> (1961, 10)

The term *discourse* is used in different contexts with different meanings, which can be a source of confusion. *Discourse* can be used in contrast to *text* to differentiate the oral expression-substance from the written substance. However, in a broad sense, discourse designates any syntactically linked semantically charged *syntagmatic chain*, regardless of it being manifested in writing or uttered orally. In this sense, it can be identified with utterance (*énoncé*), i.e., the result of the act of enunciation, regardless of its length. Discourse-utterance in this sense should not be analyzed in terms of a sentence but as a "signifying whole." Discourse-utterance is a semiotic *product* and *discoursivization* is the process of producing the utterance. On a more general note, Greimas explains:

> The concept of discourse can be identified with that of semiotic process. In this way the totality of the semiotic facts (relations, units, operations, etc.) located on the syntagmatic axis of language are viewed as belonging to the theory of discourse.
>
> ([1979] 1993, 81)

Greimas points out that *discourse* could be used as the synonym of *text* in natural languages where there exists no terminological distinction between the two terms. This is the case in Hjelmslev's terminology where *text* is the totality of a linguistic string, the material manifestation of the *process*, and constitutes the starting point of analysis to reach the underlying structures of the *system*. Hjelmslev uses the terms text or process to refer to the notion of discourse without defining utterance as the unit of speech act, and especially, regardless of the oral or written nature of the text. Hjelmslev avoids determining what constitutes an utterance on the syntagmatic chain. Insofar as there is no clear definition of an individual sign[11] nor of a unit of human behavior, the length of the discourse that forms the minimum unit of analysis remains elusive. This is due to the problematic character of sign function and what constitutes an individual structure. Structure being a dynamic process, its individuation becomes only a question of point of view and punctual circumstances, the very manifestation of *discourse*.[12]

The use of the term *process* in Hjelmslev's terminology to refer at the same time to *text* and its generative *process, production* and its end *product*, emphasizes the continuity of the creation of text and constitutes an important epistemological shift. Language as a static object fixed in its historicity is now conceived as a dynamic system where forms or structures are constantly shaped in a dynamic process. At the same time, the dynamic process of semiotization is ruled by deep structures that constitute the constant *functives* of the sign function. It is not individual linguistic objects (for instance, units of meaning) that constitute the subject of study but the relation between interdependent objects. In fact, objects are constituted by these relations. *Semiosis* is not regarded as an immutable object but as a dynamic process of *morphogenesis* and *metamorphosis* (Rastier 2017, 7). The concept of *process* or generative dynamism represents a particularly useful epistemological shift in the human sciences, similar to the theory of relativity or quantum mechanics in physics, insofar as the constancy of signs as individual objects vanishes in favor of a dynamic morphogenesis or continuous formation of relations.[13] In the context of communication, this dynamic generation of discourse could pose a serious problem, especially at the level of interpretation. If *text* is the result of a dynamic process in constant movement, then its interpretation by the addressee (or reader) must be a dynamic process as well. *A fortiori*, translation as the act of transferring discourse from one language (linguistic system) to another should be considered a dynamic process. How then is it possible to study target texts in relation to their source if discourse is by nature in a dynamic morphogenesis? The answer is in the principle of the instantaneity of analysis.[14] Just as in quantum physics where the position or spin of the particle can only be measured at the specific moment of measurement and cannot be a reference for predictability, in discourse analysis the moment the analysis is carried out is the reference for the validity of the results. The *interval of validity* for a discoursive process can be defined according to various factors such as the purpose of analysis, the length and nature of the discourse, and the diachronic variations and verbal functions involved.

Greimas postulates the concept of *generative trajectory* to describe the *process* of discoursivization. The *generative trajectory* designates the morphodynamical generation of discoursive structures from semiotic (deep level) and narrative (surface level) structures of language ([1979] 1993, 244). Greimas's semiotic model of generative trajectory can be thought of as a complementary response to Chomsky's generative linguistics in the sense that it is not solely focused on deep and surface structures of syntax deployed by a transformational system; it describes not only language but all semiotic systems as systems of signification and recognizes two syntactic and semantic components at all structural levels, including at the level of discourse. In Greimas's model, the structures of a *system* universal and independent of specific codes (specific natural languages) are divided into syntactic and semantic components operating at two superimposed levels: semiotic (deep) and narrative (surface). "The discoursive structures, less deep, are charged with taking up for themselves the surface semiotic structures and with 'putting them into discourse' by having them pass through the domain of the enunciation" (*Ibid.*, 134). The passage from the semio-narrative level to the discoursive level marks the transformation of syntactic and semantic forms from their deep linguistic – the level of system – to their *discoursive forms* – the manifestation of potential in actual. As a result of this process, the linguistic forms can be manifested every time in a different way, varying according to situational factors.

		Syntactic component	Semantic component
Semio-Narrative Structures (System)	Deep Level:	Fundamental Syntax ▼	Fundamental Semantics ▼
	Surface Levels:	Surface Narrative Syntax ▼	Narrative Semantics ▼
Discoursive Structure (Discourse)		Discoursive Syntax	Discoursive Semantics

Figure 2.5 Generative trajectory of discoursivization

As for other semiotic systems, Greimas notes that the generative trajectory and the principle of discourse can be extrapolated to other mediums of communication or semiotic systems, or even to any other system regulating human behavior. We can indeed speak of "discourse" in music, painting, architecture, political activities, social interactions, and cultural phenomena such as cuisine, rituals, and customs.

> On the other hand, by extrapolation and as a hypothesis which seems to be fruitful – the terms discourse and text have also been used to designate certain non-linguistic semiotic processes (a ritual, a film, a comic strip are then viewed as discourses or texts). The use of these terms postulates the existence of a syntagmatic organization undergirding these kinds of manifestations.
> (Greimas 1979, 81–82)

I shall use the concept of "discourse" in my discussion of the hybrid nature of the multisemiotic layers of Rumi's poetry in the next chapter.[15]

1.2.2   Dual Functioning of Language

To understand the structural nature of discourse and the passage from system to text in the process of discoursivization, we need to look more deeply into the dual functioning of language. As previously noted, structural linguistics recognize dualities at several levels of linguistic *semiosis*. The most fundamental of these dualities is found at the level of the sign's component parts. The differentiation concerns the two kinds of constituting elements of linguistic discourse based on their capacity to signify: *distinctive* elements that are meaningless and *significant* elements that are meaningful. It is again Hjelmslev (1961, 41–46) who points out the difference between signs as meaningful units and *figurae* as sign components that are not capable of *signifying* yet. The *expression-figurae* are called *cenemes* (from Greek for "empty") and *content-figurae* are *pleremes* (from Greek for "full"). Hjelmslev's *cenemes* could be understood as *phonemes* except that the former are a unit of *form* and the latter a unit of *substance*. Likewise, *pleremes* can be compared to semes in Greimas's structural semantics. Later on, André Martinet ([1960] 1980, 13–15) proposes the concept of *double articulation*[16] describing the two-fold structuring of units in language: first, the meaningless but distinctive units of sound, or *phonemes*, are distinguished based on their *pertinence* – their capacity to be combined in a language – and second, their combination creates the smallest signs, the basic meaningful units of text, called *monemes* (or *morphemes* in English terminology). In the term "un-bear-able," there are eight phonemes (ten graphemes) but only three signifying units or morphemes.

Duality does not occur only in the articulation of linguistic components. There is also a duality of the operational and functional nature of language. The operational duality exists in the differentiation between the capacity of individual sign units to signify on their own and their capacity to combine with other signs to form a meaningful *syntagm*. Another duality can be imagined in terms of the capacity of signs to *represent* or *name* versus their capacity to *communicate* a *message*. Émile Benveniste defines this linguistic capacity of naming versus communicating a message as the *double signifiance* of language (its dual signifying mode). Benveniste thus distinguishes the *semiotic* mode and the *semantic* mode of signification. The semiotic signifying mode of signs consists in their capacity to *mean*, i.e., to name, to represent, to designate. The semantic mode of signifying mode corresponds to the property of signs in combination to create syntagms that *mean* in the sense of *communicating* a message or *discourse* (1974, 63–64). As Benveniste argues, it is precisely this property of language that sets it apart as a unique semiotic system among all others. Although Benveniste's terminology is somewhat arbitrary, his dichotomy has been recognized and widely discussed by other semioticians and linguists.

Roman Jakobson largely elaborates on this twofold character of language. In his "Two Aspects of Language and Two Types of Aphasic Disturbances" (1971, 239–259), he recognizes two characteristic operations in language at the basis of discoursivization, similar to Benveniste's two modes of signifying. According to Jakobson:
Any linguistic sign involves two modes of arrangement:

(1) *Combination*. Any sign is made up of constituent signs and/or occurs only in combination with other signs. This means that any linguistic unit at one and the same time serves as a context for simpler units and/or finds its own context in a more complex linguistic unit. Hence any actual grouping of linguistic units binds them into a superior unit: combination and contexture are two faces of the same operation.
(2) Selection. A selection between alternatives implies the possibility of substituting one for the other, equivalent in one respect and different in another. Actually, selection and substitution are two faces of the same operation.

(1971, 243)

What is described by Jakobson corresponds to the utterance on the two syntagmatic and paradigmatic axes. The former corresponds to the operation of *combination* and the latter to *selection*. To give concrete examples, we can go back to the sign-function "apple" in the *system* of English. We can see how it can occur in a discourse by forming a syntagmatic chain of sign with other components of the same class. Here are some examples: (1) "She threw red apples at me." (2) "She kept looking at his ugly Adam's apple." (3) "Oh the apple of my eye!" These three chains constitute different utterances – or texts in Hjelmslev's terminology – where the potential sign-function *apple* is semiotically actualized in the discourse. The sign "apple" is used in a different context and in combination with other signs with significantly different content values.[17] What is to be noted is that in each utterance the content functive of "apple" has a different value determined in combination with the content functives of other components of the text. Each of these utterances can be taken as a single sign where the sign function "apple" is a component but each time with a different *formal* structure. What is evident is that the semantic sum of all these components is different from the sum of their individual functives. "Apple" is an English word with a predetermined semantic value (or set of values); however, it takes an *ad hoc* value every time it occurs in *discourse*. This simple example shows how potential linguistic *forms* of the system come to manifest themselves in actual *forms* of *discourse* by way of the actualization *process*. Another example shows how a deep-level syntactic form can transform into different discoursive forms: "It is recommended that he come" or "It is recommended that he should come." The syntactic structure of the subjunctive mood can be manifested as two different forms indicating both different levels of formality and two diatopic (geographic) variations: British or American English. The two discoursive forms of "Sit down" and "Be seated" are manifestations of the same semantic deep level form but imply two different situational sets of data: a classroom or a courtroom. These examples illustrate different *styles* of writing or speaking, or in other words, various ways of using the linguistic code in the text. The variations in *style* are traditionally studied by *stylistics*.

The most important take here is the formal difference between the two *signifying modes* of the sign. In brief, there are variations of content-form where the sign signifies individually or when it is combined with other signs to compose a syntagm. The central problem is the nonlinearity and nonalgebraic nature of *combination* in discourse. To clarify, there is often no equivalence between the total semantic value of a discourse and the sum of the semantic value of its individual sign units. The dual articulation means that at the two levels of analysis, the sum of the whole does not equal the sum of the parts. The passage from phoneme (or grapheme) to morpheme, i.e., from sound to sign, in a *pertinent* context, completely changes the nature of the sound. To a lesser extent, the passage from an individual word to the word in a syntagm changes its meaning to varying degrees. Therefore, the content-form of the discourse can almost never equal the linear sum of the content-form of its individual components. This conclusion also raises the question of *connotation* as opposed to *denotation*. Signs at any level of analysis – from the smallest unit of *pleremes* or morphemes, words or lexemes, all the way to longer syntagms like sentences or entire texts – have a semantic value or content substance that is different when taken individually than when in combination with other signs composing the syntagm. Denotation is then defined as the meaning of the sign as taken individually and connotation is the secondary meaning accorded to a sign by its combination with other signs.

1.2.3   Code vs. *Norm*

Language as the semiotic system par excellence displays another inherent duality, that between *code* and *norm*. Any analysis of the discoursive form must focus on the relation between the system and its use within a linguistic community. The concept of convention is at the heart of linguistic form. In fact, the arbitrariness of the linguistic sign implies that it is a sign only by convention. This principle, however, also applies to the passage from the level of code to that of discourse. What differentiates "She eats what?" as an idiomatic utterance from "What does she eat?" as the "correct" way of asking a question is not dictated by the English syntax as a *code* but by English stylistics as a conventional norm. The same formal differential imposes the morphological structure of "move-ment" rather than "mov-ure" or even "mov-ation." The generative trajectory from semio-narrative structures to discursive structures always involves transformation of structures. This transformation occurs on a conventional basis but not necessarily an arbitrary one. The difference between the linguistic structures of the system and the discursive forms found among linguistic communities springs from the existence of a secondary system of code, more localized and restrictive to certain regions of the social continuum. This secondary system called *norm* stands in contrast to *code*. Branches of language sciences such as pragmatics and sociolinguistics also deal with how code as an abstract underlying system of structures is manifested in the reality of a society and examine how variations in time, space, and social class can be reflected in the use of specific groups of the language.

> In the field of sociolinguistics, by norm is meant a model based upon a more or less rigorous observation of social or individual use of a natural language. The choice between types of usage for the constitution of the norm rests upon extralinguistic criteria; religious language, political language, literary prestige, etc.
>
> (Greimas 1979, 214)[18]

Linguistic norms are more flexible and ephemeral than linguistic codes. They vary for different reasons. Linguistic norms can also be violated in certain contexts where a literary canon is changed, improved, or rejected (See *ratio difficilis* below). In this case, older norms can even be replaced by new ones, as often attested by the work of ground-breaking authors. In general, the use of particular forms in discourse rather than other available structures in the language can be attributed to a variety of reasons including social class, historical evolution, or the lived experience of a particular user. Linguistic variations can occur at different levels and on account of different situational factors and can be classified as *diatopic* (variation in place), *diachronic* (in time), *diaphasic* (in formality of situation), and *diastratic* (in social class, culture, or educational level).[19] Any set of these discursive formal variations, with distinguishable patterns in both syntax and semantics, established by the pragmatic habits of specific groups of language users can comprise a subsystem within the general system, a language within the language, which can be referred to as *idiom, lect,* or *jargon.*

Examining the sociolinguistic dimensions of translation, Maurice Pergnier (1993, 229–232) makes a more specific use of the term *idiom* in a threefold model to describe the passage from linguistic to discursive structures: *code, idiom, instance,* i.e., respectively, standard language, use of the language by social groups and the use by an individual of the language in the discourse. This trichotomy highlights the dissociation of the canonic aspect of language from its conventional and normative aspect. *Idiom* is the collective use of the code and intercedes between language as the code and discourse as its specific use. In fact, idiom is a specificity of natural language, especially differentiating it from machine languages where the initial code is not subject to a secondary system of *habits*. Metaphorically speaking, the difference between code and idiom can be compared to that between law and custom or precedence in a judiciary framework. The *reductionist* impact of idiom is seen at all levels of sociolinguistic behavior, including in what is considered standard language. Idiom determines the choice of semantic and syntactic forms, singling them out among all other possible forms available in the code. For instance, in the previous examples, the choice of the morpheme *-ment* rather than *-tion* to form the substantive derivative of the verb "to move" is a convention imposed by idiomatic norms. Idiom also imposes the validation rules for fixed phrases and expressions. It makes the difference between the acceptable form of "It is raining cats and dogs" and the unacceptable form of "It is raining ropes."

The third component of Pergnier's trichotomy is the *instance*, namely the final stage of discoursivization where the discourse is formulated by the locutor. This is where users can make a specific use of the code and the idiom, reflecting their subjectivity. Linguistic variations result in the creation of *lectal varieties* that are defined in terms of their situational motivation as dialect, sociolect, and technolect. It is certainly within the boundaries of idiom that lectal variations occur insofar as they reflect the conventional linguistic habits of a specific community distinguished by their geographic, professional, or sociocultural characteristics. However, the lectal variety that reflects the subjective individual use of the language and idiom is called *idiolect*. Idiolect designates the general pattern that can be established by the analysis of instances of personal discourse indicating the degree to which it may deviate from both the code and the idiom.

1.3   Translation as Rediscoursivization

The process of *discoursivization* corresponds to the generation of discourse, i.e., the manifestation of semiotic forms in a meaningful syntagmatic chain or utterance. Translation, however, should be considered as a process of *rediscoursivization*: the *remanifestation* of the same utterance in a different language. In this secondary *process*, the content-substance is to remain intact while every other component, namely expression-form, expression-substance, and even content-form, inevitably change since the process of discoursivization is based upon a different linguistic *system*. But how can the content-substance remain intact while the content-form inevitably changes? In fact, the expression and content-forms regulating the formation of the source discourse in the original *system* differ from the forms of the target system regulating the formation of the target discourse. The shaping of the *purport* into *substance* definitely differs from one *system* (language) to another on the expression plane due to phonologic differences, but also on the content-plane. Hjelmslev gives the famous example of the varying segmentation of the visual spectrum in color terminologies of different languages, pointing out that different languages do not even see colors in the same way (1961, 52–53). In other words, different systems do not produce the same content-substances to refer to the same phenomenon. Certain concepts do not exist in certain languages and, as a result, no content-form corresponds to their semantic structure. At the same time, Jakobson argues that all languages are capable of representing reality, albeit using different methods. This means that the semantic content of the source utterance, i.e., its *reference* – or *object* of the sign, in Peirce's terminology – can remain intact in the process of rediscoursivization even if the content-forms are inevitably altered.

The real problem is caused by the differential between language structures and discursive forms. The process of discoursivization is not only a corollary of the semio-narrative structures of the system but also of situational factors such as the circumstances of the genesis and the author's deliberate choices. To understand the problem, one should consider that translators do not translate languages but *texts*. Translation is not the transfer of one system into another but the transfer of a discourse from one process of discoursivization to another. In effect, it is the discursive structures that need to be considered and not the linguistic (semio-narrative) structures specific to each *system*. In other words, it is the forms of *process* that count and not the forms of *language*.

This problem has been examined by several scholars such as Eugene Nida, as previously discussed, but perhaps no one has plumbed the depths of the question better than the Canadian translation scholar Barbara Folkart. Inspired by Greimas's stratified trajectory model and applying Hjelmslev's sign model to Translation Studies, Folkart proposes a comprehensive semiotic theory of interlingual translation based on the concept of discourse in an attempt to surpass the classic dichotomy of source-oriented versus target-oriented translation. Although the conclusions she draws are debatable, the quality of her detailed demonstration of the impossibility of recreating the discursive form of the ST is unmatched.[20]

As the title of her work *Le conflit des énonciations: traduction et discours rapporté* (1991) shows, Folkart considers translation, above all, as an act of re-enunciation: translation recreates an utterance previously put into discourse. The second discourse, however, must appear in a different language, which means in a different code and following a different norm. Translation, thus, is a process of rediscoursivization. As Folkart argues, discoursivization – *la mise en discours* [putting into discourse] – designates the *process* of structuring a discourse out of multilayered *prediscoursive* semiotic materials. The discourse is the final stage of the manifestation of a semiotic hierarchy at the base of which is the system (language), followed by the social polysystem (shaping the *idiom*), with the subjectivity of the enunciator forming the amorph extralinguistic continuum into an intelligible substance. All these materials and strata make up what Folkart calls *prediscoursive* purport.

Relying on Hjelmslev's concept of *purport* (translated as *matière* [matter] in French), Folkart explains how discourse is the product of a process of reshaping the extralinguistic purport by underlying (*sous-jacent*) forms or structures of language. Underlying forms of a language shape the reality into the substance of the discourse. Therefore, discoursive substance is the *manifestans* [manifester] of discoursive forms, and discoursive forms are the *manifestatum* [manifested], in Hjelmslev's terminology. These structures or sets of relations, as explained earlier, are remodeled by the combination rules of the *idiom* or sociolinguistic *norms*. In Folkart's interpretation of Hjelmslev's model, language structures, both expression-forms and substance-forms, constitute the infrastructure of the discoursive forms, hence the term "infradiscourse." The prediscoursive purport is manifested in the final discoursive substance shaped by the discoursive form. This is the final stage of manifestation that represents the speaker's subjective act of discoursivization at the instance of speech. This last stage is a crucial point insofar as it is the passage from an infradiscourse – deep structures of the language and then surface structures of the discourse modelled by the idiom – to an actualized substance by means of a speaking *subject*. Thus, the phenomenon of *mise en discours* is the deliberate operation, implemented by a speaking subject, consisting in shaping the extralinguistic continuum (phonatory and referential) bounded by a linguistic system of signs (with form, substance, and a syntactic operating mode) and by an *idiom* system (with its codes and rules of combination). Together, the linguistic and idiom systems constitute the discoursive material, towards a discoursive syntagm with its own material texture (substance) and underlying structures. Subsequently, the set of underlying microstructures constituting the form of discourse composes the infradiscoursive layer, the constituent particles, and the substance (micro-syntagms) of discourse. Folkart compares these microstructures of infradiscourse to paper seeds or screen pixels and discourse to the general aspect of a paper sheet or the image on a screen (1991, 252–274).

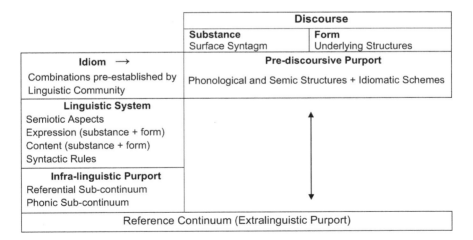

Figure 2.6 Barbara Folkart's model of discoursivization

To clarify this model, let us go back to our examples with the term "apple." The problem with the translation of the three utterances into French is not limited to the differences between the content-form of "apple" and the content-form of "pomme." The problem lies in the discoursive structure of those utterances: the discoursive content-form of the English utterance is inevitably distorted in the target French. The way "apple" is used in those three utterances constitutes the *forms of a process*, not just the *forms of a system*. For instance, translating the utterance "Oh the apple of my eye" by "Ô les prunelles de mes yeux" can only lead to a total deformation of the content-form, if not of the content-substance of the utterance: "pomme" cannot yield the same semantic value in the French syntagm as "apple" in the English one. As previously noted, forms are by nature *relations* or *functions* between terms. This is true both for semio-narrative forms of the *system* and for discoursive forms of the *process*. As two sets of relations, the semiotic forms of systems and the discoursive forms of process, themselves, stand in a relation of some sort to each other. This *process function* (the relation between discourse to code [language], process to system) is the most important parameter in translation insofar as it represents the *ad hoc* process of discoursivization in the text in question. To put this in a logico-mathematic perspective, the process function is a secondary function that has for functives the semiotic forms and discoursive forms.

Another classic example of how the preservation of discoursive forms presents a dilemma in translation is found in fixed expressions and idioms. These syntagms are normally translated by their functional equivalent in the TL – a translation technique called structural modulation. However, the precise content-form of the ST can only be altered in the process of rediscoursivization. "It is raining cats and dogs" is not exactly "Il pleut des cordes" [it rains ropes], although the two expressions are functionally equivalent. Another example showcases how the formal structure of the source discourse determined by the specific choices of the speaker (author) is altered in the process of rediscoursivization: "Starting my job hunt" and "Beginning my job search" are both functionally equivalent to "Je commence ma recherche de travail." Nonetheless, the formal structure of the discourse in the two English utterances are clearly dissimilar.

In other words, the remanifestation of the discoursive form is a theoretical aporia. By necessity, all translations imply some degree of *deformation* of the original text insofar as the process of rediscoursivization occurs upon a prediscoursive purport. Folkart's response to this theoretical conundrum is based on the preservation of reference. Like many linguists after Benveniste and Jakobson, she places the emphasis on the extralinguistic reality as reference, which calls to mind the Peircean concept of sign *object* or *referent*, not developed in Saussure's model. The content-substance of the discourse refers to something outside the semiotic system. This object is the single most important component of communication. Both the original discourse and the target discourse exist because a speaker seeks to convey a message whose content refers to a reality. The infradiscoursive structures of these discourses are fundamentally different, hence inherently unretrievable in the process of rediscoursivization. The source discoursive structures can be re-*created* by the target discourse but never re-*manifested*. Therefore, in translation, the reference is intact, but discoursive forms are recreated based on the target *infradiscourse*.

Émile Benveniste even uses the example of translation to demonstrate the dual signification mode of language, *semantic* and *semiotic*, in his paper "La forme et le sens dans le langage" (1974, 215–238). The *semantic* aspect of the utterance, as Benveniste points out, can pass from one language system to another, provided that the message is perfectly understood by the translator. However, the difficulty arises at the level of the syntagm in its materiality, its capacity for connotation and its internal articulation. Benveniste sums up the problem:

> One can transpose the *semantics* of a language in that of another, "salva veritate"; this is the possibility of translation, but one cannot transpose the *semiotics* of one language to that of another, this is the impossibility of translation. Here we touch upon the difference between semiotics and semantics.
>
> (1974, 228)

How significant is the alteration of the discoursive form caused by *rediscoursivization*? If the focus of language is after all to communicate a message containing a semantic content, why should the formal structure of the message matter? The answer lies in a functional theory of translation that considers the text not only as a system of semantic values and forms but as a means of communication.

1.4 Discourse as an Act of Communication

1.4.1 The Functional Theory of Discourse

It is mostly with Jakobson's functional theory that structural semiotics turns its attention from language as a system of values to language as a communicative tool. Language is more specifically studied as a system of communication or a code that underlies the discourse, regarded as a message. Thus, modalities of discoursivization are considered in terms of communicative functions. The change of terminology in the functional theory of language also reflects the change of perspective and rethinking of Saussurean notions: *langue* is referred to as *code* and *text* or *discourse* is more pertinently designated by *message*.

Jakobson's epistemological departure point is the work Karl Bühler, German logician and psychologist, known for his contribution to the *gestalt theory*. Bühler is among the first thinkers to distinguish the *deictic* field of language from its *symbolic* field. The deictic field of language is the capacity of language to show by pointing at – as *deixis* suggests a pointing finger – as opposed to its function of representing. "Thus, in general terms, as Bühler argues, the situation and the context are the two sources that in every case contribute to the precise interpretation of utterances" (Bühler [1934] 2011, 169). The significance of Bühler's work is, above all, due to his tripartite *organon model* of communication, considering all acts of human communication as a triangular relation between three poles: the sender of the message for whom the sign is a symptom, the addressee

82 *Translation or the Retrieval of the Discoursive Form*

(*Empfänger*) for whom the sign is a signal, and the object and fact (*Gegenstände und Sachverhalte*) for which the sign is a symbol. Modelled as such, communication involves three functions: the *expressive* function (*Ausdrucksfunktion*) for the sender, the representation function (*Darstellungsfunktion*) for the object, and the conative or appellative function (*Appellfunktion*) for the addressee.

In "Linguistics and Poetics" ([1960] 1964, 350–377), Jakobson takes Bühler's model and presents a more elaborate schema of a verbal message. Jakobson identifies six factors of communication. He proposes the following schema:

```
                    CONTEXT
     ADDRESSER      MESSAGE        ADDRESSEE
                    CONTACT
                    CODE
```

Figure 2.7 Factors of verbal communication

Each of these factors of verbal communication characterizes a function of language. Depending which of these aspects is emphasized, the discourse displays a specific function. In other words, the orientation of the communication towards one of these poles determines the function of communication. Although hardly any message can be found that fulfils only one function, the structure of the verbal message is primarily a corollary of its predominant function. Theoretically, any text, or any unit of text regardless of its length, can be analyzed at any moment in terms of its functions. It is then possible to measure the share of each of the functions as variables.

```
                    REFERENTIAL
     EMOTIVE        POETIC         CONATIVE
                    PHATIC
                    METALINGUAL
```

Figure 2.8 Jakobson's linguistic functions

The primary function of verbal communication is referential, i.e., when the emphasis is set on the *referent* or *context*. The focus of the *expressive* or *emotive* function is on the speaker and his attitude towards what he is stating. Imperative and vocative categories of grammar, which seek to act upon the addressee, are examples of the *conative* function. Certain messages that serve to "establish, to prolong, or to discontinue communication, to check whether the channel works" (1964, 355), certain fillers of speech such as "Well" in English, are examples of the *phatic* function. Discourse upon the code, the language itself, such as grammar rules or glossaries, constitute the *meta* function. Last but not least for our discussion, the orientation of the message towards itself is considered as the *poetic* function. Jakobson defines the poetic function of language as "the focus on the message for its own sake" (1964, 356). The poetic function is not exclusive to poetry, although poetry and poetic prose are archetypal examples of it. Any text in which structuring efforts are focused on the discoursive quality of the text rather than (but not necessarily at the expense of) other components of communication displays some degree of *poeticity* or *literarity*. This could include certain segments on the syntagmatic chain of an otherwise informative text.

From a structural standpoint, Jakobson defines the poetic function as the result of the projection of the *selection* operation from the paradigmatic axis of discourse to its syntagmatic axis. As previously discussed, the signifying property of a linguistic utterance is the result of a dual operation of *selection/substitution* and *combination*. Selection operates on the criterion of *similarity/equivalence* on the vertical axis of the syntagmatic chain, fulfilling what Benveniste calls the *semiotic* function of signification. Combination is based on the criterion of the *contiguity* of the constituent units of sign on the horizontal axis of the syntagmatic chain, implementing Benveniste's *semantic* mode of signification. The key concepts here are *similarity/equivalence* as the criteria of *selection* of the constituents of the utterance, and *contiguity* as the criterion of the *combination* of units with one another in order to create the syntagm. For instance, in the utterance "Jack eats pizza every day," the four sign units[21] are each selected, and can each be substituted vertically by any four sign units, such as "you," "drink," "tea," "tomorrow." This *substitution* operates on the basis of *similarity* or lack thereof (dissimilarity). However, the sign units are combined on the basis of *contiguity* in such a way that they can actually be *matched* with each other syntactically and semantically. One cannot substitute "Jack" with "apple," "pizza" with "Joe," "eats" with "eat," or "everyday" with "yesterday" to create a meaningful utterance. "Apple eat Joe yesterday" is not a meaningful utterance because the verb "to eat" is not properly conjugated and "apple" is an inanimate subject incapable of "eating" an animate direct object. Yet, in the poetic function, the criterion of similarity-dissimilarity or equivalence-difference is not only the basis of the process of *selection* but also that of the operation of *combination*.

> The poetic function projects the principle of equivalence from the axis of selection into the axis of combination. Equivalence is promoted to the constitutive device of the sequence. In poetry one syllable is equalized with any other syllable of the same sequence; word stress is assumed to equal word stress, as unstress equals unstress; prosodic long is matched with long, and short with short; word boundary equals word boundary, no boundary equals no boundary; syntactic pause equals syntactic pause, no pause equals no pause. Syllables are converted into units of measure, and so are morae or stresses.
>
> (Jakobson 1964, 371)

In other words, in the poetic function, the *signifying* property of the discourse relies on the three operations of *selection* on the basis of equivalence, *combination* on the basis of contiguity, and *combination* on the basis of equivalence. The application of the principle of equivalence to the second operation of combination means that the syntagmatic axis has now a *signifying* value. The particularity of the poetic function is that even the syntagmatic structure of the discourse has an impact on its semantic structure.[22] This has, no doubt, heavy consequences for translation. As a reminder, the general principle is translation is that the difference between the discursive forms before and after the process of rediscoursivization should not matter as long as the semantic *reference* of the utterance remains intact. This can no longer be pertinent. This principle is only applicable to texts whose primary function is *referential*, in other words, whose main purpose is the communication of an informative message. The alteration or loss of the discursive form, on the contrary, becomes as meaningfully important as the loss of the referential value of the message when the discourse has a poetic function, i.e., when the focus of the discourse is not the *referent* but the quality of the *message* itself. In the *poetic* function, the main (if not the only) purpose is to create "beauty" by means of the *semiotic* rather than the *semantic* signifying mode. In the case of poetry, it is the materiality of the discourse, the structure of its syntagm, that plays the central *signifying* role. A typical verse from Rumi – perhaps more so in his lyric works than his narrative ones – does not only seek to convey a message. Above all, it is the verse's discursive structure, comprised among other factors of its musicality, its syntagmatic harmony, and the literary devices of all type used that fulfils its *signifying* task. There is no simple extralinguistic referent. As will be discussed later, the extralinguistic referent is not even *effable*. On such occasions, translation as a process of rediscoursivization cannot ignore the *infradiscoursive purport* of the ST. Not imitating the discursive forms of a poetic ST is tantamount to the omission of certain parts of its content.

1.4.2 Discourse as Ratio Difficilis

So far, I have described the process of discoursivization based upon a prediscoursive purport composed of multiple layers of language and idiom. The poetic discourse can exhibit the utmost level of elaboration in style and rhetorical features and still remain within the infradiscoursive realm of its *code* and *norm*. Literary texts, even at their highest degree of poeticity, do not necessarily change the aesthetic canon of a language or culture. However, there exist cases where discourse is produced not by the application of rules of the code but by modifying them. That is the case of *ratio difficilis*.

Among all European semioticians, Umberto Eco is the one who most integrates Peirce's triadic sign model into his work. Combining the triadic principle with Hjelmslev's concept of *sign function*, Eco proposes a more fluid model of sign characterized by less emphasis on the fixed value of individual sign expression and content planes than on their constant mutable and transitory correlation (Eco 1976, 48–50). Eco's terminology resembles Jakobson's, with certain particularities: the *process* of discoursivization is referred to as *sign production*. It corresponds to the process of *semiosis* or the creation of an indefinite number of *messages* by the application a finite number of rules in the *code*, a closed and rigorously formalized system of governance. The relation between the sign, its *object*, and its *interpretant* is that of *inference*. Moreover, Eco's adoption from Peirce of the concept of *unlimited semiosis* means that the interpretant of each sign constitutes the object of another sign. The limitless semiosis and central role of *interpretation* result in the blurring of the border between the code and the message produced by it. The relation between sign production and code is no longer of a hierarchic and governing nature. Rather it is a correlation whereby the infinite generation of meaning and its interpretation bear on the nature of the code, reshaped through a process of what Eco, after Peirce, calls *abduction*. Abduction is the kind of inference that, unlike *deduction*, starts from the results to get to the rules, or from the manifestation of structures to the underlying structures. In the case of signs, the movement of inference is from the discourse to the organization of the *code*. In Eco's interpretation, "Abduction is, therefore, the tentative and hazardous system of signification rules which will allow the sign to acquire its meaning" (1984, 39–43). One of Eco's revolutionary ideas is in the field of semantics: the changing nature of meaning is described as the passage from *dictionary* to *encyclopedia*. Instead of the one-to-one model of *dictionary* definitions, consisting in the association of one *expression* plane to one *content* plane, Eco describes language as a dynamic augmentative repertoire of meaning, or an *encyclopedia*, in which the code is constantly enriched through a process of abduction by the association of new interpretations.

The mutability of the code in interaction with sign production and interpretation has notable implications for our understanding of the function and nature of discourse. This mutability is partially explained by the creation and addition of new signs to the code in the course of sign production in the case of what Eco calls *ratio difficilis*. To clarify this concept, signs are generated by the association of an expression plane and a content plane establishing a sign function. These functions are coded by the system in the sense that they are predefined for the users in the act of communication. The finitude of the number of signs in the system means that linguistic units of expression, such as phonemes, morphemes, and lexemes, are repeated in the discoursive chain as *replicas*. For instance, same phonemes or words are *replicated* numerous times in the course of discoursivization to create a text. Depending on the level of analysis, these expression units, occurring on a syntagmatic chain, belong to a specific class. The class is called *type* and the occurrence *token*. The *type/token ratio*,[23] which is the relation between a class of signs and its instances in the discourse, is considered by Eco to be of two sorts:

> Every replica is a token accorded to a type. Thus, every replica is governed by a *type/token-ratio*. . . . There is a case of *ratio facilis* when an expression-token is accorded to an expression-type, duly recorded by an expression-system and, as such, foreseen by a given code. There is a case of *ratio difficilis* when an expression-token is directly accorded to its content, whether because the corresponding expression-type does not exist as yet or because the expression type is identical with the content-type. In other words, there

is a *ratio difficilis* when *the expression-type coincides with the sememe* conveyed by the expression-token.

(1976, 183, emphasis in original)

In simple terms, *ratio difficilis* describes the mode of sign production in the discourse where new signs, or *new* forms in a Hjelmslevian terminology, are generated in the discourse, signs that do not exist in the system or are not sufficiently coded. This happens because there are not sufficient expressions for novel content planes. Eco speaks of the existence of an elusive *content nebula*, where the content is not perfectly defined and delineated, as a common reason for the creation of new expressions. Cases of *ratio facilis* are the signs with "a fairly simple expression-unit corresponding to a fairly precise content-unit," such as sememes (words) in a natural language. In this case where signs are replicas, the expression-token is governed by its expression-type, which is linked to the corresponding content-type. Examples given for *ratio difficilis* are less ubiquitous; they concern a veritable novelty in a wide range of stylistic practices, rhetoric figures of speech, or any particular innovative use of the code to create a uniquely formalized message including neologisms and borrowings. In this case, where signs are not replicas but one of a kind, there is no difference between an expression-token and an expression-type since there is only one token of that type that is motivated or dictated by the uncoded *content nebula*. Thus, in *ratio difficilis*, the content challenges not only the concept of replication but also the conventional sign-function in a conventional code itself. The infinity of the formation of the sign in this mode leads to an infinity of possible *interpretants*. Since *ratio difficilis* devises new discursive forms, the code is constantly enriched by it. The continuous sign production in this mode will, over time, lead to the augmentation of the code, and *a fortiori* to the unlimited possibilities of interpretation.

There can be two types of discourse as well. Discourse is by definition an aggregation of content units expressed by a syntagm of expressions, hence an uncoded sign.[24] In most cases, discourse does not present a case of *ratio difficilis* even if its content is completely new, such as a new discovery or a new scientific theory. The new content, even though formulated for the first time in history and thus completely uncoded, is semiotized by means of a *combination* of previously recoded semantic units. Eco gives the example of an astronomer discovering red elephants on a faraway planet to illustrate how even a disturbing change to the *content-system* and our worldview is still "mapped out" by an undisturbed *expression-system* (1976, 187–188). By contrast, in the case of a new and undefinable *content-nebula* that "cannot be analysed into recognizable and definable content units," a new discourse is born in which uncoded expression units are imposed by parts or segments of the content, and for which no interpretant exists yet. The example given here is that of a pictorial *text*, a painting where the painter has a vague idea of the content s/he means to express. In this case, the discourse becomes the scene of code inventing. The content nebula has to be invented and coded into content units. Then, the expression type needs to be invented and put into correlation with the newly structured content type creating a newly coded sign-function. Eco explains the difference between these two types of discourse as follows:

> The difference between mapping into the expression a new but foreseeable content and mapping into the expression a content-nebula is that between a *rule-governed creativity* and a *rule-changing creativity*. Thus, the painter has to invent a sign-function, and since sign-function is based on a code, he has to propose a new way of coding.
>
> (1976, 188, emphasis in original)

1.4.3 Translating Ratio Difficilis

As *ratio difficilis* is an act of code-making, it is *a fortiori* the quintessence of *norm-breaking*. As will be noted, remarkable examples of literary creativity are a product of the *ratio difficilis* mode of sign production. I will argue later that a major part of Rumi's work is quintessentially discoursivization in *ratio difficilis* since at all levels of textualization, he constantly changes the established code and renews and enriches it. This can only exacerbate the complexity of the translation conundrum. If translation as an act of rediscoursivization is unable to recreate the discursive forms because of the differences between source and target languages, it will be all the more incapable of rendering instances of rule-breaking *ratio difficilis*. The code and the norm of the ST are unknown to the readers of the TT. These readers can therefore not be made aware of the occasions of *rule-making* and *rule-breaking* unless the translated text is engaged in a similar process of *ratio difficilis* rule-breaking. In a rather simplifying effort, Folkart distinguishes two approaches in translation: *traduction-transitive* [transitive translation] and *traduction-pratique* [practical translation, or translation as *praxis*]. By *transitive*, she means a translation that only concentrates on the semantic content or the *referential value* of the text and disregards its discursive structure. This is the appropriate approach for technical and scientific texts, in other words, texts characterized mainly by a *referential* function. In contrast, translating texts with any degree of poeticity requires a *practical* approach, which in Folkart's terminology means a creative type or even a free style of translation, the limits and ethical problems of which will be discussed later.

> [Practical translation] privileges the semiological dimension of the utterance (for example poetic translation). Reinventing a *ratio difficilis*, practical translation aims to remanifest through the target text the idiolectal link, which in the source text, guaranteed the re-motivation of the expression by the content. The designation *traduction-pratique* emphasizes the inventiveness that the re-enunciator needs to show to follow the example of the enunciator.
>
> (1991, 456)

Thus, the choice of translation style consists principally in determining whether the original utterance represents a *ratio facilis* that conforms to a conventional discoursive purport within the established code and norm, or whether it displays a case of *ratio difficilis* of creative usage that upsets the institutionalized order. The translators' object will then be to attempt to recreate this discoursive "form" in any way possible. To understand more clearly the difference between the two types of original utterances, here is an example of two uses of the same idiomatic expression corresponding to each type. In the utterance, "She loved her horse like the apple of her eye," the use of the expression "like the apple of her eye" complies with the linguistic and stylistic norms of the English language. This example of *ratio facilis* can be translated as "Elle tient à son cheval comme à la prunelle de ses yeux." This is what Antoine Berman would describe as hypertextual translation where the translation has been adapted to the norms and style of the TT. The translation is acceptable insofar as the author shows no deviation from the sociolinguistic code of the source idiom. By contrast, in the utterance "Your friendship was the apple of my eye; you made it cider," there is wordplay relying on the connotative relation of "apple" and "cider," both terms belonging to the same semantic field. The structure of this utterance shows a combination based not only on the criterion of *contiguity* but also on that of *similarity*. The *semiotic* aspect of the expression "Apple of one's eye" here is as important as its *semantic* mode of signification. The infradiscoursive structure of this utterance is at least as important as its referential value. Moreover, the incongruity of the message evokes a case of *ratio difficilis* with some interpretative complexities: does this message allude to a betrayal in friendship?

In this example, the author breaks the conventional use of the code. He gives an *ad hoc* semiotic value to a microstructure that constitutes in itself an idiomatic and highly semiotized form. In this case, Antoine Berman, for example, would recommend a literal translation involving a *counter-idiomatic* re-enunciation process that goes against the convention imposed by the target stylistic values, precisely with the aim of recreating the original discrepancy between the discourse and the prediscoursive purport. Thus, a counter-idiomatic translation could read as "Ton amitié était la pomme de mes yeux; tu en as fait du cidre." This translation may shock the conscious reader of the English idiom, but insofar as it is an unconventional discoursive feature of the utterance, the rediscoursivized utterance must seek to hold on to the incongruity to the detriment of the stylistic convention of the French language. This kind of translation represents a "re-manifestation of the infra-discoursive layer" of the original text (Folkart 1991, 256). Folkart compared "prediscoursive purport" to the grains composing the texture or to the pixels making up the image on the screen: a counter-idiomatic translation method seeks to let reappear the disposition of the pixels forming the image, at least to some extent in the TT. In the translation of a *ratio difficilis*, it is not only the total morphological structure of the discourse that matters but also the reality of the discourse in its materiality.

The extent to which the author resorts to *ratio difficilis* is for the translators to assess and, therefore, somewhat subjective and dependent on the translators' familiarity with this prediscoursive purport of the source language as well as with the idiolectal features of the author. Examples of *ratio difficilis* are ubiquitous in the work of Rumi, not only because of its poetic genre or lyrical character, but also because Rumi is a code-breaker and code-maker *par excellence* in Persian classical literature. Rumi's relationship with language and idiom is problematic to say the least, since he considered language viscerally incapable of communicating the Truth. In the following sections and chapters, I will demonstrate how discursive forms in Rumi's text are as significant as referential values and display various degrees of *poeticity* and cases of *ratio difficilis*. The examples provided will also show what attitude Rumi translators adopted in translating Rumi's versatile and unconventional poetic discourse.

2 Connotative Semantics and Translation

As explained earlier, the most important implication of the process of discoursivization (the passage from code to text) is the modification of the semantic value (or content plane) of the sign. It is quite intuitive to see how words do not have the same meaning individually as in combination with other words in a syntagmatic chain or *context*. A more complex reality is that even the content plane of individual signs that are not actualized in discourse, i.e., signs that are absent in the text, can be indirectly evoked by way of association of meaning with the semantic content of the actualized signs, the ones present in the text. This phenomenon can obviously be reinforced when words are used in contextual combination, but in some cases, even single signs are, by nature, indirectly evocative of related concepts outside their direct content plane. For instance, the term "Indo-European" is preferred to its synonym "Aryan" to refer to the common roots of a large family of languages spoken from South Asia to Northern Europe. This is because "Aryan" evoked a series of ideas associated with it due to the historical misuse of the term during WWII. The general *primary* signification of a sign is called *denotation* and its *secondary* meaning, or the content-substance associated with *by extension*, is called *connotation*. The notion of connotation is not an easy one to define. It can have various definitions according to the context and the field in which it is examined. In broad semiotic terms, as previously noted, Hjelmslev considers a sign to be "connotative" when its *expression plane* consists of another sign. In other words, a sign in its entirety constitutes the expression to which a *content* is linked by a secondary sign function. In a structural semantic perspective, as Greimas explains:

> Connotation could be interpreted as the establishment of a relation among one or more semes located on a surface level and the sememe to which they belong, which must be read at a deeper level. Their connotation is akin to metonymy, the well-known rhetorical figure.
>
> ([1979] 1982, 53)

Metonymy or the trope of *neighborhood* is created by the association of a meaning with its neighbor by extension. Signs denote when their semes are understood only in relation to each other within the sememe they belong to, while they connote when a relation can be either subjectively or conventionally established with the semes in another sememe. Simply put, there is connotation when an utterance, by virtue of sociolinguistic norms or a subjective interpretation of the message, is associated with semantic units (semes) or concepts that are not primarily attributed to it by the *code*. The connotative character of the semantic value occurs, then, at two levels: it is either due to the *individual subjectivity* of the interpreter of the message or, more generally, imposed by the pre-established *conventional norms* of a culture. Technically speaking, it is either of an idiolectal character or governed by *idiom*. In either case, connotation represents a major challenge to translation insofar as such connotative content cannot be replicated by rediscoursivization. This is because the infradiscoursive purport of the TT is necessarily different from that of the ST on the one hand. On the other hand, the older the cultural tradition of the ST, the more complex potential connotative relations among concepts (or semes) can be.

The problem of connotation is crucial to the translation of Persian mystic literature and even more so to Rumi's discourse. The cultural difference between the ST and the TT on the one hand, and the specific technical use of terms in mystic literature, in itself a language within language, on the other hand, create a multilayered complex infradiscourse extremely difficult to replicate in the target culture. Greimas gives the example ([1979] 1993, 52) of the term *amour* and its inevitable association with sexuality in French culture as an example of connotation. This is all the more interesting that the concept of love is perhaps the most central of all in Rumi's thought and discourse. Connotative semantic problems are showcased in the following examples by idiomatic and fixed expressions in Persian, as well as the use of words and expressions belonging to different etymological origins or to various lectal registers.

2.1 Translating Fixed Expressions

Generally, the primary meaning of a syntagm is interpreted as the sum of the meaning of its constituents, putting aside its discursive structure. Fixed expressions, idioms, clichés, or what Jakobson calls *word-phrases* (1971, 242) are syntagms where the meaning of the whole is completely different from the sum of its constituents. *Pulling someone's leg* means "to fool someone" and not actually "to pull on their lower limb." Translators usually resort to the strategy of *equivalence* (Vinay and Darbelnet 1995, 38) to translate such utterances; they find for the TT an equivalent fixed expression with a more or less equivalent semantic and referential value.[25] However, for the reasons mentioned earlier, this method shows its limits when it comes to texts where the infradiscoursive structures are connotatively meaningful and the referential content denotatively important. That is why Antoine Berman adopts a controversial position in his project of foreignizing translation by advocating literal translation even for fixed expressions and proverbs (Berman 1999, 13–15). Literal translation would permit the transfer of the infradiscoursive composition of the utterance by reflecting it in its foreignness.

This position is particularly defensible in the translation of Persian proverbs and clichés for which few equivalents can be found. It is extremely relevant also for

Rumi's poetry. On the one hand, Rumi makes an abundant use of pre-existing idiomatic expressions in Persian and Arabic in an institutionalized application of the code, given the popularizing scope of his mystical-didactic poetry. On the other hand, several utterances in Rumi's poetry have risen to the rank of proverbs and fixed expressions in the Persian language and within popular culture. In other words, Rumi has created a discourse that has enriched the institutionalized code. In both cases, the impact of translation on the connotative value of the discourse is considerable. Connotative loss is inevitable, whether the translator adopts the literalist strategy or dynamic equivalence. In order to satisfy Berman's foreignizing scope and compensate for the loss of meaning, I argue that other methods should sometimes be used, not least the inclusion of abundant and detailed translator's notes.[26]

2.1.1 Institutionalized Expressions and Clichés

These are tropes, either metaphors – by way of substitutions based on similarity – or metonymies – by way of combinations based on contiguity – according to Jakobson's fundamental dichotomy of linguistic operations (1971, 243). However, these tropes are not necessarily literary devices insofar as they have lost their novelty. They have been used so often over time that they have become commonplace to the point of forming individual semantic units.[27] They are hence considered institutionalized or canonized in the language code. Clichés, moreover, are not always fixed expressions. For there to be a cliché, there must be a worn figure of speech provoking an effect of repetition and banality. These effects, often based on metaphor or hyperbole, can hinge on a single word without exhibiting syntactic rigidity (Amossy 2001, 11), as we will see in Example 2.1.

In the opening lines of one of the most famous tales of the *Masnavi*, "Moses and the Shepherd," a simple lexeme (*chāker*) constitutes a cliché par excellence due to the metasemic displacement to which it has been subjected over the centuries.

Example 2.1 M.III) 1751–1752

Did musā yek shabāni rā be rāh	ku hami goft ey gozinande elāh[28]
To kojāyi tā **shavam** man **chākerat**?	Chāroqat duzam konam shāne sarat?
Moses saw some shepherd on the way,	who was saying "O choosing God!
Where are you? That I may **become** your **slave**?	Sew your shoes, comb your hair?"

E1) Whi: p. 121–125:	E2) Wil: p. 149–158:	E3) Nim: p. 310–315:
Moses once heard a shepherd praying as follows: "O God, show me where thou art, that I may **become** Thy **servant**. I will clean Thy shoes and comb Thy hair."	Moses saw a certain shepherd by the way who was saying, "O God, O God! Where are you? that I may **become** your **servant**; that I may sew your sandals, (and) comb your hair."	Moses saw a shepherd on the way, who was saying, "O God who **choosest (whom Thou wilt)**, Where art Thou, that I may **become** Thy **servant** and sew Thy shoes and comb Thy head?"

(Continued)

Example 2.1 (Continued)

E4) At: 40, p. 132–134: ONE day Moses encountered a shepherd on the way! And heard him saying: 'O **God who electest whomsoever Thou wilt**, where art Thou, that I may **become** Thy **servant** and stitch Thy shoes and comb Thy head	E5) Bt: p. 19–22: Moses heard a shepherd on the road praying, "**God**, where are You? I **want to help You**, to fix Your shoes and comb Your hair.
E6) Moj: p. 101–106: Once Moses overheard a shepherd pray: 'O God! O God!' he heard this shepherd say. 'Where do you live that I might **serve** you there? I'd mend your battered shoes and comb your hair	E7) Lr: p. 371–373 / Ls: p. 16–18: MOSES SAW a shepherd on the road who kept crying out: O **God**, O **Lord** Where do I find you, that I might **serve**? sew your moccasins, and comb your hair

Chāker may simply mean "slave" or "home servant" but has acquired a whole connotative dimension following its use in the particular social context of Iranian culture. To be someone's *chāker* has become a token of extreme respect and humility towards a person. To say "I am your servant" with different synonyms such as *nokar*, *qolām*, or *moxles* [sincere devotee] is a coded word-phrase completely devoid of literal meaning and is used to show respect, modesty, affection, and deference. These hyperbolic expressions are not uncommon in Persian and in the Iranian culture, characterized by the phenomenon of *ta'ārof* [civilities], a mixture of hypocrisy, courtesy, and politeness. Compound verbal constructions like *chāker shodan* [become someone's servant] belonging to the colloquial register of the Persian language are characteristic of a particular sociolect, indicator of lower working social classes.

Rumi's use of the term has a specific discoursive purpose: to show the triviality of the shepherd's language. The whole tale revolves around the shepherd's inappropriate vulgar tone when addressing "the Almighty" God, a choice of words that is worthy of addressing a human being. The shepherd attributes to God anthropomorphic characteristics such as a dependence on a daily cleansing routine, arousing Moses's anger. Rumi's lexical choice helps create a connotatively rich image in the shepherd's few heartfelt cries. Yet there are no clues to these underlying connotative networks in the TT. This loss varies in degrees depending on the choices made by the translators. In E5 and E7 in particular, the substitution of the cliché "*chāker shodan*" by a verbal syntagm is particularly destructive of the familiar tone of the ST. The Persian text has an awkward choice of words to refer to God, yet the English text has nothing equivalent to shock the reader. After all, what is so unusual about a man's seeking to "serve God"?

The loss of connotative meaning is also inevitable in idiomatic expressions, as shown by Example 2.2.

Example 2.2 M.II) 116

Aql dar sharḥash **cho khar dar gel bekhoft**		sharḥ-e 'eshq o 'āsheqi ham 'eshq goft
Intellect, in explaining it (love), got stuck like a donkey in mud, The explanation of love and loverhood can only be said by love itself.		
E1) Red: I. p. 8–11: Our wits in love's affairs **stand sore perplexed**; Love only can elucidate love's text.	E2) Whi: p. 7–12: In explaining it Reason **sticks fast, as an ass in mire**; Naught but Love itself can explain love and lovers!	E3) Nim: p. 9–11: In expounding it (Love), the intellect **lay down (helplessly) like an ass in the mire**: it was Love (alone) that uttered the explanation of love and loverhood.
E4) Moj: Book One: p. 10–13: **A donkey stuck in mud is logic's fate** – Love's nature only love can demonstrate:	E5) Will: p. 16–19: The explaining mind **sleeps like an ass in mud**, for love alone explains love and the lover.	

The Persian cliché "getting stuck in mud like a donkey" is a *simile* expressing total inability to understand and act. In the absence of a direct equivalent, translators have resorted to a variety of different strategies, from the process of *equivalence* prescribed by linguists to the literality advocated by Berman (see Chapter 7). While Nicholson and later English translators have translated the simile word for word, Whinfield and Redhouse have opted for a semantic equivalence. We can thus observe the consequences of each of these strategies for the discourse. Literal translation results in the revival of a worn-out simile, reduced to the level of a periphrasis in the ST, as a fresh figure of speech in the TT. Translating literally in English a metaphor that is *dead*[29] in Persian reinvigorates its rhetorical value and therefore changes its value. On the other hand, the choice of dynamic equivalence, although preserving some of the ST's original semantic value with static verbs like "stand" or "stick," does away with the dramatizing imagery of the original discourse. The strategy of equivalence, in Redhouse's version for instance, makes the simile disappear by eliminating both terms of comparison. This shifts the semantic relationship of comparison from the syntagmatic axis (between intellect and donkey) to the paradigmatic axis. Literal translation, on the contrary, reverses a figure *in absentia* established in the paradigmatic axe – as the figurative meaning of "donkey stuck in mud" is to be sought elsewhere – to a figure *in praesentia* – as the analogy between reason and donkey are both present in the syntagm – established on the syntagmatic axis. Nevertheless, in both cases, some loss of meaning is inevitable, since the Persian cliché has the particularity of playing on both linguistic axes simultaneously: while the simile plays on the syntagm (A is like B), the fixed expression refers, metaphorically, to an idea outside the syntagmatic context.

2.1.2 Idiomatic Expressions as Ratio Difficilis

The difficulty of translating clichés reaches a whole other level when it comes to innovations introduced by Rumi and canonized by the code over time. The following two examples show two verses of *Masnavi* that have evolved into two clichés still very much in use in modern Persian.

Example 2.3 M.I) 1207

Pas zabān-e *mahrami* khod digar ast Thus, the language of intimacy is a different one. Common heart is better than common tongue.	Hamdeli az hamzabāni khoshtar ast
E1) Nim: vol. 2, p. 67: Therefore the tongue of mutual **understanding** is different indeed: **to be one in heart is better than to be one in tongue.**	E2) Lr: p. 22: The lingo the **like-minded** share is best! **Better a common heart than a common tongue!**
E3) Will: p. 76: For **intimacy's** language is quite different, **It's better sharing hearts than sharing language.**	E4) Moj: Book one, p. 76: The tongue of **intimacy** is set apart **Beyond mere words, it's being one at heart**

The second verse "Common heart is better than common tongue" has become so emblematic in Persian that it has acquired the status of a proverb. Persian speakers use it to emphasize the importance of having the same feelings and intentions.[30] And yet, regrettably, no translator of this passage has felt the need to bring this semantic phenomenon to the readers' attention by means of a translator's note, for example, or some graphic marking. Another unfortunate loss can be noted in the two compound nouns used to form a parallelism: *ham-deli* [common-heartedness], and *ham-zabāni* (common-tongue). The prefix *ham* is the Persian equivalent of the Greek syn/sym and the Latin con/com. For lack of a lexical equivalent, all the translators opted for a verb phrase to transpose the two compounds by a process of expansion.

Example 2.4 shows another of Rumi's verses that is the origin of a very common expression in Persian.

Example 2.4 M.I) 1207

Hich ādābi o tartibi maju	har che mikh^wāhad del-e tangat begu
Do not seek any rules or order.	Say whatever your pressed heart desires
E1) Wil: p. 149–158: Do not seek any forms or method; **say whatever your afflicted heart wishes.**	E2) Nim: p. 310–315: Do not seek any rules or method (of worship); **say whatsoever your distressful heart desires.**	E3) At: 40, p. 132–134: Search not after any particular rules or order of worship; **whatever your distressed heart desires, declare it.**
E4) Bt: p. 19–22: . . . God has revealed to me that there are no rules for worship. **Say whatever and however your loving tells you to.**		E5) Moj: p. 101–106: Don't bother with good manners any more, **But let your heart express what's in its core!**

The utterance "Say whatever your pressed heart desires" contains two institutionalized metaphors or periphrasis within its chain. In its entirety, it constitutes an idiomatic expression. *Del-e tang* [pressed heart] figuratively means a chagrined and distressed heart in medieval Persian, while in modern Persian it has come to mean "to miss someone or something" as well. *Del xāstan* where *del* [heart] is the subject of the verb *xāstan* [to desire/to want] denotes "to fancy, to long for, or to feel like." However, the way Rumi puts into use the language (code) and its idiom *Del-e tang* [pressed heart] gives it a whole new life and creates a new expression with a semantic content that surpasses the sum of its constituents: to express oneself freely, to vent one's feelings, to get something off one's chest. Rumi is the first to use language and idiom in this particular way. The connotative dimension of the second verse in the example greatly surpasses its denotative value. None of this richness is reflected or even hinted at in the first three classic English translations in spite of their literal character. The two modern translators have merely opted for free adaptations.

There are of course other examples of Rumi's discourse canonized as proverbs or idioms in Persian that suffer the same connotative loss in translation. One of the best-known examples is *āftāb āmad dalile āftāb* (M.II: 115) [the Sun came as proof of the Sun], a proverbial metaphor alluding to the irrefutability of a proof or of an axiomatic premise. It originates in Rumi's lyrical passage about his beloved Shamsoddin of Tabriz in a tale about an enamoured slave girl who becomes sick of love chagrin. The evolution of original verse to cliché creates a privileged communicative contact between its author and his Persian-speaking readership, a kind of cultural complicity. This bond is naturally lacking in communication through translation, even if readers are made aware of the occurrence of a *ratio difficilis* through translator's notes and comments.

These examples of various types of losses show how no translation process, either through equivalence or literal translation, can do justice to the connotative semantic value of the original utterance. Nevertheless, in the absence and impossibility of equivalence in the TT, a literal translation accompanied by a translator's metalinguistic notes pointing out these losses and recreating the reality of the situation for the reader appears to be a respectful and wise choice. Antoine Berman advocates an approach that accounts for rhythm, length, and possible alliteration of the cliché, "because a proverb is a form" and "literally translating a proverb is not a simple 'word for word'" (1999, 14). At the same time, the cliché should not be deprived of its original connotative charge in the ST. As Amossy stresses, "translation does not carry out a transfer from one linguistic system to another. It intends to reproduce a particular discourse that derives its meaning as well as its impact from the interaction between the speaker and their addressee(s)" (Amossy 2001, 12). In the end, therefore, in the absence of a solution that reproduces both the effect of Rumi's discourse and its linguistic form, the most judicious way for translators of Rumi to maintain the golden mean is to produce a literal translation enhanced by translators' comments in the margin, despite their cumbersome nature.

2.2 Translating Loanwords

A further source of connotative loss in the translation of Persian texts stems from the lexicographical heterogeneity of that language. The massive use of foreign elements, at lexical and syntagmatic levels by Rumi and other Sufi poets of his era, raises a question that goes beyond the problems of lexical semantics discussed in the previous chapter. What is at stake here is the complexity of the infradiscoursive purport of the Persian language as a result of foreignness of its lexicon. This infradiscourse manifested itself in Rumi's discourse with stylistic and rhetorical effects.

2.2.1 Persian Lexical Heterogeneity

Although an Iranian language, Persian is a heterogeneous lexical set endowed with innumerable borrowings from Semitic languages (Aramaic and Arabic) and Turkic and other Indo-European languages, much like English, a Germanic language, has up to 65% of its lexicon made up of Greek and Roman roots. The degree of the foreignness of lexemes in Persian varies according to the period and context. Rumi's epoque in the history of Persian literature could be compared to the Renaissance period in English when authors like Shakespeare enriched the language by borrowing foreign elements. Sufi literature as of the 12th century opened the door to a massive flood of Arabic loanwords into the literary canon of Persian. Beforehand, the Arabic lexicon was limited to scientific and religious domains.

Persian syntax has been subject to little evolution over the past 11 centuries, making it one of the oldest languages in the world, with works from the 9th century still intelligible for modern Persian speakers. Persian vocabulary, however, has seen several periods of alteration and enrichment. This diachronic variation manifests itself above all in the frequency of lexical elements of the Arabic language that comprise up to half of the Persian lexicon. This evolution is in conjunction with historical events: the 7th-century Arab invasion, the *de facto* independence of the Iranian kingdoms of the Iranian Plateau from the caliphate of the 9th century, the advent of Turkic tribes of Central Asia and the formation of Persianate kingdoms, the Mongol invasion, the Safavid Renaissance, etc. Persian is the spoken language of the majority of the Iranian Plateau, the crossroads of various civilizations between Asia and Europe. Mutual relations have been continuous ever since the second millennium BC when Iranian languages started to dominate the Plateau and came into contact with local languages, such as Elamite and particularly Semitic of Mesopotamia.

According to Khosrow Farshidvard (1387 [2008]), three main periods in the evolution of Persian can be recognized, each respectively marked by the Arab, Mongol, and Safavid domination of Iran. The first period, extending between the Arab and the Mongol invasion, must be divided into a period of transition (from the 7th to the 9th century) and a period of consolidation (9th to 12th) resulting in the birth of modern Persian from Middle Persian, the language of the Plateau in the Parthian and Sassanian eras. The latter period (9th to 12th) is characterized by a considerable exchange of lexicon and syntactic features between Arabic and Persian, the consequences of which proved to be eternal for both languages. For the Persian language, the impact of this era is the transition from Pahlavi to modern Persian, while for Arabic, this era represents the transition from an extremely marginalized vernacular status – due to the dominance of modern Aramaic (from Syriac) in the Semitic world – to the position of the *lingua franca* of the Islamic world. First, Arabic became the liturgical language of the Plateau, then it gradually replaced Persian as the administrative language of the caliphate at the beginning of the 8th century, and finally, during the Abbasid period, thanks to numerous translation campaigns (from Greek, Latin, Pahlavi, and Sanskrit), Arabic established itself as the *lingua franca* of science and philosophy. The consolidation of Persian is due to the rebirth of Iranian nationalism in the east of the Plateau under the Samanid dynasty, and the establishment of a modern Persian literary canon by authors such as Ferdowsi and Rudaki, among others (Xānlari 1366 [1987], 309). The lexical elements which have made their way into the vocabulary of both Persian and Arabic are those that are best integrated within each of these languages, even though Arabic tends to Arabicize aggressively any foreign borrowing, erasing foreign etymological roots.

The second era, marked by the resurgence of Sufism and the influence of Sufi poetry with figures such as Sanā'i and Aṭṭār, opens the way to a greater presence of Arabic terms in Persian, this time not as the language of the dominating power, but as a source of artistic inspiration and literary enrichment. Paradoxically, this happens while under the Mongols, Persian replaces Arabic, not only as the language of administration, but also as that of science and philosophy in the east of the Islamic world. Texts written in this period, however, regard Arabic vocabulary as a source of exoticism. The third era is the most impregnated by Arabic under the influence of the consolidation of Shiism, proclaimed the official religion of the country, and the formation of a whole Shiite liturgical and philosophical tradition. Until the second half of the Qajar reign (late 19th century), Arabic was a source of enrichment of speech with expressions and words so heterogeneous that only a literate elite was able to decipher it. The main function of Arabic elements at this time was to provide devices of euphemism in philosophical, administrative, and legal texts. This tendency abruptly ceased to exist with the advent of a modern movement of linguistic independence at the end of the 19th century. Much like Ferdowsi's campaign of purification of Persian from Semitic lexical elements, it sought to revive Iranian etymological roots.[31]

Given such a tormented history of interactions between Persian and its exogenous elements, it is not surprising that the use of Arabic utterances and terms is connotatively charged. The frequency and quality of the use of Arabic in a Persian text, as well as its context and enunciative situation, can all inevitably mark the discourse, whether deliberately or unconsciously for the author and his readership. Unlike average English speakers, who may not necessarily be aware of the non-Germanic lexicon in a text, Persian speakers, at least in the modern era, are more or less sensitized to the etymological origin of a given lexis. While this sensitivity is partly a modern phenomenon, the choice of an etymological source of lexis has always been a marker of sociolectal and idiolectal variation in the discourse. Indeed, unlike English where the vocables of Greco-Roman origin are relatively so well integrated into the lexicological landscape that they are almost inseparable from the Germanic elements, the Arabic roots present in Persian retain for a good part their heterogeneity, marked by certain letters of the Persian alphabet that have no phonetic Persian equivalent and are only used in foreign words. In addition, in most cases, the Arabic word and phrase can be replaced by a Persian equivalent without any semantic loss. In consequence, the etymological roots of a lexical choice can hardly be innocent. Depending on the context, the presence of an Arabic terminology can impact the tone, tenor, and function of the discourse, rhetorically and aesthetically. The frequency of an Arabic lexicon in a text can, for instance, be an indicator of its religious, theological, or legal nature. This reality, therefore, can have important implications for translation, especially in Rumi's texts, where Arabic terms and utterances have a remarkable presence. To understand more clearly the nature and importance of Arabic in Rumi's poetry, one needs to have an understanding of the history of Persian literature. Such knowledge can reveal, for instance, the conventionality of such a practice in relation to the norms and literary canon of the epoch or show to what extent Rumi's use is uncustomary, thus innovative.[32]

There are four major literary epochs recognized, called *sabk-e adabi* [literary school], covering the classical period of Persian literature from the 9th to the 19th century: *Khorāsāni* [of Khorasan] from the second half of the 9th until the end of the 11th century, the 12th century being a transition period with influences from Eastern Persian and Western Iranian languages; *'arāqi* [of Iraq],[33] which appeared with the Mongol invasion in the 13th century and dominated the literary scene until the advent of the Safavids in the 16th century; *hendi* (from India) corresponding to the period between the 16th and the end of the 18th century; and finally, what critics commonly call *bāzgasht-e adabi* [literary return] in the Qajar era. The four epochs are distinguished both thematically and aesthetically by the prevalence of certain literary forms (poetry or prose), poetic genre, stylistic traits, rhetorical figures, and discoursive particularities, which concern the use of language.[34]

One of these stylistic traits is the frequency and scope of Arabic words in literary texts. Borrowings from Arabic were sometimes congenial and met with favorably, sometimes with resentment, sometimes fusional, and other times conflictual. These ups and downs have been studied by Iranian linguist and language historian, Parviz Nātel Xânlari, in a chapter entitled the "Arab-Persian Conflict" (1987, 307–314). For instance, authors of the *Khorāsāni* school distanced themselves from Arabic, reversing its domination in Iranian administration, at the time of the cultural and intellectual awakening of the Iranian world. Khorasani authors, like Rudaki, use Arabic synonyms only in search of exoticism (Shamisā 1380 [2001], 25). Meanwhile, Sufi poets of the *'arāqi* school put aside this animosity, doubling the volume of the Persian lexicon by massive loanwords and expressions from Arabic vocabulary in every imaginable field.

This fact is notably corroborated by recent lexicographical studies, such as Gilbert Lazard's chapter on Arabic borrowings in Persian prose from the 10th to the 12th century (1995, 163–177). He makes particular reference to the statistical work of Shalmowski on the occurrences of Arabic lexicons in four ghazals of Hafez and Sa'di, showing a 20% token rate and a 40% type rate of Arabic (Lazard 1995, 163). Nonetheless, such statistical studies only focus on the quantitative nature of

Arabic terms at the expense of the qualitative reality of the phenomenon, in spite of its higher importance in the context of literary discourse. Counting the number of occurrences in the text does not take into account the fact that Arabic terms are not all characterized by the same degree of heterogeneity within the Persian lexical landscape and discoursive context. This degree varies according to the history of the appearance of loanwords, the lexical field to which they belong, the situation of their enunciation, etc. While certain borrowings come across as exotic, others have been well integrated in the Persian code, such as *'eshq* [love], *Sufi*,[35] and *ḥāl* [(spiritual) state of being]. But outside this category, the greatest number of lexies, especially phrases and compound words of Arabic origin, are easily identifiable by the average user of the language who would find them, if not evocative of a feeling of strangeness, at least endowed with an important connotative charge.

2.2.2 Foreign Lexica in Rumi's Text

Rumi is classified as a poet of *sabk-e arāqi*, although his use of language also bears characteristics of the *Khorāsāni* school, certainly because of his Khorasani origins (Shamisā 2001, 226–229). *'Arāqi* differs from the school of Khorasan on two accounts: thematically, following the advent of Sufi poetry with its mystical ideas and symbolism, and stylistically, because of the massive use of Arabic terms and certain syntactic variations present in western dialects of Persian. Rumi's liberal use of foreign languages, perhaps due to his multiculturalism and multilingualism, resulted in an unprecedented frequency in his work of non-Persian elements at all levels of utterance: morphology, lexical choice, lexical composition, syntactic structure, sentence, and even entire verses and poems. However, the sources are not exploited equally: while there are poems, sentences, verses, syntagms, and words in Turkish and Greek, the main foreign source of foreignness is Arabic for obvious reasons. Rumi's Arabicizing style especially in the *Masnavi* can be explained by his career as a preacher, theologian, and specialist of Islamic jurisprudence with a traditional education steeped in an absolute mastery of the Arabic language and the study of the Koran and hadith.

The use of foreign elements in Rumi's poetic texts can be classified in different ways. Nastaran Pezeshki's essay on the use of Arabic words and phrases in Rumi's poetry (1388 [2009]) suggests a typology based on two factors: first, she divides the occurrences of Arabic elements in speech into two groups, according to their familiarity and frequency in – modern but not necessarily contemporary – Persian: Persianized Arabic lexicon used unconsciously by average speakers, and affected and unusual elements uncommon in discourse. Then, she identifies lexicological categories in each group: isolated words, phrases, sentences, and quotes from the Koran and hadith.

I suggest a dual approach to classify Rumi's use of Arabic in his texts: one based on morphology and the other on pragmatics. On the syntagmatic axis and from a morphological standpoint, Arabic occurrences in utterance can be divided into single lexemes – whether they are simple or compound – and entire clauses or sentences. Borrowings exist in the form of simple morphemes like *ṣanam* [idol], mixed compound lexemes like *porshekāyat* [plaintive] consisting of Persian prefix *por* [full], and Arabic *shekāyat* [complaint], fully Arabic compound lexemes like *sadrey montahi* (M. III: l. 1788) [the tree that marks the end of the seventh heaven], noun phrases like *dār o-shshafā* [house of healing/hospital], adjective phrases like *dar safā* [joyful], adverbial phrases like *an qarib* [immediately], or entire clauses turned to single lexemes in Persian like *shaq al-qamar* [the moon split] used in Persian to refer to impossible tasks or *alast* [am I not?] referring to the covenant, and finally, independent clauses, simple or complex, which form verses or even entire couplets in Arabic such as the second verse of M. III) l.1753:

Tā tavāni pā maneh andar ferāq
[As much as you can, do not tread (in the way of) separation]
abqazo l-asyâ e 'endi at-talâq
[The ugliest thing for me is divorce.][36]

The grammatical category and the length of the borrowed element on the syntagmatic axis influence its heterogeneity. A simple Arabic morpheme used in lexical composition marks speech less visibly than does an entire sentence that has become a fixed expression. The degree of foreignness also varies according to the era; an Arabic expression that enters Persian for the first time through the stylistic choice of an author in the 19th century can be trivialized over time to such an extent that it loses its exoticism.

The stylistic effect sought by the author in his selection constitutes another important critical basis for a typology of Arabic occurrences in Persian texts. In a discoursive semiotic perspective, much as his use of clichés, Rumi's recourse to Arabic elements can be described as both conventional and code changing. While the majority of loanwords were already present and commonly used in Rumi's era, the existence and extent of the occurrence of certain elements can only be classified as *ratio difficilis* and attributable to Rumi's creative utilization of the linguistic code and norm. The first group is, of course, that of Arabic words and phrases that already existed in Persian, surviving the purgatory period of the school of Khorasan. In the stylistic analysis of a poem by Rudaki, Shamisā notes, "one of the linguistic peculiarities of the school of Khorasan is that despite the limited number of Arabic words, sometimes certain regular and high frequency Persian words are substituted with Arabic; for example, *sa'b* instead of *saxt* [hard/difficult], and *ḥarb* instead of *jang* [war]" (Shamisā 1380 [2001], 25). This could be explained by authors' quest for a larger lexicon more conducive to creating rich rimes and formal figures of speech. These lexical elements became an integral part of the language and have little or no connotative value, unlikely to attract average Persian-speaking readers' attention.

The second category, on the other hand, concerns a much more deliberate choice that no longer involves the use of signs from the canonized Persian repertoire. These are borrowings, either unprecedented or of low frequency, that constitute a *ratio difficilis*. Whether they are simple words, phrases, or entire sentences, the author's stylistic choice cannot be without consequence on the discoursive structure. Whether the author's intentions are aesthetic, rhetoric, or didactic is unclear.

Translation or the Retrieval of the Discoursive Form 101

What goes without saying is that the use of these elements cannot leave the reader of the original language indifferent. Foreign elements strike, slow down the reading process, and make the reader do research. Features of intertextuality, the quotations taken from external sources, mainly from the Koran and hadith but also from Arab folklore, constitute an important part of the occurrences of Arabic especially in the *Masnavi*. It is these Koranic references that have undoubtedly given this book the reputation of being a commentary on the Koran, even a "Koran in Persian."[37] Whatever the size of the foreign syntagm and the context of enunciation, these elements represent the highest degree of discoursive heterogeneity, pushing even a native speaker of Persian to resort to exegetic commentaries to understand the text. How can the translator transfer such a connotative charge from Persian to a foreign language without serious consequences for the TT?

2.2.3 Translating the Foreignness

Utterances in the ST in other languages than the ST's main language are difficult to reflect in the TT. There seem to be few options. Graphic markers in the TT, translator's notes, or the use of an equivalent language variation in the target language (TL) are some of the tools in the translator's toolbox; however, none of these devices can be regarded as a satisfactory solution. These foreign elements are part of the discoursive structure of the ST and have important connotative significance. In translations of Rumi, little effort has been made to mark the foreignness of the discourse and to compensate for the connotative loss in any way. An exception should perhaps be made in the case of certain modern academic translators who often mark significant citations from the Koran and hadith. That is the case of Mojaddedi in Example 2.5.

Example 2.5 M.III) l.1814–1815

Meil-e *ruḥat* chun soye bālā bovad Var negunsāri sarat suye zamin	dar *tazāyod marjaʻat* ānjā bovad *Āfeli, haqq lā yoḥebbo lāfelin*	
If the proclivity of your soul is towards high, On the *increase*, your *reference* is up there. But if you are upside down (you are miserable), your head towards the Earth *You are declining, "God does not like decliners."*		
E1) Wil: p. 149–158: When the inclination of your spirit is upwards, you will **increase** and **advance** till you **return**. To those Heights. But if you hang your head, (if) your head (inclines) towards the earth, **you are one who declines; God loves not things which decline.**	E2) Nim: p. 310–315: When the propensity of your spirit is upwards, (you are) in (the state of) **increase**, and that (lofty) place is the place to which you will **return**; But if you are upside down, (with) your head towards the earth, (then) **you are one that sinks: God loves not them that sink.**	E3) Moj: p. 101–106: If your soul longs to soar up through the sky, You will **gain** much and soon **return** on high, But if your head points downwards, don't forget: You'll **sink**, and **God loves not *the ones that set*!**[38]

This verse is the quintessence of Rumi's wordplay based on the alternation between Persian and strikingly heterogeneous Arabic elements. The two lines contain conditional clauses followed by the main clause in the second hemistich, creating a syntactic parallelism. The first hemistiches are almost devoid of Arabic elements (there are only two words highly integrated in Persian in the first line), while the second hemistiches are composed almost entirely of Arabic terms. The first line is affected by two Arabic words, *tazāyod* [incremental augmentation], very rare in Persian, and *marja'* [the place of return/reference]. The second hemistich of the second verse contains only one Persian morpheme, *i* in *āfel-i*, the verb *budan* [to be] conjugated in the second person singular. The rest is a quotation from the Koran (6:76) which Rumi puts in free reported speech by changing the starting term, *haqq* [the truth], one of the names of God. *Āfel* [descending] is in no way comprehensible for average Persian speakers without the help of a dictionary. Only Mojaddedi puts the whole utterance in the second verse in italics and adds a translator's note giving the reference to the verse of the Koran. This practice is systematic in Mojaddedi's translations. However, even Mojaddedi did not try to compensate for the originality of the lexical selection of the source text in the first verse. For instance, one might have expected a somewhat uncustomary lexical choice for *tazāyod*, in English where there exists a wide range of words belonging to the same semantic field: *augmentative, crescendo, crescentic movement*, etc. All translations show a distinct impoverishment of the extremely verbose tone of the ST.

Example 2.6 M. II) l.105

Bikhabar budand az ḥal-e darun	**asta'iẓo llah mem-mā yaftarun**
They ignored the interior state	*I seek refuge with God from what they contrive*
E1) Red: I. p. 8–11: The case has been from first misunderstood. Protect us, Heaven! A blundering brotherhood!"	E2) Nim: p. 9–11: They were ignorant of the inward state. I seek refuge with God from that which they invent."
E3) Moj: Book One: p. 10–13: They'd failed to see the ailment deep within – *God save us from what theft they are dabbling in!*	E4) Will: p. 16–19: They did not understand her inner state: *I seek God's refuge from what they contrive.*'

In this passage, a lovesick patient is being visited by a doctor, who criticizes his colleagues for failing to diagnose the spiritual and psychological source of the disease. The line is part of the doctor's speech. Verses in which one of the hemistiches is in Persian and the other is in Arabic are very typical of Rumi's style, especially in the *Masnavi*. Whereas most of such verses contain a famous citation from the Koran or elsewhere, this one is different: the second hemistich is not a quotation, but a statement constructed by the author, hence belonging to the diegetic realm of the tale. One would expect the translators to mark this discoursive heterogeneity graphically, in the manner of two contemporary academic translators. Not only does this care not exist in Redhouse's text, his translation of the second hemistich can at best be qualified as an adaptation. Clearly, there is a higher level of sensitivity in modern translators from academic backgrounds than in classic translators, including Nicholson, with regard to the question of borrowings and foreign utterances in the ST. One explanation is that modern translators are more aware of the attitude of Persian speakers towards Arabic elements in their language. The lack of sensitivity displayed by some 19th-century translators is also

Translation or the Retrieval of the Discursive Form 103

epitomized by their method of transcription that systematically confused Persian and Arabic. In many cases, Persian words of Arabic origin are transliterated as if they were used in an Arabic text, with disregard for the correct Persian pronunciation: *Mathnawi* instead of *Maṣnavi* or *Maulana* instead of *Mowlānā*.[39] Such loanwords have an Arabic root and have been well integrated, thus their pronunciation is Persian. This kind of error has been perpetuated in the modern versions/adaptations by Barks, Helminsky, and Harvey, who are unfamiliar with the source language and culture. Arberry, notably, made a difference by changing this tradition and systematically avoiding any confusion caused by transliteration, including in the title of his translations.[40]

One can readily expect translators to indicate the presence of long Arabic citations or utterances in the ST. It is much more challenging, however, to mark more subtle stylistic traits of the original discourse produced by an author's industrious mélange of native and foreign terms. As we saw in Example 1.10 in the previous chapter, some translators such as Mojaddedi and Williams are sensitive to more idiomatic borrowings like *ebnolvaqt*, which they translated in italics. However, these italics notify the untranslatability of the term in English rather than the presence of an Arabic term in the Persian text. In the case of well-established loanwords, translations understandably lack markers of foreignness. In Example 1.12, there are two occurrences of loanwords, *lik* [but] with a very high frequency but belonging to a literary and archaic register, and *samā'* [sky] with low frequency and of exotic character. It is impossible to compensate for the loss of the archaism associated with first loanword, but in the case of *samā'*, there is a wide range of choices in English, unlike in French or other romance languages, to recreate the nuance: *sky*, *heaven*, and the adjective *celestial*. Lewis's choice seems to have been made in this view. Unfortunately, elsewhere in the same ghazal, the situation becomes far more complex for translators in the face of the discursive symphony created by loanwords and Arabic citations well integrated in the Persian syntagm.

Example 2.7 D) G. 464, l.6–8, 11

Az mah-e u mah shekāft, didan-e u barnatāft māh chonān bakht yāft, u ke kamine gedāst Bu-ye khosh-e in nasim az shekan-e zolf-e ust **sha'sha'e**-*ye* in **khiāl** zān rokh-e chun **vażżoḥā**st Dar del-e mā darnegar, har dam **shaqolqamar** Kaz **naẓar**-e ān **naẓar**, chashm-e to ān su cherāst . . . Āmade mowj-e **alast** kashti-e *qāleb* bebast bāz cho kashti shekast, *nowbat*-e **vaṣl** o *laqā*st
By her/his moon, the moon split. It couldn't endure beholding her/him. The nice scent of this breeze is from the curl of her/his hair. The glitter of this ***imago*** is from that "by the morning light"-like face. Behold, in our heart, a "moon-splitting" every moment. Why are your eyes looking that way to **see** that **vision**? . . . The wave of "Am I not" has come, it bound the ship of the mold (body). Once it breaks the ship again, it will be the turn of union and rejoining.

(*Continued*)

104 *Translation or the Retrieval of the Discoursive Form*

Example 2.7 (Continued)

E1) Nid: IX,[41] p. 32–37: This gale's sweet scent is from the curl of his tresses, This **thought's radiance** is from a cheek like "**by the morning bright.**" By his cheek the moon was split: she endured not the sight of him; Such fortune the moon found – she that is an humble beggar. Behold a continual "**cleaving of the moon**" in our hearts, For why should the **vision** of that **vision** transcend thine eye? Came the billow of "**Am I not?**" and wrecked the **body's** ship; When the ship wrecks once more is the time of **union's** attainment.	E2) Am: tome I, # 55, p. 49–50: At his moon the moon was split,[42] it could not endure to behold him; the moon attained such luck-she, a humble beggar. The sweet scent of the breeze is from the curl of his tress, the **glitter** of this **phantasm** is from that cheek like the **forenoon**.[43] Behold in our hearts every moment **a splitting of the moon**, for why does your eye soar beyond the **vision** of that **vision**? ... The wave of **Alast**[44] came along and caulked the body's ship; when the ship is wrecked once more, the turn of **union** and **encounter** will come.
E3) Cow: p. 67–68:[45] The wind's sweet smell comes from his curly hair, This **thought's radiance** from a cheek 'as bright as the morning' Cut by his cheek, the moon turned away; Such is her fortune while in her heart beggared In our hearts this unending '**cleaving of the moon**' Allows knowledge of that **vision** to transform us. Came the wind billowing, '**Am I not?**' to wreck my foundering body; When it founders again **union** is **attained**.	E4) Ls: p. 162–163: Our pride in life, the Chosen One By His bright orb the moon was split (it would not turn its gaze away) And so luck smiled upon the moon the lowly moon that begs its light! The wind's sweet scent drips from his locks His **image** shines with brilliant **rays** from his bright face, reflecting from *And the sun in its zenith*[46] ... Over our boat just like a wave broke *Am I not*[47] Our ship's ribs staved, the boat will sink our time has come for **reunion**, to meet with God.
E5) Hom: p. 73–74: A tender breeze brings the scent of his milken hair, the allure of every **illusion** is from his sacred **light**. Every instant witnesses the resurgence in our hearts Like seabirds we are born in an ocean of spirits and we head towards turbulent flows all together, as we exist within him. Why look away when he casts his gaze upon you? Let raging waters ferment in the sea of your hearts. Here comes the wave of **creation** to wreck our ship and it's time for **jointure** and **union**	E6) Bb: #80, p. 134–135:[48] Like ocean birds, human beings come out of the ocean Do not expect to live inland. We hear a surging inside our chests, an **agreement we made in eternity**. The wave of that **agreement** rolled in and caulked the body's boat. Another wave will smash us. Then the **meeting** we have wanted will occur.

Theses verses depict allegorically the inner restlessness of the Sufi who constantly seeks to travel beyond his body, compared to a *qāleb* [mold], in the earthly life in order to join with the beloved creator, whose anaphoric references, neutral in Persian, are *masculine* in all TTs. In this journey, the leader of the caravan is the prophet, referred to in line 5 by one of his names, *Mostafā*. What follows revolves around a central theme: Mohammad's only miracle, splitting the moon. Mohammad's feat is then reduced to an illusion, a vision, a reflection of the splitting of the beloved's hair. Such splitting of the moon occurs every second in the mystic's heart. After recounting a few other adventures, the poem summarizes earthly life in a maritime metaphor: the divine creation, alluded to in the story of the Covenant – evoked by *alast*, short form of the Arabic *alastu birabbikum* [Am I not your Lord?] – is compared to a sea wave that caulks a vessel – the human body. The same wave, when it returns, will shatter this "mold," thus allowing the final reunion with the beloved.

This semantic imagery is of course supported by the global and internal rhythm of the verses (see Chapter 3), but above all, by a progressive movement from the concrete to the abstract, from the terrestrial to the celestial, from Persian to Arabic. Line 6 contains no Arabic words, despite referring to Mohammad's miracle. The first hemistich of verse 7 is entirely in Persian too. Suddenly, the second verse strikes with a low-frequency, downright foreign Arabic word, *sha'sha'e* [radiance] as the inanimate starting term and agent of a predicative clause. The sentence continues with the copula "to be" which makes the link of attribution between two derivative nominal compounds, the "radiation of this image" and its ablative attribute: the radiation comes from this daylight-like face. The complement of the noun *xiāl* [mental image, thought] is a common Arabic term in Persian. The second shock lies in the choice of the qualifying epithet, *chun va'ẓẓohā*, [like "on the brightness of the day"], a citation from the Koran, where God invokes various natural phenomena including the brightness of early morning. Rumi's impressive skills are at work here with the nominalization[49] of a lengthy clause. Verse 8 follows the same path with the nominalization of another full clause taken from the Koran, but this one is of higher frequency and is placed as the passive object of the verb: *shaqqolqamar* [the moon split]. The culmination point is wordplay founded on the homonymy of an Arabic word *nazar*, containing multiple sememes, only some of which are commonly used in Persian. The common meaning of *nazar* is the noun "look," as in "to take a look," or "view," as in "in someone's view." However, in *nazar*'s second occurrence in the verse, it is used in the sense of "sight," thus creating a *jenās-e tām*, one of several formal figures of speech based on homonymy. The fact that this pun is missed by all translators shows the complexity of their task, rather than their lack of skill. The alternation between Persian and Arabic is far from trivial as a rhetorical tool. The miracle (of splitting the moon by the prophet) is described using purely Persian lexicons but its metaphorical reworking is decorated with Arabic, as if the poet were suggesting a return to the origins of the story.

The extracts of translations cited earlier show that there are few ways of rendering this elaborate discursive structure. Apart from Barks's and Homayounfar's adaptations, all other translators have merely added explicative notes to mark the origin of the Koranic citations. The italicization of sections of the text as well as their placing in quotation marks are a code established by contemporary translators to mark cases of intertextuality in the ST. Certain commendable attempts at compensation can be observed in English translations; for instance, the preservation of the nominalized clauses ("I am not" or "moon splitting") by most translators. Nicholson's choice of the hyponym "thought" for the complex sememe *khiāl* represents a sheer reduction, while Arberry's choice of "phantasm" is a successful bet on a somewhat unusual Greek element that compensates to some extent the lost rhetorical effect of the discourse in other places.

What this example most strikingly demonstrates is the inevitable disappearance of an important component of the discursive layout of the ST. The harmony created by the juxtaposition of heterogeneous syntagms – not only etymologically but also stylistically and connotatively – has not been recreated in any of the translations. This loss is all the more unfortunate that one can only suppose two main reasons for Rumi's original stylistic practice. Firstly, the choice of lexicon marks the discourse in its connotation, transforming the modalities of the communication of the message by modifying the images associated with the signs. The Arabic sign does not create the same effect on the Persian-speaking reader as etymologically Persian words: *māh* and *qamar* are synonymous and denote the same content, but they don't have the same functional effect because they connote differently. Secondly, the cadenced use of Arabic and Persian to construct two utterances referring to the same extralinguistic reality constitutes a semantic figure of speech similar to periphrasis (see Chapter 4). Rumi's *ratio difficilis* is realized at multiple levels: a syntagmatic construction, as in the nominalization of Arabic clauses; formal figures of speech, as in the aforesaid pun around *naẓar*; and semantic substitution, periphrasis being a type of trope. All this mastery is lost in translation.

To draw a parallel about the loss of the connotative value of foreign lexicon in the process of translation, I share Jean-Louis Cordonnier's observation about the presence of non-Germanic terms in German. He cites a German author and translator (1995, 185):

> philosophical terms in German are, on the one hand, derived from the roots of the language itself, which are immediately recognizable. On the other hand, they come from the Greco-Latin vocabulary. The translation is, therefore, incapable of revealing the immediate accessibility of the texts by Fichte (*der Grundsatz*) or Hegel. It is also unable to bring out the vocabulary of foreign origin: *Subjekt, Objekt, Prinzip, Reflexion.*

Cordonnier seeks the solution elsewhere than in the language itself, that is "at the level of the historicity of the German cultural unspoken (non-dit)." Following Antoine Berman's path, he advocates for the deepening of the knowledge of foreign culture to facilitate the translating operation. It is the same historicity of the unspoken in the Iranian culture that translators like Arberry, Lewis, Mojaddedi, and Williams have tried, with some success, to render evident.

3 Linguistic Variations and Discoursive Heterogeneity

The question of the discoursive form and its elusive re-creation in the TT is not limited to the lexical and syntactic levels at the microstructural level. At the macrostructural level, i.e., that of the message and even that of the entire work, the prediscoursive purport of the text bears on the discoursive form. Features like tone, tenor, organization, and, in case of narrative texts, narrative polyphony, are some of the ways in which the discoursive form of Rumi's text suffers often inevitable alterations in the translation process. The loss is most significant in Rumi's work for two reasons: on the one hand, the aesthetic and rhetorical canon of classical mystic poetry diverges considerably from the norms imposed by the target culture. On the other, Rumi's discourse is characterized by *ratio difficilis*. His style is both code-breaking and code-making. In the last part of this chapter, I examine two cases of linguistic variations that illustrate both features of Rumi's discoursive form and how translators have tackled the challenge.

3.1 Diachronic and Diatopic Variation

According to Shamisā (2001, 91–92), although Rumi is considered a poet belonging to the *'arāqi* school in vogue from the 13th century, his style bears certain characteristics of the Khorasan school that flourished in his native region, the cradle of the Dari version of Persian.[50] This dialect is strongly characterized by the existence of archaic forms, at both lexical and syntactic levels. Rumi lived at a time of complete linguistic, stylistic, and aesthetic transformation. He belongs to the *'arāqi* period in thematic and aesthetic terms, but his style is also influenced by his native Dari dialect. Rumi's language is dynamic. He freely mixes the modern and the old, the formal and slang, just as he juggled liberally with Arabic utterances of all types. His text consists of mixtures of archaic and dialectal Persian that constitute an idiom in itself, or idiolect, or what one could even call a *Rumiolect*. These discrepancies create two opposite problems in translation: either an ennoblement of the original discourse or, conversely, its impoverishment.

3.1.1 The Disappearance of Archaism

The first translation effect that can be observed, particularly in more recent translations, consists in constructing neutral or modern syntagms to translate diachronic or even dialectical variations. Shamisā underlines the *Khorasani* characteristics of Rumi's syntax and specifies that the language of *Divan* is more modern than that of the *Masnavi*. Some of the archaic features are, for example, the emphatic *be* at the beginning of the stem of the preterite verb: *be-khoft* (he lay, he slept) in Example 2.2; the use of the negative adverbial affix (morpheme) *ma-* instead of *na-* in negative imperative verbs: *maju* (don't search!) instead of *naju*.

Example 2.8 D) G2131, 1.11

Guyad soleimān **mar** to **rā**	beshnow *lesān oṭṭayr* rā
dāmi o morq az to ramad	**row** lāne sho **row** lāne show
Solomon tells thee: "hearken the birds' language." You are a trap and birds escape you. Go become a nest. Go become a nest.		
E1) Shg: p. 134: Solomon speaks with the language of the birds – Listen! Don't be the trap that falcons flee – become a nest, become a nest.	E2) Ls: p. 121–123: Though Solomon has told you: Listen to the language of the birds like a trap the birds fly from you nestle them and be their nest	F1) Taj: p. 180–184: Écoute, te dit Solomon, Le langage de ces oiseaux Tu es piège et l'oiseau te fuit, Le nid deviens, le nid deviens.

The main archaic marker of the school of Khorasan in this example is the use of the preposition *mar* along with the postposition *rā* to indicate the first or second complement (accusative or dative case), which is the disjunctive pronoun *to* [thou]. The other characteristic is the omission of the affix *be* at the beginning of the imperative *row* [go] in verse 2, and the maintenance only of the present stem of the verb to form the imperative, in contrast to its retention in another imperative *be-shnow* [hear/listen]. Although this choice is probably made for reasons of metric, the discoursive alternation between the archaic and the modern constitutes a microstructure of opposition, which also manifests itself in the use of the unidiomatic Arabic phrase *lesān ot-tayr* [language of birds] and the Persian *morq* [bird]. It should be specified that by archaisms, I do not mean the literary or formal register of Persian, which often resembles archaic use. I mean manifest discrepancies between the 13th-century norms and Rumi's style. None of the translating languages have, at least in their contemporary forms, the necessary tools to transpose this archaism, especially as recourse to Old French or Middle English would make the translation unintelligible. In French, Tajadod/Carrière seem to have recovered the original infradiscourse with syntactic manipulations such as the interjected syntagm like the inverted incise *te dit Solomon* or the inversion in the imperative *le nid deviens*. English grammar, on the contrary, does not allow for such syntagmatic liberties. Lewis resorts to alliteration and paronymy with his lexical choice nestle/nest to compensate for the loss, whereas Shiva's lexical choice (falcons flee) transforms the content without any apparent gain in the discoursive form.

Example 2.9 D) G 441, 1. 2, 14

Ey āftāb ḥosn borun **ā** dami ze abr	kān chehre ye moshaʻshaʻ-e tābān**am** ārezust
Di sheikh bā cherāq **hami gasht** gerd-e shahr	kaz div o dad malulam o ensān**am** ārezust
O sun of beauty, come out, for a moment, of the cloud As that dazzling glowing face is my desire. Yesternight, Sheikh, with a lamp, turned around the city, [Saying:] "I am sick of devil and beast; human is my desire."	

Translation or the Retrieval of the Discursive Form 109

E1) Nid: XVI, p. 65–69: O sun, **show forth thy** face from the **veil of cloud**, **For** I **desire** that radiant glowing **countenance**. . . . **Yesterday** the Master with a lantern was roaming about the city, Crying, 'I am tired of devil and beast, I desire a man.'	E2) Am: vol. I, #51, p. 45–46: Sun of beauty, come forth one moment out of the cloud, for that glittering, glowing countenance is my desire. . . . Last night the shaikh went all about the city, lamp in hand, crying, "I am weary of beast and devil, a man is my desire."
E3) Khf: n°12, p. 22–23: come out from behind the clouds i desire a sunny face . . . yesterday the wisest man holding a lit lantern in daylight was searching around town saying	E4) Cow: p. 81–83: O Sun, reveal your face from the **veil of cloud**, I want to see the glow of its countenance. . . .

    The two lines of the previous example belong to one of the longest and most famous of Rumi's ghazals. They present several occurrences of diachronic variations that create a constant alternation between the language norms of the time and archaisms: the imperative *borun ā* [get out!] instead of *biā*, the imperfect preterit in its repetitive or iterative verbal aspect (it is unclear which) is formed with the prefix *hami-* instead of *mi-*, the displacement of the possessive morpheme *am*, normally attached to the attribute in the form of a noun phrase, is placed in the position of the argument of the copula *budan*, breaking the canonical order of the sentence, as well as the highly archaic lexical choice of *di* [eve].

    Among translators, only Nicholson's Victorian style does justice to the original discursive forms: the low-frequency phrasal verb *show forth*, the archaic possessive *thy*, common in other 19th-century British translations, the use of *for* as conjunctive adverb, as well as the choice of qualifying adjectives. The downside is probably the choice of *yesterday*, which could have been substituted by a more literary and accurate term like *yestereve*. The metaphorical compound of the veil of cloud, nonexistent in the original, can also be seen as a compensatory strategy used by Cowan, whose version is based entirely on that of Nicholson (like many other contemporary translators). Arberry, whose style in the translations of Rumi's quatrains is very close to that of 19th-century authors, favored a literalist approach in his translations of ghazals, resulting in the flattening of Rumi's archaic speech in this example.

    The modern translations provided in the previous example seem totally disconnected from the discursive reality of the original text, preferring readability to recreating the ST's discursive forms. The erasure of the archaism of Rumi's

110 *Translation or the Retrieval of the Discoursive Form*

style by recent translators and its preservation by most classical English translators is not limited to this specific passage. This phenomenon can be explained in general by diachronic variations within target languages themselves. The further one advances in the 20th century and the further one moves away from the poetic and stylistic norms of the Victorian literary polysystem, the less the archaisms are reflected in translators' styles.

3.1.2 The Over-Archaization of the Discourse

Although the general trend seems to be that of the erasure of the archaic forms, there are several cases of an opposite effect when translators render the discourse more archaic sounding by their lexical or syntactic choices. This is common in the translation of the *Masnavi* where Rumi often shows a simpler, more modern, and even banal language, closer to contemporary everyday Persian. Sometimes the common register and ordinary tone of the ST are subject to archaization by translators like Redhouse, Whinfield, and Nicholson, who raise the degree of sophistication of the text. This is illustrated in Example 2.1, among others, where the difference between Mojaddedi's and Wilson's discoursive choices and the Victorian archaizing prose translation of Whinfield, Nicholson, and Arberry is quite significant. Whereas the diegetic reported speech of the shepherd is characterized by a high degree of orality, the occurrence of archaisms such as *thou, thy, art, wilt, choosest,* and *electest* brings the English-speaking reader back to the Saxon or Frisian origins of their language (*wilt* in particular is akin to Low German). Such a destructive shift in tone defeats the purpose of Rumi's rhetoric, which highlighted the illiteracy and simplicity of the protagonist. This stylistic deformation can also be observed in the translation of ghazals, as shown by Example 2.10 where Nicholson's bombastic Victorian tone seems disconnected from Rumi's orality, as if the original text was not literary enough for the canon of the target polysystem.

Example 2.10 D) G. 1521, l.1, 9

Man az 'ālam to rā tanhā gozinam neshinam		ravā dāri ke man tanhā
Bejoz chizi ke dādi man che dāram?		Che mijuyi ze jayb o āstinam
Of the world, I only choose you.	Do you accept that I sit alone?	
Apart from what you gave, what do I have?	What are you looking for in my pocket and sleeve?	
E1) Nid: XXX, p. 121–123: **Thee** I choose, of all the world, alone; **Wilt thou** suffer me to sit in grief? I have nothing, except **thou hast bestowed** it; What **dost thou** seek from my bosom and sleeve?	E2) Am: vol. I, #186, p. 154–155: Out of all the world I choose you alone; do you deem it right for me to sit sorrowful? What do I possess other than the thing you have given? What are you searching for in my pocket and sleeve?	E3) Cow: p. 111: Of all the world I choose you alone; Will you allow me to sit in grief? I'm nothing, except what you've bestowed; What do you seek from my breast and sleeve?

This ghazal from the *Divan* has an exceptionally short and simple meter and displays a style devoid of the stylistic complexities and syntactic verbosity typical of Rumi's ghazals. It reads like a contemporary nursery rhyme that even a Persian-speaking schoolboy could understand. There are no archaisms, no lexical hermeticism, no unexpected borrowings from Arabic, no formal or literary structure, and very few figures of speech. Nicholson's translation, however, has an archaic and affected tone: in addition to old syntagms, the lexical field is rich in literary diversity: *bestow, seek, sit in grievance*. The example of the professor was not followed by his disciple, Arberry, who offers a sober and literal translation.

Nicholson's translation shows how the translator's idiolect can be superimposed on the author's, causing a certain interference at the idiomatic level of the discourse and relation to the norm of the SL. Nicholson's translation is marked by the idiom imposed by the Victorian polysystem on the one hand and the archaism dominating most of Rumi's texts on the other. As Pergnier states:

> What is put in contact in translation are not two abstractly defined systems, but two idioms having a sociolinguistic status. The message is sent in an idiolect specific to the sender. . . . The translator, for his part, approaches a translation with his own idiolect in the source language and in the target language. . . . the translator, therefore, operates on a plurality of juxtaposed and superimposed "codes" that fit together.
>
> (1993, 204–205)

Nicholson's idiolect is the result of the superimposition of Victorian norms on the ST. These norms orient Nicholson's adoption of a uniformly literary and archaic style, applied even in the case of source texts marked by orality and simplicity.

3.2 Lectal Inconsistency in Rumi's Text

The problem of the ennoblement and *literarization* of the discourse in translation, considered a *deforming tendency* by Antoine Berman (see Chapter 6), is exacerbated by *diastratic* variations of language. In fact, certain translators of Rumi, namely those of the 19th century, tended to ennoble his discourse with a more elegant and affected style in the TT, even though some of his texts are – sometimes even unusually – marked by infradiscoursive elements belonging to informal, colloquial, and even vulgar registers of Persian. Pergnier underlines the problem, citing Wandruzska:

> We all have "several languages at our disposal. One correct and official, another colloquial, a third vulgar, a fourth slang, and we pass with the greatest ease from one style to another, sometimes in the middle of a sentence." These different "languages" rub shoulders, interpenetrate, marry, and – not at

the level of the language, but at that of the rhetoric – constitute the "styles", the "registers", or "language levels."

(1993, 197)

This superimposition of registers reaches an unprecedented level in Persian literature with the work of Rumi. He does not hesitate to mix genres, as well as registers, sometimes within the same tale or ghazal. Rumi's nonlinear narrative techniques in the *Masnavi* combine didactic and analytical discourses with a diegetic discourse that can vary tremendously in tone and sociolect. On the mimetic side, Rumi does not hesitate to alternate between colloquial sociolects in his characters' dialogues and theological and metaphysical technolects of his own analyses. He even goes as far as producing the same amalgam within narrative discourse, in his own language, with various registers immediately juxtaposed within the same line. There is no homogeneity of idiolect either in Rumi's work viewed as a whole, or yet in a single tale, or even in a single line. An example of this *polylogical* style in modern literature can be found in James Joyce's *Ulysses*, whose translational effects have been studied by Barbara Folkart (1991).[51]

3.2.1 Diegetic and Narrative Polylogy

The inconsistency of lects, registers, and voices in Rumi's work manifests itself in the style of both his diegetic and his narrative discourses. Polylogy is present in length either from one tale to another or within a single tale. In the same passage, the voices of the characters stand in contrast to each other or oppose that of the narrator. One of the best illustrations of this phenomenon is the tale of Moses and the shepherd, already cited in Example 2.1, in which we saw how the connotative semantic value of *chāker* could be totally lost in translation. The passage shows the translators' lack of sensitivity regarding the discursive forms that rely on a subtle use of lectal variations to mark the distinct voices of the shepherd, Moses, the narrator, and God. Lectal markings and diastratic variations of Persian facilitate the articulation of different voices in the text. Nicholson's archaic and heavy syntagms, however, as well as those of his predecessors, stand in clear contrast to the words of an illiterate shepherd. The loss of discursive form is thus twofold: stylistic, since the rhetorical effect of lectal contrasts is lost, and pragmatic, since the polylogical articulation of the text is absent in the TT. In the English version of this tale, God, the prophet, and the shepherd all speak in the same way. Rumi's skillful polylogy even marks the evolution of the shepherd's voice from the beginning to the end after he has been reprimanded by Moses. The tale unfolds in three stages: the conversation of the shepherd and Moses, the dialogue between Moses and God, and finally, Moses's apologies to the shepherd, whose voice now sounds like the mystic narrator's. In Example 2.11 the breakpoints between the shepherd's voice and the narrator's voice, as well as the lectal disparity in the shepherd's voice at two different points in the story, are revealed.

Example 2.11 MIII) l. 1723–1725, 1790

Dastakat busam bemālam pāyakat	vaqt-e khāb āyad berubam jāyakat
Ey fadā-ye to hame bozhā-ye man	Ey be yādat hey hey o hey hā-ye man
In namat bihude migoft ān shabān	goft musā bā ke ast in ey folān
...	
Maḥram-e nāsute mā lāhut bād	āfarin bar dast o bar bāzut bād
That I give kisses to your little hand, that I rub your little foot when the time to sleep comes, that I sweep your place (clean your bed) O you, for whom may all my goats be sacrificed! O you, in whose honour are all my 'hey hey' and 'ha, ha' So spoke the shepherd Then said Moses: "Whom is this talk with? O so and so!" ... Let the intimate of our *nāsut* (material world) be *lāhut* (divine nature) Kudos to your hand and your arm!	
E1) Wil: p. 149–158: That I may kiss your little hands, (and) rub your little feet, (and when) the time of sleeping comes I may sweep out your little room, O You for whom (all) my goats be sacrificed! O You "in commemoration of whom are all my cries and shouts!" In this fashion the shepherd was foolishly speaking, (when) Moses said, "To whom are these (words) of yours (addressed), man?" ... The Divine Nature has become the intimate of my human nature: – praise be to your hand and arm!	E2) Nim: p. 310–315: That I may kiss Thy little hand and rub Thy little foot, (and when) bedtime comes I may sweep Thy little room, O Thou to whom all my goats be a sacrifice, O Thou in remembrance of whom are my cries of ay and ah!" The shepherd was speaking foolish words in this wise. Moses said, "Man, to whom is this (addressed)?" ... May the Divine Nature be intimate with my human nature – blessings be on thy hand and on thine arm!
E3) At: 40, p. 132–134: Kiss Thy little hand and rub Thy little foot, sweep Thy little room when bedtime comes, O Thou to whom may all my goats be a sacrifice, O Thou in remembrance of whom I cry ah and ah! The shepherd was talking nonsense after this fashion. Moses said to him, 'Whom are you addressing?' ... May the Divinity be intimate with my humanity: blessings be 'upon your hand and upon your arm!'	E4) Bt: p. 19–22: to kiss Your little hands and feet when it's time for You to go to bed. I want to sweep Your room and keep it neat. God, my sheep and goats are Yours. All I can say, remembering You, is ayyyy and ahhhhhhhhh." Moses could stand it no longer. "Who are you talking to?" ... The Divine Nature and my human nature came together. Bless your scolding hand and your arm.
E5) Moj: p. 101–106: I'd kiss your little hand, and rub your feet, And sweep your bedroom clean and keep it neat; I'd sacrifice my herd of goats for you This loud commotion proves my love is true.' He carried on in this deluded way, So Moses asked, 'What's that I hear you say?' ... May God stay close to human beings like me, And may He bless your hand eternally!	E6) Lr: p. 371–373 / Ls: p. 16–18: Kiss your little hands and rub your feet and at bed time sweep your place to sleep. May my goats all be your sacrifice, in whose name I call my hoes and hoes. "Who's that you're talking with?" asked Moses, hearing shepherd voice such silly hopes. ...

The first two lines are the shepherd's words, clearly marked by colloquial lexical and syntagmatic choices, such as childish terms of endearment to address God or imitations of a shepherd's song for the sheep. The discursive form matches the semantic content of the utterances: personification of the divine being by evoking human properties and habits and the association of the almighty with the animals attended by the shepherd. The colloquial character of the syntagm is reinforced by the addition of the diminutive suffix -*ak* indicating parts of the body. The use of nonlexicalized elements (*hey hey* and *hey hāy*) simulating the sound of a wordless song the shepherd sings to his goats also indicates the poverty of the speaker's vocabulary. The contrast between the sublime and the grotesque, a typically romantic theme, is epitomized by the juxtaposition of *fadā-ye* [may be sacrificed] and goats, or again of *be yād* [in honor of] and onomatopoeic terms: this creates an association of ideas that borders on the humoristic.

The effects of Rumi's discursive form are lost in every single English translation except Mojaddedi's and Barks's. Mojaddedi uses contractions (I'd kiss) that indicate the informal register. Barks succeeds in creating a colloquial tone, especially in his choice of words, but unfortunately this success can be attributed to the contemporary character of his language rather than to his effort to translate all the effects of Rumi's discourse: Barks indeed fails to mark the lectal rupture between reported speech and narration. The use of capital letters for terms referring to God by everyone except Lewis and Mojaddedi is also another distorting choice. The translators' deification of God goes against the shepherd's simplistic, light-spirited, and down-to-earth concept of divinity he compares to his beloved goats. Rumi opposes the childish words of the shepherd to his own narrative voice and that of Moses as of line 1724, which starts with a formal and archaic adverb, *zin namat* [in this manner] followed by a moralizing speech delivered successively by the prophet, God, and once again by the narrator. The change of register, for example, is actualized by the more complex syntax of Moses's speech. Another contrast in the idiolect of the shepherd occurs in his second conversation with Moses when he suddenly uses a lexicon belonging to the Sufi technolect – *nāsut* [earthly world] and *lāhut* [transcendent world of divine nature] – to express his aspiration towards transcendence. None of the translations cited earlier, all hypertextual in nature, has been able to recreate these discursive forms of the ST.

My examples also show the limits of literal translation as a strategy that seeks to recover the infradiscoursive material as it manifests itself in the syntagmatic microstructures rather than in the discursive forms of the utterance. The classic translations of Rumi, while literal, sometimes show great gaps in their indifference to the relationship that exists between the Persian language, its idiom, its sub-idioms (lects), and especially their articulation in Rumi's discourse, vested perhaps more than any other classical poet in *ratio difficilis*.

3.2.2 Translating Vulgarity

Another one of Rumi's code-breaking and code-making practices in Persian classical literature is his use of slang or even of vulgar language in his didactic mystic work of the *Masnavi*. Originally a theologian and preacher, Rumi freely touches on all aspects of human life, sometimes in its most abject and degenerate forms.[52] He seems to pursue several objectives in his use of obscene language in his tales: a strong rhetorical effect to shock the reader (or disciple), the drawing of mystical lessons by demonstrating the contrast between the abject and the sublime, and the use of symbolism to refer to evil forces, including one's ego.[53] Tales dealing with controversial issues and containing coarse language have been the subject of much debate and controversy but of little serious critical study.[54] Such tales are also the perfect terrain for the mixture of opposing registers, since the author hides the obscene under euphemisms, especially by resorting to Arabic terminology (just like the *resāle* [legal treatise] of Islamic jurisprudence) while at the same time displaying a whole panoply of extremely explicit and vulgar terms in Persian. Yadollah Royāyi, contemporary poet and literary critic, known for his polemical positions in relation to classical literature, has addressed the role of the obscene in Rumi's work in an article (2007), counting no fewer than six occurrences of the use of vulgar terminology.[55] Royāyi admires the frankness of Rumi's language. Without precedent among classical writers, and despite the indignation of purists of his time, Rumi does not deny the existence of sexual parts in his poetry. Although *tanz* [humor], *hajv* [satire], and *hazl* [facetious obscene writing] were common genres in classical Persian literature, the use of obscene language (*hazl*) in serious mystical didactic texts only started with Sanāyi.[56] The particularity of Rumi's style, however, is his constant switching between registers in the middle of the text in a heteroclite diastratic mélange within the same tale.

Translators' reactions to this incongruity are surprising. Example 2.12 shows how Nicholson and the French translator, whose version is entirely based on the former, use an uncommon strategy to refrain from repeating Rumi's "swear words."

Example 2.12 M.IV) l.1334, 1336–13382

Dastān-e ān kanizak ke bā khar-e khātun **shahvat mirānd** va u rā chun boz va khers āmukhte bud **shahvat rāndan**-e ādamiān va kaduyi dar **qazib**-e khar mikard tā az andāze nagozarad khātun bar ān vofuq yāft . . .	
Ān khar-e nar rā be **gā** khu karde bud	khar **jemā'**-e ādami pey borde bud
. . .	
Dar **zakar** kardi kadu rā ān 'ajuz	tā ravad nim-e **zakar** vaqt-e **sapuz**
Gar hame **kir**-e khar andar vey ravad	ān **rahem** vān **rudehā** virān shavad
Khar hami shod lāqar o khātun-e u	mānde 'ājez kaz che shod in khar cho mu
The story of the maid who had sex with the mistress's donkey, and taught it human copulation, and put a squash on the donkey's virile member so that it would not exceed the limit; the mistress (of the house) noticed it . . . She had accustomed that male donkey to fucking. The donkey had discovered human coitus . . . That old woman (witch) put a squash on the penis so that only half of the penis entered her during penetration If all the donkey's dick penetrated her Her uterus and guts would be ruined The donkey became thinner and its mistress Remained helpless (wondering) why this donkey became [thin] like a hair?	

(Conitnued)

Example 2.12 (Continued)

E1) Nim: vol. 3 p. 82–87:   *Story of the maidservant who cum asino herae suae libidinem exercebat et eum tanquam caprum et ursam docuerat libidinem more humano exercere et veretro asini cucurbitam affigebat ne modum excederet. Her mistress discovered it . . .*   Asinum ad coitum assuefecerat: asinus ad concubitum hominis viam invenerat. . . .   Cucurbitam peni indiderat ilia anus ut trudendi tempore dimidium penis iniret;   Si totum asini veretrum earn iniret, uterus ejus et viscera diruerentur.   The ass was becoming lean, and his mistress remained helpless, saying, "Why has this ass become as (thin as) a hair?"
F1) Vm, livre cinquième, p. 1172–1177:   *Histoire de la servante qui avec un âne herae sua libidinem exercebat et eum tanquam caprum et ursam docuerat libidinem more humano exercere et veretro asini cucurbitam affligebat ne odum excederet. Sa maitresse le decouvrit,*   Asinum ad coitum assuefecerat: asinus ad concubitum hominis viam invenerat. . . .   Cucurbitam peni indiderat ilia anus ut trudendi tempore dimidium penis iniret;   Si totum asini veretrum earn iniret, uterus ejus et viscera diruerentur.   L'âne maigrissait, et sa maîtresse restait impuissante, disant: "Pourquoi cet âne est-il devenu mince comme un cheveu?"
F2) Kud: p. 124–126:   Une esclave, sous l'empire du désir, avait appris à un âne à faire l'amour avec elle et l'animal y avait pris goût. L'esclave utilisait une courge afin de contrôler les assauts de l'âne. C'est-à-dire qu'au moment de l'union, cette chienne enfilait la courge sur le membre de la bête afin de n'en recevoir que la moitié car, sans cette précaution, son vagin et ses intestins eussent été déchirés.   La maîtresse de l'esclave s'étonnait de voir son âne dépérir de jour en jour.

This text is an excerpt from the tale that displays most blatantly and expressively Rumi's lectal mixture: it's the story of a slave girl who copulates with an ass. The opening paragraph in prose summarizes the tale, which is followed by a poem. A few occurrences of obscene language occur in the previous example. Example 2.13 shows a different situation: a single verse makes a sudden and shocking digressive move in the middle of a passage about a sermon by the third Rashidun caliph, Osman. Rumi shifts quickly away from the philosophical analysis of the moral of a tale to vulgarity. In this instance, the author is demonstrating the importance of hypothetical thinking (*tamsil*) in rhetoric.

Example 2.13 M.V) l.511

Khāle rā **khāye** bodi khālu shodi	in be taqdir āmadast ar u bodi
If aunt had **balls**, she would be the uncle It is by chance (that one says): "if it was that."	
E1) Nim: vol. 4 p. 300: Mateterae si **testiculi** essent, ea avunculus esset: this is hypothetical – "if there were."	
F1) Vm: p. 866: "**Si ta tante était un homme**, elle serait ton oncle" – ceci est hypothétique : "si elle était. . . ."	

Let us first note that these passages have very rarely been translated. They only appear in the complete compilations of the *Masnavi* and in a French prose adaptation. Nicholson and Vitray-Meyerovitch would most certainly have omitted these passages from their compilation had they not set out to translate the entire *Masnavi*. Indeed, the vulgar utterances are rendered by neither the British nor the French translator into their respective languages. Nicholson translated them into Latin. Vitray-Meyerovitch, not having access to the original text, did the same, or changed the content as in Example 2.13. Nicholson's choice can be explained by his conformity to the norms of his polysystem. The French translator's choice, however, is all the more unexpected since she published in the second half of the 20th century and was thus not bound by the literary norms of the Victorian era.

In any case, the archaizing choice of Latin has three major possible impacts on the discourse: firstly, it makes the plot totally incomprehensible to the ordinary Western reader; secondly, it removes the shock effect sought by the author; and thirdly, this brazen act of ennoblement completely erases the discursive structure of the ST created by the contrast of registers set up by Rumi. Rumi employs a vast lexical field of sexuality and alternates between technical (anatomical and legal) terminology of Arabic root and explicit vulgar terms. This back and forth between the vulgar, such as *gā* [fuck] or *kir* [dick], and technical/scientific terminology like the Arabic *jemā'* [coitus], *zakar* [penis], and *sapuz* (from Middle Persian *sapuzidan* [penetration]), and metaphorical images such as using *qazib* [tree branch in Arabic] to refer to the donkey's penis confers a multiplicity of shocks on the reader. Clearly, the author is not using the Arabic term *qazib* euphemistically since he does not shy away from vulgar equivalents elsewhere in the same text. Likewise, the term "balls" violently shatters the mood set by the passage of Osman's story at a point where an account of hypothesis and analogy in rhetoric is being given.

This incongruity being the hallmark of Rumi's stylistic and aesthetic *ratio difficilis*, Nicholson's puritan and annexionist choice seems egregiously unfortunate. Can his choice be merely explained by the norms dominating his Victorian polysystem or are other factors at play? The existing translations seem dysfunctional at more than the aesthetic level.

Notes

1. It is common in many contexts to use the term "language" by metonymy, to refer to any semiotic system, for instance, the language of music. Hjelmslev uses the same term *sprog* to refer to both language in particular and semiotic systems in general.
2. Contemporaries of the School of Prague, André Martinet ([1960] 1980), (1962), and (1965) and Émile Benveniste are noteworthy French linguists and semioticians who made great contributions to the School of Paris's functional theory.
3. That post-structuralism ever shed its original linguistic paradigm is questionable. Thinkers like Derrida or Foucault, for instance, are commonly considered post-structuralists. Yet their methods can be described as a less systematically rigorous application of the rules of structuralism.
4. For further information on the history of structuralism, see, among others, Nöth (1990, 295–309).

5 *Matter* and *purport* are two English translations of the Danish *mening*. The French translation of *mening* is *matière*. *Mening* is akin to *meinung* in German, *meaning* in English, but also, interestingly, to *maynu* [spirit, sense, meaning] in Avestic, and *ma'nā* [meaning, spirit] in modern Persian and Arabic.
6 Dependences in the *system* or in the *process* are of three types: *interdependence* (*solidarity* in a *process*, *complementarity* in a *system*) in which two terms presuppose each other, *determination* (*selection* in a *process*, *specification* in a *system*) where one term presupposes the other, and *constellation* (*combination* in a *process*, *autonomy* in a *system*) when two terms are correlated with no presupposition (Hjelmslev [1943] 1961, 24–25).
7 Function in the logico-mathematical sense of the word, i.e., the dependence between two terms, e.g., $y = f(x)$.
8 See Thom's preface in Petitot's monography (*Morphogenèse du Sens* 1985).
9 See Petitot ("Forme" n.d.).
10 Postulating the existence of *a priori* structures obviously harks back to the Kantian concept of *a priori* categories of the understanding, a central source of inspiration for structural linguists.
11 For practical purposes, various units have been devised in semiotics to designate the smallest constitutive particles of pertinent sound (phoneme), meaning (seme and sememe), grammar (morpheme), etc.; however, the length of a sign is not determined by the length of its expression plane.
12 On the ontological ambiguity of structure, Umberto Eco asks a rhetorical question: "Is structure an object as it is structured, or a set of relations that structure the object and that can be abstracted from the object?" (1968, 285).
13 As Petitot argues, the epistemological revolution of Saussurean linguistic formalism is the shift of interest from "physics to logical organization" (Izard, Puech, and Chiss n.d.).
14 See Eco on "Structural method and operative procedures" (*La struttura assente* 1968, 285–287).
15 Umberto Eco, like many French structural semioticians of the School of Paris such as Roland Barthes, is particularly concerned with a unified theory of signs capable of explaining all cultural phenomena. In consequence, as of his *Trattato di semiotica generale* (1975), he systematically engages in a broad project of theorization of codes that govern the functioning of a variety of *natural* and *artificial languages*: olfactory signs, tactile communication, kinesics, proxemics, music, etc.
16 In American terminology, this property of language is called *duality of patterning* (Nöth 1990, 239–240).
17 It is of course possible to imagine an utterance composed only of the sign *apple*. Such an utterance is a set containing only one member. As *apple* is one lexeme (or lexical morpheme), it constitutes one sign, the smallest unit of meaning. From a functional perspective, such an utterance heavily relies on the extralinguistic context, in the absence of any co-text, to have any communicative value: for instance, the context of a person in a grocery store.
18 The concept of *norm* is also of utmost importance in Translation Studies and has been thoroughly analyzed in polysystem theory (see Chapter 6).
19 Respectively, these variations can be shown in the differential between the following: "underground" vs. "subway", "you" vs. "thou", "dude" vs. "gentleman", "to call (to purchase in the financial jargon)" vs. "to call somebody".
20 Dismissing the myth of source-oriented translation and translator's invisibility, Folkart advocates a creative approach to translation in which a translator can freely and remorselessly abandon certain aspect of the ST in order to recreate the formal relations in the TT. Folkart's central argument is that since the creation of the discursive forms of the ST is a logical impossibility, translation must take its independence vis-à-vis the source discourse in order to reproduce discoursive structures that are aesthetically

inspired by the source, but functionally and pragmatically, only its continuation. I shall argue against this view in Chapter 7 on the ethics of translation.
21 Six morphemes (Jack, eat, -s, pizza, every-, day) constituting four lexemes (Jack, eats, pizza) and three semantic units.
22 The projection of the principle of equivalence on the combination axis means the end of the duality of the sign in the poetic function. The relation between the expression-plane and the content-plane is no longer of an arbitrary nature. Content is motivated by the structure of the expression.
23 The distinction between *type* or class of objects, and *tokens* or individual instances of that class, is central to logic. In linguistics, the relation between the type and the tokens of that type is an important factor in lexical and textual analysis, for instance, to measure lexical density: "in statistical linguistics and lexical studies, a measure of the difficulty of a text, using the ratio of the number of different words in a text (the 'word types') to the total number of words in the text (the 'word tokens'); also called the type/token ratio (TTR)" (Crystal 2003, 276).
24 Although many texts can be replicable, hence coded, like the utterances on a legal document, texts are often first incidences of their semiotization.
25 This classification of translation procedures has later been criticized by Chuquet and Paillard (1987, 10). From a technical standpoint, equivalence is only a specific form of *modulation*, called *lexicalized modulation*.
26 The topic of translator's notes is broad and will be discussed in detail later in Chapters 5 and 6.
27 See Chapter 5 for a discussion on tropes and Paul Ricœur's idea of dead and live metaphors.
28 In certain editions, the last part of the second verse reads as *ey khodā o ey elāh* [o God o Lord!].
29 A dead metaphor, as Paul Ricœur explains, is one that has lost its discursive value as an image and become part of ordinary language. It is opposed to a *live* metaphor, which is a freshly creative figurative image (see Chapter 5).
30 The verse is extracted from a passage referring to the Biblical and Koranic tale of Solomon, who spoke the language of animals. This should be understood in the light of Rumi's particular relationship with language. Rumi constantly criticized language's incapacity to express the true nature of phenomena and frequently expressed his preference for the language of heart.
31 Similar phenomena can be noticed in the Ottoman Empire in the same era and later in the Indian subcontinent, where Turkish and Hindi were purged of much of their Arabic and Persian lexical influence.
32 There are several references for the history of Persian literature, but to name the most important ones in English, I shall evoke Ṣafā (2535/1355 [1976]) in Persian and Arberry (1956) in English, both of great technical value. Edward Browne's *A Literary History of Persia* should also be mentioned as the first work of this type.
33 In the geography of the Persianate world, Iraq, a toponym of Persian origin, designates the entire western region of the Iranian Plateau up to Mesopotamia. This region is divided into Arab Iraq, or Mesopotamia, and Ajam Iraq (foreign/Persian Iraq), which covers the entire mountainous region of the west of the plateau.
34 See Shamisā (1380 [2001]).
35 Many of these lexies have no Arabic or Semitic etymological root and are only the Arabicized version of a foreign word. Some of them like *sa'at* [hour] and *eshq* are even of Middle Persian origin, Arabicized, and then loaned back into modern Persian.
36 A hadith attributed to Prophet Mohammad.
37 There are several comparisons between the *Masnavi* and the Qor'an. As per a famous quote attributed to the Persian mystic poet, Jami (d.1492):

> Maṣnavi-e ma'navi-e Mowlavi / hast qo'ān be lafẓ-e pahlavi [Mowlavi's Maṣnavi is the Koran in the Pahlavi language].

Or this quote from the Shia philosopher Sheykh Bahā'l (d. 1621):

> *Man nemiguyam ke ān 'ālijenāb / hast peighambar vali dārad ketāb* [I do not claim his excellency to be a prophet; however he does have a book.

38 TN: "*the ones that set*: Qur'an 6: 76. See note to vv. 299–300 above."
39 If many classical translators including Nicholson can be criticized for their negligence in this matter, other translators like Whinfield or Wilson seem to have had a better understanding of necessary distinctions between the two transliteration systems.
40 Lack of geographical distinctions as well as cultural amalgamation have seemingly been the hallmark of the Anglophone, and to a lesser extent Francophone, academy as far as the approach to the Islamic world is concerned. Simplistic overgeneralization is most noticeable when considering that most universities and research institutions in the Anglophone world still use outdated terms such as "Near and Middle Eastern Studies," relics of the colonial era, to refer to West Asia, one of the most culturally diverse and heterogeneous regions in the world.
41 In Nicholson's edition, less accurate than Foruzānfar's, ghazal 463 and 464 are considered as one with a slight difference in the sequence of the verses.
42 TN for the verse 6: "The miracle alluded to in Koran 54 :1." P. 179.
43 TN: "Like the forenoon": Koran 93: 1.
44 TN: Alast: the day of God's primeval covenant with man, see Koran 7:171.
45 Cowan's version is based on Nicholson's, combining the two ghazals (463 and 464).
46 TN: [K 93:1]
47 TN: [K7:172]
48 Barks translated the ghazal 463 in separate publications. The first translation seems to be based on Arberry's version and the second on Nicholson's.
49 Nominalization or substantification is the syntactic transformation of a clause into a noun (or substantive).
50 The diatopic variation of the Persian language still in use in an evolved version in the east of the Persian-speaking world, i.e., in Afghanistan and Central Asia (Tajikistan, Uzbekistan).
51 Polylogy, or the plurality of voices, is a narrative phenomenon whereby the author uses specific registers, tenors, and tones to create an idiolect or a narrative *voice* for each of the characters as well as the narrator. According to Folkart, voice designates a macrostructure based on the alternation of registers in the text to create a specific discourse then attributed to a character or to the narrator: "Very simply, the same voice can manifest itself through several registers. The register thus constitutes the raw material that will be worked on by the author to shape a voice . . .; a voice is a bundle of textual traits that gives the impression of being at a single center of enunciation" (Folkart 1991, 127).
52 Much like in the Talmudic tradition, Islamic jurisprudence claims to regulate all aspects of human life, material or spiritual, with a complete set of rules called *sharia*.
53 According to Rumi:

> *Hazl* is education, listen to it seriously.
> Do not get stuck on its obscene surface.
> Any serious stuff is *hazl* for *hazl*-writers.
> *Hazls* are serious for sages.
> (M.IV: section 133, l.15–16)

54 Eroticism in the *Masnavi* is the topic of the Iranian Canadian scholar Mehdi Touraj's monograph (*Rūmī and the Hermeneutics of Eroticism* 2007), one of the rare examples of scientific research on this subject.
55 Five such accounts are found in Book *V* (l.1333, 3325, 3716, 3780, 3831) and one in Book *VI* (line 3843). Explicit language is witnessed throughout the *Masnavi* even if the tale does not broach such subjects (*cf.* Book *IV*, l.511).

56 As previously mentioned, Sanāyi's work made a deep impact on Rumi's thought and style in the *Masnavi*. Sanāyi responds to his detractors about his use of vulgarities to teach mystical lessons:

> My *hazl* is not *hazl*; it is education.
> My verse is not verse; it is a climate.
> What do you know about how, in this climate,
> The wise man's intellect educates?
> (Hadiqat ol-haqiqah va shari'at ol-tariqah,
> Book X, Chapter 5, 1.83–84)

References

Amossy, Ruth. 2001. "D'une culture à l'autre : réflexion sur la transposition des clichés et des stéréotypes." *Palimpsestes (Le cliché en traduction)*, n° 13.

Arberry, Arthur John. 1956. *Classical Persian Literature*. London: George Alien and Unwin Ltd.

Barthes, Roland. 1957. *Mythologies*. Paris: Seuil.

Barthes, Roland. 1967. *Système de la mode*. Paris: Seuil.

Benveniste, Émile. 1974. *Problèmes de linguistique générale*. Vol. 2. Paris: Gallimard.

Berman, Antoine. 1999. *La traduction et la lettre ou l'auberge du lointain*. Paris: Seuil.

Bühler, Karl. [1934] 2011. *The Theory of Language: The Representational Function of Language (Sprachtheorie)*. Translated by Donald Fraser Goodwin. Amsterdam: John Benjamin's Publishing Company.

Chomsky, Noam. [1965] 1969. *Aspects of the Theory of Syntax*. Cambridge, MA: M.I.T. Press.

Chuquet, Hélène, and Michel Paillard. 1987. *Approche linguistique des problèmes de traduction. Anglais-français*. Gap/Paris: Ophrys.

Crystal, David. 2003. *A Dictionary of Linguistics and Phonetics*. 5th ed. Oxford: Blackwell.

Eco, Umberto. 1968. *La struttura assente*. Milano: Bompiani.

Eco, Umberto. 1975. *Trattato di semiotica generale*. Milano: Bompiani.

Eco, Umberto. 1976. *A Theory of Semiotics*. Bloomington: Indiana University Press.

Eco, Umberto. 1984. *Semiotics and the Philosophy of Language*. London: Macmillan.

Farshidvard, Khosrow. 1387 [2008]. *Tārix-e moxtaṣar-e zabān-e fārsi: az āghāz tā konun* [A Brief History of the Persian Language from the Beginning Until Now]. Tehrān: Zavvār.

Folkart, Barbara. 1991. *Le conflit des énonciations : traduction et discours rapporté*. Montréal: Balzac.

Greimas, Julien Algirdas, and Joseph Courtes. [1979] 1982. *Semiotics and Language: An Analytical Dictionary*. Translated by Larry Crist et al. Bloomington: Indiana University Press.

Greimas, Julien Algirdas, and Joseph Courtes. [1979] 1993. *Sémiotique: Dictionnaire raisonné de la théorie du langage*. Translated by Larry Crist et al. Paris: Hachette Supérieur.

Hjelmslev, Louis. [1943] 1961. *Prolegomena to a Theory of Language*. Translated by J. Francis Whitfield. Madison: University of Wisconsin Press.

Izard, Michel, Christian Puech, and Jean-Louis Chiss. n.d. "Structuralisme." *Encyclopædia Universalis [en ligne]*. www.universalis.fr/encyclopedie/structuralisme/.

Jakobson, Roman. [1960] 1964. "Linguistics and Poetics." In *Style in Language*, edited by Thomas Sebeok, 350–377. Cambridge, MA: M.I.T. Press.

Jakobson, Roman. 1971. *Selected Writings II. Word and Language.* The Hague: Mouton.
Lazard, Gilbert. 1995. *La formation de la langue persane.* Paris: Peeters.
Martinet, André. [1960] 1980. *Éléments de linguistique générale.* Paris: Armand Colin.
Martinet, André. 1962. *A Functional View of Language.* Oxford: Clarendon Press.
Martinet, André. 1965. *La linguistique synchronique.* Paris: Presses universitaires de France.
Nöth, Winfried. 1990. *Handbook of Semiotics.* Bloomington, IN: Indiana University Press.
Peirce, Charles Sanders. 1931–1958. *The Collected Papers of Charles Sanders Peirce.* Edited by Charles Hartshorne, Paul Weiss, and Arthur W. Burks. 8 vols. Cambridge, MA: Harvard University Press.
Pergnier, Maurice. 1993. *Les fondements sociolinguistiques de la traduction.* Lille: Presses universitaires de Lille.
Petitot, Jean. 1985. *Morphogenèse du Sens.* Paris: PUF.
Petitot, Jean. n.d. "Forme." *Encyclopædia Universalis.* Accessed July 31, 2022. www.universalis.fr/encyclopedie/forme/.
Pezeshki, Nastaran. 1388 [2009]. *Hamāhangihā ye vājegāni e 'arabi va fārsi dar she'r-e Masnavi; bā takye bar janbehā-ye musiqāy-e Masnavi va Ghazaliāt-e Shams* [The Coordination of Arabic and Persian in Masnavi]. Tehran: Āzādmehr.
Propp, Vladimir. [1926] 1968. *Morphology of the Folktale.* Translated by Laurence Scott. Austin: University of Texas.
Rastier, François. 2017. "Cassirer et la création du structuralisme." *Texto! Textes et cultures* XXII, n° 4.
Ṣafā, Ẓabiḥollah. 2535/1355 [1976]. *Seyri dar tārix-e zabānhā va adab-e irāni* [A Review of Iranian Languages and Literatures]. Tehrān: Showrā-ye Farhang va Honar, Markaz-e Moṭāle'āt va hamāhangi-e Farhangi.
Saussure, Ferdinand de. [1916] 1995. *Cours de linguistique générale. "Grande bibliothèque Payot".* Edited by Tullio de Mauro. Paris: Payot.
Shamisā, Sirus. 1380 [2001]. *Sabkshenāsi-ye she'r* [Versification and Poetic Genres]. 9th ed. Tehrān: Ferdows.
Sørensen, Hans. 1955. *Studier i Baudelaires poesi.* Copenhaguen: Festskrift udgivet af Københavns Universitet.
Svend, Johansen. 1949. "La notion de signe dans la glossématique et dans l'esthétique In." In *Recherches Structurales,* 288–303. Copenhagen: Travaux du cercle linguistique de Copenhague 5.
Touraj, Mehdi. 2007. *Rūmī and the Hermeneutics of Eroticism.* Leiden/Boston: Brill.
Xānlari, Parviz Nātel. 1366 [1987]. *Tārix-e zabān-e Fārsi* [The History of the Persian Language]. Tehrān: Nashr-e now.

3 Recreating the Poetics of Rumi

This chapter is dedicated to possibly the most important feature of the infradiscoursive purport of Rumi's text and one that furthermore constitutes a strong challenge to any attempt to recreate the discoursive form in any target language. I will focus here on the question of the poetics of Rumi's text and, more specifically, on the problem of rhythm and how it represents the core problem of the untranslatability of Persian classical poetry and *a fortiori* of Rumi's verse insofar as his poetry is, according to many experts, the epitome of musicality in Persian literature. This subject has been separately broached in detail in two of my previously published articles.[1] My central argument in these articles is that Rumi's use of music in his discourse possesses semiotic complexities that surpass the sole semiotization of extralinguistic reality by natural language and alludes to the existence of a systematic utilization of nonlinguistic semiotic systems. As I have argued in those papers, Rumi's relation to music in his verse creates a unique semiotic situation in which certain portions of his poetic text are of a dual hybrid semiotic nature, simultaneously musical and verbal, on account of the unprecedented and systematic use of rhythm and rhyme he makes, especially in his ghazals. Although I take advantage in this chapter of certain content points and extracts from my previous articles, my main goal here is to demonstrate how this hybridity presents an unsurmountable challenge to translation.

Rumi's success in creating a multisemiotic medium of expression can be ascribed to the existence of an infradiscoursive material relatively unique in nature, namely the structural intermingling of Iranian music and Persian poetry. Associating music and poetry as two related artistic forms of expression is nothing intrinsically new. In fact, it is quite commonplace in many cultures. However, in few traditions are these two means of expression as closely and systematically related as in the Persianate world. Ehsan Yarshater duly points out:

> In Iranian culture, the arts are not as clearly delineated as they are in the Occident. Being an artist is defined first by an internal feeling that can be expressed through different mediums, such as poetry, calligraphy, painting, and music. Many musicians were also calligraphers or wrote the texts of their own songs. . . . Many parallels could be drawn from various achievements in

DOI: 10.4324/9781003157960-4

different artistic fields, but [as far] as the Persian arts are concerned, no two of them are more intimately related than poetry and music.

(Yarshater 1974, 153)

The association of music and poetry in Iranian civilization is not manifested only thematically or metaphorically. It doesn't only appear in the guise of recurring allusions to music, dance, or the performance of troubadours (*moṭreb*) in the poetry of Rumi, Nezami, Sa'di, Hafez, or other mystic poets. The connection between these two art mediums is formal, structural, even existential, as if they were derived from a single overarching aesthetic paradigm of common values and semantics. On the one hand, Persian prosody has a particularly rhythmic character due to its use of a Persianized version of *'aruẓ* meters and heavily enriched rhyme patterns facilitated by morphological, lexical, and phonetic characteristics of the Persian language. On the other hand, depending on the pieces and the genres, a particular form of Iranian music, *sāz o āvāzi*, has a rhythmic structure that can be partially or entirely reliant on poetic meters. Taking classical Persian poetry and Iranian classical music as two separate semiotic systems, I can show how in certain contexts, for instance in Rumi's ghazals, the simultaneous use of language and poetry creates an unusual and highly original single hybrid system which lends itself to mystical expression.

1 The Music of Persian Poetry

1.1 Basic Principles of Persian Versification

What constitutes poetry in Persian? Shafi'i Kadkani, a contemporary Iranian linguist and poetician, dedicates an entire modern treaty of Persian poetics, entitled *Musiqi-e she'r* [The Music of Poetry] (1989), to this question. Inspired by Russian formalists, he considers poetry as the resurrection of words that are by default in a dead state in neutral language and devoid of any aesthetic appeal to the interlocutor. He determines the source of poeticity as being of two types, musical and linguistic (1368 [1989], 13–15). In the linguistic category, he counts several figures of speech such as those of substitution or syntactic ones, the presence of which is essential for a text to be considered poetic. This could include poetry in the conventional sense of the term or poetic prose or *nasr-e mossajja'* [decorated prose].[2] In terms of musicality, i.e., the phonic and chronometric form of the utterance, four *sine qua non* conditions are required for a text to be considered a poem: meter, rhyme, *radif* [anaphoric rhyme complementary to ordinary rhyme], and an array of phonetic figures of speech akin to alliteration and assonance (see Chapter 4). Shafi'i Kadkani recognizes rhythmic properties in classical Persian poetry that he describes as musical components. They consist of metric rhythm, rhythm created by ordinary and anaphoric rhythms, and sound harmonies (alliteration, consonance, and *jenās* figures). It is this same typology of musical traits that he applies to the poems of the *Divan* in an analysis that serves as the introduction to his anthology of the ghazals of Rumi (2008).

Kadkani considers a fourth musical component that he calls semantic music created in the content of poetic utterances.

> Music or melody in poetry is classified as follows: 1. *External music* (*'aruz*); 2. *Peripheral music* (*qāfie* and *radif*, and everything related to them such as anaphors [and internal rhymes]; 3. *Internal music* (corresponding to all the harmonies generated by the chords and contrasts of consonants and vowels in the verse; for instance various types of *jenās* are an example of this); 4. The music of meaning (all the hidden underlying relations of the elements of a *meṣra'* [verse] which are realized through contrasts, equivalences, and confrontations; as well, the repetition of the central theme of the poem in its variations).
>
> (1387 [2008], 23)[3]

As far as the metrical and prosodic aspects of poetry are concerned, Arabic and Persian versifications – and consequently those of Turkish and Urdu, which were shaped on the basis of Persian poetry towards the High Middle Ages – have common prosodic principles. This common base consists above all in following the same metric models, the same prosodic logic and structures of rhyme, and the same forms (*robā'i*, *maṣnavi*, *qaside*, ghazal, etc.), even the same poetic genres, especially in the case of the last three languages because the Persian literary tradition shares very little simultaneous evolution with Arabic. The following analysis is far from exhaustive, its purpose being only to give a contrastive overview of the versifications of Western target languages and those of Persian. This is all the more important since the prosodic principles of Western versification, unlike their rhetoric common roots in Aristotelian rhetoric, are fundamentally different from Persian and Arabic: the classification of meters, the metric scansion, the definition of the foot, even the definition of the hemistich and of the stanza are all unique to these languages.

One of the most important distinguishing factors in Persian poetry is the graphic deployment of verses on the page as well as the structure of the verses. The graphic organization of verses constitutes a visual effect that can only be lost in translation. According to Homāyi's treatise on Persian versification (1367 [1988], 93), the basic unit of rhythmic utterance is the *meṣra'* [Arabic term designating each of the components forming a double-leaf door], while the discursive unit of the poem is the *beyt* (tent/house in Arabic), which is composed of two juxtaposed *meṣra'* forming a line. In this definition, *meṣra'* should be considered the equivalent of a verse and *beyt* corresponds to a *couplet* in Western poetic systems. This definition is radically different from the one used in Arabic versification, which takes *beyt* as the basic unit of poetry. This has been a source of confusion for many Western scholars who applied the Arabic principles to Persian versification, taking *beyt* as the equivalent of a verse and translating *meṣra'* by 'hemistich'. We can talk about hemistich in Persian poetry only when the meter of the verse lends itself to a *caesura*, i.e., a meter whose number of feet (*ajzā-ye 'aruz*) is even and the size of each foot is equal, namely a symmetrical meter (*baḥr e sālem*) with no elisions. This distinction is important for the analysis of the rhyme structure and the formation of an internal rhyme, often employed by Rumi.

Poetic forms (or *qāleb* [mold]) are defined according to formal factors such as number, meter, rhyme positioning, vertical grouping and arrangement of verses (*beyts*), as well as discoursive characteristics such as theme, genre, and the function of the text. These forms are comparable to those in the Western literary system such as sonnets, odes, ballads, or even quatrains added to the Western canon thanks to translations of Omar Khayyam (Lefevere 1992, 8–9). The high diversity of forms in Persian poetry is that on top of the forms borrowed from Arabic such as the *qaside* and *robā'i*, there are forms that have been devised by the Iranian literary polysystem. This is particularly the case of the *do-beyti* (literally "two couplets") that was modeled on the rhyme model of the *robā'i* but on a lighter meter, invented by Baba Tāher in the 11th century. Some other forms are *masnavi, ghazal, qet'e, chārpāre, tarji'band, tarkib-band, mostazād, mosammat,* etc. (Homāyi 1367 [1988], 100–221). Regarding the forms used by Rumi, they come down to four: *masnavi, ghazal, robā'i,* and *tarji'band*. Masnavi (or *dogāni* [couplet] in Persian) is the most widespread form in Persian poetry based on the quantity of verses composed.[4] It consists of a series of couplets (*beyt*), two horizontally juxtaposed verses, with a single rhyme. The number of *beyts* is undetermined but they all have the same meter. Furthermore, only the two verses (*meṣra'*) of each couplet (*beyt*) rhyme with each other.

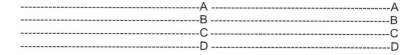

Figure 3.1 Rhyme structure of *masnavi*

Thanks to the possibility of changing the rhyme in each couplet, the poet enjoys a certain freedom in his selection, on the paradigmatic axis, of the final term of each line. For this reason and the indefinite number of lines, the *masnavi*, like the French *alexandrins*, is the first choice of an author in the composition of long narrative, historical, epic, or didactic poems. The great masterpieces of Persian literature, such as Ferdowsi's *Shāhnāme*, Nezami's *Khamse* and Attār's *Manṭeq al-ṭeyr*, are all in *masnavi*. *robā'i* or *chahār-gāni* [quatrain" in Persian] is a short poem similar to a stanza in Western languages. It is composed of two *beyts* or four verses of identical meter, of which verses 1, 2, and 4 have the same rhyme.

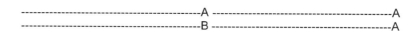

Figure 3.2 Rhyme structure of *robā'i*

An Iranian innovation taken up by Arabs, as Homāyi argues based on the etymological origin of the term (1988, 152), the robā'i is one of the most widespread poetic forms in Persian. Its thematic content and genre can vary widely depending on the period and the poet, as evidenced by the diverse nature of philosophical robā'is by epicurean Omar Khayyam, the moralizing nature of Sa'di's, and the lyrical and mystical quatrains of Rumi and Abusa'id-e Abalkheyr. The conciseness of this poetic form provides for a stripped down and incisive discourse.

Closely related to the *qaside* [ode], a popular form in Arabic poetry, the ghazal is the archetype of Persian lyric poetry. Brought to its peak of poetic perfection by Sa'di and Hafez, it has become the most popular form among Persian readers. The Arabic term ghazal means "gallantry, flirtation, amorous word." However, this form evolved with Sanāyi in the 12th century, who made it the vehicle of his mystical teachings. What distinguishes the *qaside* from the ghazal, apart from the length, is the content and the organization of the discourse. The particularity of the ghazal is the multitude of themes addressed within a single poem (Homāyi 1988, 125). This imposes an extralinguistic multireferentiality in the sense that the message communicated by the discourse is variable and not necessarily coherent on the logical level of the discourse. Generally between five and nine lines (*beyts*), rarely going up to 19 (in Rumi's case), the ghazal maintains the same meter and especially the same rhyme as established in the first *beyt* (both verses) and occurring at the end of each consecutive *beyt*.

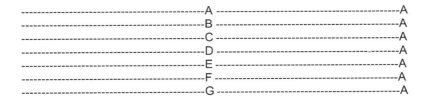

Figure 3.3 Rhyme structure of ghazal and *qaside*

The preservation of the same rhyme for the entire length of the poem makes the composition of ghazal a rather daunting task. Another peculiarity of the ghazal lies in the practice of *takhalloṣ* [release, exit from the poem], which consists in including either a dedication (to an important character) or, more often, the author's pen name as signature in the last or penultimate line of the poem. This integration takes place within the utterance in such a way that the proper name in question becomes an element of the syntax: a starting term, an object adjunct, an appositive, and very often as a vocative function. Rumi's penname is *Shams*, in his companion's honor, or *khāmush/khamush* [silent].

Finally, the *tarji'band* is the result of the joining of several poems (ghazals or other forms) by means of a linking *beyt* that is repeated at the end of each poem, much like a stanza, and that is different in rhyme but identical in meter. The result is a large block of text resembling that of a long *masnavi*.

1.2 The 'Aruẓi: A Chronemic Quantitative Accentual Meter

The most important musical component of Persian classical poetry is its metric system insofar as the chronemic nature of Persian prosody is what assimilates the most linguistic utterances to musical phrases. The metric system of classical Persian poetry is based on the *owzān-e 'aruẓi* [meters of the *'aruẓ*], a *chronemic* or *quantitative* metric model, inherited from Sanskrit by Arabic and Persian,[5] similar to those used in the versification of ancient Greek and Latin, with the difference that the numerical values of syllables and meters are calculated on the basis of a nonsyllabic distinction. To simplify things and to bring out the increased complexity of the Arabic-Persian metric system compared to quantitative meters, it should be noted that the number and the length of syllables are not the only factors that count in the construction of a meter.[6] In addition to those factors, it is the relative positioning of syllables according to their length in the enunciative sequence in addition to the tonic (accentual) character of syllables that is considered to distinguish various factors. The distinguishing feature of the *'aruẓ* is that, unlike most metric systems, such as the *syllabic* meter in Romance languages or *accentual-syllabic* or *syllabotonic* meters in Germanic languages, the smallest unit of scansion is not the syllable but a combination of *morae* forming short, long, and augmented syllables, called *arkān-e 'aruẓ* [foundations of *'aruẓ*].

The founding blocks of the meter are three phonological units, *sabab*, *vatad*, and *fāsele*, corresponding to a sequence of phonetic units with a specific number of morae. These sequences are of two sorts: a *motaḥarrek*, a consonant followed by a vowel, and a *sāken*, a consonant not followed by a vowel. In other words, what counts in addition to long and short syllables is the relative position of consonants and vowels in relation to each other. For instance, a *vatad e najmu'*, which consists of two *motaḥarreks* followed by a *sāken*, can manifest itself in two short syllables (U U) of which the second ends in a consonant, like *falak*; or in a short syllable followed a long syllable (U–) like *mara*. Persian recognizes three kinds of syllables: short (indicated by 'U': *ma/mo/me/*. . .), long (indicated by '–' : *mā/man/*. . .), and elongated (indicated by U–: *mard/māl/mānd/*. . .). It is then not only the number or the tonal quality of the syllables that must be accounted for in scansion, but also their length and relative position.[7] Comparing various prosodic systems, Roman Jakobson summarizes the syllabic difference between the quantitative and syllabotonic metric schemes, explaining:

> In quantitative ("chronemic") verse, long and short syllables are mutually opposed as more or less prominent. This contrast is usually carried out by syllable nuclei, phonemically long and short. But in metrical patterns like Ancient Greek and Arabic, which equalize length "by position" with length "by nature", the minimal syllables consisting of a consonantal phoneme and one mora vowel are opposed to syllables with a surplus (a second mora or a closing consonant) as simpler and less prominent syllables opposed to those that are more complex and prominent.
>
> (Jakobson [1960] 1964, 360)

Recreating the Poetics of Rumi 129

The phonetic units of the *motaḥarrek* and *sāken* in Arabic, or their equivalent short, long, and elongated syllables in Persian, in turn form larger units called *ajzā-ye 'aruẓ* [components of *'aruẓ*], similar to the notion of foot in Greco-Roman quantitative meters. There are 8 main feet and 12 ancillary feet in Persian poetry, which are based on the sequence of the aforementioned units. The various combinations of these feet give rise to 19 basic metric structures called *baḥr* [ocean] from which the meters are derived. Each of these global structures can give rise to several meters (up to 30 different meters) according to two variables: the number of feet in each *meṣra'* [verse] (2, 3, 4 feet) as well as potential modifications (like elision of one or more phonetic units in one of the feet) or lack thereof (Ahmadnezhād and Kamāli Aşl 1385 [2006], 16). In order to name each meter, one begins by naming the *baḥr*, followed by the number of feet in each *beyt*, then by the nature of the modification undergone by the meter. For example, *baḥr-e ramal-e mosaddas-e maḥẓuf* is a meter of the basic structure of the *ramal* containing 6 feet in each verse (*mosaddas*: hexameters), and which is missing a long syllable (*maḥẓuf*: elided). That is the meter used in the composition of the entire *Masnavi*.

از جدایی‌ها شکایت می‌کند	بشنو از نی چون حکایت می‌کند
Beshno az ney | chun hekāyat | mikonad	az jodāyi | hā shekāyat | mikonad
– U – – | – U – – | – U –	– U – – | – U – – | – U –

Figure 3.4 The meter of Masnavi MI) l.1

The fixed metric models imposed by these components of *'aruẓ* designate the exact *position* of syllables according to their length (number of morae) and accentual quality in Persian in relation to one another.[8] The result is a precisely measured sequence of sounds with specific *ictuses* at the beginning of certain feet. When recited continuously, the poem can constitute the beat of simple musical phrases (Figure 3.5). This highly precise chronometric measuring of the sign sequence as well as the symmetrical structure of the rhyme creates linguistic utterances that are structurally similar to musical phrases. This prosodic structure is reinforced by the more fluid phonetic articulation due to the low number of accumulated consonants and the high number of syllables per unit.

Yār marā | ghār marā | 'ishq i jigar | -khʷār marā
مفتعلن| مفتعلن| مفتعلن|مفتعلن
Mufta'ilun | Mufta'ilun | Mufta'ilun | Mufta'ilun
– U U – | – U U – | – U U – | – U U –
tum ta ta tum | tum ta ta tum | tum ta ta tum | tum ta ta tum

Figure 3.5 Graphic indication of a *Baḥr-e Sari'* used in D) G.37

130 *Recreating the Poetics of Rumi*

This figure shows the metric structure of Example 3.2 in three transcription modes.[9] It demonstrates how each foot is equivalent to a 6/8 bar in music, corresponding to an eighth followed by two sixteenths and a final eighth. The verse then has four measures of 6/8 divided by three bar lines on an imaginary score. In a conventional method of reciting the poem, it is appropriate for the first syllable of each foot to be accented, as if the "downbeat" (le temps fort) of each should be stressed and pronounced with more intensity. This practice, along with the accentual character of the language, makes Persian prosody comparable to the quantitative syllabotonic meter of Germanic languages, although the latter is devoid of the exact time measures found in *'aruẓ*.

1.3 The Rhyme Structure: **Radif** *and* **Qāfie**

According to Shafi'i Kadkani, the second indispensable musical component of the poem, after the meter, is the rhyme. Indeed, classical Persian prosody is based on two main pillars: rhythm (metric) and rhyme, insofar as no poem can exist without rhyme, and this since Middle Persian, that is before the common evolution of Arabic and Persian versifications. The wealth of rhyme in Persian medieval verse cannot be exaggerated. This is due to the simple empirical fact of the numeric wealth of the Persian lexicon, which it owes to its character as an Indo-European language enriched by massive Semitic and Altaic loanwords. This phenomenon of lexicographic accumulation can also be observed in English, a Germanic language with a heavy Greek and Latin influence. The primordial status of rhyme in Persian poetry has been emphasized by Western scholars such as Arberry, Nicholson, and Lewis. Lewis points out the impossibility of having a poem in Persian devoid of particularly rich rhymes: "All medieval Persian poetry observes rhyme; there is no equivalent of blank verse (Lewis 2007, 332). He emphasizes the sheer length of common Persian rhymes in comparison to English, where a similarly large numbers of repetitive phonemes in a rhyme would be frowned upon and remind the reader of nursery rhymes.

Persian rhyme has two variants: *qāfie* and *radif* [row, list]. The first variant is the equivalent of rhyme in Western languages. It consists of nonrepetitive terms at the end of a *beyt* or *meṣra'* (depending on the poetic form in question), whose phonemes are fully or partly alliterative, the last consonantal phoneme(s) of which are identical: the larger the number of recurring phonemes, the richer the rhyme (Ahmadnezhād and Kamāli Aṣl 1385 [2006], 103). *Radif* designates the anaphoric rhyme, i.e., the recurring lexemes placed after *qāfie* at the end of the verse to increase the number of identical phonemes making up the whole rhyme structure. Note the rhyme structure in a Rumi quatrain, where *qāfie* is bolded and *radif* is bolded and underlined:

Example 3.1 D) R. 1891

مستم کن و از هر دو **جهانم بِسِتان**	ای دوست قبولم کن و **جانم بِسِتان**
آتش به من اندر زن و **آنم بِسِتان**	با هرچه دلم قرار گیرد بیتو
Ey dust | qabulam kon | o jānam be|setān	Mastam ko|n o az har do |jahānam be|setān
− − U | U − − U | U − − U | U −	− − U | U − − U | U − − U | U −
Bā har che | delam qarār | girad bi | to	ātash be | man andar za|n o ānam besetān
− − U | U − U − U | U − − − | −	− − U | U − − U | U − − U | U −
O friend! Accept me and take my life Make me drunk, and from both worlds take me away From all that in which my heart finds peace without you, Set me ablaze and seize that away from me.	

In this quatrain that puts to work a tetrameter in the *bahr e hazaj*, the typical meter used in *robā'is*,[10] there is a complex rhyme structure: including the anaphoric rhyme, *besetān* [take away], the rhyme has a total of five identical syllables repeated at the end of verses 1, 2, and 4: ā/nam/be/se/tān. The syllables belonging to a *bestān* in anaphoric position should not be confused with the repeated syllables of the other three lexemes constituting *qāfie*. *Besetān*, repeated three times, is the *radif*, whereas *jānam* [my life], *jahānam* [world], and *ānam* [that] constitue the *qāfie*. This degree of prosodic richness created thanks to the chronemic accentual meter of the quatrain as well as the number of repeating phonemes, typical in Rumi's poems, has no equivalent in any other Indo-European language, including the target languages.

Furthermore, in longer verses, some poets use an internal rhyme. This means the use of a rhyme not only at the end but also in the middle of the verse, reinforcing the visual symmetry and increasing the sound harmony. Internal rhymes can be simple (*qāfie* alone) or compound (*qāfie* + *radif*), taking place in the middle of the verse (*meṣra'*), either at the end of each hemistich (if the number of feet is even) or at the end of each foot (if the number of feet is odd). The use of internal rhyme is Rumi's signature in his ghazals. Note Example 3.2 where external rhymes are shown in bold while internal rhymes are in italics and anaphoric rhyme is underlined.

Example 3.2 D) G37, l.1–2, 5[11]

یار تویی غار تویی خواجه نگهدار **م‌را**	یار م‌را غار م‌را عشق **جگرخوار م‌را**
سینه مشروح تویی بر در اسرار **م‌را**	نوح تویی روح تویی فاتح و مفتوح تویی
روضه امید تویی راه ده ای یار **م‌را**	حجره خورشید تویی خانه ناهید تویی
Yār *mārā* ghār *mārā* 'eshq-e jegar-kh"ār *mārā*	Yār *toyi* ghār *toyi* kh"āje negah *dār* **mārā**
− U U − | − U U − | − U U − | − U U −	− U U − | − U U − | − U U − | − U U −
Nuḥ *toyi* ruḥ *toyi* fāteḥ o maftuḥ *toyi*	Sine-ye mashruḥ *toyi* bar dar-e asrār **mārā**
Ḥojre-ye *khorshid toyi* xāne-ye nāhid *toyi*	rowze-ye ommid *toyi* rāh deh ey yār **mārā**

(Continued)

132 *Recreating the Poetics of Rumi*

Example 3.2 (Continued)

The companion is mine, the cave is mine, heart-consuming love is mine The companion you are, the cave you are. O Khawaja [master]! Save me! Noah you are, the soul you are, the conqueror and the conquered one you are. The torn-open bosom you are, at the gate of secrets, for me. The store of the Sun you are, the house of Venus you are. The cut open bosom you are. Let me in o companion!		
E1) Ls: p. 66–67: I HAVE THIS friend I have this cave I am gutted by love[12] you are that friend you are that cave my lord, don't cast me off	E2) Helr: p. 147–148: Beloved, You are my cave. You are the fire of love that consumes me. The beloved is You; the cave is You.	E3) Shg: p. 96–97: Be a lover for me, a cave for me, The sweet burn of love for me. O master, protect me!
F1) Vo: p. 69–70: O compagnon, compagnon de la Caverne! Amour qui dévore le cœur! Tu es mon compagnon, tu es ma caverne : ô Maître, gardemoi!		F2) Taj: p. 109–110: A moi l'ami, à moi la grotte, A moi l'amour mangeur de foie, Tu es l'ami, tu es la grotte, Ô mon maître, protège-moi.

According to our calculations, in this passage, there are on average 10 words (between 8 and 11) in each verse for an approximate total of 60 words (lexemes, not morphemes). Of this whole, only 11 words do not belong to some sort of rhyme group, interior or exterior. There is also a strong alliteration between the three terms that are not part of the rhyme: *ḥojre*, *xāne*, and *rowẓe* in verse 5. This veritable verbal symphony is by no means devoid of a deep semantic content; quite the contrary, this ghazal is built on semantic symmetry and teems with various tropes, from top to bottom. This symmetry is both the consequence and the cause of the prosodic choice. The meter that serves as the background and undertone of this ghazal is a tetrameter formed by four occurrences of the foot "*mofta'elon*" following a symmetrical plan. The poet has found a certain way to pace the verse using inner rhymes, otherwise the result would have seemed rather monotonous. It is therefore a metric choice that both facilitates and requires the creation of the inner rhyme.

2   Music and Poetry in the Persianate World

If classical poetry imitates the rhythmic structure of musical phrases, Iranian music too is of unparalleled orality. It is therefore not only the Persian language that comes close to Iranian music; Iranian music too, in its classical form, is remarkably similar to the Persian language in that it can reproduce a particular linguistic effect because of its almost total dependence on poetic rhythm.

2.1   Poetic Rhythm in Iranian Music

It is necessary to distinguish two cases of the coexistence of the poetic system with the music of the Iranian world: the sacred practice of *samā'*[13] and the secular pieces of *āvāzi* (cantabile) whose rhythmic structure is based on the poetic rhythm (meter) of Persian. In the sacred chants of the mystics, the linguistic component occupies a central place: either liturgical *zekr* [incantations][14] or mystical poems. The same rhythm can serve as the basis for the famous ritual dance of *samā'*, practiced typically by the Mevlevi brotherhood – they are the descendants of a Sufi branch founded by the disciples of Rumi, and several essays about them have appeared since the 19th century. The mystics of these dervishes are above all characterized by the practices of *samā'* and *zekr* governed by the rhythm of Rumi's odes and accompanied by a percussion instrument called *daf*. Schimmel remarks in particular (2011, 180–186) that Rumi's originality as a Muslim mystic lies in his conceptualization of the three elements of music, poetry, and dance as a form of spiritual path-faring (*tariqat*) or journey towards the union with God and as a means of entering into harmony with the universe. The combination of these three elements raises the soul of the practicing mystic to a state of ecstasy (*vajd*) by bringing him closer to the creator (2014).[15]

The secular form of Iranian music can be divided into two main categories from the point of view of rhythm: on the one hand, classical pieces whose ordinary rhythm is characterized by equal intervals, and on the other, arrhythmic pieces characterized by a free or timeless rhythm. While it often happens that the rhythm of rhythmic pieces such as songs is based on the meter of the poem being recited, it is the second category of arrhythmic pieces that is particularly marked by the orality of poetry. This is the *āvāzi* form (literally *cantabile*, although the *āvāzi* form can also refer to instrumental pieces). The rhythm of *āvāzi* is not measurable in a conventional way, since the musical phrases do not follow one another regularly in a regulated chronometric sequence. This unmeasured rhythm, or free-paced rhythm as Jean During calls it (During et Mirabdolbaghi 1991), is partly structured by classical prosody.

Among all forms of the Persianate musical tradition, *sāz-o avāzi* (literally "instrumental cantabile") is of particular interest to our study. *Āvāzi* is in fact an arhythmical recital, with or without a vocal component, in which the melody follows a "free rhythm" formed by a series of discontinuous musical phrases played by "pulsation." Interestingly, the individual pulsations often imitate the rhythm of a verse. The melody is therefore played – or vocalized – phrase by phrase, with long or short intervals of silence, in a manner similar to the way one recites a poem. An *āvāzi* piece, therefore, doesn't flow like a conventional musical piece; its flow is similar to the recitation of poetry, as if the instrument didn't play music but *literally* spoke.[16]

The melody in an *āvāzi* piece is played sometimes timelessly, sometimes by "pulsation," sometimes with a discontinuous rhythm, sometimes in a mixed modality (of the three) and this, unexpectedly, in the space of a few musical phrases. The rhythm of pulse-played phrases is based entirely on the feet of a poem's meter, even if the melody in question is played by an instrument and not by the vocalist. This type of musical interpretation resembles the rhythm of the reading of a Persian poem: one can sometimes declaim a poem continuously and successively without pause, sometimes pause after lines or even in the middle of lines, sometimes by accentuating the syllables; in other words, one can read by pulsation, in a disjointed way. A piece of *āvāzi* is therefore marked by the orality of the poetic rhythm even if there is no sung poem and if the piece is entirely instrumental.

2.2 Musical Content in Composition

In my analogy of the intersystemic interferences of music and poetry, I presented the musical categories proposed by Shafi'i Kadkani. He pursues his analysis by comparing the rhymes in a poem to musical instruments. This metaphor is elaborated in the following manner: if a poem is assimilated to a set of harmonious sounds, like those of a musical piece, the poem's meter can be compared to the musical rhythm, the tonality of its constituent monemes to musical pitches, and the rhyme to the sound character represented by each instrument with various sound qualities. Can we consider Rumi's ghazals, mostly owners of a rich inner rhyme, as polyphonic, symphony-like pieces? Can we even push this metaphor further and consider the "music" generated by the discursive content of the poem to create a particular psychological state or mood: nostalgia, hope, sadness, joy, grief, or ecstasy?

A classical piece in an Iranian concert is, in fact, characterized by constant musical modulations. The melodic component of Iranian classical music has a dual modal and tonal character. Like the Ancient Greek musical system, some residues of which appear in Gregorian chants, the use of quartertones allows for a larger potential of modulation and a higher number of scales, represented by *dastgāh*. The tonal property of Iranian music is represented by its 12 *dastgāh* (scales), three of which are akin to the major and minor scales in modern Western music. Iranian music displays a modal character insofar as each scale or *dastgāh* contains several tonal modes called *gushe*[17] Each *dastgāh* consist of several *gushe* (literally: corners), which can be compared to the modes or *maqām* in a modal musical system. Some of these *gushe* are common between different *dastgāh*, allowing the passage from one scale to another (Zonis 1973, 62). The disposition of the modes of the *dastgāh* prepares fertile ground for a minute combination of modes and scales and makes the player-composer modulate nonstop in his performance, even in a short instrumental piece. Moreover, the existence of quartertones means a higher mathematical probability of creating scales and modes in the Iranian system compared to the Western musical system, which is limited to minor and major scales.

Each modal disposition evokes a certain mood; each *gushe* conjures up a particular emotion. In an *āvāzi* recital, the modulation process is usually in accordance with the semantic content of each verse. In other words, the content of the linguistic utterance tends to match the mood created by the melody and rhythm, i.e., content of the musical utterance, that accompany the verse. The modulation in *āvāzi* pieces takes on particularly interesting semantic dimensions. Indeed, it is important for the player/vocalist to associate the semantic content of the recited poetic utterance with the mode in which the verse is sung. The concern for compatibility between musical and linguistic statements is reflected in the appearance of melodic *gushe* specifically used to accompany certain poetic forms. This semantic connivance characterized by a rhythmic base common to music and poetry creates a unique mode of expression whose statements are both musical and verbal in nature. It is possible, within a single singing performance, to go through a multitude of modes, crossing the borders between *dastgāh*, to sing a single ghazal by Hafez or Rumi or a selection of several poems. What motivates the choice by the musician of the mode, or modes (by modulation), in order to sing one verse, or several verses? According to our hypothesis, at least in part, the linguistic content has an important role to play because it is necessary to establish a parallel between the content of the poem and the mood evoked by the melody in the mode, which is associated with the verse, i.e., between the linguistic sign and the musical sign.

An instance of this phenomenon is a *gushe* called "*Masnavi.*" It is a composed *gushe* (itself comprising several passages to other modes by modulation), with an unmeasured (free) rhythm, of the *Afshāri*, a subscale of the *Shur dastgāh*. As its name suggests, this part of the radif is reserved for the singing of the verses of the *Masnavi-e Ma'navi* by Rumi. Like the melodic and rhythmic structures of this *gushe*, there are also other *gushe* in other *dastgāh* that are associated with this poetic form, proof of the importance of a musical tradition based on the poetry of the *Masnavi* in addition to the preponderant place of the Rumi ghazals in dance and song. But why *sing* the *Masnavi*, poems that have a mainly mystical-didactic character and that consist in a series of statements whose semantic aim takes precedence over its aesthetic form? Is there a part of the poet's mystical message that is conveyed only in conjunction with another semiotic system than language? Is there a hidden dimension released only in the presence of another form of expression whose expressiveness is close to that of the Persian language, namely Iranian music? One can imagine this other dimension insofar as it is customary to *sing* the same poem in various modal systems in order to provide it with spiritual qualities and to reveal its different aspects.

This phenomenon leads to the revelation of a completely different dimension of classical Persian poetry, not really found in the content of the discourse but well hidden in its prosodic form, in particular in its rhythm, in all its typological multitude. It is no longer only the signified of the sign that carries the message in combination with other linguistic signs, referring to a precise extralinguistic reality, but also its signifier. We no longer seem to be dealing with a *double*, semiotic-syntactic significance, as Benveniste specifies, specific to language, but with a *triple* significance. Or perhaps this third mode of significance is found elsewhere, in another semiotic system, somewhat despised by the linguist as being incapable of constructing utterances endowed with "syntax but no semiotics" (Benveniste 1974, 56). A certain injustice is being committed against music here because, at least in its Iranian form, music too can convey a "verbal" message, to actualize an extralinguistic reference. This actualization can take place in conjunction with the *sung* verses or even without them. In a way, *āvāzi* pieces seem to imitate verbal language when their free rhythm (accompanied or not by a poem) follows a pattern that bears resemblances to the phonological, tonic, and rhythmic pattern of linguistic utterances.

3 Hybrid Semiotic Systems

3.1 Intersemiotic Relations Between Language and Music

Jakobson defines the poetic function of language as one in which the scope of the similarity/equivalence criterion is shifted from the vertical axis of selection to the horizontal axis of combination. In other words, unlike other linguistic functions, in a poetic discourse, words are selected based on their similarity to the other words on the chain of utterance. The effort is concentrated on creating the best harmonic effect: rhyme, alliteration, rhythm. In Persian poetry, the principle of equivalence is accentuated by the equity of *time measures* in the sequence, which is the same foundation as in musical discourse. This phenomenon virtually makes Persian verse utterances the equivalent of musical phrases. On the other hand, we explained how Persian music takes up a whole different signifying dimension by its association with the poetic rhythm which shapes the *āvāzi*.

The association of music and language occurs at three levels in Iranian prosodic and musical arts: first, within the poetic statement, notably in classical Sufi verse; second, in Iranian classical music, whether in its *āvāzi* form where the musical rhythm is partially that of the poetic meter or else in sacred *samā'* concerts and secular songs where almost always the rhythm is metric; and third, where the content of the linguistic utterance is associated with that of the melody in a song (sacred or profane). We are therefore faced with a hybrid meaning production system whose signs come from the domain of both language and music.

However, according to Émile Benveniste, semiotic systems cannot be mixed. Recognizing the existence of intersemiotic relations, types of generation, homology, and interpretation, Benveniste imposes two principles: nonredundancy and nonsynonymy. Each sign system being unique by its type of operation and by the value of its signs, these signs never mean the same thing despite material resemblances between signs belonging to different systems. According to the principle of nonredundancy, what is expressed by one system cannot be expressed by another, except in the case of systems of the same nature such as written and oral language or even the graphic alphabet and Braille. According to Benveniste's principle of nonsynonymy, "we cannot 'say the same thing' through speech and through music, which are systems with different bases." In the event of the existence of common signs between different semiotic systems, these systems are never synonymous, says Benveniste, because "the substantial identity of a sign does not count, only its functional difference" (1974, 53). In other words, if the content-substances of two signs can be identical, the content forms of two signs, namely their functional differential, are different.

Benveniste's theory does not seem to us to take into account the existence of hybrid semiotic systems, whose signs contain elements from several semiotic systems. These systems must necessarily be in a formal correlation in order to be able to be combined. This relation of isomorphism between semiotic systems, in the jargon of Benveniste, is called homology. By virtue of this relationship, there are similar shapes, characteristics, or structures, so that one can establish "correlations" between specific parts of two or more semiotic systems. For Benveniste, isomorphism can only occasionally be observed between specific sections of semiotic systems, and even then, they cannot be systematically theorized. "This relationship is not observed but established by virtue of connections that one discovers or that one establishes between two distinct systems. The nature of the homology can vary, intuitive or reasoned, substantial or structural, conceptual, or poetic" (1974, 61).

In other words, these relationships are not holistic or global but occasional and sporadic. Isomorphism can be found between specific components of semiotic systems or within a single system among various subsystems, which are derivatives of a parent semiotic system. In the light of Benveniste's classification, one can postulate that the intersemiotic relationship between music and language in the occurrences already cited is of a homological nature.

Now what can be said of music and language in relation to each other as two semiotic systems? In a comparative analysis, Benveniste proposes two axiomatic principles: the *nonredundancy* and *nonconvertibility* of semiotic systems. Sign systems are not redundant insofar as the same exact message cannot be conveyed by two systems of different kinds. Hence their nonconvertibility: "two different types of semiotic systems cannot be mutually convertible."

There is no possible "synonymy" between semiotic systems; one cannot "say the same thing" through words and through music, which are systems with different foundations (1974, 53).

How can we then explain the ties between similar semiotic systems? Benveniste actually recognizes three intersemiotic relationships: a *generative* relationship by which one system is generated by another, oral language and writing systems for instance; *interpretance*, whereby one system interprets and explains another. As per Benveniste, language is the one that interprets all other semiotic systems. Finally, *homology* or isomorphism can be observed in similar forms and features of different sign systems. Such "correlations" can be established only between *particular parts* of these systems. The relationship between Persian poetry and music should be considered of this type.

3.2 Rhythm: Significance on the Syntagmatic Axis

If the semiotic aspect of language manifests itself above all at the level of words and its semantics in the syntagm, this dichotomy is indeed undermined in the poetic function of language. Connotative syntagmatic choice, rhythm, rhyme, figures of speech playing on homophony, idiomatic phrases, fixed expressions, etc. are some of the ways in which the sequence of words can acquire semiotic value. In his essay on the conflict of enunciations, Folkart distinguishes three levels at which the prosodic pattern of the utterance plays a role in the construction of discourse and can generate a shift, or an invariance, within the re-enunciation (Folkart

1991, 220–221). It may be a "simple configuration based on rhythmic and phonetic recurrence" or else a configuration inscribed within a polysystem (in particular syntagms charged with a historical or cultural connotation), or intervention of this prosodic scheme in the process of the meaning of the text. She then gives the example of James Holmes's analysis of a ballad by Auden translated into French. The ballad in anapestic tetrameter has been translated into Alexandrian verse, which amounts to saying that a quantitative meter has become syllabic in French; this is the first level of analysis. The second angle of view consists in identifying the difference in the cultural status of these two poetic forms in French, where the ballad is a scholarly form, unlike in English. But the more complex question is how the prosody is "engaged with meaning in the poem." But what is rhythm?

In an etymological analysis, Benveniste (1974, 327–335) rejects the hypothesis concerning the meaning of the Greek word "rhythm" that associates it with "flow." He finds the origin of the term in a Greek synonym for the word "form," but it is not just any form. Analysis of the semes of the root of this word reveals a multifaceted meaning: "distinctive form; proportioned figure, disposition" of a phenomenon in transformation, "form of movement," "measured form of flow." Especially in the use Plato makes of it, the word takes on the meaning of "that form which is henceforth determined by a 'measure' and subjected to a mathematical order."

Among the literary theorists of modern times, no one has studied the question of rhythm more than the French Hebraist and translator of the Old Testament (1970) Henri Meschonnic, who attributes to rhythm a dimension beyond the simple metric measure of verse. For Meschonnic, "rhythm (both prosody and rhythm, intensity, breath and gesture) carries more meaning than the signified itself" (1973, 270). Meschonnic showcases his argument by a sharp criticism of the translations of the Old Testament, of the Hebrew Bible, into Western languages, which he judges as starting from an erroneous principle of the linguistic sign. He proposes the notion of the inseparability of the meaning of the sign from the form of the sign in the case of Hebrew and the prophetic and poetic discourse of the Bible. The famous myth of the duality of the sign is then undermined by Meschonnic's emphasis on the orality of language and the rhythm of the statement as a signifying element (Meschonnic and Dessons 1998). By broadening the aim and the domain of poetics so that it becomes an analysis of all the phenomena at work within discourse, he maintains that the poem is the manifestation par excellence of these phenomena.

In agreement with Meschonnic, I also argue that the projection of the principle of *equivalence* from the paradigmatic axis onto the syntagmatic axis – as per Jakobson's definition of the poetic function – entails indeed the inseparability of the expression and content planes in the poetic mode of significance. Another term describing Meschonnic conception of poetic significance is "serial semantics." It consists in the capacity of the utterance to signify by the sole juxtaposition of the expression plane on the syntagmatic axis, regardless of the syntactic rules of *combination* that hold these signs together. According to Benveniste, language's *semiotic* mode of significance is realized on the paradigmatic axis while its *semantic* mode is achieved on the syntagmatic axis of the utterance. In the light of this definition, I can argue that the application of *equivalence/similarity* to the axis of *combination* is the projection of a *semiotic* principle unto a *semantic* object. In other words, the poetic utterance, by virtue of the chronemic equivalence of its rhythm, shifts its *semiotic* mode of significance to its *semantic* mode of significance. We can then conclude that the semantic mode of significance in a rhythmic poetic utterance relies on the *equivalence* of its constituent signs. Considering that the equivalence in question is only established between the expression planes of these constituent signs, the signifying mode of the poetic utterance depends not only on its content plane but also, and especially, on its expression plane. This is how I demonstrate the pertinence of Meschonnic's argument about the inseparability of letter and spirit in the Hebrew Bible, and by extension the Koran. Rumi's poetry epitomizes Meschonnic's theory of rhythm and poetic significance among profane texts. It is indeed possible to establish a relationship of analogy between Rumi's poetry and sacred or liturgical texts because of their prosodic character (alliteration, inner rhymes, etc.) and the central role of rhythm in their significance. If the letter of Rumi's poetry is not separable from its spirit, just as sacred texts, then the implications for translation are significantly serious.[18]

3.3 Connotative Semiotic Systems

While Benveniste does not elaborate much on isomorphism, the pivotal works of Louis Hjelmslev, particularly his notion of connotative signs, are of great relevance here. Louis Hjelmslev's model illustrates the operating modes of hybrid semiotic systems resulting from the association of systems that are already in a homological relationship. In his glossematic theory, Hjelmslev distinguishes three types of signs, depending on the existence of the elements of another sign on the level of expression or on that of content: denotative, metasemiotic, and connotative. A metasemiotic sign is one whose content plane corresponds to an entire sign with its two planes and four elements. Scientific language or grammar offers examples of a metasemiotic system. Hjelmslev defines *connotative* signs as ones whose *expression-plane* itself is composed of another sign. This is the case of stylistic forms, styles, vernaculars, or regional languages that have language as a denotative sign (Hjelmslev [1943] 1961, 145–146). If a given language is a denotative semiotic, then units of style such as tone, vernacular, dialect, etc., are its connotative signs.

Still according to Hjelmslev, there can be connotative signs that can contain elements not only of language but also of other semiotic systems on their *expression plane*. One can then imagine the existence of *hybrid* connotative signs whose expression plane contains denotative signs belonging to a different semiotic system (*Ibid.*, 146). It is possible to imagine nonlinguistic connotative semiotic systems such as multimedia utterances as some examples of this phenomenon. Based on this model, we can consider Persian mystic poetry as a connotative semiotic system displaying in its most elaborate rhythmic forms elements of more than one denotative system: in addition to language, there is music, not to mention calligraphy, drawing, and decorative arts. The following model can describe the functioning of the semiotic hybridity of a classical Persian poem and its recitation.

140 *Recreating the Poetics of Rumi*

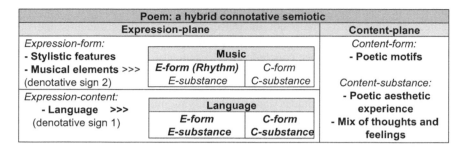

Figure 3.6 The semiotic structure of Persian classical verse

Persian classical poetry is a hybrid connotative sign whose plane of expression consists of the form of musical signs in addition to that of linguistic signs. The musical poetry recited in a piece of *āvāzi* constitutes a second hybrid connotative sign that can be called a hybrid sign in the second degree. This latter hybrid sign in the second degree already has on the plane of expression or, more precisely, as substance of expression, a hybrid sign which corresponds to the poetic statement; it has, moreover, as a form of expression, the musical sign. It should therefore be emphasized that, unlike ordinary multimedia utterances, made up of signs belonging to various semiotic systems and whose semantic content is the linear sum of the contents of each of the signs composing them, the content plane of a hybrid sign, first or second degree, has a value that greatly exceeds the simple sum of its component parts. The hybrid sign transcends, so to speak, the semiotic capacities of the denotative or connotative signs that constitute it.

Āvāz: a second-degree hybrid connotative semiotic	
Expression-plane	**Content-plane**
E-form: The structure of the musical composition	*Content-form:* - **Poetic/musical motifs** *Content-substance:* - **Aesthetic experience** - *Je ne sais quoi*

Figure 3.7 The semiotic structure of *āvāzi* composition

The combination of connotative hybrid signs occurs at the level of the expression-figurae, i.e., the components of form belonging to the musical and linguistic systems.

Thanks to its chronemically measured prosodic structure, Persian poetry is uniquely musical, ostensibly more harmonious than its modern counterparts. This prosody is best used by Rumi in his mystical odes. Iranian music, too, is affected by a high degree of orality since the rhythmic structure of its *āvāzi* form is entirely based on the poetic meter. The mixture of the two semiotic systems, both in *samā'* concerts and in secular musical performances, forms a hybrid connotative semiotic system whose content plane contains a semic quantity that exceeds the sum of its components.

3.4 Semiotizing the Insemiotizable

The purpose of this transcendent semiotic system, insofar as it is supposed to surpass any means of expression, can be understood within the framework of mystical metaphysics, which exhibit the desire to communicate and to know a meaning that is by nature ineffable. Both the divine properties and the reality of the mystical experience is, for the mystics, of the order of the ineffable. The human intellect is fundamentally incapable of understanding the transcendent reality of God. These mystics viewed human language as fundamentally inadequate for communicating the essence of Truth. The meaning of transcendence is totally unspeakable, even *insemiotizable*. Devising such hybrid semiotic systems is, in a way, the response of human ingenuity to the impossibility of communicating the ecstatic experience of the divine presence. Since the human intellect is incapable of apprehending divine transcendence, man must access an intermediate world between the world of matter and that of pure intelligence, in order to allow himself to be apprehended by the object of knowledge. It is to facilitate access to this intermediary world that the Sufi poets have devised hybrid languages whose signs not only signify but lead to ecstasy. These poetic signs form an intermediate space between the sensitive and the intelligible, a space between two worlds that Henry Corbin (1990, 8–13) describes as the *'ālam-e meṣāli* or "imaginal world" *(mondus imaginalis)*, inspired by Sohravardi's Oriental philosophy *(Falsafe-ye eshrāq)* and adopting a common in medieval Scholastic philosophy. This key notion in Iranian Mazdean as well as Islamic cosmogony refers to a middle world that lies between the world of pure ideas and the manifested terrestrial world. In this perspective, one can consider the transcendent hybrid sign as a *para-semiotic* attempt to access or to make the interlocutor access this "imaginal" world, this space par excellence of divine epiphany where the pure forms manifest themselves not by semiotization but by direct incarnation – in the eyes of the mystic.

According to mystics, the elusive, *insemiotizable*, and transcendent nature of the Absolute Truth[19] cannot be known by human intelligence through its logical or dialectical means, of which language is a part. The idea of the inaccessibility of knowledge of the nature of the True has its roots in the conception of knowledge by ontological unification in mystical theosophy. As Henry Corbin argues (1974, 1076), the essence of the Divine True cannot be the *object* of dialectical knowledge but the *subject* of ontological knowledge. God cannot be *known* as a mathematical rule or a natural phenomenon can be *known* by humans. The knowledge of God is initiated by God Himself, who becomes the *subject* of knowledge in an active process. This process involves the manifestation of God to the mystic's purified heart, such as the reflection of a beam of light in a mirror. One cannot therefore semiotize the Truth nor hold it as an object of knowledge. Transcendent truth cannot be "represented by"; it can only be experienced and *lived* (*erlebt*). The truth must reveal itself to the knowing subject, who will only reach it by coming out of his ipseity and by drowning himself in the transcendence of the supreme being. This type of knowledge is realized in an ontological union between the object and the subject of knowledge. It is in this perspective that a mystic like Rumi undertakes to push the formal limits of various languages to achieve a transcendent semiotic system that does not only appeal to the intellect but to all the senses. This new system will no longer serve to speak the ineffable truth of the Absolute but to make it felt through a state of ecstasy (the state of one who stands outside of himself), a state in which the addressee lives the meaning in its own existence. We can therefore assume nonsemiotic properties for the poetic sign which, while retaining its capacity to represent, is occasionally transformed into a signal, that is to say into a sign that stimulates.

4 Translating Rumi's Hybrid Discourse

4.1 *Rumi and Poetry*

Music is omnipresent in Rumi's poetry, both thematically and structurally, in the guise of rhythmic meters and extraordinarily rich rhymes. The latter have been noticed by Franklin Lewis:

> Rumi makes full use of the rhyme richness of Persian; he frequently uses internal rhyme so that the rhyme word will occur two, three or even four times as often as prosody requires in a given line. He also tends to choose the more fluid meters and employ them rhythmically, as one would expect for poetry extemporaneously composed to a turning dance. The use of refrains in many of the ghazals also contributes to the highly cadenced and song-like rhythm.
>
> (2007, 334)

The richness of rhythm in Rumi's poetry is celebrated a number of ways in Iranian music: there are *gushe* dedicated to his *Masnavi* and *samā'* ritual dances based on the rhythms of his ghazals, and his poems are reinterpreted in songs, including modern ones. Rumi's poetry never ceases to fascinate lovers of poetry as well as those of music, if we can really separate those two forms of art from each other. If Rumi's poetry fascinates, according to Shafi'i Kadkani, it is because

> Of all the classical poets of Iran, the one who grasped the music of poetry and the relationship of these two [systems] is Jalāleddin Môlavi, in the ghazals of Shams. In this divan, as we have seen, all the rhythms are musical, which shows how much Môlavi cared about the musicality of the poem. . . . Despite appearances, and Rumi's reputation, and what he said himself: 'rhyme or the aruz let them all be washed away!'. . . reading this divan, everything the

world can feel that Rumi paid attention to the musical role of rhyme more than any other poet, for in addition to the main rhyme he was concerned with inner rhyme; if one examines the other Divāns of classical poetry, none attains the richness of the interior rhyme of the Divān e Kabir. . . . In addition to inner rhyme, he uses a kind of "emphatic" rhyme, which reveals his passion for rhyme. We will then see that this singular predisposition for rhyme is due to the fact that his poems were declaimed to the rhythm of percussion [*zarb*]. This practice divides the verse and makes the existence of the inner rhyme mandatory.

(1368 [1989], 52–53)

Shafi'i Kadkani highlights two essential points about Rumi's poetry: that it is the epitome of a hybrid semiotic discourse associated with *samā'* or cantabile music, and that this achievement was surprisingly rejected and criticized by Rumi himself. How could one of the most prolific poets in the history of world literature hate rhyme and *'aruẓ*? Rumi's seemingly contradictory position towards poetry and more generally towards natural language is reiterated in more than one place in his extensive work, such as in this ghazal:

I fled from this *beyt* and this ghazal, O king and sultan of *azal* (eternity without beginning)
Mofta'elon Mofta'elon Mofta'elon killed me!
Qāfie and sophism, let them all be washed away!
There is only skin, only skin, in the brain of all poets!

(G.38, 1.2–3)

What can we make, then, of the fact that Rumi composed no fewer than 62,000 verses (124,000 distiches), a remarkably large poetic corpus? Rumi's frontal attack on poetry and poems seems senseless at first glance, but it is understandable in context, given the historical circumstances of the transition to the school of *arāq*, where this kind of denigration of the profession of poet was quite common among intellectuals for different reasons, including the excessive financial dependence of poets on people in power. Intellectuals, even if they composed poetry as a leisure activity or for some other reason, refused to consider themselves professional poets. Rumi was no exception to the rule, even though he was dean of the main school of an important city in Anatolia. As Fatemeh Keshavarz argues in her *Reading Mystical Lyric* (2004, 15–16), Rumi's apparent hatred of poetry should be understood as making two stands. Firstly, Rumi was negative towards professional court poets because of their hypocrisy, servility, and the way they indulged the whims of rich patrons and rulers. Secondly, Rumi's attack on poetry stems from a more profound problem he perceived regarding the inadequacy of human language as a medium to express a semantic content that transcends human intellectual power.

Rumi thus tried to devise a semiotic system capable of transcending the *semioticity* of communication in favor of a direct experience of meaning thanks to the new system's hybridity. The direct effect of the hybrid musical, verbal, and visual stimuli that constitute the melodic text of a ghazal is to bring listeners to such a spiritual level that they can experience "the ultimate meaning." Rumi's poetic discourse is meant not only to *signify* but also to make feel. The direct experience of "Truth" is impossible for Rumi unless individuals step out of their ipseity in a state of *vajd*, or *ec-stasy*, literally, "standing out of self."

4.2 Translating the Ineffable

What a desperate case for translation! What a conundrum! What to sacrifice? Linguistic utterances with a complex prediscoursive form present serious challenges for translation as the act of recreating forms. What kind of difficulties will the translators of a hybrid connotative discourse face? What will the translators of this poetry do if they do not intend to stick only to the semantic content of the discourse but wish to recreate the discursive semiotics of the utterance in the TT? How should one translate into natural language what is deemed to be "unspeakable," a "Truth" that spurs the speaker to surpass the limits of verbal communication? How should one translate into linguistic discourse an original discourse that by nature is not limited to linguistic signs? Translating Rumi's music epitomizes what Ricœur describes in translation as a source of sorrow and joy at the same time. Should the translator sacrifice the semantic content on the altar of a verse translation that recreates the rhythmic form of the discourse? Or should the translator be content with scholarly footnotes in which the difficulties of translating Rumi's hybrid discourse are described? And what if new multimedia technologies could offer a solution, for instance by accompanying literal translation with audio recitals of the same verse where the reader could listen to the musicality of the text in the original language while accessing the semantic content in the TT?

Our reference texts provide an overview of all translation attempts over the past two centuries. Translations of Rumi's poetics form a continuum of types at one end of which are translations of Rumi's poetry in all its formal elaboration into prose (horizontal advancement of text in blocks organized in paragraphs) and at the other end are translations of Rumi's poetry into rhythmic and rhyming verse. In the translation of Persian poetry, two aspects are of paramount importance, the preservation of the visual aspect of the poem and the recreation of its sound aspect, namely the prosody (rhyme and rhythm) of the poem.

4.2.1 Recreating the Graphic Effect

What is striking, at first sight, in Rumi's translations is that almost no translator has attempted to respect the graphic aspect of the original text or to share it with their reader. Whether for technical reasons such as the complication at the level of the layout or whether the choice is linked to the reception of the text by the

Recreating the Poetics of Rumi 145

readership of the target language, the total disappearance of the graphic aspect of the original text raises a semiotic problem insofar as the visual aspect of Persian verses constitutes in itself a semiotic value. There are, nonetheless, some sporadic attempts by certain translators to create some graphic form in the TT, seemingly to reconstitute some sort of equivalent effect. Lewis, for example, is quite innovative in this field, both in the ghazals and in the couplets of the *Masnavi*, which he rearranges according to short, long line clauses in stanzas of variable size. See MI in Ls, tome II or in the following translation of one of the emblematic ghazals of the *Divan*:

Example 3.3 D) G. 95, l.1–3

چه نغزست و چه خوبست چه زیباست **خدایا**	زهی عشق زهی عشق که ما راست **خدایا**
چه پنهان و چه پنهان و چه پیداست **خدایا**	چه گرمیم چه گرمیم از این عشق چو خورشید
که جان را و جهان را بیاراست **خدایا**	زهی ماه زهی ماه زهی باده همراه

Zahi 'eshq zahi 'eshq ke mā rāst **khodāyā**
Che naghz ast o che khubast o che zibāst **khodāyā**
Che garmim che garmim az in 'eshq(-e) cho khorshid
Che penhān o che penhān o che peidāst **khodāyā**
Zahi māh zahi māh zahi bāde ye hamrāh
Ke jān rā o jahān rā biārāst **khodāyā**

What love, what love, which belongs to us! O God!
How pleasant it is, how good, how beautiful! O God!
How warm we are, How warm we are, by this sun-like love/by this love like the Sun!
How hidden, how hidden, and how manifest it is, O God!
What a moon, what a moon, what accompanying wine (companion wine)
Who beautifies the soul and the universe, O God!

E1) Ls: p. 139:
EXQUISITE LOVE, what exquisite love we have	**O God!**
How fine, how good, how beautiful,	**O God!**
How warm, how warm this sun-like love keeps us –	
How hidden, hidden, yet how manifest,	**O God!**
The moon, the exquisite moon, and exquisite wine – both here with us	
adorning the spirit and the material world,	**O God!**

F1) Vo: p. 121–122:
Quel merveilleux amour, quel merveilleux amour est le nôtre, ô mon Dieu!
Qu'il est exquis, qu'il est bon, qu'il est beau, ô mon Dieu!
Combien nous brûle, combien nous brûle cet amour pareil au soleil!
A la fois caché, caché et apparent, ô mon Dieu
Ô lune, ô lune, ô vin qui l'accompagne,
Par quoi l'âme et le monde sont remplis de grâce, ô mon Dieu!

F2) Jam: n°91, p. 202–203:
Le bel amour, le bel amour qui est nôtre, ô Dieu!
Quelle merveille! et qu'il est bon! et qu'il est beau, ô Dieu!
Comme nous brûlons! que nous brûlons de cet amour comme un soleil!
Comme il se cache, comme il se cache! et comme il se montre, ô Dieu!
Lune gracieuse! lune gracieuse! vin délicieux son compagnon
Qui sauvent rime et le monde, ô Dieu!

146 *Recreating the Poetics of Rumi*

The distance that separates "O God" from the rest of each line in Lewis's formatting is very significant: it emphasizes the *radif* (anaphoric rhyme) as the refrain at the end of each line, reinforcing its anaphoric effect. At the same time, Lewis gives a separate value to this vocative by separating it, rightly, from the rest of the statement because on the propositional level, it is independent. Thus, he prevents this refrain from passing unnoticed among all the other terms in anaphoric position, especially the exclamatory clauses. This innovative method cannot be found with French translators, except perhaps Leili Anvar's few translations not cited in these examples.

In the same creative category, we can place the translations illustrated by Persian calligraphy or the original poem written in Persian appearing opposite. This is notably the case of many recent translators who have published short anthologies composed mainly of *robāʻis*. The inclusion of the original text, however, was not without precedent: it was Nicholson who implemented this practice in his anthology of ghazals, where he accompanies his translation of each ghazal of the original text as well as a multitude of explanatory notes and above all, indication of the meter in which the poem was composed. Ibrahim Gamard also, for the sake of unfailing "fidelity," chose to accompany his translation first with the original text, then with a word-for-word translation before proposing his own fully annotated translation.

Example 3.4 D) R. 447

Har ruz delam az qam-e to **zār-*tar ast***	az man del-e birahm-e to **bizār-*tar ast***
bogzāshtiam gham-e to magzāsht marā	haqqā ke ghamat az to **vafādār-*tar ast***
Day by day, my heart is more chagrined in your sorrow, Of me your ruthless heart wearier. You left me; your sorrow didn't. Indeed, your sorrow is more faithful than you are.	
E1) Ar: p. 134: Daily my heart, that grieveth sore For Thee, doth sorrow more; Daily Thy heart, so merciless, Careth for me still less. Thou leavest me, and yet my grief Leaveth me no relief, Proving the sorrow of my heart More faithful than Thou art.	E2) Shr: p. 49: *every day – my heart – in – the sorrow of – you – more painful it is* *and with – me – heart of – merciless of-you – more weary it is* *you have left me alone – sorrow of – you – hasn't left me alone* *in truth – that – your sorrow – of – you – more dedicated it is* Every day my heart falls deeper in the pain of your sorrow. Your cruel heart is weary of me already. You have left me alone yet your sorrow stays. Truly, your sorrow is more faithful than you are.
E3) Sab: n° 78, p. 248: Everyday my heart is weaker in its suffering for you While your pitiless heart is more hateful of me You left me alone, your suffering did not. Indeed your suffering is more faithful than you are.	E4) GaFa: n°557, p. 173: Every day my heart is more miserable in the longing for you, And your merciless heart is more weary of me. You abandoned me, but the longing for you has not left me. Truly, this longing for you is more faithful than you.

F1) Tch: n°8, p. 22:	F2) Vr: p. 147:
Le souci que j'ai de toi rend chaque jour mon cœur plus plaintif; Mais ton cœur sans pitié est chaque jour de moi plus las. Tu m'as abandonné, mais Mon chagrin ne m'abandonne pas; A dire vrai, Mon chagrin est plus fidèle que toi	Chaque jour, mon cœur est plus affligé de douleur pour toi Et ton cœur sans tendresse a de la haine pour moi Tu m'as quitté, mais le chagrin pour toi ne me quitte pas; Il est clair que ce chagrin est plus tendre que toi-même.

Of all translators, Shahram Shiva's initiative shows remarkable ingenuity by offering an intermediary literal translation in addition to the calligraphic version of the original text. Including the original text seems a good way to keep some of the "gold dust" of the graphic scheme of the ST. Shiva's literal version would have been the ultimate solution to an inevitable case of untranslatability caused by the infradiscoursive texture of the ST had his translation not been teeming with errors ("of you" instead of "than you," "of Me" instead of "with me", "merciless heart" instead of "heart of merciless," etc.) and respected the English syntax more closely.

4.2.2 Translating the Music

As for the most important features of Rumi's verse, rhythm and rhyme, few translators, classical or modern, have attempted to recreate the prosody of the original text by means of a versified form in the target language. Apart from a few more or less successful attempts at translation into rhythmic and rhyming verse, most of the poetic translations are in free verse. The translation choices are understandably based on the primacy of semantic content over discursive form. Rumi's top translator, Nicholson, for instance, focused on making accessible the semantic content of the discourse in the TL as efficiently as possible. Nevertheless, the choices of retranslators, like Barks, who are largely poets themselves and do not hesitate to compose fresh rhythmic verses in English at the expense of the semantic content, do not seem justified either. The translations of line 1 in Example 3.1 illustrate this lack of effort to retain any of the original music. Understandably, professional translators who take on the task of translating large amounts of texts do not have the opportunity to invest enough time in the reworking of the prosodic form of verses. On the other hand, one can question the usefulness of the efforts of retranslators who concentrate only on short passages of the work without making the slightest effort to recreate its original poetic form.

Efforts at poetic re-creation, however few they are compared to all the translations listed, do nevertheless exist, especially among the classics. In general terms, the following translators have offered verse translations: Sir William Jones, Redhouse and, more recently, Mojaddedi and Williams have all translated *Masnavi*'s verses into verse; only, the first two sometimes deviate substantially from the content of the discourse but their versification enjoys a better aesthetic quality (see MI: translations 1, 2, 10, and 11). As for Williams, his verses are in "blank (unrhymed) iambic pentameters." In other words, he completely dispenses with rhyme for two reasons, according to him: respecting the rhyme would be impossible without sacrificing meaning; thus, the final rhyme in English "infantilizes" (nursery rhyme) or "ridicules" (as in the 18th-century satirical rhyming) except in the hand of an accomplished poet. Nicholson also retranslated some of poems in *Masnavi* to offer a more poetic version in his anthology (1950) (see IM: translation 5). All other (re)translators of *Masnavi* have preferred a prosaic approach resulting in unrhythmic and arrhythmic verses, thus erasing all the musicality of the original work. Regarding the translation of ghazals, only Lewis sometimes gets close to a rhythmic and rhyming poetic translation. All other English translators produced translations either in prose with separate lines (Arberry) or in free verse (without rhyme or any particular rhythm). Arberry, however, reaches the summit of poetic art in his translations of *robā'is*. In Example 3.4, Arberry's brilliant verse translation shines among all others, enjoying both adequate rhyme and rhythm. With each *beyt* of the ST transformed into a quatrain alternating between octosyllables and hexasyllables, Arberry doubles the number of rhyming stanzas of a rich and highly musical character.

Unlike the rhythmic structure doomed to being lost in translation, the re-creation of rhymes is not in the realm of the impossible, especially anaphoric rhymes (*radif*), insofar as, very often, the terms are repeated in the same spots of the syntagm as in those of the re-enunciated discourse. In Example 3.1, the words *friend* and *cave* can constitute the anaphoric rhyme in the TT without particularly great effort on the part of the translator, since they are already repeated in the original. This brings us back to the question of the inner rhyme, which is well considered by Lewis, who creates a new rhyme at the end of each of his verses. Lewis also offers the only real verse translation. The other translations, despite their appearance thereof, are not in verse: neither rhyme, nor rhythm, nor equal meter are respected. This represents a double loss, because these translations distance themselves quite considerably from the content of the original speech without gaining anything in return: no re-creation of rhythm and no rhyme even close to a similar effect as in the ST. Another example is Helminsky's translation, which is nothing more than an English free verse poem inspired by Rumi.

The anaphoric rhyme *khodāyā* (oh my God) in Example 3.3 is also the subject of a successful literal translation, as are the repeated terms in verses 1, 3, 4, and 5, especially in Lewis. On the contrary, the nominal constituents of the rhyme (*qāfie*) as well as its verbal component (*ast*, "is") can only disappear, even in Lewis, in order to respect the canonical form of the sentence in English and French. The *robā'i* of Example 3.4 is also indicative of the possibility of the reconstruction of the rhyme, although this form represents a less elaborate musicality than the ghazals in the elongated meter. Unlike all the other translators, Arberry wins his bet wonderfully: the double quatrain he composes to translate Rumi's quatrain is based on the structure of the AABB-CCDD rhyme and the alternation between the octosyllable (of odd verses) and the hexasyllable (of even verses), which generates a rhythmic movement with ups and downs evoking the sound of a sea wave. The enjambments dividing all the complex sentences distribute the clauses among the even and odd verses in order to create a certain effect of suspense. The whole is haloed by an almost perfect recovery of the semantics of the original discourse. In a word, it is the example par excellence of translation-re-creation, on which Efim Etkind, a fervent theoretician of the translation of poem by poem, insists. The poetic translation he advocates is one that "creates the whole while retaining the structure of the original" (cited in Oseki-Depre 1999, 89).

One must admit that the rhythmic chain of discourse is broken even in the translation of Arberry in Example 3.4. If the rhyme can be partially restored by an effort led by the translator, the pace of Persian poetry remains elusive. It can only be imitated, copied, mimicked, much more effectively in English and French, but never rebuilt. To use Kadkani's metaphor, this practice looks like using the same instruments (rhymes) to sing the same poem (semantic content) but with a different melody and rhythm and in a different musical mode. Avoidable disappearance of the original rhyme is explained first by the absence of an equivalent rhythmic system in the target language. This is what has led some translators to explain the problem of the loss of musicality in their *metalinguistic* comments and notes. In English, it is especially Lewis who specifies the major loss of prosody in translation in detail. Even Nicholson, who indicates the metrical pattern of each ghazal in his anthology, does not give a full account of the sustained semiotic loss in translation. But more than any other translator, Williams's latest analysis is comprehensive and recognizes the semantic value of rhythm in Rumi's poetry significance mode (Williams 2006, xxix–xxxii).

Although the examples do not generally show translations in other languages, it is worth mentioning how translators have reacted to the problem of rhythm in other languages. In French, for example, it is Tajadod and Carrière in particular who attract the reader's attention to the fact that, despite their effort to versify the translated text, the rhythmic character of the ST is such that any translation attempt leads to a major loss of musicality (1993, 33–34). Leili Anvar compares Rumi's poetics to the literary movement of surrealism on account of its novelties and rhythmic particularities, without underlining the semiotic significance of musicality (Anvar 2011, 13 and 16). Vitray-Meyerovitch, for her part, makes no mention of the problem of rhythm or rhyme. She is content to speak of the impossibility of "passing" some of the odes to a foreign language because of the existence of "alliterations, puns, assonances popular at the time, impossible to render" (2003, 18).

Notes

1 See Sedaghat (2020a and 2021).
2 The best example of this highly frequent literary genre in Persian literature is Sa'di's *Golestan*. The closest equivalent in Western European languages is *prose poétique*, which owes its existence to French symbolists of the late 19th century such as Baudelaire.

150 *Recreating the Poetics of Rumi*

3 My translation from Persian.
4 There are few *masnavis* in Arabic literature, and this form is a Persian specificity. See M. Shafi'i-Kadkani (1350 [1971], 360).
5 There is no consensus about the origins of *'aruẓ*. Some trace it back to Sanskrit prosody or to the Poetics of Aristotle according to Iranian polymath Abureyhān-e Biruni (973–1048). But according to the legend, Al-Farāhidi of Basra, the father of the "science of *'aruẓ*," received it as divine revelation during a pilgrimage to Mecca. Xānlari (1345 [1966], 84–85) supports Biruni's thesis, evoking astonishing similarities between the Sanskrit metric system and that proposed by Al-Farāhidi, especially regarding units of scansion, feet, and the chronemic structure. Whatever its origins, the principles of *'aruẓ* bears the prosodic mark of a Semitic language comparable to the rhythmic character of sacred texts such as the Koran and the Hebrew Bible as described by Henri Meschonnic.
6 There are two major works in English on Persian prosody: Elwell-Sutton (1976) and, more recently, Theisen (1982). I refer here directly to the abundant references in Persian like Xānlari (1345 [1966]).
7 Although it is not syllables that count in the original Arabic measuring system of *'aruẓ*, in modern poetics, experts use the concept of syllables based on the number of morae in Persian, which, as an Indo-European language, depends more on syllabic division of meter. See Xānlari's critical analysis of the shortcomings of the principles of scansion in Persian (1345 [1966], 91–108).
8 Unlike in Arabic poetry, the accentual component is important in Persian where the stressed and unstressed syllables take up semantic value. For instance, in example 3.1, the stress must be on the first syllable of *toyi* [you are] for the proposition to be meaningful.
9 In traditional transcription of *'arūẓ*, the metric scheme of a *bahr* is indicated in mnemonic characters of Arabic using the triliteral root of *f ' l* (فعل) and its derivatives.
10 With a small deviation in verse 3 which should be considered a poetic license, a practice that occurs quite often.
11 The cited translations refer to the first line only.
12 TN: [K9:40] The two friends in the cave is an allusion to an episode mentioned in Koran 9:40, describing Muhammad's flight from Mecca with Abu Bakr. As the pagan Meccans pursued Muhammad, attempting to kill him, they hid in a cave. A spider is said to have spun a web over the entrance, making it appear as though no one had entered the cave for some time, so the pursuers did not look inside.
13 There has been extensive research work on *samā'*, studying the phenomenon both from the Sufis' perspective and a modern point of view by both Iranian and Western scholars. See Annemarie Schimmel ((1993) 210–221 and 2011, 178–88) and Leonard Lewisohn, whose exceptional work on *samā'* and the concept of *vajd* [existence/finding] and ecstasy in Sufi literature (1995), (1997), (2014) is of great value. For a more technical monograph on mystical ecstasy, see During (1988).
14 "Immersion in the heart; recollection; souvenir" here is the definition proposed by Henry Corbin for *zekr (1389 [2008])*. Indeed, this practice is similar to the repetition of sacred sounds in Vedic religions. It consists of repeating monosyllabic or plurisyllabic words in order to reach states of ecstasy or elevation of the spirit in a meditative process.
15 Also see During (1988 and 1989) on the role of musical rhythm in mystical ceremonies.
16 More specifically on *āvāzi* songs, see Miller (1999).
17 See Farhat (2004) on the specificities of the *dastgāh* system.
18 I already mentioned in the Introduction that the translation of the Koran from Arabic has never been canonized, neither in Sunnism nor in Shiism. The translation of the Koran in any language is by no means considered as its equivalent and cannot, for instance, be used in liturgy. No Muslim can say his obligatory daily prayers in any other language than Arabic. Muslim theologians explain the untranslatability of the Koran to

the fact that the letter of God's word cannot be separated from its meaning; however, I attribute this attitude to the same old Semitic tradition that consists in the inseparability of letter from spirit.
19 Truth is *Haq* in Arabic and is one of the most important names of God.

References

Ahmadnezhād, Kāmil, and Shiva Kamāli Aṣl. 1385 [2006]. *'Arūḍ va qāfīya* [Rhythm and Rhyme]. Tehrān: Āyīj.
Benveniste, Émile. 1974. *Problèmes de linguistique générale*. Vol. 2. Paris: Gallimard.
Corbin, Henry. 1974. "La philosophie islamique depuis la mort d'Averroës jusqu'à nos jours." In *Histoire de la philosophie, tome III*, edited by Yvon Belaval, 1065–1188. Paris: Gallimard.
Corbin, Henry. 1990. *Corps spirituel et terre céleste: De l'Iran mazdéen à l'Iran shï'ite*. Paris: Buchet-Chastel.
During, Jean. 1988. *Musique et extase, l'audition mystique dans la tradition soufie*. Paris: Albin Michel.
During, Jean. 1989. *Musique et mystique dans les traditions de l'Iran*. Paris/Leuven: Institut français de recherche en Iran/Éditions Peeters.
During, Jean, and Zia Mirabdolbaghi. 1991. *The Art of Persian Music, Lessons from Master Dariush Safvat*. Translated by Manuchehr Anvar. Washington, DC: Mage Publishers.
Elwell-Sutton, Laurence Paul. 1976. *The Persian Metres*. Cambridge: Cambridge University Press.
Farhat, Hormoz. 2004. *The Dastgah Concept in Persian Music*. Cambridge Studies in Ethnomusicology. Cambridge: Cambridge University Press.
Folkart, Barbara. 1991. *Le conflit des énonciations: traduction et discours rapporté*. Montréal: Balzac.
Hjelmslev, Louis. [1943] 1961. *Prolegomena to a Theory of Language*. Translated by J. Francis Whitfield. Madison: University of Wisconsin Press.
Homāyi, Jalāleddin. 1367 [1988]. *Funun-e balāghat va ṣanā'āt-e adabi* [Rhetoric Techniques and Literary Devices]. Tehrān: Nashr-e Namā.
Jakobson, Roman. [1960] 1964. "Linguistics and Poetics." In *Style in Language*, edited by Thomas Sebeok, 350–377. Cambridge, MA: M.I.T. Press.
Lefevere, André. 1992. *Translation, Rewriting, and the Manipulation of the Literary Frame*. London: Routledge.
Lewis, Frankin D. 2007. *Rumi Past and Present, East and West: The Life, Teachings, and Poetry of Jalal al-Din Rumi*. Oxford: Oneworld.
Lewisohn, Leonard. 1995. *Beyond Faith and Infidelity: The Sufi Poetry and Teachings of Maḥmūd Shabistarī*. Richmond, Surrey: Curzon Press.
Lewisohn, Leonard. 1997. "The Sacred Music of Islam: *Samā'* The Persian Sufi Tradition." *British Journal of Ethnomusicology* 6: 1–33.
Lewisohn, Leonard, ed. 2014. *The Philosophy of Ecstasy: Rumi and the Sufi Tradition*. Bloomington, IN: World Wisdom.
Meschonnic, Henri. 1973. *Pour la poétique II. Epistémologie de l'écriture. Poétique de la traduction*. Paris: Gallimard.
Meschonnic, Henri, and Gérard Dessons. 1998. *Traité du rythme: Des vers et des proses*. Paris: Dunod.
Miller, Lloyd Clifton. 1999. *Music and Song in Persia: The Art of Āvāz*. Salt Lake City: University of Utah Press.
Oseki-Depre, Inès. 1999. *Théories et pratiques de la traduction littéraire*. Paris: A. Colin.

Schimmel, Annemarie. 1993. *Triumphal Sun: A Study of the Works of Jalaloddin Rumi.* Albany: State University of New York Press.

Schimmel, Annemarie. 2011. *Mystical Dimensio–ns of Islam.* Chapel Hill: University of North Carolina Press.

Sedaghat, Amir. 2020a. "Rūmī's Verse at the Crossroads of Language and Music." *Mawlana Rumi Review* 9, no. 1–2 (2018): 91128.

Sedaghat, Amir. 2021. "Semiotic hybridization in Persian poetry and Iranian music." *Semiotica* no. 241: 275–310.

Shafi'i-Kadkani, Moḥammad Reẓā. 1350 [1971]. *Ṣovar-e khiyāl dar she'r-e pārsi* [The Forms of Imagination in Persian Poetry]. Tehrān: Enteshārāt-e Nil.

Shafi'i-Kadkani, Moḥammad Reẓā. 1368 [1989]. *Musiqi-ye she'r* [Music of Poetry]. Tehrān: Enteshārāt-e Khāvarān.

Shafi'i-Kadkani, Moḥammad Reẓā. 1387 [2008]. *Ghazaliyyāt-e Shams-e Tabrizi.* Tehrān: Soxan.

Theisen, Finn. 1982. *A Manual of Classical Persian Prosody: With Chapters on Urdu, Karakhanidic and Ottoman Prosody.* Wiesbaden: Harrassowitz Verlag.

Xānlari, Parviz Nātel. 1345 [1966]. *Vazn-e she'r-e fārsi* [Metre of Persian Poetry]. Tehrān: Bonyād-e Farhang-e Irān.

Yarshater, Ehsan. 1974. "Affinities between Persian Poetry and Music." In *Studies in Art and Literature of the Near East*, edited by P. Chelowski. New York: New York University Press.

Zonis, Ella. 1973. *Classical Persian Music; an Introduction.* Cambridge, MA: Harvard University Press.

4 Translating Rumi's Rhetoric

1 Comparative Rhetoric: An Elusive Classification

Several discoursive features in Rumi's text can be considered *ratio difficilis*: rhythm, alliteration, narrative and discoursive polyphony and mixing of genres and registers, massive use of foreign elements, etc. Rumi's elaborate use of figures of speech in his poetry, however, constitutes the quintessence of *ratio difficilis* insofar as the author explicitly distances himself from the institutionalized use imposed by *code* and *norm* with the aim of creating an extraordinary discoursive form for aesthetic or rhetorical purposes. Some of the discoursive features I have studied so far are indeed considered figures of speech in the classical rhetoric of Western languages. For instance, the construction of the rhyme in Persian may correspond to a wide range of concepts in English or French poetics: refrain, anaphora, paronymy, paronomasia, etc. On the contrary, many figures of speech in English, like *ellipsis* or *zeugma*, are not considered as such in Persian but rather as simple stylistic choices.[1] What is more, what can be considered a figure of speech in prose is not necessarily one in poetry.[2] There are in fact conceptual differences between the rhetoric systems of source and target languages because of the theoretical and historical gap separating the two polysystems.

Thus, the main obstacle that a study of comparative rhetoric must face is a common basis for the classification of figures of speech in the systems in question. The typology of figures of speech has always been a source of debate and controversy among experts (philologists, rhetoricians, linguists, etc.). While the rhetoricians of antiquity favored a classification according to the change of meaning to distinguish between tropes, figures in which the word changes meaning, and nontropes, figures of speech that are outside this class (either in a negative-sum definition), today linguists rely on much more nuanced criteria such as the nature of discoursive alteration, the desired effect, and the context. Modern linguistics has deepened the typological vision of stylistic figures by considering the nature of stylistic figures, their effect, the referential context, as well as their syntagmatic formation. It distinguishes, beyond the trope/nontrope dichotomy, figures affecting syntax, word order, lexicon, sounds, and discourse. It is therefore of utmost importance to lay down a common framework of analysis to study the occurrence of figures of speech in the ST and their potential loss or deformation in the TT.

DOI: 10.4324/9781003157960-5

154 *Translating Rumi's Rhetoric*

Following the model of classical Persian rhetoric,[3] the figures of Rumi's rhetoric can be classified on two main axes: stylistic figures that relate to "expression" (graphic and sound forms as well as the placement of words) and those based on "content" (discourse semantics). This categorization, however, seems somewhat arbitrary and outdated and contrary to our general idea of the inseparability of form and content of the poetic sign. According to Persian traditional classification, there are two categories of rhetorical figures, *ṣanāye'-e badi'-e lafẓi* [figures of expression] or *ārāye-hāye biruni* [external ornaments], and *ṣanāye'-e badi'-e ma'navi* [figures of meaning] or *ārāye-hāye daruni* [internal ornaments]. In the first category, I count all the figures that are realized by the substance of the syntagm, i.e., the expression-plane of the sign, "so that the quality of the ornament is dissipated if we change the words while keeping their meaning" (Homāyi 1367 [1988], 37). In the second category are placed all the figures of speech based on the semantic aspect of the discourse, "in such a way that the quality of the ornament remains even if we change the words while keeping their meaning" (*Ibid.*, 38). According to this definition, figures such as *alliteration, anaphora,* and *parallelism* are placed in the first class whereas *tropes, allusion, hyperbole,* and *antithesis* are classified in the second. Most modern Iranian linguists tend to distinguish tropes by placing them in a separate category. Kazzāzi, for instance, relying on an even older taxonomy[4] in his work on discoursive linguistics, does not count the figures of substitution[5] – *tashbih* [simile], *este'āre* [metaphor], *majāz* [certain types of metonymy], and *kenāye* (equivalent of circumlocution, allusion, or catachresis depending on context) – among the "ornaments of discourse" but considers them rather "manners" or "poetic stratagems" of expression. He then divides the rest of literary figures into two classes of *lexical* and *semantic* figures (Kazzāzi 1368 [1989], vol. I, 26). This conception is similar to the Western classical typology of rhetorical figures of speech that separates tropes from nontropes or *schemes*. One can then imagine two major divides, the first between expression-based and content-based figures of speech, and the second between tropes and schemes.

The main objective of this chapter is neither to make a list of all the figures of speech implemented by Rumi nor to define a figure of speech based on Persian rhetoric as opposed to target languages. I aim to identify the most recurrent figures of speech and, above all, to demonstrate the most problematic ones in terms of translation. In fact, no categories of figures of speech are an equal challenge to translation. One can easily imagine that the figures that affect the materiality of discourse, i.e., the utterance in its infradiscoursive purport, present a far greater challenge to transpose in a different language than tropes or semantic figures of speech insofar as their essential mode of functioning is linked to their semantic content, which, as discussed previously, is *a priori* transferable between linguistic codes. A figure like the *simile*, for example, is not necessarily likely to present a major obstacle to transfer from Persian to English, whereas *alliteration* is virtually impossible to translate. On the other hand, certain Persian figures of speech, in particular those with no equivalent in Western classical rhetoric, such as *ihām* (see later) pose serious difficulties to the translating operation. The greatest challenge is then the incompatibility of certain notions in the two rhetorical systems – Persian and that of European languages, as well as in the difficulty of identifying equivalents for Persian figures in the other system, in which case, both source and target rhetoric traditions should be taken into account.[6] On the Western side, I rely on two contemporary works in modern rhetoric by French rhetoricians Henri Suhamy ([1981] 2004) and Patrick Bacry (1992), while keeping a comparative eye on the terminology of rhetoric in English outlined by Chris Baldrick's *Oxford Dictionary of Literary Terms* (2008). These sources have slightly different but equally valid approaches in their successive classification of figures of speech in target languages.

The organization of concepts should consider not only the differences between classical Persian and modern Western rhetorical systems, but also most importantly the level and nature of difficulty presented by the specific figures of speech for translation. My classification is therefore based on the linguistic criteria of lexicon, syntax, syntagmatic organization, semantics, and substitution rather than the outdated dichotomy of expression versus content. Lexical, syntactic, and organizational categories are studied in this chapter, whereas figures of thought,[7] both semantic-based figures and figures of substitution, are relayed to the following chapter dedicated to the cultural and hermeneutical problems of translation. This approach is far from arbitrary since the figures of substitution and the figures of thought do not consist in a deviation from the conventional use of the code in its discursive materiality. They do not affect the infradiscursive expression substance of the utterance but rather its semantic content-form and -substance. As such, the translative challenges presented by figures of thought and substitution are of a fundamentally different nature from the difficulties posed by the figures of style that act upon the materiality of discourse. The discursive novelty of tropes, in particular, is deeply rooted in the cultural polysystem of the ST. The problems related to the translation of tropes, therefore, are of a hermeneutic and cultural rather than a linguistic or semiotic nature.

2 Lexical Figures of Speech

Following Bacry's typological model (1992), I categorize lexical figures based on the modality of their formation: semantic content-substance in a glossematic sense – or their phonetic aspect – expression-content.

2.1 Sound-Based Figures of Speech

Two main phonetic-based figures of speech, *tajnis* and *tasji'* [bird's song], characterize Persian classical poetry. *Tajnis* has three and *tasji'* nine variants covering, by analogy, a large number of figures of speech in Western rhetoric, ranging from alliteration and assonance to the paronomasia, polyptoton, or even homeoteleuton. The criteria of formation of these two types of rhetorical devices are approximately the same as Persian prosodic system, insofar as not only the sound quality of the phonemes but also the number and the nature of syllables, defined according to the basic elements of *sāken* and *moteḥarrek*, count in the choice of lexical elements on the syntagmatic chain. That is why Shafi'i Kadkani considers them as one of the four types of music in poetry (see Chapter 3). As such, they represent one of the greatest challenges to translation.

2.1.1 Tasji' *or* Saj'

Saj' consists in juxtaposing terms sharing the last phoneme(s) and/or terms that have the same syllabic pattern (in terms of the sequence and quality of syllables) in the syntagm at varying intervals. The effect is the accrued musicality and rhythm of the text. In fact, the definition *saj'* resembles that of rhyme or constituents of meter, and the designation of figure of speech or inner rhyme becomes only a question of perspective. For instance, in Example 3.2, line 1, the terms *yār*, *qār*, *xār*, and *negah dār* present the same metric scheme and have the same last two phonemes. In verse 5, *hojre*, *xāne*, and *rowze*, on the one hand, and *khorshid*, *nāhid*, and *ommid*, on the other, follow the same syllabic pattern. This is called *saj'-e motavāzi* [parallel *saj'*] that satisfies both criteria. In line 2, the words nuḥ, ruḥ, *maftuḥ*, and *mashruḥ* form a *saj'-e moṭarraf* [lateral *saj'*] since the terms only have the last three phonemes in common but not the meter. For the translation, the problem is of the same order as the recreation of rhythm; consequently, few translators have even tried to recover the infradiscoursive elements and have given priority instead to the semantics of the discourse at the expense of its expression form.

The metric (syllabic) equivalence of terms is what differentiates *saj'* from Western equivalents such as *paronomasia*, although *saj'-e moṭarraf* can be compared to *homeoteleuton*. While *saj'* can be compared to the inner rhyme in poetry, so characteristic of Rumi's ghazals, it is just as important in Persian classical prose and stands as a sign of stylistic richness and eloquence. In a sense, this figure of speech is as frequently used in classical poetry as in *naṣr-e mossajja'* [harmonic prose], epitomized by Sa'di's *Golestān*.[8] When deployed amply in classical prose, it gives birth to *naṣr-e moraṣṣa'* [jewel-decorated prose]. *Tarṣi'* [decoration with jewelry] consists in rhyming all the constituents of the syntagm two by two. As such, the problem of rhythm manifests itself in the translation of prose, as Henri Meschonnic points out in his "poetic project."[9] Indeed, it is not only within the purview of sacred texts such as the Old Testament and the Koran to give a particular semantic scope to the rhythm of discourse; many literary texts in Semitic languages or Persian display the same discoursive expressivity by means of rhythm.

2.1.2 Tajnis *or* Jenās

In a literal sense, *jenās* designates the accompaniment of objects of the same material (*jens*). According to Homāyi, *jenās* "is the choice of similar lexicons" (1367 [1988], 48) on the syntagmatic axis. Garcin de Tassy translated it as "alliteration" and, for lack of equivalent in French, forged new phrases like "compound alliteration," "identical alliteration," "imperfect alliteration," etc. to designate its

11 variants. While some of its variants overlap with *tasji'*, its general formation does not consist in forming metrically equivalent elements, nor necessarily in presenting identical final phonemes. What takes precedence is the resemblance between the components of *jenās* rather than their meter or final phonemes. There is a panoply of modalities of formation, such as the following: all phonemes are identical, constituting *phonetic homonymy*, akin to *pun*; all the phonemes except one vowel are identical or, alternatively, all the consonants are the same with all different vowels, creating *graphic homonymy*, akin to *paronomasia*; identical phonemes with one or more extra phonemes in one of the components; components with identical phonemes but forming different syntactic functions, akin to *kakemphaton* (one of the variants of pun in English rhetoric); consonants are different but the vowels remain the same, which is frequent in Persian where several graphemes correspond to the same phoneme (four graphemes with the same sound /z/: ز ذ ض ظ). The following extract from the prelude of *Ney* displays two types of *jenās*:

Example 4.1 M.I) l.11 and 15

Ney ḥarif-e hark-e az yāri borid **Ruz**-hā bā **suz**-hā hamrāh shod	**parde**-hāyash **parde**-hāye mā darid dar gham-e mā ruz-hā bigāh shod	
Ney, companion of all who broke up with a friend His notes/melodies tore off our veils In our sorrow, days became momentless Days and burns became companions		
E1) SWJ in Ap: p. 118: plaintive wand'rer from my peerless maid, The reed has fir'd, and all my soul betray'd . . . Alternate hope and fear my days divide: I courted Grief, and Anguish was my bride.	E2) Red: p. 1–2: The absent lover's flute's no toy; Its **trills** proclaim his **grief**, his **joy**. . . . Each day of sorrow, torment's pawn. My days are waste; take thou no heed,	E3) Whi: p. 3–5: The flute is the confidant of all unhappy lovers; Yea, its **strains lay bare my inmost secrets**. . . . Through grief my days are as labor and sorrow, My **days** move on, hand in hand with **anguish**.
E4) Nim, p. 5–6: The reed is the comrade of every one who has been parted from a friend: its **strains pierced our hearts**.[10] . . . In our woe the days (of life) have become untimely: our **days travel hand in hand with burning griefs**.	E6) At: p. 21–22: The reed is the true companion of everyone parted from a friend: its **melodies** have **rent the veils shrouding our hearts**. . . . Untimely the days have grown in our tribulation; **burning sorrows** have travelled along with all our **days**;	E7) Be: p. 17–19: melts into wine. **The reed is a friend to all who want the fabric torn and drawn away**. The reed is hurt and salve combining. Intimacy . . . [?]

(*Continued*)

158 *Translating Rumi's Rhetoric*

Example 4.1 (Continued)

E8) Her: p. 146–147: **The reed is a comfort to all estranged lovers.** Its **music tears our veils away.** Have you . . . Our **days** grow more unseasonable, these **days** which mix with **grief and pain** . . .	E9) Lr: p. 362–364: The reed, soother to all sundered lovers – its **piercing modes reveal our hidden pain:** . . . **In our sadness time slides listlessly by the days searing inside us as they pass.**	E10) Moj: p. 4–6: The reed consoles those forced to be apart, Its **notes** will **lift the veil** upon your heart, . . . The day is wasted if it's spent in **grief,** Consumed by **burning aches without relief** –
E11) Will: p. 7–9: The reed is friend to all who are lovelorn; its **melodies** have **torn our veils apart.** . . . In all our grief the days turned into **nights,** the **days** fell into step with searing **pains.**		

While it is rare for a verse to be composed without there being at least one figure of speech, the case of the second verse of line 11 is particularly interesting because it exposes four figures of speech: two tropes, *ihām* [insinuation by polysemy], and alliteration (*jenās*). The juxtaposition of *parde* [musical note or the frets on a musical instrument] and *parde* [veil] constitutes a *jenās-e tām* [perfect pun] or "identical alliteration" according to Garcin de Tassy. This figure is rather akin to *antanaclases* than to alliteration or assonance insofar as the two signs involved have identical expression planes but different content planes, which can also be construed as simple polysemy. The first *parde* is a *majāz-e morsal* [metonymy] taking the cause – the holes of the wind instrument – for the effect – the notes produced by the instrument – while the second *parde* is part of the verbal compound *parde daridan* [tearing the veil], which constitutes a *catachresis* in that it means, by metaphor, "to reveal the secrets (of a hidden love)." It is obvious that no translation strategy allows, as in any case of *antanaclases*, a recovery of the infradiscoursive layer of this utterance in the materiality of its syntagm. No attempt has been made either to compensate for the loss, although Helminsky's retranslation introduces alliteration by playing on the repetition of the vowel /e/ and /ei/ in *tears*, *veils*, and *away* and assonance between *veils* and *away*.

The following line reveals a variant of *jenās-e nāqes* [imperfect alliteration] called *jenās-e motarraf* [lateral] between two paronyms where one consonant differs from the other: the paronyms *ruz* [day] and *suz* [burning sorrow] are only short of one consonant to become homonyms. A partial recovery could be imaginable in the TT restituting *paronomasia* by some sort of alliteration. Lewis, Mojaddedi, and Williams have tried to take up the author's *ratio difficilis* by various translation strategies. Lewis creates an assonance with no less than 12 occurrences of the phoneme /s/. The dominance of the sonority of this verse by the sound /s/ evokes the noise generated by the burning of flesh on the fire: *searing inside us*. . . . Mojaddedi's strategy seems convincing, and his beautiful rhyme and iambic meter are impressive. Williams creates a slight assonance with /s/ plus an alliteration between *days* and *pains*, which can almost be qualified as paronyms given the nonnegligible role of tonic accent in English. These translation feats prove the existence of the famous "great difficulties and small joys of translation" to which Paul Ricœur alludes in his *On Translation* (2004, 7).

I evoke Yarshater's quote about the consubstantiality of the arts and the mixture of artistic means of expression in Iranian civilization. The multilayer hybrid semiotics of Rumi can also show a graphic component that consists in the visual harmony created by the arrangement of signs on the syntagmatic chain of Persian couplets. What Example 4.2 demonstrates is another aspect of *jenās* whereby the graphic component of the verse plays an important role in the creation of the general harmony of Persian poetic music. Given that poetry was traditionally published (edited or in manuscript) in the form of calligraphy (*nasta'liq* or *shekaste*) (Lazard 2006, 37), the graphic aspect of the words has always had particular importance.

Example 4.2 G. 527, l.8

افتد عطارد در **وحل**، آتش درافتد در **زحل** ژهره نماند ژهره را تا پرده ای خرم زند		
Oftad 'atārod dar **vaḥal**, ātash dar oftad dar **zoḥal** zahre namānad zohre rā tā parde i khorram zanad		
Mercury will fall in the mud, fire will fall on Saturn Bile will stay in Venus to play a joyous melody.		
E1) Ls: p. 111–112: **Mercury** sinks into **mire**, and **Saturn** goes up in **flames** **Venus** grows **pale**, untuned its happy music	F1) Vo: p. 263–264: Mercure sombrera dans la **boue**, Saturne s'embrasera. **Venus**, chanteuse du ciel, ne jouera plus ses mélodies joyeuses.	F2) Taj: p. 207–209: Mercure tombe dans la **boue**, Le feu s'empare de **Saturne**, **Vénus** n'a plus aucune **bile** Pour frapper un rythme joyeux

The first occurrence of *jenās* in the first verse equates *vaḥal* and *zoḥal* on the axis of contiguity, constituting, as in the previous example, a *jenās-e moṭarraf*. The type of *jenās* that stands between *zahre* and *zohre* is called *jenās-e nāqeṣ* [imperfect] or *moḥarraf* [alphabetic]. Both types of *jenās* have been translated by Garcin de Tassy as "writing alliteration" and placed in the same category (Garcin de Tassy [1873] 1970, 124–127). The main function of this *jenās* is the graphic

160 *Translating Rumi's Rhetoric*

equivalence established in addition to the phonic alliteration or assonance of paronyms. As is obvious in the original Persian script, without the diacritical marks, *zohre* and *zahre* are written exactly the same way. Due to the graphic proximity of /ز/ and /و/ as the first graphemes of *vahal* and *zohal*, a similar effect can occur in the first verse as well.

It should also be noted that these two verses put into practice no fewer than nine occurrences of seven stylistic figures: two variants of *jenās* (paronomasia and alliteration); *majāz-e morsal* [metonymy] in the verbal compound of *parde zadan* [to play a melody]; *talmih* or allusion to the mythological roles of the stars; *ihām* [illusion] created around *parde*, explained further later; metaphor transformed into a catachresis in the two compounds of *zahre namānad* [no bile is left] meaning "one dares no more" and *dar vahal oftādan* [to fall in the mud] which, just as in Example 4.4, designates "helplessness"; and especially hyperbole. This constellation of sound, visual elements, semantic figures of speech, various types of tropes and *ihām*, and figures of thought such as allusion and hyperbole is accompanied by the perfect musicality created by the interior rhymes. Furthermore, Rumi's elongated meter gives birth to a multilayer semiotic symphony evocative of Wagner's opera rather than the French quatrain by Tajadod or the bland prose by Vitray-Meyerovitch. Lewis's attempt to create an assonance between *Mercury* and *mire* or an alliteration between *flames* and *pale* hardly does justice either. In the eyes of an Iranian musician, this verse vocalized with a melody in the *dastgāh* of *Homāyun* or *Chahārgāh* can bring this hybrid semiotic constellation to a whole different level of synesthetic perfection.[11] Such examples can seriously undermine the legendary scenario according to which Rumi, the maddened poet, circled around a column while singing and composing his ghazals, which were then notated by his disciples.

The following passage, although a puzzle to read, lends itself a little more to a resumption of infradiscourse.

Example 4.3 Q. VII) 1.8

| **Mashk** beband ey **saqā**, mey nabarad **khonb**-e mā |
| **Kuze**-ye edrāk-hā **tang**[12] az in **tangnāst/tang**-tar az **tangnāst**[13] |

| Close your wineskin, O *saqā* [cupbearer], our pitcher cannot carry wine. |
| The jug of perceptions is narrow because of this straight / |
| The jug of perceptions is narrower than straight |

E1) Nid: IX, p. 32–37:	E2) Cow: p. 67–68:	E3) Ls: p. 149:
Tie up the skin, O cup-bearer, fetch wine from our jar: The vessel of perceptions is straiter than a strait pass.	O cup-bearer, tie up the skim Fetch wine: The jar of insight is filled with a pure draught.	Seal up the skin, my host, no vintage can convey us there The jug of apprehension's bottlenecked in those straits

The complexity of this line caused a major discrepancy between the two editions of the *Divan*. The main semantic divergence occurs in the first verse while the second verse leads to a difference of interpretation. In the first verse, both versions make sense, but Foruzānfar's choice seems more correct in the second verse for two main reasons, grammatical and stylistic. Grammatically speaking, in Nicholson's version, the use of *tangnā* ("narrowness" in a literal sense, "embarrassment" in the figurative) without a determiner (neither article nor demonstrative) seems to correspond to a reference to a generic notion; nonetheless, this term cannot constitute a generic notion in its singular form (embarrassment in general) whereas the choice of situational pinpointing by Foruzānfar (*this particular* embarrassment/narrowness) makes better contextual sense. Be that as it may, the two terms *tang* [narrow] and *tangnā* [narrowness] constitute a case of *jenās-e zāyed* [paronymy by derivation] comparable to polyptoton. While Nicholson's translation renders this figure of speech perfectly by a repetition of the same adjective in the comparative and absolute forms, the other translators have neglected this discursive peculiarity. This line also displays several other figures of speech discussed later in the chapter: *tanāsob*, *morā'atonnazir* ("convenience" according to Garcin de Tassy) by way of several lexical elements of the same semantic field relating to alcoholic beverages, the metaphorical nominal phrase of *kuze ye edrāk-hā* [the jug of understandings], as well as *ihām* [illusion] around *tang* and *tong* [amphora] discussed later.

2.2 Figures Based on Lexical Semantics: Ihām *and* Ihām-e Tanāsob

Ihām is difficult to classify in the Western rhetoric. In the category of lexical figures of meaning, for instance, Bacry includes, in addition to what will be studied here, archaism, neologism, and polyptoton, which I have mentioned in Chapter 2. Another example of this typological divergence is one of the most recurrent figures of Persian stylistics, the *ihām* [double meaning, ambiguity, illusion] or *towrieh* [concealment], which has no direct equivalent in Western rhetoric theories. *Ihām* is the use of a polysemic term or phrase that denotes more than one meaning, but only one meaning can be taken in accordance with the referential or the syntagmatic context while all other meanings should be disregarded. In this sense, the definition of *ihām* is close to that of metaphor or symbol; nonetheless, there is one major difference. Depending on their definition, in metaphor or symbol,[14] both the primary and secondary meanings of the sign are semantically pertinent whereas in *ihām*, only one logical meaning, and no secondary content, can be taken into account. In fact, other possible meanings of the term are nullified by the context. In a sense, the first meaning could be concealed by or mistaken for another possible meaning that is irrelevant to the context. A simple example in English is *Jill gave a* tip *to the waiter: "never rush while serving illustrious clients."* In this sentence, the term *tip* could mean both "advice" or "gratuity," but given the context only one of these can be kept. Consequently, *ihām* is not considered a trope but a lexical figure of speech in Persian rhetoric insofar as it does not represent a displacement or replacement of meaning – i.e., no *metasemia*. Similarly, *ihām-e tanāsob* [ambiguity by connivance] is a variety of *ihām* by which the speaker reinforces the position of the *illusory* meaning at the expense of the *real* meaning by juxtaposing the concerned term with elements belonging to the semantic field of the *illusory* meaning within the syntagmatic context. In this sense, the example of *tip* could be considered a case of *ihām- e tanāsob* insofar as it is used in the sentence in the vicinity of terms belonging to the lexical field of dining. In other words, in *ihām* both the referential and syntagmatic contexts allude to the *real* meaning while in *ihām-e tanāsob* only the referential (or logical) context alludes to the real meaning and the syntagmatic one seem misleading. According to Garcin de Tassy:

> Cette figure qu'on nomme aussi ایهام, insinuation, c'est-à-dire insinuer ce qu'on veut dire, le faire conjecturer, consiste à employer une expression dans sa signification éloignée, en s'appuyant sur une analogie cachée.
>
> ([1873] 1970, 136)

In Example 4.1, the first word *parde* (in the musical sense) in the presence of its homonym (in the sense of veil) conjures up a wrong illusory meaning at first glance: "her/his veil tore up our veils." Reading more attentively and tracing back the referent of the possessive adjective "-sh" in *parde-hāyash* [its frets], the reader notices that the narrator is referring to *ney* [reed flute], thus, he is referring to the *parde* [musical notes/melodies/frets] of that musical instrument. In Example 5.2, the same term, *parde* [melody], used by metonymy,[15] can also allude to a different referent, that of "the curtain of drama stage" hence conjuring up the image of setting up a stage in theatre: "Venus can no longer put out a joyful play." Yet metaphorically speaking, the planet Venus can very well put on a beautiful show just as it can play a beautiful melody. Here, *ihām* reaches its zenith insofar as the ambiguity caused by the author cannot be clarified definitively. This is, on the contrary, what assimilates *ihām* to tropes – i.e., figures of substitution (metonymy, metaphor, catachresis, allegory, etc.) – since there is no certainty about the intended meaning.

Ambiguity is created differently in Example 4.3, where, in the absence of diacritical marks, *tang* [narrow] and *tong* [amphora] are written the same and can both make perfect sense, especially in the vicinity of the lexical field of alcoholic beverage and its related paraphernalia, thus forming *morā'āto-nnaẓir* [convenience],[16] the message of the verse being construed as: the barrel of understanding, in this embarrassment, is only a pitcher! It is, therefore, not only the figurative meaning that is open to interpretation, but also the syntagmatic and paradigmatic organization of the utterance. This amounts to saying that the figure of speech in question poses not only a great challenge in terms of the transposition of the discoursive form, but also, and above all, a hermeneutic challenge, just as in Example 4.4:

Example 4.4 D) G. 436, l.8

Khāmosh ke gar beguyam man nokete-hāye u rā	az khʷishtan bar āyi ney dar bovad na bāmat
Silence! Since if I say more about her/him, You will get out of yourself, you will have neither door nor roof.	
E1) Nid: XIV, p. 55–57: **Peace!** if I should utter forth his mystic sayings, You would go beside yourself, neither door nor roof would restrain you.	E2) Am: tome I, n°50, p. 44–45: **Silence!** For if I were to utter his subtleties you would come forth from yourself, neither door nor roof would remain to you.	E3) Be: p. 77–78: **Now silence.** If I told more of this conversation, those listening would leave themselves. There would be no door, no roof or window either!
E4) Cow: p. 77–78: **O peace!** if I should shout aloud his mysteries Neither door nor roof would restrain you.	E5) Her: p. 197–198: **Silence.** If I were to utter more, you would be completely gone. left without a door or roof.	E6) Sta: p. 98: **Now it is time for silence.** If I told you about His true essence You would fly from your self and be gone, and neither door nor roof could hold you back!
E7) Sch: p. 83–85: **Be silent!** If I'd utter here the secrets fine he told me, You would go out all of yourself, no door nor roof could hold you!	E8) Ls: p. 80–81: **Silence!** For if I tell you of his attributes you will lose yourself and find yourself homeless completely without prospects	

As explained in Chapter 3, along with *Shams*, *khāmush* [silent], *khāmushi* [silence], and *khamush* [[be] silent!] are Rumi's pennames (*takhalloṣ*). A common/generic rather than a proper noun (anthroponym), *khāmush* creates a double meaning and ambiguity almost in every instance creating contextual polysemy. It can both be interpreted as the author's penname in a vocative or appositive function and be read as part of the sentence. Its meaning changes according to whether it is taken for an isolated noun, an adjective, or part of an imperative structure: "quiet!" Syntactically speaking, the term can take the role of an apostrophe (vocative) by which the poet addresses himself in an interpellation or a single-term clause. In this example, a literal translation, preserving the capital "s," can do the trick insofar as the ambiguity sought by the author remains intact in the re-enunciation "Silence!" because it is not automatically determined, either in the ST or the TT, whether it should be understood as a penname in an appositive or vocative position, or the nonverbal clause "be quiet!" However, only Arberry and Lewis seem to have perfectly achieved this goal. The informed reader who knows about the practice of *takhalloṣ* in Persian ghazal remains undecided as to the true semantic value of "silence!" Is this the pen name or an imperative?

164 *Translating Rumi's Rhetoric*

It is precisely the same ambiguity that is created in the last line of Example 1.7. The poet repeats anaphorically his penname, twice in the first verse in its archaic form (*khamush*), followed by its substantive form *khamushi* [silence], creating a polyptoton, and once in its current form (*khāmush*) in the second verse. While each of the occurrences of the term can be construed as the penname, it is the last *khāmush* that corresponds perfectly to the idea of the double meaning sought by the *ihām*: here silence is a metaphor for "death," in line with the main theme of the poem. What or whom do the author's addressees hate? Do they hate Rumi, the silence of death, or both?

3 Figures of Syntagmatic Construction

This section is not restricted to Persian figures of speech. It includes some of the literary devices that are dependent on the syntagmatic chain of discourse in general, such as ellipsis and hypallage. These discoursive structures do not usually pose a serious challenge to translators. What can be observed in this section, then, is the difference between translators' attitude where the structure and stylistic habits of the target language (TL) often allow for the recreation discoursive form in the ST.

3.1 Figures Affecting the Syntax

Persian syntactic word order is among the most malleable of all Indo-European languages. The general order of the components of propositions with a verbal predicate is as follows: $C0 + C1 + C2 + \ldots +$ process (verb), or in classical terminology, subject + complements + verb. Likewise, in propositions with a nominal predicate: $C0 + C1 +$ process (copula) (Lazard 2006, 193–197). However, this order is often upset for various reasons, especially in poetic discourse. This practice is so widespread that none of the numerous stylistic figures in Western classical rhetoric, such as hyperbaton, ellipsis, and inversion, is considered as such by classical Persian rhetoric. Mir-Jalāleddin Kazzāzi discussed some of these stylistic features and not as figures of speech in the second volume of his work on Persian aesthetics and rhetoric, dedicated to *ārāyehāy-e ma'navi* [semantic figures] (Kazzāzi 1368 [1989], vol. II).

3.1.1 Hypallage

Hypallage upsets the syntactic order and semantic content of the discourse by displacing a term within the syntagm, giving it a syntactic function that is conventionally attributed to another term of the syntagm. In Example 4.1, the more probable syntactic arrangement of terms in the first verse of the second line should be *dar qam, ruz-hā-ye mā bigāh shod* [in sorrow, our days became timeless]. In other words, it is not "days in general" that have lost their sense of time "in our sorrow," but rather "we" who have lost the track of time in "our days" out of chagrin. This use of hypallage by Rumi has led to different readings by translators, unlike in Example 4.5.

Example 4.5 D) G. 2039, l.5

Khire-kosh**ist mā rā**, dārad deli cho khārā	Bokshad, **kasash naguyad**, tadbir-e khunbahā kon
There is a surprise-killer/weak-killer for us. He/she has a heart like flint. He/she kills, no one tells him/her: "[Now] think of blood money."	
E1) Am: tome II, n°253, p. 42: A tyrant we have who has a heart like flint; he slays, and no one says to him, "Prepare to pay the blood-money."	E2) Hel: p. 23: While a tyrant with a heart of flint slays, and no one says, "Prepare to pay the blood money:'	E3) Ls: p. 56: Impudent, brazen, he murders me, stony his heart none dares demand money to atone my blood

The hypallage occurs in the second verse with the displacement of the personal indirect object pronoun *–sh*, which is attached directly to the starting term (subject) of the verb, the indefinite pronoun *kas* [nobody/somebody] instead of the verb (*naguyad*) itself. This is such a widespread practice in medieval Persian poetry that it is no longer considered a figure of speech. In fact, the different forms of hypallage are so often practiced in Persian poetry that it is almost impossible to find a verse where the syntactic order of the words is perfectly respected. In the first line of the same passage, for example, the second-order complement (indirect object) *mā rā* (for us/to us) is positioned after the verb, almost like an ornamental epithet, even though it has major semantic value. This unusual location, common in poetry, creates a certain effect of suspense and reorientation by the reactualization of the referent: "there is a killer, . . . who belongs to us/ who kills us" instead of "we have a killer. . . ." This is precisely the discursive effect that Arberry's astute choice of starting term or Lewis's use of an ornamental epithet seek to reproduce. On the other hand, the displacement of the pronoun in the second line is not reproducible in the more rigid structure of the target language.

3.1.2 Enjambement and Hyperbaton

Suspense is omnipresent in the syntactic construction of Persian verse, where enjambment is a norm rather than an exception in the majority of verses. We can distinguish two types of enjambments: one type separates the main and subordinate clauses of a complex sentence, and the other type distances the syntactic functions of the same clause, constituting a hyperbaton.

Example 4.6 MII) l.1741–1742

Garche yek jensand mard o zan hame Garche khosh-ru o ḥalim o sāken ast	gar to mardi rā bekhāni Fāteme qaṣd-e khun-e to konad tā momken ast
Although man and woman are all of the same substance, if you call a man 'Fatima' No matter how nice, patient and calm he is, He will shed your blood if he can.	

(Continued)

166 *Translating Rumi's Rhetoric*

Example 4.6 (Continued)

E1) Wil: p. 149–158: If you call a man Fatima – although men and women are all of one kind – He will try as far as possible to kill you, although he be good tempered, mild, and quiet.	E2) Nim: Moses and the Shepard, p. 310–315: If you should call a man 'Fátima' – though men and women are all of one kind – He will seek to murder you, so far as it is possible (for him), albeit he is good- natured and forbearing and quiet.	E3) Bt: p. 19–22: but if you call a man Fatima, it's an insult. Body-and- birth language
E4) Moj: p. 101–106: If you address a man by Fatema's name, Though man and woman are inside the same, He'll still seek vengeance for it if he can, Even if he's a calm and patient man	E5) Lr: Poem 29, p. 371– 373: If you call some man by "Fatima" though men and women are one species though this man's a calm one and serene he'll try to slit your throat	F1) Vm: p. 400–405: "Si tu appelles un homme "Fâtima" – bien que les hommes et les femmes soient tous d'une seule espèce – "Il cherchera à te tuer, si cela lui est possible, bien qu'il ait bon caractère, qu'il soit patient et calme.

These two lines (four verses) are composed of a single complex sentence: a main clause and four adverbial clauses of condition, time, and concession. Three of the subordinate clauses are spread over the first three verses and the main clause is placed in the last verse, followed by a last subordinate clause. The utterance keeps the reader in suspense for a long time, setting the stage with various conditions and concessions before presenting the final result. This does not constitute a hyperbaton but represents an unusual discoursive case, so much so that the reader would need to return to the beginning of the statement in order to remember the circumstances of the action described in the main clause. Rumi's discoursive structure does not really have an aesthetic function but rather a rhetorical one. These are the words of Moses (hence the quotation marks in the French translation) reproaching the shepherd for his impudence towards God. The diegetic speaker is putting forward his arguments like a philosopher. The sequencing of his rather banal analogy is what gives it a scholarly aspect. Hence the macrodiscoursive organization giving priority to propositions of condition and concession constitutes a rhetorical device that should be preserved in translation. However, despite the linguistic possibility of recovering the infradiscourse in the TT, most translators have erased this feature. Only Lewis and Mojaddedi partially seem to notice the rhetorical function of the author's choice.

In the first line of Example 1.4, the conventional syntactic order of Persian is upset with important rhetorical effects. The break of the verbal predicate in the main clause of the interrogative sentence corresponds to the proper definition of hyperbaton although no equivalent figure of speech exists in Persian rhetoric. By means of a parenthesis,[17] the direct object (the description of that friend . . .) is distanced from the verb by an incisive clause. The complex syntactic construction of the relative subordinate clause "for whom there is no friend" also contributes to the unusual structure of this utterance. Redhouse's poetic translation recreates this effect albeit with different means, in an attempt to create dynamic equivalence (in Nida's terms): the distance separating the relative pronoun "whose" from its "me" constitutes a hypallage, and the separation of a lover's woe from the main verb imitates the hyperbaton in the ST. Whinfield rationalized the stylistic strangeness of the speech even though no linguistic constraint in English prevents the translator from recreating the discursive form. Nicholson takes up the original structure, while modern translators adopt different stands. Mojaddedi's freestyle poetic translation preserves neither the expressive form nor the content. Williams uses the same structure while offering a paraphrase, a hypertextual translation (in Berman's terms), of the second verse: "the friend who has no friend" is a paraphrase for God in monotheistic discourse.

3.1.3 Ellipsis

What constitutes an ellipsis in a language depends mainly on the language's syntactic system (code) as well as on the idiomatic norms imposed by the stylistic polysystem (norms). Since an ellipsis is not considered as one in Persian but as a stylistic effect, its translation into English could be problematic. In the first line of Example 5.1, for instance, it is the copula that has been omitted. For the sake of rhythm, Rumi took the liberty of deleting the verb, thus creating a syntagmatic fragment that does not constitute a clause. Although the transposition of this figure is perfectly possible by a figure of the same category, apposition, all except one of the translators distanced themselves from the ST by adding either a copula or another verb. Lewis, more attentive to the infradiscoursive layer of the poem, imitates the syntactic structure while respecting the constraints imposed by English, by giving the proposition an appositive function by adding commas and isolating the subject argument, *ney*. This singularization of the subject argument recreates the emphasis in the ST on the central theme of the discourse, the personified hero of the story. Lewis's sensitivity to the modalities of Rumi's discoursivization is not new in his translation process. Lewis does not always prioritize the semantics of the discourse to the detriment of its semiotic materiality.

3.1.4 Symmetry: Parallelism and Chiasmus

The symmetrical structure of the majority of *beyts* [couplets (couple of verses constituting a line)] is a banality rather than a novelty in Persian prosody. This symmetry manifests itself as parallelism or chiasmus, in case of syntactically similar hemistiches. Symmetry is necessary for the formation of inner rhyme, particularly ubiquitous in the ghazals but also elsewhere in Rumi's poetic work. Moreover, the very principle of an anaphoric rhyme (*radif*) on top of the regular rhyme (*qāfie*) prepares the ground for various syntactic symmetries. The *robāʿi* of Example 3.4

168   *Translating Rumi's Rhetoric*

is an illustration of this. The typical pattern of parallelism (A-B | A-B) manifests itself in the syntactic structure "A is more B in the circumstances C":

> Everyday, *my heart* **is more afflicted** in your sorrow | *your cruel heart* **is more disgusted** by me [Given that] you left me, but your sorrow didn't, | indeed, *your sorrow* **is more faithful** than you.

The C0 (subject argument) is indicated in italics, the predicate in bold characters, and the rest (other complements and adjuncts) in normal characters. The pattern "copula + comparative epithet" is repeated in verses 1, 2, and 4, the ones that are also rhymed. The copula and the attribute complement (C1) constitute together the compound rhyme, i.e., *qāfie* (comparative epithet), plus *radif* (the copula *ast* [is]). It goes without saying that this syntactic construction cannot be transposed into any one of the target languages because of their different syntactic order (subject + verb + complement); however, in Arberry's translation, a schematic equivalent has been reconstructed for the translation of at least the first line:

A: Daily my heart ≃ Daily Thy heart
B: sorrow more ≃ still less

No other translator shares either the insight or the poetic artistry of the British Rumi specialist, Arberry. This is a typical example among thousands, as parallelism is found everywhere in the corpus, especially within the ghazals with an elongated meter that can accommodate whole propositions in each hemistich. Chiasmus, or inverted symmetry (A B | B A) is another less frequent form of symmetry that abounds in Rumi's work.

Example 4.7 D) R. 846

Har shab ke *del*-e **sepehr** golshan gardad Sad *āh* bar-āvaram ze **āyine ye del**	'ālam hame sāken cho *del*-e man gardad āyine-ye del ze *āh* roshan gardad
Every night when the heart of the firmament becomes a garden The universe becomes all peaceful like my heart A hundred sighs I exhale from the mirror of heart The mirror of heart, with sigh, becomes clear	
E1) Ap: p. 35: Flowers every night Blossom in the sky; Peace in the Infinite; At peace am I. **Sighs** a hundredfold From my *heart* arise; My *heart*, dark and cold, Flames with my **sighs**.	E2) Be: p. 320: Flowers open every night across the sky, a breathing peace and sudden flame catching.	E3) GaFa: n°1284, p. 398: Every night when the sky-like heart becomes a rose-garden, The whole world becomes still, like my heart. I bring forth a hundred sighs from the mirror of the heart, And the mirror of the heart becomes luminous from these sighs.[18]

Rumi's poetic art and Arberry's translation skills are at their height in this quatrain displaying two cases of chiasmus: one is of a syntactic and semantic nature and the other is based on the repetition of terms. The A B | B A pattern can be found in **heart** + of + *firmament* | *universe* + like + **heart** in the first couplet, and then more clearly in the second line: **sigh** + verb + *mirror of the heart* | *mirror of the heart* + preposition + **sigh**. Rumi's exquisite imagery is based on the juxtaposition of *real* and *metaphorical*. The inverted symmetry on the syntagmatic axis corresponds to the semantic inverted symmetry of metaphors: the sigh comes from the heart (compared to a mirror), and the mirror is cleaned by a sigh (a breath). The counterpoint is shaped by the inverted juxtaposition of figurative meaning against real meaning, poetic image against technical image, the *sublime* against the *earthly* in the following pattern: A-B against B-A. Is it by chance that Rumi uses chiasmus, the figure of inverted images (AB-BA), to speak of a mirror?!

Arberry's translation represents the perfect incarnation of a translation-recreation insofar as his two quatrains recover the infradiscoursive form of the original utterance up to its syntagmatic materiality. Arberry replaces the first chiasmus by a parallel structure A-A | B-B: Flower – blossoms | peace in – at peace. Then, with the noun phrase B, there is a chiasmatic microstructure of C-D | D-C, C being the noun *peace* and D the *preposition*. The second line is even more impressive. The British scholar defies the very idea of untranslatability by an extraordinary feat of skill. Not only does Arberry restore the metaphorical interplay of this couplet by substituting the image of a sigh clearing a mirror with the image of a sigh stoking a fire, but he also succeeds in imitating the syntagmatic microstructure of the chiasmus existing between the two verses: A B | B A (sighs – heart | heart – sighs). Colman Barks's self-declared mission of "liberating" Arberry and Nicholson's poems from their dry and arcane frame to make them more readable certainly falls flat in the face of this amazing feat of translation.[19] Barks's own total sacrifice of the ST's content suggests that free translation can cost tremendously while bringing little benefit (see Chapter 7 for further discussion).

3.2 Word Order and Syntagmatic Organization

The main criterion that governs the figures of this category is not the syntactic function of the terms but the syntagmatic organization of the ideas expressed by them, i.e., the arrangement of their semantic content on the syntagmatic axis in a such a way that there be a certain relationship of *equivalence* between the semic groups. The lexical figures studied so far touched on the syntactic structure of the utterance, whereas I now turn to the figures that affect the semantic distribution of the discourse.

3.2.1 Repetition: Anaphora and Concatenation

Although repetition in most variants is not considered a figure of speech by classical Persian rhetoric, it is very often practiced in the form of rhyme, inner rhyme, or at the beginning of couplets or verses. Repetition has a central role in Rumi's discoursive semiotics considering the association of his poems (especially his ghazals) with

170 *Translating Rumi's Rhetoric*

the meditative and ritual Sufi practices of *zekr* and *samā'*. One could suppose that these kinds of figures would not pose major difficulties for translation since their formation does not depend essentially on syntax but rather on the lexical component of the utterance. However, Example 4.8s do not support this hypothesis.

Example 4.8 MIII) l.1754

در حق او شهد و در حق تو سم	در حق او مدح و در حق تو ذم
Dar ḥaq-e u madḥ o dar ḥaqq-e zam	dar ḥaq-e u shahd o dar ḥaqq-e to sam
For him, it's praise, for you, it's slander	
For him, it's honey/juice, for you, it's poison	

E1) Whi: p. 121–125: What is poison for thee is honey for him. What is good in him is bad in thee,	E2) Wil: p. 149–158: From him it is praise, but from you it would be blame; from him it is honey, but from you it would be poison.	E3) Nim: Moses and the Shepard, p. 310–315: In regard to him it is (worthy of) praise, and in regard to thee it is (worthy of) blame: in regard to him honey, and in regard to thee poison.
E4) At: 40, p. 132–134: In regard to him it is praiseworthy; in regard to you it is blame-worthy; in regard to him it is honey, in regard to you it is poison.	E5) Bt: p. 19–22: What seems wrong to you is right for him. What is poison to one is honey to someone else.	E6) Moj: p. 101–106: What he thinks virtuous you deem scandalous: This person's meat to you seems poisonous.
E7) Lr: Poem 29, p. 371–373: What to some is praise, to you is blame What's honey to his taste, your poison		

The organization of the syntactic elements in this couplet constitutes a parallelism following the scheme A-B | A-B. However, symmetry goes beyond syntactic microstructures; it also resides in the semantic content of terms. Each verse consists of nine separate lexia for a total of 18 terms in a row, all forming four noun phrases in the absence of a copula, which also represents an ellipsis. Each verse (*meṣra'*) consists of two hemistiches formed by each of these noun phrases with repeating elements except for four lexia: *madḥ, zam, shahd,* and *sam*. These are the only terms that change in each hemistich and the rest, i.e., 14 terms, are only repeated elements, either twice: *u* [him], *o* [and], *to* [you], or four times: prepositional phrase *dar haqq-e* [in the right of, in the case of, for]. This pattern constitutes an *anaphora* according to Western rhetoric and create the inner rhyme in Persian prosody. However, most translators have neglected this remarkable discoursive form with its powerful contrastive effect on the reader: "what is good for A is not good for B." In prose translations like Nicholson's, the anaphoric structure has been at least partially respected by repeating comments in parentheses, despite Nicholson's primary goal of clarity in his commentary-worthy translation. Wilson, on the other hand, does not pay attention to the anaphora despite the perfect possibility of recreating the infradiscoursive structure in the target language. In order to create coherence in speech, he adds conjunction adverbs "but" and processes (verbs) as well as the verbal mood with conditional "would be," changing noun phrases to noun clauses. On a different note, Nicholson's addition of parenthetical information "worthy of" shows a hermeneutic trap, where the translator's attempt to clarify the ST misleads him as well as the reader. Nicholson's choice suggests that the object of "praise" or "blame" is the shepherd's or Moses's respective actions. However, these actions are the active subjects of "praise" and "blame": "in his case, this action is considered to be a praise while in your case, this same action is considered to be an offence."

The discoursive effect of the original anaphora is only recreated in Whinfield's translation and much less effectively in Lewis's. By combining chiasmus (A-B | B-A: for thee, for him versus in him, in thee) with anaphora (repetition of "What is" at the beginning of each line), Whinfield tries to recover the discursive form of the initial statement. Lewis, in turn, favored rhythmization and alliteration as a discursive strategy, which only makes sense in the context of his entire stanza. He also plays on the graphic aspect of the poem, taking advantage of graphic design as a compensation strategy. Transposing commonplace lexical repetitions are shown to be less straightforward than expected. What of rarer and more elaborate repetition figures such as concatenation and epanalepsis? Will they be even more difficult?

Example 4.9 D) R. 1104, l.2

دل را چه کنم بهر چه میدارم **دل**	گر من به غم عشق تو نسپارم **دل**
del rā che konam bahr-e che midāram **del**	Gar man be gham-e 'eshq-e to naspāram **del**

If, to the sorrow of your love, I don't give the heart,		
With the heart, what shall I do? What for do I have this heart?		
E1) Erc: p. 61:	E2) Shr: p. 146:	E3) GaFa: n° 686, p. 213:
If the pain of Love doesn't fill this Heart, I don't care if I have it or not	If I don't offer my heart to the sorrow of your love What do I need it for? What other purpose can it serve?	For if I don't entrust my heart to the longing of love for you, What can I do with my heart? Why else do I have a heart?

These two verses of a quatrain display two figures of lexical repetition with the term *del*. First, the repetition of *del* forms a concatenation at the caesura of the two verses, corresponding to the pattern "... A | A ...". Second, an epanalepsis creates the enunciative schema "A ... | ... A" in the second verse, i.e., the placing of identical elements at both ends of the utterance.[20] As this example shows, none of the contemporary translators make the slightest attempt to recover this particular discursive form even though the syntax of the TL allows it, as is shown in our literal translation. All that is required is to exchange the regular position of C1 (direct object argument) and of C2 (indirect object argument) in the first verse, and to put the marker "heart" in the position of the starting term (C0). The first intervention constitutes a hypallage and the second a fairly common emphasis in English. Yet the repetition of "heart" has totally disappeared from two of the translations, making these hypertextual and disrespectful of the original discursive formatting. Nevit's version deviates from both the expression and the content of the ST, and Shiva's version is equally disrespectful of the poeticity of the ST. Only Gamard's

172   Translating Rumi's Rhetoric

version imitates to some extent the discoursive form. Gamard provides a prose commentary, however, rather than a poetic translation of the original text.

3.2.2   Laff o Nashr *[Reunion and Dispersion]*

A figure affecting the construction of the syntagm both in the lexical choice and in the syntactic organization, *Laff o Nashr* does not correspond directly to any equivalent figure in Western rhetorical systems. According to Garcin de Tassy:

> This figure consists in first expressing different things in an either detailed or succinct manner, then mentioning, without particular designation, what relates to each of them. In the first case, it is either regular . . . or irregular. . . . It is regular when the arrangement of the first part of the sentence, that is the *reunion* . . . is in conformity with that of the second part or *dispersion*.
> ([1873] 1970, 113)[21]

As shown in Example 4.10 and the second line of Example 4.11, this figure should not present an important challenge to translation if enough care is taken to reproduce the macrosyntagmatic order of the original utterance.

Example 4.10 D) R. 1104, l.2

آن شب شب زلف تست ومهتاب رخت	گفتم که شب دراز خواهم مهتاب
Goftam ke shab-e derāz khʷāham mahtāb	ān shab shab-e zolf-e tost o mahtāb rokhat
I said, [in] a long night, I need the moonlight That long night is the night of your hair and the moonlight, your face.	
E1) Ar: p. 122: 'The night is dark and long', I said; 'Bright,' bright the moonshine that I seek; That night, the tresses of Thy head, That moon, the lustre of Thy cheek.	E2) GaFa: #202, p. 66: I said, 'I want a long night of moonlight.' That night is but your dark curls and the moonlight is your face.

In the first verse, there are two semantic elements that are actualized in an independent simple proposition. These same elements are repeated in the second verse in order to provide complementary information. The second set of elements do not need to be identical either in terms of the syntactic function or on a lexicographical level but should belong to the same semantic field: it is in fact a question of two or more ideas actualized by a first part of the statement and then developed in its second part. In this case, the same order of evocation of ideas is respected in the second part. The same is true in all the translations that respect the syntagmatic and semantic organization of the enunciation. There is however an error of interpretation in Gamard's text because of the ellipsis that takes place in the first clause, blurring the logical relationship between the adverbial (circumstantial) complement "long night" and C1 (complement of rank 1: direct object) "moonlight." In reality, the poet does not desire a long moonlit night as implied by the TT, but moonlight in a long night. The length of the night is not the object of his desire; it is the cause and the circumstance. The figure of speech is best reproduced in the TT in Arberry's rhythmic and rhymed text that reorganizes each element in a separate verse.

3.2.3 Tanāsob *and* Tazād: *Metabola and Antithesis*

These two antithetical figures are among the most important in the Persian rhetorical repertoire, and they enjoy similar frequency and importance in Western rhetoric. *Tanāsob*, translated by Garcin de Tassy as "convenience," is akin to *metabola* and to a lesser extent to *gradation*; however, unlike French or English stylistics, which tend to disfavor "the accumulation or succession of quasi-synonyms" deeming it useless (Bacry 1992, 171–172), Persian stylistics encourages it. This is the case of the next example, which perfectly illustrates the use of metabola in a discourse where synonymy evokes semantic anaphora.

Example 4.11 D) G) R. 1315

Mā **kār** o **dokān** o **pishe** rā sukhte im **she'r** o **ghazal** o **dobeyti** āmukhte im Dar 'eshq ke u *jān* o *del* o *dide*-ye māst *jān* o *del* o *dide* har se bardukhte im	
We have burned work, shop, and craft In love, which is our soul, heart and eye, We have learned poem, ghazal, and quatrain We have sewn soul, heart and eye	
E1) GaFa: #1, p. 1: I have burned my business, shop, and trade, *And* I have learned verses, odes, and quatrains. In [the fire of] love, which is my soul, heart, and sight, I have burned all three – soul, heart, and sight.	E2) Shg: p. 30: We have burned all trace of work and profession; We have nothing but poetry and love songs now. We sing of heart, soul, and the Beloved – Only to burn all trace of heart, soul, and Beloved.
E3) Bo: p. 20: We've given up making a living. It's all this crazy love poetry now. It's everywhere. Our eyes and our feelings focus together, with our words.	E4) Ls: p. 55: We've left our job and craft and store in flames We've learned ghazals and lyrics, lines of verse In love, he's heart and soul, our very eyes We've left all three – heart, soul and eyes – in flames
E5) Khd: p. 196: we set fire to our shops jobs and trades we chose to learn poetry love songs and lyrics instead in the journey of love where love is our soul and heart and eyes we riveted all three to love in turn	

What counts is less the quasi synonymy of the components of this series than their connotation reinforced by collocation. There are three successions of juxtaposed lexia, the first two of which are linked by denotative relations and the third on a connotative basis. There is also *laff o nashr* insofar as the series in the subordinate clause of the third *meṣra'* is repeated in the main clause of the fourth *meṣra'*. The third series of associated lexia, unlike the first two, where the elements all come from the same semantic field, has an additional particularity: the three terms constituting the series actually form very strong collocations two by two: *jān o del* or *del o jān* [soul and heart] and *del o dide* [heart and eye]. As for the serial semantic structure of *metabola*, it has been taken up, more or less authentically, by all translators. In contrast, the connotative value in the last series is completely lost in the TT. There are also modifications in the translation of certain terms, which sometimes seem essential (the eyes instead of the eye) sometimes superfluous (our business). Gamard's translation appears to intend to increase the *readability* of his text to the detriment of the ST: the change of voice from the first plural person to the singular, the addition of the possessive "my," the addition of the coordinating conjunction "and," as well as the addition of comments in square brackets. His version goes far beyond the definition of translation and falls under commentary. It is not exactly a literal translation, contrary to what he claims in his introduction, but an exegesis of Rumi's text, which he treats as a sacred text.

Tażād [contrast], the equivalent of *antithesis*, is illustrated in Example 4.8 where it is deployed between two verses in a symmetrical way. Obviously, its translation presents no difficulty provided the semantic content of the utterance is respected.

As the examples show, the discoursive formation of these two figures of speech does not pose any difficulty in translation, insofar as their mechanism consists in bringing semes together in specific elements of the syntagm, either according to resemblance (*metabola*) or on the basis of dissimilarity (*antithesis*), just like the figures of thought and the tropes. Nonetheless, the cultural connotations constituting the infradiscoursive layer of the utterance do not make the task of the translator easy. The complications are of a hermeneutic order or, in other words, appear at the level of the reception and interpretation of the text. The association of *del* (heart) and *dide* (eye), for instance, is specific to Persian culture. Their collocation makes no sense in European target languages.

Notes

1. A simple figure such as alliteration corresponds to 11 types of *tasji'* and *tajnis* in Persian rhetoric depending on the modality of lexical formation (Garcin de Tassy [1873] 1970, 120–135).
2. This is particularly the case with *saj'*, which in poetry is nothing other than the inner rhyme (see Chapter 3).
3. Persian rhetoric, *Badi'* from the Arabic radical /b d '/ meaning innovation, novelty in speech, or its Persian equivalent *soxan-ārāyi* [speech ornamentation], designates the study of figures of rhetoric, *ṣanā'āt-e adabi* [literary creations] or *ārāye-hāye adabi* [literary ornaments]. See Kazzāzi (1368 [1989], 25) and Homāyi (1367 [1988], 34–41).

4 One of the oldest treatises of Persian rhetoric and poetics in European languages is a French work by Garcin de Tassy ([1873] 1970). It is inspired by a Persian treatise written by an 18th-century Indian Persian by the name of Shamseddin Faqir-e Dehlavi, entitled *Hadāyeq ol-belāghat* [Gardens of eloquence].
5 Tropes are *metasemic* figures of speech whereby the first meaning of the utterance is doubled or altered by a second meaning that prevails in the interpretation.
6 Such differences should not be exaggerated either. In fact, apart from figures based on prosody, i.e., the phonetic characteristics of language, the use and definition of literary devices in European languages, like French and English, are not far apart, at least in their basic principles, from Eastern languages and Arabic, both having common sources in Hellenic rhetoric.
7 To use Henri Suhamy's terminology, *figures de style de pensée*, without necessarily sticking to the rhetorical figures he places in this category (Suhamy [1981] 2004, 83–89 & 108–114). This term is also common in English rhetoric.
8 This popular Persian and Arabic medieval genre can be considered a precursor to *poetic prose*, which appeared only in the late 19th century in European languages with French symbolists like Baudelaire.
9 Meschonnic's immense work on poetics, published in five volumes of *Pour la poétique* (1970b) among other titles, is not restricted to poetry or the problem of translation but to the question of rhythm, ignored for long in what he calls "Hellenized Indo-European languages" starting with Septuagint, the translation of the Hebrew Bible into koine Greek.
10 TN: Literally, "rent our veils."
11 These are two modes or scales of the Iranian musical system capable of generating a mysterious and epic mood. Given the themes evoked in this verse and the spirit of its content-substance, these modes would seem the best modal choices for a possible musical composition for this poem.
12 *Tang* or *tong* [?]. See section 2.2.
13 Nicholson offers two versions for this *beyt*.
14 As discussed in Chapter 5, symbol and metaphor can have opposite definitions according to theorists. Umberto Eco, for instance, calls "symbolic mode of expression" what Paul Ricœur calls a "live metaphor," i.e., a metasemic sign whose primary and secondary meanings are both valid and the primary meaning should not be ignored in favor of the secondary one.
15 Part (notes) replacing the whole (melody) or the concrete (keys or frets of the instrument) standing for the abstract (notes, melodies).
16 A figure comparable to *gradation*.
17 *Parenthesis* as a figure of speech compared to *ḥashv* in Persian rhetoric (Homāyi 1367 [1988], 331–334).
18 TN: Line 4: a reference to the saying [hadith] of the Prophet Muhammad, "There is a polish for every mirror, and the polish for the mirror of the heart is the recollection of God [dhikr-u-'llah]." Mawlānā is here saying that the sighs of longing for the nearness to God are polishing the metal-like mirror of his heart.
19 What started Barks's long and rich translation adventure was his friend and mentor Robert Bly's suggestion to "release these verses from their cage," referring to Nicholson's and Arberry's translations.
20 Concatenation and epanalepsis are roughly the equivalent of a figure of speech with the uncommon name of *radd al-'ajoz 'al a-ṣṣadr* except that the unit of enunciation is more strictly defined in the Arabic and Persian rhetoric system and depends on the definition of *beyt* and *meṣra'* (Homāyi 1367 [1988], 67–73).
21 In this sense, *laff o nashr* corresponds to no figure of speech in any Western classical rhetoric, but similar textual phenomena have been extensively studied by Greimas's theory of structural semantics in the auspices of his theory of semantic isotopy ([1979] 1993, 163–165).

References

Bacry, Patrick. 1992. *Les figures de style: et autres procédés stylistiques.* "Collection Sujets". Paris: Belin.

Baldrick, Chris. 2008. *Oxford Dictionary of Literary Terms.* New York: Oxford University Press.

Garcin de Tassy, Joseph. [1873] 1970. *Rhétorique et prosodie des langues de l'orient musulman; et spécialement de l'arabe, du persan, du turc et de l'hindoustani.* Amsterdam: Philo Press.

Greimas, Julien Algirdas, and Joseph Courtes. [1979] 1993. *Sémiotique: Dictionnaire raisonné de la théorie du langage.* Translated by Larry Crist et al. Paris: Hachette Supérieur.

Homāyi, Jalāleddin. 1367 [1988]. *Funun-e balāghat va ṣanā'āt-e adabi* [Rhetoric Techniques and Literary Devices]. Tehrān: Nashr-e Namā.

Kazzāzi, Mir-Jalāleddin. 1368 [1989]. *Zibāyishenāsi-e Sokhan-e Parsi* [Aesthetics of Persian Discourse]. 3 vols. Tehrān: Nashr-e Markaz.

Lazard, Gilbert. 2006. *Grammaire du persan contemporain.* Téhéran: Institut français de recherche en Iran.

Meschonnic, Henri. 1970b. *Pour la poétique I.* Paris: Gallimard.

Suhamy, Henri. [1981] 2004. *Les figures de style.* Paris: Presses universitaires de France.

5 Hermeneutics of Translating Rumi

1 Translating as Understanding

The challenges of translating Rumi were discussed from a linguistic and then a discoursive semiotic standpoint. So far, the formatting of the message by the speaker was the center of our attention; it is now the reception of the message that will be studied as a source of difficulties for translation. I have already discussed the procedures and modalities of the actualization of forms in the semiotization of Rumi's thought; now what matters is the thought itself rather than its way of expression, the reference rather than the sign function. The following two chapters raise the question of translation to a whole different level beyond language: to that of the interpretation of Rumi's mystical discourse. Here, I use *mystical* both in its contextual meaning of Iranian gnostic thought and in its literal sense akin to mystery. Interpretation is the basis of translation at two levels: at the moment of first reading and at that of the second reading. The first reading is when the translator, just like any other ST reader, comes into contact with the text. The second reading is when the target reader comes into contact with the author through the TT, which is a second enunciation or re-enunciation. Put simply, the discourse must be understood before being reformulated in another code system with a different prediscoursive purport. It is hence up to the translator to extract this message, understand it, rephrase it, and recommunicate it to TT readers. At both contact points, translation raises serious and hard-to-answer hermeneutic questions. Difficulties of understanding can have important consequences for the act of translinguistic and transcultural communication.

1.1 Rumi's Philosophical Poetry Project

The challenge of translation is only tremendously exacerbated in the case of Rumi, whose text, much like sacred texts, teems with hermeneutic complexities and is often already in need of exegesis in Persian. The hermetic character of Rumi's poetic text, as previously explained, is partly due to the archaism or the diachronic distance between his language and contemporary language and idiom. It is also caused by the very character of the "reference," the *sign-object* in Pierce's semiotic model, the *intention* of the author, what he *means* to say or *refer* to.

DOI: 10.4324/9781003157960-6

In effect, there is an extralinguistic subcontinuum to which Rumi's discourse refers. His poetry is not only an aesthetic project but also a primary way to express ideas that, in mystics' view, cannot be expressed except by an *ad hoc* multilayer hybrid semiotic system. Indeed, the interpretation of Rumi's message is all the more important since his poetry is ultimately not a poetry of discursive form alone, but is entirely based on language games, sounds, and rhythms that are used to animate *samā'* and on lyrical and bacchanalian imaging. It is, in fact, a poetry of otherworldly meaning and substance; this not only in the didactic *Masnavi*, but also in his lyrical *Divan*. The hybrid semiotic structure of his discourse, composed by a combination of prosody, rhythm, interior rhymes, lexical figures, alliterations, musical harmony, calligraphy, and natural language, is not his finite goal, as he specifies: "God knows that I am not a poet! Whence is poetry, whence am I?!" (*Fihe mā fih* 2006, 235).

As mentioned in Chapter 3, Rumi's ostensibly declared contempt for poetry and poets should not be taken at face value but as alluding to two facts: the negative halo around professional court poets in mystical and intellectual circles given their hypocrisy and servility, and most importantly, Rumi's general criticism of the inadequacy of natural language as a medium to express transcendent meanings beyond human intellectual grasp. Rumi, as Leonard Lewisohn argued, is much more than a poet, and poetry is the least of his arts. Poetry is Rumi's principal way of reaching ecstasy, defined as a state of being where understanding the Ultimate Truth is made possible by the reunion with it (Lewisohn 2014, 78–80). Rumi is a philosopher, or as Henry Corbin puts it, a "theosopher," whose poetic project is a philosophical one. Rumi's poetry is above all a metaphysical poetry, with mystical substance and philosophical commitment. Like his contemporaries from the *'arāqi* school[1] already did in the Middle Ages before him, Rumi can be considered a precursor of 19th-century German idealists such as Hegel, Hölderlin, and Schelling when they aspire to make poetry "the teacher of humanity again" (Pinson 1995, 21–24). Another rare example of Rumi's avant-garde attitude towards poetry can be seen in 20th-century French poet and essayist Yves Bonnefoy who, unlike his contemporaries, took a stand against the "textualism" dominating poetry of the 20th century and advocated poetry as philosophy (*Ibid.*, 156–157).

In the case of mystical metaphysics, the importance of poetic discourse is all the greater since, faced with the impossibility of semiotizing transcendent *reference*, the poet is trapped in an inner conflict between the desire to "say" and the incapacity of "saying." Many Sufi commentators have attributed, perhaps hastily, the reticence of the mystic poet to "say" to the inability of audiences of noninitiates, to "understand" what the poet-theosopher sees and experiences, or to the deontological interdiction to reveal divine secrets. In either case, revealing too much of the secrets might have involved the kind of misunderstanding by the commoners and the gatekeepers of the religious dogma that led to the fate of Sohravardi and Hallaj. However, assuming that the likes of Rumi resorted to a complex poetic discourse only to dissimulate a dangerous message and save their lives appears simplistic. If Rumi resorts to the poetization of his message and to the language of tropes, i.e., resorts to substituting a figurative meaning for a real one, it is most likely not for fear of reprisal by religious authorities. Rumi's poetic discourse was the way he devised to semiotize the *insemiotizable* and that the lack of understanding of the audience is due to the nature of the experience that he shares. As Leili Anvar, the French academic and Rumi translator, once put it in an interview, "the only true poetry is necessarily mystical, and the only true mystical language is necessarily poetic" (2015, 14:30).

The idea of poetry as the sole understandable mode of expression for metaphysics finds an echo in the German idealists' attitude towards poetry, also reflected in Martin Heidegger's idea of "residing in the poet." As Pinson explains:

> The finitude of comprehension, as thought by Heidegger, has for an inevitable consequence the refusal of anything that could lead to an intellectual intuition of Being: Being can never be given as full presence. Yet, whatever the extent of the "destruction" of this metaphysics of presence in which Heideggerian meditation indulges, it is not incongruous to suggest that his thought still belongs, as a philosophy of poetry, to the realm of romantic thought. This is because he is not content only with relativizing the language game of scientific understanding (the "vocabulary" of *Verstand*), but posits, like Romantics, that only that of poetry is capable of resounding with the echo of a supreme truth.
>
> (Pinson 1995, 22)

Heideggerian finitude of comprehension is indeed an ontological finitude, not an epistemological one in the Cartesian manner. I argue that Rumi's approach to poetry is precisely in this "romantic" line of thought, even though a deep gap separates Heidegger's irreligious philosophy from Iranian mystics' theosophy. Rumi's method of semiotizing the supreme transcendent Truth is a self-generated multilayered semiotically hybrid poetry. On the one hand, just like German idealists, he pursues a program of *bildung* through poetry, as attested by his intentions in the *Masnavi*; on the other hand, he finds in poetry but a glimmer of hope that he succeeds to reflect a ray of the supreme light that enlightened his mystic's mind. How then will interpreters-translators themselves succeed in grasping this faint ray in the lines of Rumi's text and how will they bring out the elusive extrasemiotic "referent" of this discursive labyrinth and reutter it in the target languages?

1.2 Translation and the Interpretation Field

Rumi's poetic language, as previously explained, presents the epitome of what Umberto Eco defines as *ratio difficilis*. This mode of semiotization, in which the relation between content plane and expression plane is not arbitrary but in which the former is shaped by the latter, happens specifically when there is no previously established sign to communicate a novel semantic content. In other words, Rumi had to invent his own code, his own idiom, to communicate what he deemed was impossible to be *said* in human language. If this is the condition of the creation of the message, *quid* of the conditions of the reception? Reception takes place at different times and in various sociocultural and ideological circumstances. This is what is called "deferred reception," a communication *in absentia*, as opposed to direct oral communication *in presentia*. In case of written texts, especially the ones that survive the test of time, the process of understanding relies on a multitude of factors related to the moment of reception. The interpretation of Rumi's polysemous message varies according to the circumstances of interpretation. While this is true about any act of discoursivization and communication, the complexity is all the more accrued in the instance of a metasemic discourse, as per Michèle Prandi's demonstration in *Grammaire philosophique des tropes* (1992, 146). Prandi's work on the hermeneutics of tropes is of great utility in our analysis, not only because we are here concerned with the translation of Rumi's metasemic discourse, but also because Rumi uses a semiotic approach to communication by which metasemia can be understood in terms of Peirce's sign model and of Bühler's theory of communication (see Chapter 2). What is at stake here is not only communication *in absentia* through the text but the interpretation of a metasemic *conflicting* utterance, that is the language of trope, second meaning, metasemia. Prandi adopts the definition of trope as a structurally conflictual utterance in which a primary content and a secondary content are simultaneously present. In such utterances, meaning does not correspond to the sum of the values of the constituent signs and, most importantly, there is a conflict between the first apparent meaning and a *second* meaning that, according to classical rhetoric, is considered as the main *real* meaning.[2] This kind of *conflicting* discourse can be found all over Rumi's poetry at the microstructural level: there are tropes in individual utterances, as well as at the macrostructural level, i.e., in the work as a whole. As will be discussed in the section that follows, the structures of the *Masnavi* and of the lyrical *Divan* seem so incoherent in their organization that the general meaning appears to unfold *metasemically* at a different level of reading.

The scheme proposed by Prandi is based on the Peircean concepts of *symbol* (a linguistic sign or a sign by convention) and *index* (a sign by inference) applied to the context of communication. In communication, the *indexical* character of the message is opposed to the *symbolic* character of the utterance. This differentiation is akin to Benveniste's distinction between the semiotic function of language and its semantic function, the former destined to "signify" and the latter to "communicate" (Benveniste 1974, 225). While the semiotic content of the utterance only has a structural value, arbitrary for sure but predictable because imposed by the system (code) and convention (idiom), the semantic component also has an indexical one and as such, "the index receives a contingent positional value at each use" (Prandi 1992, 146). In other words, communication is based not only on the structural organization of language but also on the contextual indexes that are found within and without the language. The same utterance can mean different things when associated with different indexes. For instance, the utterance "It is noon" can have different meanings whether it is uttered by a speaker who looks towards the kitchen or one who looks at his watch. Taking up Bühler's definition of the referential function of the sign, Prandi calls *field of indication* "the field of objects and forces which gives the *index* its positional value" (*Ibid.*). Although on the symbolic/semiotic side of our "It is noon" example, the structural value of meaning is limited to the announcement of a time – noon; according to the extralinguistic indexes, in the first context, the semantic content by logical inference may be that "the speaker is hungry." On the other hand, the same utterance can mean, "the speaker is expecting something or someone," especially if the observer or interlocutor knows that the speaker has already eaten. In oral communication, *in presential*, where there is *demonstration ad oculos*, the visual extralinguistic indexes like the direction of the speaker's look make up the field of indication. In the case of written communication, *in absentia*, the field of indication is far more complex and dependent on linguistic (semiotic) indexes. These *indexical* expressions are internal to the language and can be of the deictic type, such as pronouns *I*, *you*, *this*, or of anaphoric/cataphoric nature, like the third person or relative pronouns. While anaphoric/cataphoric indexes refer to elements within the language, deictic elements of the field of indication refer above all to the referential context of discourse, found outside language. Together, anaphoric and deictic indexes provide the field with most of its constituent elements, but extralinguistic indexes are still indispensable even in written communication. The field of indication consists of the whole set of indexes that give the utterance its positional meaning at the moment of *genesis* or production of the discourse. On the other side of the communication is *reception*, which takes place in a corresponding force field named *field of interpretation*:

> The field of interpretation, on the basis of which the value of the message of the utterance is defined, can be described as a second-degree force field. Specific in its structure, this second field is functionally the development of a primary field of indication.
>
> (Prandi 1992, 148)

The *field of interpretation* is ideally intended to be a true copy of the original *field of indication*, which may be thinkable in certain simplified contexts of communication *in presentia*. In practice, however, the field of interpretation diverges from the field of indication to various degrees depending on time and space, the historicity of the text, and the cultural and idiosyncratic gap between the sender (author) and the receiver (reader) of the utterance. This divergence increases tremendously in the communication *in absentia*. If the utterance "It is noon" is in writing, such as in a novel, in the absence of extralinguistic indexes, the primary and secondary fields differ to the point that the reader will never have the same interpretation as the interlocutor unless extra information is added to the context, this time by means of linguistic indexes. Figure 5.1 shows the process of reception as described by Prandi.

As Michèle Prandi argues, communication in figurative utterances has a different operating mode from that of ordinary speech. In the case of metasemia, "unlike coherent utterance, trope presents a conceptual conflict – a contradiction – at the level of one or more connections giving shape to its semantic content"

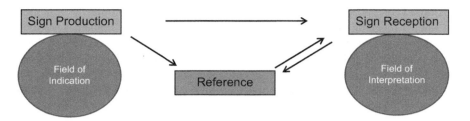

Figure 5.1 Fields of indication and interpretation

(Prandi 1992, 169). If there is a conflict in the primary *field of indication*, there will *a fortiori* be one within the secondary *field of interpretation*. Furthermore, the indicative expressions in the text are not limited to *anaphora* and *deixis*; there is a third element in the case of tropes and poetic imagery, recognized by Conte, quoted by Prandi. It is the indicative expressions in reference to an imaginary field of indication, called *deixis am phantasma*. An example of such an index is the deictic element "there" in the following utterance devoid of any metasemia: "you should follow the road till you reach a church. There, you should turn right" (1992, 148). Now in poetic imagery, it is precisely this imaginary *am phantasma* deictic function that constitutes the heart of the field of indication. This is true *a fortiori* in mystical poetry, which has the primary objective of redeploying the esoteric rather than the exoteric aspect of truth and of semiotizing the *transcendent* rather than the *physical*.

Evidently, these hermeneutic stakes are only raised in translation, i.e., in an act of re-enunciation, and hence of *re-reception* for the TT reader. Translators are above all readers and therefore interpreters of the message. Yet, they are only the first intermediary readers, whereas the readers of TT are the second and end receivers of the message. What effect, then, do the circumstances of first reception by translators have on the translation? The semiotic problems of *discourse production* at the moment of the genesis of the work are matched in scope and caliber by the hermeneutic problems encountered at the moment of reception. George Steiner, in his *After Babel* (1975), was the first to place the fundamental problem of *understanding* at the center of translation problems. He developed his notion of *hermeneutic motion*, "the act of elicitation and appropriative transfer of meaning" (Steiner 1975, 312), according to which the act of translation is carried out in four stages: *confidence* or thrust, *aggression* or penetration, *incorporation*, and *restitution* or compensation. These are also the stages through which the translator, confident of the existence of meaning in Rumi's hermetic discourse, attacks the utterance, penetrates it in order to appropriate it, in order then to import into his TL the meaning in its discursive form.

Yet in the case of mystical poetry, this sought-after meaning cannot easily be the object of understanding and therefore of appropriation in the way Steiner suggests. In mystical poetic discourse, the primary field of indication is already complexified by the conflicting indexical elements provided by the author. Moreover, at the moment of reception, the secondary field of interpretation diverges from the primary field because of the wide diachronic and cultural gaps separating the translator as first reader from the text. In the case of Sufi poetry, hermeneutic difficulties also arise from the ideological charge and the polemical character of the discourse. The difficulties associated with Rumi's figurative discourse are thus manifested at two levels: first, the complexity of its field of indication stemming from the displacement of the intention of the message in relation to the semantic value of the symbol; second, the variations of the field of interpretation of Rumi's mystical discourse depending on the distance in time and space and especially the cultural distance that separate the mystical discourse from the interpretative paradigm of the modern Western reader. What is more, any intervention by the translator with a view to clarifying or interpreting the message further harms the process of comprehension by the Western reader.[3] In short, the hermeneutic difficulties of translating Rumi can be conceived along three main lines: the difficulty of understanding the intended message due to the unusual and conflicting discursive formatting of ST; the role of the reader-translator's subjectivity in orienting the process of understanding and hence translation by *polluting* the TT field of indication; and the distorted reception of the message by the target language-culture that has rarely been exposed to the ST indexes and hence has an impoverished and distorted field of interpretation.

Steiner also famously declares that to *understand* is to *translate*, i.e., to appropriate meaning. Any act of understanding passes by an act of *intralingual* translation in the mind, even if the process is unconscious. While this usually happens at the individual level, in certain cases, this primary translative process becomes a necessity at the collective level. This phenomenon manifests itself quintessentially in the exegeses and the commentary of hermetic and obscure texts of a religious or philosophical nature. Native readers often need exegetic commentaries to understand such texts. One can easily imagine the challenges presented by secondary *interlingual* translation when a ST should already be *intralingually* translated to be understood. Translating Rumi's discourse takes a whole different dimension when we consider that his text, like sacred texts, is typically subject to various conflicting and often arbitrary interpretations within Persianate culture. Any interlingual translation of Rumi will then necessarily come from an arbitrary interpretation of his message, a sort of extension of the work in some direction. Even at the height of objectivity, Rumi's translator always faces a perennial dilemma steeped in the shared history between commentary and translation as two inter- and hypertextual activities. Rumi's translators have almost never been able to avoid being also his commentator, not only because of the hermeticism that characterizes his text, but also because they are motivated by a certain ideological tendency or political agenda (see Chapter 6).

2 Mystical Discoursive (In)Coherence

The structural conflict of mystical discourse appears both at the microstructural level, that of individual utterances such as propositions or verse, and at the macrostructural level, that of the entire text, i.e., the poem or even the entire work. This conflict is not always of a metasemic nature, which is the case of tropes. The semantic structure of Rumi's discourse is sometimes conflictual because of an apparent lack of coherence in discursive organization and in narrativity.

2.1 Narrative and Discoursive Puzzles

The semantic organization of Rumi's text has certain features that may be considered an obstacle for an unfamiliar reader's understanding, be they the translator or the end reader. I have already mentioned certain microdiscoursive sources of what can be perceived as incoherence or lectal inconsistency: lack of punctuation, graphic problems, use of foreign elements, archaisms, and alternation of registers, idiolects, and technolects. At a macrodiscoursive level, too, Persian classical literature can challenge some of the basic principles of composition in European stylistic systems. Modern readers are used to a certain logical coherence in the organization of texts and in the articulation of content points and themes. These are fundamentally absent in classical texts, whether of sacred or of profane nature. However, the stylistic difference mentioned here is less a matter of era than one of different rhetorical logic and literary norms. Western rhetoric, especially since classicism,[4] has a much stricter definition of coherence than does Persian literature that includes lyrical and mystical poetry in a major way.[5] Even in narrative texts, either in the poetic form of *masnavi* or in poetic prose as in Sa'di's *Golestān*, where thematic consistency should be respected within the same story, the general organization of the work seems unconventional. Rumi's *Masnavi* is the epitome of this apparent lack of cohesion, since even within the same story the flow of plot is consistently interrupted by the author's meanderings, parenthetical accounts, and metaphysical discussions, often marked by abrupt lectal variations. The consequent hurdles for translation created by the apparently random organization of the *Masnavi* and its lack of narrative consistency was mentioned by early translators such as Wilson:

> The principal [difficulty] is undoubtedly the subtlety of the Author's thoughts and the obscurity of his expression. Touching the latter, it may be more particularly said that the Author often in accordance with the requirements of his disquisitions applies untechnical words to Sufi senses. To this may be added that he often changes the significance of his own terms in the course of a few lines, a practice which has sometimes led even the Turkish Commentator into misconception.
>
> (1910, vii)

This phenomenon studied in Chapter 2 can be explained by Rumi's constant alternation between linguistic variations, mostly diastratic ones. Whether in direct speeches, within diegetic events, or within his own metanarrative comments, Rumi does not hesitate to mix the vulgar with the sublime, a practice that appeared much later in the West during Romanticism.

Another difficulty is to trace the connection between lines and lines, but this is not so uncommon in Persian poets, whose imagination is peculiarly vivid. No less a difficulty is it sometimes to distinguish who is speaking. When the author, for instance, has been quoting the words of another, he wanders on occasions so insensibly into reflections of his own as to bewilder the Commentators, from whom, it will be remarked in the Notes, I have sometimes ventured to differ. Then, too, the object of address may occasionally be open to doubt. After one person has been addressed, the speaker may almost insensibly transfer his address to another, but in such terms as to leave it a little uncertain whom he is addressing.

(*Ibid.*)

Wilson's euphemistic reference to the Persian poets' "particularly vivid imagination" hides in fact a deeper criticism by 19th-century orientalists often aimed at Iranian authors regarding their exaggerated use of digression when making a point in a piece of dialectic reasoning or within the narrative structure. This practice was at its height with Rumi, but its origins can be found in two places: first, in the structure of sacred texts such as the Old Testament and the Koran, where the importance of the moral of a story supersedes the perfection of its plot. In such texts, considered to be God's words by believers, the author's objective is not storytelling for entertainment but to make a divine point. From a profane perspective of textual analysis, the inconsistency in these texts is attributed to their fragmentation and loss, collective authorship, and transcription errors.[6] However, for mystic thinkers like Rumi, the organization of sacred books was a model to imitate. Second, in Rumi's worldview, natural language and dialectic reasoning are intrinsically inept at expressing divine truth. His *Masnavi* is neither a historical work, a work of fiction, nor a philosophical treatise. His teaching method is far from conventional.

This general attitude along with the more material particularities of the infradiscoursive structures, such as lack of punctuation and gender markings, leads to texts that are inherently difficult to read, especially for a 19th-century Western translator. Wilson can barely hide his annoyance at the near impossibility of distinguishing descriptive and narrative utterances from reported speech. This difficulty in following the plot – or the author's line of thought – is exacerbated by the constant use of the phatic function and apostrophes, where the author addresses an imaginary interlocutor who may be God, the reader, a diegetic addressee, his scribe Hesāmeddin Chalabi, his beloved Shams, or his own self. This writing style is indeed too peculiar for the Victorian taste of Rumi's first translators, a conservative literary era preceding by a number of years the advent of narrative techniques used by surrealists such as *mise en abyme*, stream of consciousness, the nouveau roman, etc.[7] At least, Wilson's critical tone is much softer than his predecessor's, Whinfield, who points out the imperfections of Rumi's style:

it is not always easy to follow the meaning. When the poet is telling his stories he is constantly "going off upon a word," – drawing a fresh moral from every

incident in the course of the story. "Il moralise tout," some French critic says of him, and this unfortunate habit of his is somewhat of a trial to his readers.
(Whinfield 1887, xli–xlii)

The general organization of the *Masnavi* has indeed two characteristics that can leave the unfamiliar reader/translator perplexed and liable to misread, due to the disturbances in the *field of indication* at the macrostructural level.

First, the sequential organization of the stories exhibits no apparent chronological or thematic logic. Narratives and compositions on morality and philosophical teachings can follow one another indifferently, without any unity of theme or of genre. Philosophical fables follow street folk tales; fictitious stories are followed by biblical and Koranic accounts accompanied by allusions to the traditions of Muhammad (*hadiṣ*); stories of mystical saints alternate with obscene scenes. There are no chapters within the six books of the *Masnavi*; the only marker of the topic is a title preceding each passage. This can be a short title, like "Moses's Denial of the Shepherd's Prayer" (M.III), or a long title functioning as a summary of what comes after, like the tale of the servant girl and the donkey (M.IV).

Second, individual narratives usually follow a nonlinear and polyphonic scheme. Rumi is a master of the *mise en abyme* even before Diderot in *Jacques le Fataliste et son maître* or André Gide in *Les faux-monnayeurs*. In most tales of the *Masnavi*, the author digresses to tell one or more other stories that may or may not be directly related to the main plot. The deviation can lead to unfinished or hastily botched up main plots. The narration can also be suspended at any moment to make room for philosophical commentaries and moral reflections made by the narrator or one of the characters, assuming the speaker can be pinpointed. As Keshavarz points out, "the poems themselves are the mystical experience and the meaning, not a container holding them" (2004, 19). In other words, it is not so much the content and the plot of the tales as the metaphysical discourse and the moral Rumi alludes to that counts. This narrative pattern is also typical of sacred texts, especially of Koranic tales, where the plot is usually interrupted with parallel narratives and commentaries and remain sometimes even unfinished.

2.2 The Intrinsic Order of the Chaos

While discoursive cohesion has a much looser definition in Persian classical literature, Rumi's style should nevertheless not be taken as the literary norm of the Persian narrative literature of the time. Rumi's stylistic traits are hardly found to the same extent with Nezami, Sa'di, Attār, Sanāyi, or other mystic-didactic authors of that epoch. They are therefore idiosyncratic to Rumi's creations. Yet characterizing Rumi's work as incoherent is unjust: it has actually been shown to follow a pertinent logic of its own. Recent studies shed light on the hidden aspects of its organization, especially on the macrostructural level. Fatemeh Keshavarz's indispensable contribution (Keshavarz [1998] 2004) evokes several apparent problems of discoursive and narrative inconsistency: in each case, it turns out that the *ad hoc* effect was actually intended by the author. Another important study,

Safavi, Ghahreman, and Weightman's *Rumi's Mystical Design* (2009) focuses on the macrostructural thematic organization of the *Masnavi*. In their structural analysis of the six books of the *Masnavi*, the authors propose the theory of its *circular composition*, based on thematic similarities and the recurrence of certain characters and topics.[8] They find a symmetrical relationship between certain sections of the six books forming a chiasmatic pattern. In the introduction to his translation of *Book I* (2006, xvi–xxxv), Alan Williams broaches the question of organization, citing J. Baldick's thematic study, which compared the structure of the *Masnavi* to that of Attār's *Elāhināme*. Williams also explains how key ideas are regrouped two by two: *Books I* and *II* around the vices of the *nafs* [humans' lowly "self"], *Books III* and *IV* see the recurrence of "wisdom and reason" embodied in the biblical character of Moses in the face of the "illusory imagination" personified by Pharaoh, and the accounts of *Books IV* and *VI* are united by the idea of the "total denial of the self" in order to reach God.

Williams also distinguishes narrative voices of the *Masnavi* in an attempt to let TT readers fully appreciate the narrative logic and coherence of Rumi's discourse. He identifies seven narrative voices (2006, xxvi–xxviii), which he underlines in a passage from *Book I*. The first is the "voice of the author," by which the author addresses the reader as in the Prelude of *ney*; the second, the voice of narration, which is the classic narrative voice in the third person. The third is the "analog voice" where the author interrupts to make a comparison with a situation outside the story to clarify his point of view. Fourth, the "dialogical voice" relates to the characters' speech in the dialogues. The "voice of moral reflection" – number five, similar to the "voice of the author" – is addressed to an imaginary addressee using the second person pronoun "you," which could be the reader or not. This voice is used to give moral lessons, normally after having made an intertextual allusion to the Koran or *ḥadis*. Through the sixth "voice of spiritual discourse," the narrator addresses God, more or less in the same way as he addresses the reader. The last voice is what Williams calls the "voice of hiatus." This is the voice of silence:

> The 'voice' of hiatus signals the limit of spiritual discourse and the return to silence. Hiatus questions the wisdom of continuing to speak, having reached the very brink of incoherence because of the unattainability, or inexpressibility, of what the poet is trying to evoke. Sometimes Rumi says that he cannot say more because of the reader's incapacity to understand, as in 1. 18[9] of the very opening of the poem. . . . Accordingly, the *Masnavi* should have ended here, 25000 couplets early, but this is a rhetorical device. Sometimes Rumi wishes for silence to reign, as being more expressive of 'inner' truths than sensual words.
>
> (2006, xxv)

Rumi's penname, "silence," to which Keshavarz devoted a chapter in her monograph (Chapter 4, "Rumi's Poetics of Silence"), constitutes a figure of speech on its own. It is as if he means to constantly remind the addressee of his discourse of the impossibility of expressing the truth and the necessity to remain silent. It is striking to see Rumi's leitmotif reverberated in the work of a distant philosopher like Wittgenstein, with a fundamentally distant worldview and epistemology, who draws the same conclusion at the end of his influential *Tractatus Logico-Philosophicus* about speaking the truth: "*Wovon man nicht sprechen kann, darüber muss man schweige* [Whereof one cannot speak, thereof one must be silent]" (1922, §7). This is not an ancillary position or a rhetorical technique. Silence is an essential theme of Rumi's work and of his mystical thought. The absence of words, sounds, ideas, thoughts, preoccupations; the absence of self, death of the self:

> Die, die, die of this love,
> Once you have died of this love, all of you will be recipient of the spirit.
> (G. 636, l.1)

This metaphoric (or real) death of self and reincarnation in the beloved is Rumi's way of knowing God. A knowledge (gnosis) that is not of a dialectic nature; it is an ontological one. It is realized by the reunion of the subject and object of knowledge.

Can the polyphonic character of Rumi's narration and the hybridity of his semiotic system be attributed to his frustration at not being able to express his experience of God? The answer is overwhelmingly Yes. The overlapping of voices in a single verse, as happens all over the *Masnavi*, is most certainly symptomatic of the author's quest for a narrative point of view that does justice to the unspeakable nature of his intended message. For example, there are no fewer than 25 changes of points of view in *Neynāme*. According to Williams, the more one progresses in the *Masnavi*, the more the articulation (change) of the voices accelerates and the markers become rare.[10] This polyphonic scheme, therefore, is based on a well-thought-out structure presenting a dissimulated coherence. Through careful analysis, scholarly students of Rumi would succeed in identifying and perceiving the well-calculated architecture of his work that unfortunately does not conform to the conventional idea of coherence in Western stylistics. In the development of his story, Rumi does not feel compelled to follow the traditional sequential structure of a plot: initial situation, disturbing element (problem), adventures (climax), outcome, final situation. He seeks to *go beyond* this schema, in the same way as he seeks to *deconstruct* any other intellectual schema that reigns through conventions. For a mystic like Rumi, these conventions are only illusions for the spiritual wayfarer, and the reader of his work is supposed to be on a spiritual path. In the flow of his speech, Rumi imitates nature; it is pure mimesis because it reproduces nature in its enthalpy. His work looks more like an English garden, well-groomed but looking like wild woods, than a French one, an image of perfect symmetry, the sign of the human domination of nature. Any attempt at organization, any desire for classification comes from the human intellect (*aql*). Calculating reason, in mystical teachings, is considered a veil (*hejāb*) covering the Truth. This view does not prevent Rumi from having a coherent pattern in his discourse; if only in the constancy of his incoherent structure throughout the *Masnavi*. There is an intrinsic organizational logic hidden both in the work as a whole and in the structure of isolated narratives. The lack of punctual *cohesion* between constituent parts of the text hides the wholistic *coherence* of the discourse. The distinction between cohesion and coherence relates to the distinction between text and discourse, that is between the material manifestation of utterances and the externalization of the thought in its discoursivization.

2.3   Translating the Disorder Into Order

Primarily concerned with the text, translation is above all responsible for preserving the *cohesion* of utterances constituting the text rather than worrying about the *coherence* of the discourse. In the absence of cohesion in the *Masnavi*, some of Rumi's translators have lost track of its discursive coherence, which spurred them to establish one that suited their own idea of organization. This is not the case of translators who undertook to translate the entire work in its original configuration. Even classical and modern translations of some parts of the work, such as *Book I*, mostly preserved the exact sequence of stories and verses.[11] However, two types of hypertextual activities have led to the rearrangement of passages and ultimately to the establishment of a new organizational coherence in the work: translation into prose and selective translation. Prose translation concerns specifically the *Masnavi*, while translation of passages extracted from different works to rearrange them in a particular thematic order concern all of Rumi's texts, including his speeches and correspondence. These practices are aimed at facilitating the reading for the target audience and popularizing Rumi: after all, the inestimable value of Rumi's texts can be better appreciated when they are actually read by large numbers of readers. On the other hand, these practices, though sometimes necessary and useful, can be qualified as rationalizing and homogenizing towards the ST, which raises an ethical problem as discussed in Chapter 7.

It is with this popularizing concern that shortly after Nicholson's translation of the entire *Masnavi*,[12] Arberry, Nicholson's student, decided to provide an abridged version in prose with an anthology of the most fascinating emblematic stories. Although verses were transformed into prose in Arberry's version, it is quite close to Nicholson's literal and moderately annotated text. What differentiates the two is Arberry's more restrained lexical choice, his meticulous attention to punctuation, and above all the deletion of passages that would interfere with the coherence of the text. The result is a much more "readable" text than the original with a better fluidity of speech; unfortunately, the discursive effect sought by Rumi through his narrative game, a game that impresses, shocks, teases, and keeps the reader in endless suspense, is completely absent. Arberry distinguishes Rumi's narrative aim from his didactic and moralizing aim and underlines the need to separate the two functions for fear of illegibility.

> It must however be admitted that as it stands the huge work makes very difficult reading. 'The poem resembles a trackless ocean,' wrote Professor R. A. Nicholson who devoted many years to meticulous study and fastidious

interpretation. 'There are no boundaries, no lines of demarcation between the literal "husk" and the "kernel" of doctrine in which its inner sense is conveyed and copiously expounded.' Written down sporadically over a long period of time, without any firm framework to keep the discourse on orderly lines, it is at first, and even at repeated reading, a disconcertingly diffuse and confused composition.

(Arberry 1961, 12)

None of the classical translators, even the ones with the most literalist and foreignizing approach, seem to have really managed to perceive the latent coherence of Rumi's *difficult* style or to appreciate the inner cohesion of his text marked by acute polyphony. It is therefore with the aim of establishing a certain civilized coherence in a somewhat barbaric discourse in which the author jumps from one subject to another that the translator decides to put some order in the stories, arranging them according to a specific theme and removing digressions in favor of the plot. But there is also the concern for "readability" that preoccupies the translator:

Nicholson himself however would have been the first to concede that the rich fruits of his single-minded and unremitting labours were digestible with extreme difficulty, and even then only by scholars having the same kind of specialist equipment as himself. Yet the poem obviously deserves a far wider circle of readers than that. How can that larger circle be reached and satisfied?

(*Ibid.*, 12)

This second goal is laudable insofar as it is an attempt to popularize Rumi's otherwise inaccessible thought. It should be noted that Nicholson also made attempts to popularize his own translations by making them more palatable to a wider audience in two late anthologies.[13] In French, there is a selection of the *Masnavi* tales, thanks to the efforts of a Turkish speaker, Ahmed Kudsi (1988), published two years before Vitray-Meyerovitch's full retranslation based on Nicholson's English translation. However, Kudsi himself rightly admits that his anthology is an adaptation and not a translation. Tales are subject to significant mutilation, the omission of passages, and the addition of commentaries. In this respect, Arberry's translation differs substantially from Kudsi's adaptation; while Arberry proceeds to a systematic suppression of nonnarrative voices, the French text allows all voices to resurface but selectively and arbitrarily.

The popularization attempts begun by Nicholson took on a completely different dimension with modern late-20th-century translators who sometimes, but not always, take all imaginable liberties to recontextualize short passages arbitrarily. The increasingly common practice results in mixed anthologies composed of disparate excerpts from various sections of the *Divan* and the *Masnavi* regrouped at the translator's arbitrary discretion. They are simple collages of translated or adapted texts – imitative or hypertextual translations – comprising chapters with a perceived common theme. The fragments usually come from various unidentified sources, and sometimes verses are merged together from various poetic genres (*robā'i*, ghazal, *masnavi*) to shape longer poems. It is a popular practice in particular with Colman Barks and Kabir Helminsky who do not read Persian, but also with specialists like Lewis, Schimmel, and other specialists.[14] What is striking is that this intertextual collage activity does not systematically bear the label of adaptation.[15] This practice can be observed in our Examples 1.1, 1.2., and 1.3 from the *Neynāme*, with the versions of Barks, Helminsky, and Lewis that appeared in thematically organized chapters in their respective collections.

It is easy to imagine the interest raised by these kinds of translation-adaptations: modern Western readers avoid getting lost in the author's discursive labyrinth. Such anthologies offer them the luxury of a fluid reading thanks to the organization of the collection. The reader can also appreciate a whole different aesthetic dimension thanks to the regrouping of poems with similar themes. Unfortunately, the inevitable consequence of this intertextual practice for the original text is the total breakdown of its underlying networks of meaning.[16] The recontextualization of the utterance can result in the creation of a message that is sometimes radically different from the original one. Taking utterances out of their original context – and co-text – can be detrimental to their referential value due to radical changes made to the objects and forces found in the *field of indication*, and as a consequence to the reader's *field of interpretation*. This problem is one of the contributing factors to the phenomenon of second-degree deformation, discussed in Chapter 7.

3 Translating Figures of Thought

Depending on the typological approach, the figures of speech called *sanāye'-e ma'navi* [*conceptual figures*] by Persian rhetoric, may or may not include figures of substitution or tropes. As discussed in Chapter 5, they are not realized at the microstructural-level discourse; therefore, they do not pose a problem to the process of linguistic transfer of utterances. Their importance for translation is of a hermeneutic nature in several respects. They render the message complex for the translator in the first place, raising the probability of error. Secondly, figures of thought and substitution usually lose a large part of their rhetorical impact and aesthetic value in the cultural sphere of the target language. Here, they are discussed separately given the particular importance of tropes in Rumi's poetic discourse.

3.1 Semantic Figures of Speech

The rhetorical impact of these figures is of a semantic nature. Unlike figures of substitution, however, figures of speech function not by way of replacing the meaning of the utterance or adding a secondary semantic level but by altering either the conventional organization of semantic content or the discursive point of view, just as tropes, the rhetorical impact, and connotative semantic values of figures of speech are bound more or less to the cultural and historical realities of the ST.

3.1.1 Litotes and Antiphrasis

While these two figures are among the most common in the rhetoric of European languages, they are very rare in Persian literature although quite widespread in everyday language. A few *litotes* occur in our corpus and are mostly found in reported speech, namely the dialogues between various characters of the *Masnavi*. Example 5.1 is taken from God's words to Moses.

Example 5.1 MI) l.1758

Man nagardam pāk az tasbiḥeshān	pāk ham ishān shavand o dorfeshān
I don't become pure by their praise, It is they who become pure and full of pearls	

In the first verse, the statement attributed to God about himself is an example of "saying less to suggest more." It is a religious dogma that God does not need the adoration of the created and does not need either to purify or sanctify himself. God makes this understatement in response to Moses, who was deeply offended at the casual way the shepherd praised God. God's words are translated word for word, but the force of the understatement of the original saying is not readily conveyed to the unscholarly reader who will most certainly miss it.

Antiphrasis too can be identified mostly in the reported speech of various characters. This figure has a distant equivalent in Persian rhetoric under the name of *shive-ye shirin* [the sweet way]. The sweetness comes from the humorous nature of this figure. It can also be found in Moses's monologue rebuking the shepherd for having spoken to God as if he were speaking to his aunt and uncle.

Example 5.2 MI) l.1735

Jesm o ḥājat dar ṣefāt-e zoljalāl	bā ke miguyi to in bā 'amm o khāl?
Body and needs, [talking] about the attributes of the *Owner of Magnificence*? Whom are you saying this to? To the paternal aunt and maternal uncles?	

In the absence of punctuation in the original manuscript, it is difficult to determine with certainty the voice of the utterance. The last elliptical proposition can be taken either for a (rhetorical) question like the rest of the statement or for an affirmation. In either case, the tone is sarcastic and comical, meant to ridicule the shepherd. The (diegetic) speaker, Moses, attempts to caricature the words of the poor shepherd by mentioning that his manner of speaking to God is rather worthy of his aunt and uncle. Moses says this with a significant critical distance, which does not show up to the same degree in translation. Most translators considered the sentence interrogative (except Lewis).[17] What is more notable is the lexical impoverishment stemming from lack of vocabulary in the TL for the attributes of God (*zoljalāl*) or to distinguish paternal and maternal aunt and uncle.

3.1.2 Hyperbole

Unlike the rarely used *litotes*, *hyperboles* are among the most frequently used tropes in Persian poetry and in Rumi's. Amplification and exaggeration are ubiquitous in Persian poetry, whereas they are used with moderation and constraints in Western literatures – the reverse was the case for understatements. According to an Arab-Persian poetic principle, it is the nature of poetry to distort reality. Ancient rhetoricians went so far as to call poets "liars" (Homāyi 1367 [1988], 267), so recurrent are the poetic processes that produce figures like hyperbole. Homāyi quotes a verse from Nezami on this subject: "Don't think too much about poetry and its techniques, because its most falsifying form is the best." This attitude shows how large the gap between the aesthetic principles in source and target cultures is, particularly in terms of didactic and philosophical texts. Rumi, given what we know about his style, is among those who used hyperbole most lavishly. Hyperbole is widespread throughout his corpus, as found in Examples 1.6 and 2.6, to name only two. The translation of this figure is not particularly difficult, but the target text may become somewhat shocking or excessive for the Western reader unfamiliar with the style of Persian poetry with its cosmic images such as those of the spraying of the universe or the disappearance of the oceans.

3.1.3 Rhetorical Questions and Dialogism

Affecting the organization of the discourse, *dialogism* is a narrative technique involving dialogue. The Persian version of dialogism is called *porsesh o pāsokh* [question and answer], even though it does not necessarily imply questions and answers or even a dialogue. It consists of a more or less symmetrical organization of direct reported speeches exchanged between the narrator and a character or two characters, more akin in reality to an interior monologue than to a real dialogue. Whether many dialogues of the *Masnavi* constitute *porsesh o pāsox* is debatable. For instance, ghazal 436 of the *Divan*, where the majority of the verses are organized around a dialogue between the poet and his beloved, is one among many examples of *porsesh o pāsox* in Rumi's poetry, and there are many other examples in Persian classical poetry. In ghazal 1393, from line 3 to line 11, Rumi stages a series of reported speeches attributed to an unknown character to explain the origin of the transformations he has undergone. This latter dialogue is a more typical example of *porsesh o pāsokh* than its Western counterpart *dialogism* insofar as only one side of the dialogue is expressed in the text. Another element that differentiates between *porsesh o pāsokh* and Western-style dialogism as it exists in the target languages is that the identity of the speakers is almost never revealed in Persian classical poetry, nor is their gender, as Persian pronouns are gender neutral.

Rhetorical questions are also one of the most widespread figures in Rumi's poetry, both in the *Divan* and in the *Masnavi*. In addition to Example 5.2,

Example 5.3 probably shows the most well-known rhetorical question in all of Rumi's work:

Example 5.3 MI) l.1751

To barāye vaṣl kardan āmadi	yā barāye faṣl kardan āmadi?
Have you come to reunite	or have you come to separate?

This question is one God asks Moses and has almost attained the status of a cliché in Persian. It is used in the context of a person who is supposed to bring people together but who on the contrary sows discord in a group or a couple.

3.1.4 Digression, Reticence, and Suspense

Often seen as a sign of lack of coherence in Rumi's discourse, "digression" and "suspension" characterize the narrative organization of the *Masnavi*. While the structure of a ghazal is designed not to deal with a single subject but to hop from one to another, the relative freedom of the *maṣnavi* [couplet] genre makes it conducive to storytelling without worrying about finding the right rhyme. Yet Rumi can never stick to a plot; he constantly puts the narration in suspension to tell a story within a story, to give moral lessons, to refer to another story, to make a philosophical analysis, etc. One of the numerous examples of this practice at the macrostructural level is manifested in the story of the king who falls in love with a servant girl in M.II (Example 1.4). Although the narrator is telling the story of the doctor's visit to the servant, he gradually slips from line 109 into a metaphysical discourse on love. Then, as if under the effect of an external force, for 34 couplets, the poet is inflamed by evoking the memory of Shams-e Tabrizi, who is the incarnation of love.

Rumi is also a master of *reticence*. I have already underlined the paradox of the poet in his relentless inner struggle between the desire to express himself and external and internal constraints. The poet sometimes seems torn apart by an inner conflict that very often resurfaces in his discourse. This fact is best illustrated in the passage where he feigns the existence of an interlocutor who seems to be constantly urging the poet to continue telling the story of love (M.II, l.130–140). Meanwhile, the narrator seems too reticent to continue being a poet, pretexting that "it is better that the secret of the beloved be told in the history of the others." The notion of "secret" is central to Rumi's mystical thought, which explains the high frequency of reticence in his poetic work.

3.1.5 Correction or Palinode

Correction, another ubiquitous figure of speech in the *Masnavi*, is easily translatable as well. Most corrections occur within the same line (distich) and relate to a small part of speech; in effect, *palinode* has a lower frequency insofar as it concerns the organization of discourse at a larger scale. Corrections appear often in the form of a rhetorical question:

Example 5.4 D) G. 464, l.2

Dorj-e 'atā shod padid, ghorre ye daryā rasid   sobḥ-e sa'ādat damid, sobḥ che nur-e khodāst
The pearl of generosity has emerged, the roar of the sea has arrived The dawn of happiness/fortune has risen. What is dawn?! This is God's light!

E1) Nid: IX, p. 32–37: The billow of largesse hath appeared, the thunder of the sea hath arrived, The morn of blessedness hath dawned. Morn? No, 'tis the light of God.	E2) Ls: p. 149: the sea foams white, casts its treasures: Fortunate dawn, morn of the light of God!

In the second verse, "what is dawn" is a negative rhetorical question. It actually means "there is no dawn" or "dawn is nothing." The poet corrects his previous statement about the arrival of "dawn of joy and prosperity." This apparent rhetorical question indeed constitutes a *correction*. English perfectly allows for the recovery of the ST discursive form of correction, yet in Lewis's hypertextual translation, this figure disappears entirely. Nicholson on the other hand modifies the syntagmatic structure of the figure of speech by adding a negative answer to the rhetorical question. This way, he perfectly manages to recreate the ST's discoursive form.

3.2 Talmiḥ *[Allusion]*

Talmih, or *chashmzad*, means "to point out by the corner of the eye." This figure corresponds approximately to *allusion*, in which the author evokes a source external to the text, by various discursive means, directly or indirectly (metaphorically). The reference can be of sacred or secular nature: a folkloric story, hadith, proverb, anecdote, or parable can be alluded to for rhetorical purposes such as the confirmation of the author's point of view or for exemplification. An open manifestation of intertextuality, allusion takes varied forms in Rumi's text: direct quotation, paraphrased quotation, direct allusion, concealed allusion, metaphor referring to a well-known biblical or Koranic story, etc. Some instances were discussed in Chapter 2 on the use of Arabic utterances, in Examples 2.7 and 2.8 and the citation from M. III) l.1753. In the latter, there is a direct quote, and in Example 2.7 an indirect quote (paraphrase), whereas Example 2.8 shows an indirect reference to the biblical story of Solomon. The cultural difficulties of translating such allusions are discussed in the next section where translators are faced with the dilemma of adding explanatory or exegetic notes, regarding both religious and secular sources.

4 The Hermeneutic Conundrum of Mystical Imagery

Translating figurative meaning highlights three interconnected but distinct difficulties of interpreting texts from the perspective of translation: the problem of interpreting the utterance in its metasemic relationship, that of the referential interpretation due to variations in the field of interpretation, and finally, the problem of interpreting the *hidden* meaning of symbolic language in a given ideological context. The first question falls within the domain of linguistics or, more precisely, that of rhetoric insofar as metasemia, the metaphorical or metonymic displacement of meaning, is above all a linguistic phenomenon. This challenge is of lesser importance for translation than the other two since a literal translation into any language can happen to recreate the same poetic image in the TT as the one existing in the ST. The real problem of loss of meaning in translation resides in the question of cultural referents, their absence or transformation in time (diachronic) and space (between source and target cultures), as well as in the hermeneutic issues associated with the interpretation of the displaced, conflicting, or incoherent utterance in a field of interpretation distorted by ideological and political forces.

4.1 Tropology of Rumi's Poetry

Rumi's text is the manifestation of Persian poetic imagery[18] in some of its most exquisite forms. The occurrence rate of metasemic utterances in his discourse is so high that in certain passages of the *Masnavi* and almost all of the *Divan* it is easier to count the number of verses devoid of conflict or displacement of meaning than the ones displaying some type of metasemia. Some of these images are rather conventional: they are institutionalized metaphoric images regularly used in poetry in general or mystical poetry in particular. Some of these *dead metaphors*[19] – perfect examples of *ratio difficilis* – have even been integrated in the *code* and are used as proverbs not only in the Persianate culture but also in European languages.[20] By contrast, some of Rumi's images seem to come from the same chimeric realm as surrealist poetry:

> O wine, I'm worse than you! I am more wine than you!
> I am more effervescent than you. Hush! Hush! Slowly!
> (*Divan*, G. 1446, l. 6)

Such imagery is unique and almost matchless in Persian classical poetry despite its extensive use of tropes. In Persian, just as in Western languages, both influenced by Aristotelian rhetoric, tropes are defined as *displacement* of meaning (the definition of *meta-semia*) and are derivatives of *simile* (*tashbih*) in the absence of the comparator, and sometimes of the *tenor* (the subject of comparison) and the *event* (state or act).[21] In other words, in tropes, namely metonymy or metaphor, it is only the object of comparison and often the *event* that remain, and in the absence of the indicators of comparison, the secondary meaning of the sign must be construed according to the context, i.e., other linguistic and extralinguistic elements of the *field of indication*. This displacement or substitution can take place on the paradigmatic axis based on similarity (metaphorical displacement) or on contiguity (metonymic displacement). Jakobson defines the two main types of semantic displacements as follows:

> The development of a discourse may take place along two different semantic lines: one topic may lead to another either through their similarity or through their contiguity. The metaphoric way would be the most appropriate term for the first case and the metonymic way for the second, since they find their most condensed expression in metaphor and metonymy respectively.
>
> (Jakobson 1971, 254)

In Persian rhetoric, the fundamental distinction is not made at the level of metaphor and metonymy, i.e., the orientation of substitution – on the paradigmatic or syntagmatic axis, but rather on the degree and quality of substitution. Persian classification is more global than it is detailed, in the sense that there is no separation between *antonomasia, synecdoche,* or *prosopopoeia.* Persian tropology is simpler: *majāz* [virtual or unreal in Arabic] generally means trope, englobing all metasemic figures. On the macrostructural level, *tamṣil* is the equivalent of *allegory.* At the level of positional utterances, *este'āre* (literally "borrowing") is the equivalent of metaphor and *majāz-e morsal* is close to the concept of metonymy insofar as in the former the relationship between the substituent and the substituted is that of *shebāhat* [similarity] and that in the latter is that of *qerābat* [neighborhood/proximity]. Moreover, there is a third level of substitution, *kenāye* [implicitness] corresponding to several figures in Western rhetoric, depending on the context and the modalities of use: *synecdoche, antonomasia, catachresis,* or even *periphrasis.* What differentiates *kenāye* from the rest of tropes, according to Persian tropology, is that in *kenāye* both the proper and figurative meanings are valid in the semantic context whereas in other types of *majāz* only the secondary, figurative meaning is to be taken into account (Homāyi 1367 [1988], 256). In other words, *kenāye* is a transitional stage between figurative and real.[22] *Kenāye* occurs in Example 2.2 where two figures of speech are simultaneously used: the *simile* between intellect (*aql*) and donkey (*xar*) and *kenāye* in the syntagm "to lie in mud" which figuratively means "getting stuck due to clumsiness and stupidity." The other example is 4.1 where the first literal meaning of "dropping the veil" can be taking in the sense of "[a woman] revealing her face," whereas the figurative meaning is closer to the contextual field of indication: "revealing the secrets."[23]

The omnipresence of tropes in Rumi's poetry can be exemplified by any ghazal randomly chosen from our corpus: in G. 1759 of the *Divan,* for instance, at least one case of trope can be found in every single one of the 12 couplets.[24]

Example 5.5 D) G. 1759, l.1,4

Vah che birang o **bineshān** ke manam Baḥr-e man gharqe gasht andar khʷish	kei bebinam marā chonān ke manam bol ʿajab baḥr-e bikarān ke manam
Wow! How colorless and traceless I am! My ocean sank in itself Stupor!	When will you see me the way I am?! What a shoreless ocean I am!
E1) Ls: p. 159–160: OH, HOW colorless and formless I am! When will I ever see the am that I am? My sea has drowned within itself; what a strange and shoreless sea I am!	E2) Hom: p. 70–71: **What Am I?** Colors and features I've none when will I see myself? Lay open your secrets, my soul says. My sea drowns in itself what a boundless ocean I am
F1) Taj: p. 294–296: **LA LANGUE N'EST PAS ARRIVÉE** Ah! Que sans la moindre couleur Et sans aucun signe je suis! Et quand donc pourrai-je me voir Enfin comme vraiment je suis ? Mon océan, c'est en lui-même Que lui aussi il s'est noyé. Quelle stupeur, cet océan Sans aucun bord, et que je suis.	F2) Lel: p. 48–49 **"Moi"** Oh oui, je suis sans couleur et sans signe moi! Quand me verrai-je tel que je suis moi! Mon océan s'est noyé en lui-même Étonnant océan sans rivage que je suis moi!

This example shows that even though the re-creation of discursive forms can be quasi-impossible, the transposition of tropes in the TT is only a matter of the translator's choice. There is obviously no difficulty in recreating the discursive form of the tropes of the ST in the target language, certainly with some stylistic liberties on the translator's part. Things get complicated however, with the translation of *bineshān* [featureless, traceless], which is a *kenāye* [periphrasis] for "insignificance". "Look how insignificant I am!" Although a literal translation can preserve the discursive form, the connotative semantic charge in the St cannot be conveyed to the target languages. In Persian, the idiomatic compound *bi nam o neshān* [without name or trace] is a fixed expression, a conventional metaphor that has no equivalent in the target languages. At a higher level, the fact of being *bineshān*, empty and insignificant, is an allusion to the state of selflessness aspired by mystics, not only in the Persianate world but also in all Vedic traditions. The second verse of this line is a rhetorical question reinforcing the argument proposed in the first verse: since there is no sign or color of me, since I am effaced, how can I even perceive *me*? The choice of object pronoun *marā* [me] instead of reflexive pronoun *khod* or *khʷish* [myself] is also a significant choice, suggesting that the speaker is in *ex-tasy*: he is *standing outside* himself and looking at *him* not from within but without. This effect is totally lost in French translations due to the impossibility of recreating the discursive form: in French the first person reflexive pronoun and object pronoun are the same. However, this loss could have been avoided in English, yet isn't so in E2. Lewisohn, on the other hand, finds an ingenious solution to compensate for this loss by manipulating the infradiscoursive purport of English: *am* ceases to be a verb to become a direct object: "When will I ever see the am that I am?"

Beyt 4 offers different challenges as Rumi's surreal symbolic imagery at its peak: "the ocean of me/my ocean" forms a metaphorical phrase (*eẓāfe-ye tashbihi* [comparative phrase]) by which the poet compares himself to an ocean and, as a result of the personification of the ocean, attributes a human act to it: the ocean sinks in the ocean. However, the same phrase could be interpreted differently while still being translated in the same way. It could be read as a *majāz-e morsal* [metonymy] in which *baāhr-e man* means *the ocean within me*; it is not "me" that is an "ocean" but the ocean that is contained in "me" and "I" am the container. The *content* is then taken for the *container*, thus creating a metonymy. The second verse of the line takes up the metaphor formulated in the first verse and reshapes it in a predicative relation and now changes the image into a metaphor. The translations all do more or less justice to the imagery, which is well recovered in the two target languages. This shows the ease of translating tropes in their discursive structure since both readings of the same trope can be had in both target languages. The difficulty is not of a linguistic but of an interpretative nature.

4.2 Translation and Cultural Gap

4.2.1 Variations in the Fields of Interpretation

To put it simply, the principal source of this difficulty is the distance that separates the initial field of indication and the secondary field of interpretation that results in the absence of certain objects and forces in the secondary field. As previously discussed, tropes represent a conflictual utterance insofar as their primary literal meaning is shadowed by a secondary figurative one and the field of indication is formed primarily around *deixis am phantasma*. The conflictual structure of the field of indication can only be accrued in the corresponding field of interpretation. Now in the case of translation, the conflicts in the semantic structure of original utterances increase exponentially in the field of interpretation of the TL reader. This is because translation is in itself a new act of communication with its own fields of indication and interpretation. In the translation process, the two fields are doubled in the sense that the translator is once the receiver of the message, hence in a primary field of interpretation, and subsequently the sender of the same message, ideally, hence in a secondary field of indication. Any complexity, conflict, or variations in the primary field of indication is reflected in the secondary field of indication and *a fortiori*, the secondary field of interpretation, that of the TT reader. This is due to the nature of re-enunciation where the secondary fields are partially functions of the primary ones. The possibilities of interpretation increase exponentially with the rising combination of constituent indexical elements.

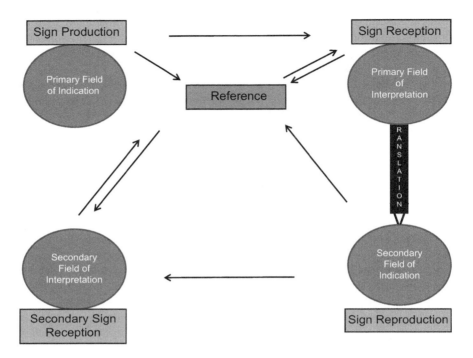

Figure 5.2 Fields of indication and interpretation in translation

The further apart the source and target languages and cultures are, the greater the conflictual forces in the secondary fields will be in relation to the primary ones. To make an analogy with target shooting, the slightest movements of the shooter will result in large variations of the bullet placement down range. The longer the distance between the shooter and the target, the greater the variations caused by the same movement. Given the cultural distance between the source and the target polysystems in the case of Rumi's poetry, one can imagine how the slightest variation in the indexical forces and objects of the translated text can result in missing the target. In other words, the complexity of the transfer of figurative meaning in mystical poetry stems from two sources: on the one hand, the conflictual character of the poetic metasemic utterance blurring the primary, and hence the secondary, fields of indication and interpretation; on the other, the absence of pertinent referential indices or even the false resemblance of these indices due to the cultural gap.

In his theory of poetic imagery, Shafi'i Kadkani explains that imagery in the text is realized on two axes, a horizontal one and a vertical one. The vertical axis refers to the construction of images (tropes or other imaginative devices such as *hyperbole*) by the substitution of real meaning for a figurative one at the microstructure of the figure. The horizontal axis corresponds to the macrostructural presence of images in the discourse. In the *Neynāme*, one can find a vertical organization of the images at almost every couplet, for instance the metaphor of tearing the veils (l.11). But the allegory of the *ney* – the symbol of the individual longing for the reunion with his primordial origins and the chagrined lover lamenting about separation – constitutes a horizontal axis throughout the poem. Similarly, the resumption of the metaphorical use of *parde* [veil, musical note] constitutes a network of images deployed on a horizontal macrodiscoursive plane. The significance of the imagery rests at least partially on the horizontal plane of images without which isolated tropes lose part of their semiotic value. This horizontal network constitutes a fairly pertinent field of indication. However, this semantic network of images cannot always be preserved in the TT.

One obstacle is obviously linguistic: the word *parde* cannot be translated in the same way throughout the text. Translation of disparate extracts does not help either because the recontextualization of individual images by the translator cuts the internal underlying semantic chain. However, the greatest challenge is that the concept of veil does not carry the same connotative effect in Persian language and culture, in the Sufi *idiom*, in Rumi's *sufiolect*, and in the TL and culture. The metasemic utterance is placed in a broader field of indication formed not only by linguistic indices but also by a set of social, cultural, ideological, political, and aesthetic data. This set provides a certain number of reference points, milestones, and clues that facilitate understanding. By migrating to the TL and culture, this field is fundamentally altered; it loses some of its objects and forces and gains other new elements native to the new environment. Example 5.6 demonstrates how some allegories and allusions to Islamic sources can be hard to translate or, rather, easy to translate literally without losing their original field of indication for the target reader.

Example 5.6 MIII) l.1766–1768

> If he says faults, don't call him faulty
> If the martyr is full of blood don't wash it
> Blood is better than water for martyrs
> This fault is worth more than a hundred good deeds
> Inside the *Kaaba* there is no question of *qibla*
> What does it matter if the diver has no shoes?

The three metaphors here are in fact cases of *kenāye* insofar as they have two semantic layers, a perfectly acceptable literal meaning, and a more distant figurative meaning, both making the same point: the spirit of law is more important than its letter. Contrary to common Islamic jurisprudence, dead bodies must be washed according to specific rituals before inhumation, yet the bodies of martyrs are an exception: no need for treatment and embalmment. Moreover, blood is considered untouchable (*najes*) in Islamic law but, again, as Rumi argues, the martyr's blood is "better and cleaner than water." The other image, less invested in specific prediscoursive contextual data is the fact that inside the *Ka'aba* there is *qibla*, geometrically speaking. Finally, the point of the third metaphor, a rhetorical question, is quite clearly made because of the cultural universality of the image. Therefore, the three metaphors deploy different degrees of hermeticism ranging from nil (the diver's not needing shoes) to the highest degree of complexity (the martyr's blood not being unclean) where understanding certainly requires a fair amount of expertise in Islamic law on the Western reader's part. The second meaning in the metaphor of the martyr is distant enough in time that even the average Persian-speaking reader is likely not to grasp the author's intent despite understanding the content of the utterance. In brief, the recipient of the message in a foreign language, even though there exists an identical re-enunciation of the message in its full discoursive form, would *a fortiori* not be able to understand the utterance without additional information provided by an explanatory and exegetic note by the translator. Apart from Nicholson, whose commentaries on the text are features in separate volumes from the translation, no translator has provided any note on this verse.

The extralinguistic pieces of information helping to grasp the secondary meaning of these images are all of a deictic – or imaginary (*am phantasma*) deictic – kind in the sense that they hint to external sources (Islamic jurisprudence). There are also examples of *anaphoric* hints, i.e., ones that refer to information within the text. This is the case of the digressive passage of MII on love (for Shams), from 1.109 to 1.142 in the middle of the tale, where the poet, roused by the mention of the name of his beloved, as if struck by lightning, goes on one of the most incendiary amorous serenades in Persian literature. The knowledge of the name "Shams" [Sun] constitutes an anaphoric clue. Two semic isotopes, sun and love, reappear in different forms, each time creating a different exquisite metaphor. The uninformed recipients of the message find themselves faced with a series of vivid metaphors whose focal point is the sun, without suspecting the double meaning of the statements displaying cases of *kenāye* and not simply *este'āre*. Cases of intratextual references to Rumi's own work are abundant, especially in the *Masnavi* given the period of its composition at the end of Rumi's life and its didactic genre. In these cases, translators' informative notes could be a good means of establishing coherence without hurting the discoursive form of the ST. As Cordonnier points out (Cordonnier 1995, 181–186) regarding intertextuality, misunderstandings and confusion that arise may be the result of insufficient translation. Establishing consistency is an important aspect of the practice of translation, and the secondary field of indication can be enriched by translators' relevant, factual, and explanatory data.

4.2.2 Cultural Cognates and Faux-amis

The wealth of Rumi's imagery is not always difficult to restitute in the TT because the secondary field of interpretation is fairly close to the primary field of indication, especially for Western educated readers. Common cultural referents in

Iranian and Western cultures are to be thanked for this relative ease of communication. In addition to biblical stories and characters,[25] there are multiple references to ancient Greco-Roman mythological characters whose presence in the Persianate culture is due to the vast influence of the Hellenistic era on both the Western world and the Persianate world, as well as Rumi's proximity to the land of Rum (Anatolia).

Example 5.7 D) G. 527, 1.7

Merrikh bogzārad nari, daftar besuzad moshtari Mah rā namānad mahtari, shādiy-ye u bar gham zanad
Mars will leave virility, Jupiter will burn the Book No grandeur will be left for the Moon; its joy will turn to sadness
E1) Ls: p. 149: Mars drops its manliness, Jupiter's celestial books burn up The moon wanes in grandeur, its joy turns to grief
F1) Vo: p. 263–264: Mars perdra sa bravoure, Jupiter brûlera le Livre du monde, La Lune ne gardera pas son empire, sa joie sera ternie de chagrin.
F2) Taj: p. 207–209: Mars a perdu virilité,[26] Feu au livre de Jupiter,[27] Plus de majesté pour la Lune Et sa joie frappe un rythme triste,

Some of the images of G. 527 (also cited in Example 4.2) exhibit a great deal of cultural proximity to the Western world, with imagery focused on celestial bodies and multiple references to Greek mythology and astrology. The first verse is a metonymy in which the acts of the stars are associated with the mythological roles of the gods representing them: Mars, Roman god of war, symbol of bravery, and Jupiter, the keeper of the Book of the world. This figure is part of a broader imagery deployed on multiple lines of this poem, showing by hyperbole the consequences of the release of a breath from the soul of the lover. The entire cannot endure for a moment the sight of God if s/he manifests his/her true self. As Example 5.8 shows, literal translation isn't problematic in any of the target languages, although Tajadod has chosen to include explanatory notes to clarify the message further. On the other hand, this proximity should not be exaggerated and the ease of interpretation of common cultural reference points naively taken for granted. Despite the universalism of his message, Rumi still belongs to the Islamic and Iranian world and his use of common biblical or pagan intertextual references may differ from the Western narrative, as evidenced by the character of Khizr, of utmost mystical importance in Sufism and in the tales of the *Masnavi*.

Example 5.8 MII) l.125

In nafas jān dāmanam bartāftast Bu-ye pirāhān-e yusof yāftast	
On this breath (at this moment), the soul has grabbed my skirt It has found the perfume of Joseph's shirt	
E1) Nim: p. 9–11: At this moment my Soul[28] has plucked my skirt: he has caught the perfume of Joseph's vest.	E2) Nir: p. 175–176: My soul plucks my skirt: she has caught the perfume of Joseph's vest.[29]
E3) Moj: Vol.1, p. 10–13: Hosamoddin has flung me by my skirt So I can breathe in scent from Joseph's shirt:[30]	E4) Will: p. 16–19: Upon this breath my soul has scorched my skirt and caught the perfume of the shirt of Joseph,

This example displays multiple metaphors found in the fiery digressive passage on love and the sun in the middle of the lovesick maiden. The first verse deploys two metaphorical images – or rather two cases of *kenāye*: "on this breath" means "at this moment" and "grabbing someone's skirt" implies "soliciting insistently." The second verse is an allusive metaphor to the biblical-Koranic story of Jacob and his son Joseph. According to the Koran, Jacob's sight, lost by dint of weeping during years of separation from his beloved son, is restored by the smell of his son's shirt. The figurative meaning of "finding the scent of Joseph's shirt" is "to reach salvation." The speaker is expressing his jubilation and effervescence as soon as the memory of his beloved is conjured by the recollection of his/her name. Meanwhile, the anecdote concerning the recovery of Jacob's sight triggered by the scent of Jacob's shirt does not exist in the Old Testament. We can therefore see how intertextual references to Jacob and his son Joseph that are understandable in both source and target cultures can actually be a source of confusion. Indeed, Mojaddedi chose to add an explanatory note citing the original Koranic verse. Nicholson did the same but only in a later commented version of his translation.[31]

The two previous examples draw our attention to what I call cultural cognates and *faux amis*, in reference to lexemes of the same root in two languages that have the same meaning – i.e., cognates – or ones that have partially or totally different meanings – i.e., *false friends*. Cultural false friends occur when the same concept is associated with different connotations between source and target polysystems. The divergence in connotations stems from significant differences in the structures and compositions of the primary field of indication and of the secondary fields of indication and interpretation. This difference is due to variations in the connotative value of utterances, itself a function of time and space. In the same way that language and idiom (code and norm), which constitute the linguistic field of indication, are subject to diatopic and diachronic variants, the interpretative value, i.e., the possible understandings of the message, can be subject to similar changes. The result is the divergence between the author's *a priori* intent – fluid and unstable though it might be according to the partisans of postmodern new criticism – and the reader's *a posteriori* understanding. In less technical terms, the semantic content of the discourse as well as its message (referent) take various interpretative directions and hermeneutic dimensions depending on the sociocultural context of reception. Variations in the fields of indication and interpretation are more significant in established texts such as medieval mystical poetry with totally different circumstances between the genesis of the ST, the genesis of the TT, and the reception of the TT. They are also more important between culturally distant polysystems.

In Prandi's definition, the field of indication is a set of real objects and forces that confer on the index its positional value, just as magnetic electromagnetic force fields determine the value and orientation of physical objects inside them. In consequence, bacchanalian images of wine drinking in the company of moon-faced, silver-bosomed female cupbearers omnipresent in Sufi poetry from Sanāyi to Khomeini[32] cannot be understood in the same way within its own Iranian culture as in the Western cultures. It is in fact the very discursive form of the text that varies depending on the quality, composition, and disposition of objects and forces within the field of interpretation. Referring to its most basic definition evoked in Chapter 2, *form* is a type of relation between two points on a continuum: form corresponds to rupture at a specific point on the continuum of the *control space* creating a positional difference. *Difference* implies relation between two points of the control space. What makes *man* meaningful is the difference that separates it from all other possible phonemic combinations: *nam, jan, mon*, etc. The semantic form of *man* [adult male human] takes shape in its difference from *woman* [adult female human].

According to this definition, a change of relations in the field of interpretation implies a change of the semantic discursive form of the message as it is understood, because a message is only a message when it is received and interpreted by someone.[33] In this sense, even such fundamental concepts as *love, wine,* and the beloved's *hair* conjure up completely different pictures and have fundamentally divergent connotative effects when they are placed within the field of interpretation of a 21st-century Western reader or that of a practicing Muslim. The same concepts are understood in a completely different way since the positional relation between the normal term "God" in a religious discourse and the abnormality of a singing female cupbearer in décolleté to refer to the same referent is not the same in the two fields of interpretation. To refer to the love of God, *mey* [wine] cannot mean the same for a Muslim, for whom alcohol is *harām* by sharia, as for a Catholic for whom wine is the blood of Christ and is imbibed in the Eucharist every Sunday. The image of wine drinking in the words of a theologian like Rumi cannot have the same effect on an Iranian reader, who could be punished for drinking alcohol, as on a French reader who drinks wine at almost every meal. Similarly, a notion as banal as "love" has radically different positional values depending on the field of interpretation shaped by theological forces: depending on the context, Islamic or Christian, the romantic feelings towards God don't feel exotic to all in the same way. In a religion where the Son of God sacrifices himself on the cross out of *love* for mankind, where the word "love" is a leitmotiv of every homily, the image of *love* cannot have the same strength or feel as exotic and original as in a religion where the term is not found a single time in its holy scriptures.

4.3 Conflicts of Meaning, Conflicts of Interpretation

4.3.1 The Polemic of Mystical Symbolism

Mystical symbolism in general and Rumi's imagery in particular have traditionally been subjected to a naïve simplistic reductionism. The semantic conflict of Rumi's metasemic language has led to a hermeneutic conflict between two opposing views. The first more traditional idea is that a mystical metaphor is purely symbolic and refers directly to pure spiritual realities. There is no first-level reference to earthly realities such as erotic love. The second view sees in the bacchanalian images of mystical poetry some form of poetic lyricism and romantic eroticism entirely devoid of any mystical intent.

There is a myriad of positions between these two poles, but they can all be measured according to their distance from the two extremes. This opposition regarding the interpretation of Rumi's poetry exists in the source language and culture, and to some extent in the Sufi milieux of the entire Islamic world and, as Leonard Lewisohn argues (1989), among Western orientalists as well. In a sense, this hermeneutic dialectic has its roots in conflicting views over the nature of mysticism in Islam and its relation to the core tenets of this Abrahamic religion (see Introduction). At the core of this dialectic rests the question of whether Sufism should even be regarded as an endogenous mystic movement to Islam, or if it should be seen as part of an Indo-Iranian reaction – not unlike Shiism itself – to an ideological and civilizational onslaught from Semitic religions.

Even among scholars who have a nonpolemical conception of Iranian mysticism and its relation to Islam, the question of mystical metasemia, more commonly referred to as Sufi symbolism, is still a problematic one and subject to interminable debates. Lewisohn summarizes two pertinent positions in the field of classical Persian literary criticism in the West:

1 Scholars such as A. J. Arberry and more recently Michael Hillmann, and Annemarie Schimmel, who treat the Persian ghazal form primarily from an aesthetic and literary standpoint, usually interpret the Sufi motifs . . . as an 'imposed allegory.' The truly allegorical quality in Sufi poetry is seen as a disguise for eroticism, and the metaphysical, archetypal nature of the ghazal is considered as a whitewash over a profane romanticism. They speak of tensions to resolve the dichotomy of erotic and metaphysical love, hence using concepts which unconsciously reflect, as Henry Corbin observed, the situation of *conscience maheureuse*.

2 Those who approach the ghazal as a statement of archetypal logopoeia, that is to say, as a communication derived from the imaginal world (*'âlam-e methâl*)

or the realm of archetypal significances (*'âlam-e ma'nâ*), understand it as an expression of precise symbolic meanings working systematically at a supraconscious associative level.

(Lewisohn 1989, 177–178)

Lewisohn, himself member of the second school,[34] seeks to apply the principle of *logopoeia* not only to Iranian metaphysical doctrines at a macrodiscoursive level like many others have done, but also at the microstructural level of poetic symbols. Lewisohn's metaphysical theory applied to the field of aesthetics relies on the hermeneutics of mystical language formulated by the 14th-century Iranian thinker Mahmoud Shabestari in the *Masnavi of Golshan-e Rāz* [Garden of Mystery]. Developing Rumi and other mystical thinkers' view that natural language with its dialectical modes of signification is unable to communicate archetypal meaning,[35] Shabestari considers the "language of the *heart*" as the only way to understand and communicate transcendence. The speaker, i.e., the mystical poet, artist, or musician, uses a surface language that communicates meanings to the mind but, in depth, the true archetypal meaning is "tasted by the heart-savor" (*zowq* [taste]) of the initiated purified mystic.

Shabestari's theory of aesthetics is based on a science of mystical states, rather than the study of rhetoric and prosody. It is an aesthetics of intoxication, an awareness of the non-sensible and supernatural, the heart's own humour, an *aesthesis* and appreciation of beauty to which the external eye and ear are only a mute audience, rather than direct participants. Every word, phrase, or turn of speech in the lexicon of the Sufi symbolist poets conveys an intricate ecstatic 'taste' to the heart, and relays a subtle noetic light to the soul.

(Lewisohn 1989, 200)

The image[36] of direct communication "through the ears and eyes of the heart" is an attractive metaphor of what I have tried to analyze semiotically regarding Rumi's hybrid system of communication. However, the material necessities and structural modalities of this type of communication "through the heart" are not clarified. A more methodic explanation is necessary to shed light on the functioning of this gnostic realm for those who do not have the luxury of receiving the "noetic light." Shabestari's romantic account of Sufi symbolism is somewhat simplistic regarding the functioning of sign systems and semantic production. In his view, there is a fundamental dichotomy between *haqiqat* [Truth] and *majāz* [the unreal/virtual] not only in existence and universe but also in the incarnation of the *word*, i.e., of the linguistic sign in our terminology. The hermeneutic conclusion that is drawn from Shabestari's philosophy in the field of rhetoric and aesthetics is that *majāz* – which also means tropes – is only the material surface, the skin of the expression, and that the *haqiqat* – that which is to be held – is the archetypal meaning contained within the content.[37] Expressed in semiotic terms, it is as if a sign were a container holding some content. This is a naïve concept of the sign that ignores important aspects of communication such as sign function, expression and content planes, form, and substance. Indeed, I consider this view simplistic and unconstructive since it leads to the theologizing of a fundamentally hermeneutic and semiotic question. More often than not – and perhaps unconsciously – supporters of the pure metaphysical significance of Sufi symbolism and mystical imagery deny the "earthly" erotic character of the utterance. It is not a coincidence that this earthly character constitutes the first semantic value of metasemic utterances. The tenants of this view insist on the *symbolic* value of tropic signs at the expense of their *iconicity*.

Moreover, the reductionist view held by certain Western scholars and translators of Sufi literature,[38] who interpret the profane and erotic imagery of mystics as a pure symbolic code, gives the poetic discourse an exclusively religious destiny. The aesthetic dimensions and semiotic structure of mystical discourse simply disappear in favor of a theosophic dimension of the text. In this castrating perspective, Rumi's poetry becomes a type of religious hymn, a musical reinterpretation of the Koran. This approach seems disconnected from and out of touch with the complex nature of mystical imagery. In fact, it resounds like the politically motivated claims of those mystics who, to survive in a society ruled by the Islamic law, had to justify their antimonious discourse by explaining it away as a simple symbolic code, a professional jargon, a Sufi technolect. In this metalinguistic code, every sign from natural language simply corresponds to another sign: female beauty refers to God, wine is nothing but the love for God, erotic acts are acts of worship, and the aspired union is a metaphor for death and reunion with God. This is the official position promoted by Sufis in their writings. Yet one can clearly doubt the sincerity of their account. If the sacred text of the Koran has multiple layers of truth, according to Shias and Sufis, the deeper layers of which are only accessible to God's *olia* [friends of God], why should Sufi's theoretical treatises be taken at face value? If texts have such complexity, why should the official stance on Sufi symbolism be considered so simple? Furthermore, this argumentation may only partially and pragmatically justify the use of profane language in a religious context; yet the Sufi use of metaphoric imagery is not restricted to bacchanalian poetic images and profane descriptions of debauchery and intoxication. Tropes are utterances with a fundamentally conflicting semantic structure that are used in other contexts. This is especially true in Rumi's poetic discourse which, unlike that of Hafez, Sa'di, and Nezami with their high degree of allegorical lyricism, deploys an epic tone that fosters a kind of unsober and untamed mysticism. More than romantic lyricism, Rumi's poetry is teeming with images of the tearing off of veils and clothes, breaking the chains of earthly life, sacrificing the self, setting ablaze the fabric of the intellect and logic, shattering the mold of the material body, dying to oneself to reach reunion with the beloved.

4.3.2 Live Metaphor and the Symbolic Mode of Signification

My position on the interpretation of mystical texts and the conflict it generates is different. I suggest taking both the primary and the secondary meanings of the tropes of mystical poetry, i.e., their literal and figurative senses, as being equally legitimate. No meaning can be, or should be, excluded from the field of interpretation in favor of the other, no matter how conflicting or even paradoxical they may be. The inner tension of a trope is the result of a semantic dialectic whose synthesis is the combination of thesis and antithesis. There is no resolution to this tension that does not imply some sort of regrettable reductionism towards the semantic structure of the discourse.

To understand the structural tension that lies within tropes, one should refer to the very semantic structure of metasemia. As per definition, a metaphor[39] consists of a sign that has a primary meaning as well as a secondary or connotative content. In Hjelmslev's model, a metaphor is a connotative sign insofar as its first meaning constitutes the expression plane for a secondary connotative sign. Yet the main issue is to define the relation between the connotative content plane and the denotative expression or, to put it more simply, the relation between the first literal meaning of the utterance and its secondary meaning. Peirce's trichotomic division of signs into icon, index, and symbol is a useful contribution to the discussion. Icons are *natural* signs in the sense that the relation between representamen and sign object is *motivated* by natural resemblance. Conversely, a symbol is a *conventional* sign in which the relation between expression and content planes is established by convention, in the arbitrary code of the language. In this perspective, metaphor as sign belongs to the domain of icons: in a metaphorical utterance, a sign refers to another by virtue of the similarity between them. To say "the torch of the sky" to refer to "the sun" thus constitutes a metaphor by way of shared *semes* between "torch" and "sun" – source of light and heat. Iconicity, however, is not the only characteristic of all figurative utterances. In the case of worn-out metaphors, so widely used in language that they have lost their novelty, for instance "the ruby of lips" in Persian poetry, there is a degree of conventionality proportional to the familiarity of the image in a given culture. Conventionality can reach its zenith in fixed metaphors or catachresis: e.g., the arm of an armchair, the Big Apple (for NY).

The dialectical tension between the primary and secondary meanings of a metaphor can then be a function of how "*live*" a metaphor is, to use Ricœur's term. In his pivotal essay, *La Métaphore vive* (1975), on the phenomenology of tropes and metasemic discourse, Ricœur differentiates clearly between the *live* metaphors' innovative imagery and *dead* metaphors whose imagery has lost its vivacity and that have become incorporated in the linguistic and cultural norm, or even in the code, akin to clichés (Ricœur 1975, 273–321). As such, a dead metaphor has a high degree of conventionality. Clichés are conventional and arbitrary, just as simple (nonconnotative) signs of a given linguistic code. In Peirce's terminology, clichés and dead metaphors are "symbols" for which only the secondary meaning of the metasemic utterance remains while the first meaning, the expression plane of the metaphoric sign, is discarded. On the other hand, *live* metaphors are innovative and represent the epitome of *ratio difficilis*. As a reminder, *ratio difficilis* takes place when the nature of the content plane is such that no expression plane exists to stand as a sign function in relation to it. In Eco's terminology, the expression plane and the content plane are related by more than a conventional arbitrary relation. They actually have the same form with different substances. They represent newly invented signs that are added to the code. New content requires new expression to form new signs in which the formal composition of expression plane and content plane are identical. Metaphoric imagery seen under this light constitutes connotative signs in which the expression and content planes are formally (but not substantially) identical. The primary meaning or expression plane of the connotative sign should therefore not be ignored in favor of the content plane. The primary meaning is then as valid as the secondary meaning. In this light, "wine" in mystical poetry is not just a simple symbol for "divine light" and "love" as it is not a denotative sign whose expression is dropped and whose semantic content only is held. Mystical wine refers as much to the intoxicating red liquid extracted from fermented grape juice as to the divine light warming the heart of the mystic.

In very sharp contrast to the consensus held by semioticians and rhetoricians, Eco inverts the meaning of symbol and metaphor in his own terminology. He calls *metaphors* what Ricœur calls "dead metaphors," namely institutionalized clichés whose primary meaning is discarded in favor of their secondary content. Conversely, *live* metaphors, the connotative signs whose primary and secondary meanings are in a dynamic tension and are both equally valid, are described under a specific process of sign production that Eco calls the *symbolic mode of sign production* (Eco 1984, 223). For Eco, this is the apex of *ratio difficilis* and the quintessential mode of discoursivization of the kind of content that has no expression associated with it in the code. In this symbolic mode of semiotization, utterances that deploy both a literal reality and a metaphorical truth are created and are used in what Ricœur considers a *redescription* of the extralinguistic referent.[40]

The question of whether to abandon the literal meaning in favor of the metaphorical meaning is at the center of both of these authors' epistemological enterprise. Both authors demonstrate in opposing terms how certain forms of metasemic connotative signs need to be treated differently from conventional ordinary signs. In live metaphors or the symbolic mode of semiotization, unlike with dead metaphors or the allegorical mode of semiotization, both the literal and figurative meanings are bearers of sense. The symbolic mode of semiotization is the only way that the signifier can signify the signified, which is by imitating the form of the signified, since the referent is not signifiable by any other sign present in the language. As Eco argues by giving examples from the Kabbalah, this is the typical mode of expression for mystics. On the hermeneutic side, Eco evokes the kabbalist idea that a symbol is a sign whose interpretation is infinite. Because the content plane imitates the formal structure of the expression and since there is no fixed content associated with the newly created expression, a symbolic sign, in this sense, has infinite interpretation.

Ricœur places less emphasis than Eco does on the hermeneutic aspect of *live* metaphors. Ricœur argues that metaphors are the high place of an ontological tension between "being" and "not being," i.e., between the literal meaning which *is not* and the secondary figurative meaning which *is*. Live metaphors are those in which both the primary and secondary meanings *exist*. In this sense, live metaphors are the bridge between the two, between what *is* and what *is not*, i.e., they *are* and *are not* at the same time. On the interpretation side, there is an ontological tension at the heart of metaphor. This tension can only be solved case by case. The ability both to mean and not to mean is what Sufis call the "language of heart," which conveys meaning only to the pure heart of the mystic endowed by *zowq* [taste].

I have tried to show that Rumi's hybrid connotative sign system constitutes the perfect example of a symbolic mode of signification in Persian mystical literature. Despite the presence of dead metaphors – mostly clichés – most of Rumi's poetic imagery (such as "I am more wine than you are") is characterized by provocative innovation unequaled in his classical times, so much so that some of his utterances can sound absurd. Rumi's metaphor is metaphor *par excellence*, i.e., its literal meaning cannot simply be dismissed in the name of some codified Sufi technolect or religious ideology, neither by Muslim institutional Sufis nor their Western scholars. On the infradiscoursive side, most of his uses of tropes can be reproduced in the TT. This means that the field of indication can more or less be recreated in the translated text. It is on the interpretative side, however, that most translations become problematic because of a simple but unfortunate fact: most translators of Rumi's poetry are either fervent supporters of the reductionist theologizing view, who interpret the metasemic utterance exclusively in religious terms, or modern popularizing retranslators who romanticize and lyricize an infinitely complex discourse by their textual and paratextual choices, their deforming translations, and their distorting exegetic notes.

Notes

1 According to Shamisā (1380 [2001]), the main marker of the passage from the *Khorāsāni* school to *'arāqi* is the advent of rich content and gnostic substance in poetry.
2 I do not call the second meaning of metaphoric utterance *real* since, as I will explain, it has no superiority to the first apparent meaning.
3 See "Second-Degree Deformation" in Chapter 7.
4 For example, the three unities in French classical drama: "That in one place, on one day, one accomplished action be held until the end of the full theatre," wrote Boileau in *L'Art poétique* ([1674] 1872).
5 In a poetic form like the ghazal, multiple unrelated themes often occur in a few verses with little organizational cohesion.
6 The critical study of the Pentateuch, called the documentary hypothesis, was initiated by Julius Wellhausen (1894) and has never ceased to develop. Although with more difficulties caused by political reasons and pressure from the Muslim world, similar analytical techniques have been applied to the study of the Koran as of the late 20th century.
7 Indeed, the nonlinearity of Rumi's narration and the erasing of the plot can only be found in the works of such new novelists as Michel Butor and Alain Robbe-Grillet.
8 They were inspired by similar circular patterns in the Holy Bible.
9 This is the ending verse of *Neynāme*. TL: The state of a ripe, no raw understands / so the word must be short. *Vassalām!* [That's all].
10 These enunciative markers are of a grammatical nature such as the use of second person pronouns or comparison prepositions (like, etc.).

11 The only discrepancies in the verse sequence are due to the differences between editions.
12 Nicholson's version is also considered prose in the sense that the utterances are devoid of rhythm, meter, and rhyme. However, each couplet appears in one line or paragraph, which partially preserves the appearance of the original poem. The term "prose" has been used by both Nicholson and Arberry to describe this type of translation, although these presumed prosaic texts display more poeticity than most of the later translations, which have a vocation for poetry without really crossing the threshold of poetic prose. Thus, I differentiate this intermediate state between prose and poetry from proper prose translations exemplified by Arberry's and Kudsi's (in French), where the graphic organization of the text is properly prosaic.
13 *Tales of Mystic Meaning* (1931/2000) and *Rumi: Poet and Mystic* (1950).
14 The difference is, of course, that specialists have a mastery of the original work and know what they are doing.
15 Barks, for example, admitted in his early collections that he knew no Persian and that all his translations were, in fact, retranslations either from Nicholson's and Arberry's versions or from drafts made by a Persian-speaking colleague. In more recent editions, however, this reminder often disappears.
16 This is a deformation tendency according to Berman. See next chapter.
17 Translations are not cited here to save space.
18 Shafi'i Kadkani presents a theory of poetic imagery (*Ṣovar-e khiyāl dar she'r-e pārsi* [The Forms of Imagination in Persian Poetry] 1350 [1971]). For him, imagination is the *sine qua non* substance of poetry, and it is incarnated in poetic imagery. He includes in the notion of image, "everything that refers to an external dimension of the apparent semantics of the utterance; not only metaphor and simile and their derivatives (periphrasis, allegory, metonymy, etc.) but also hyperbole and especially personification" (1971, 38–40). In other words, the poeticity of the text relies on the presence of tropes.
19 To pick Paul Ricœur's terms.
20 Although the origins of the English proverb "A fish rots from the head down" is older than the first translations of Rumi in European languages, according to Sir James Porter (1768), a similar proverb was used in Turkish that came from M.III) l.3080: *Nafs-e avval rānd bar nafs-e dovom / Māhi az sar gande gardad ney ze dom* [the first self overruns the second self // fish rots from the head not the tail].
21 A *simile* has four components. In the utterance "her eyes shine like the sun," "her eyes" is the subject of comparison or *topic/tenor* (*moshabbah*), "the sun" is the *vehicle* or the object of comparison (*moshabbahon beh*), the preposition *like* is the comparator (*adāt-e tashbih*), and process "shine" is the event (*vajh-e tashbih*) (Homāyi 1367 [1988], 228).
22 As I will argue in the next section, most occurrences of tropes in mystical poetry should be understood as *kenāye* and not *este'āre*. In the bacchanalian and profane language of mystical poetry, the literal and primary meaning of supposedly metaphoric and metonymic utterances should not be systematically and unceremoniously dismissed in favor of a secondary hidden and esoteric meaning, as has been customary in the Islamic world.
23 This constitutes a *metonymy* in Western rhetoric by way of the cause-effect relationship: "un-veil" in English or "dé-voiler" in French.
24 If T = *tashbih*, E = *este'āre*, M = *majāz-e morsal*, and K = *kenāye*, the occurrence of tropes in each couplet is as follows: 1: K, 2: K, E, 3: E, E, 4: E, M, E, 5: E, K, 6: T, E, 7: E, K, 8: K, 9: M, 10: T, K, E, 11: M, M, 12: K, E.
25 The most important is Moses whose presence in the *Masnavi* is more ubiquitous than any other historic or religious figure, including Mohammad or Muslim saints.
26 TN: Mars is the symbol of bravery, of a warrior.
27 TN: Jupiter is the scribe of the world, hence the book.

28 TN: Husāmu'ddin.
29 TN: "My soul" said by the commentators to signify Husamu'ddin, with whom the poet feels himself mystically one. "The perfume of Joseph's vest," smelt from afar by Jacob (*Qur'an* XII, 94), describes spiritual rapture.
30 TN: *So I can breathe in scent from Joseph's shirt*: the scent of Joseph's shirt was perceived by his father Jacob before it even reached him, informing him that Joseph was still alive and restoring sight to his eyes after he had gone blind through weeping over his favorite son's disappearance (see further Koran 12: 93–96).
31 Another notable event here is Nicholson's and Mojaddedi's assumption that "soul" refers to Hesāmeddin Chalabi, Rumi's scribe. This is one of those occasions of textual polyphony where Rumi speaks of, and to, a mysterious interlocutor. This explanatory note seems over the top since it restricts the hermeneutic scope of the text with speculative information. See Chapter 6 on *second-degree deformation*.
32 Astounding as it may sound, the founder of the Islamic Republic of Iran, Ayatollah Khomeini, has a far less known side of the character: he composed several ghazals containing profane images typical of mystic poetry.
33 The definition of *intentionality* in Husserl's phenomenology is as follows: "the characteristic of consciousness whereby it is conscious of something – that is, its directedness toward an object" (*Encyclopedia Britannica*, intentionality).
34 According to him, this school of thought includes other philosophers like Henry Corbin, Seyyed Hossein Nasr, and William Chittick. Nonetheless, I argue that the case of Henry Corbin is different from those scholars who are fervent supporters of an Islamizing view of Sufism and its imagery. Corbin's position is significantly more subtle and hard to elicit from his gigantic work.
35 The creation of linguistic *form* as explained before is based on the *difference* between constituents. Communication is therefore based on the mutual agreement of the speaker and the addressee over a set of codes that *differentiate* meaningful from unmeaningful sounds. Understanding is then a dialectical process that consists in a back-and-forth movement that differentiates signs from simple sounds based on the principle of *pertinence*.
36 Because this can only be a metaphorical image itself. Lewisohn's borrowing of Shabestari and other Sufis' terms, although he does not admit it, is also an example of using figurative meaning and metaphoric imagery to make a point: taste, heart, divine light, etc. can only be understood metaphorically in a semiotic analysis.
37 This simplistic dichotomy is applied to any profound and abstract concept such as love. *'Eshqe majāzi* [virtual love] is a term used even in modern Persian, opposed to *'eshq-e ḥaqiqi* [true love]. The former signifies erotic and earthly love whereas the latter is simply love for God.
38 Vitray-Meyerovitch and Leili Anvar fall in the same category in the French-speaking world.
39 Here I use the term in the way Paul Ricœur does (*Métaphore vive* 1975), that is as a hypernym referring to all sorts of tropes.
40 In fact, Eco speaks of the same differentiation as Ricœur but in other terms: Eco's symbolic mode – the case of invention in sign production – is the equivalent of Ricœur's live metaphor, and Eco's allegorical mode – the case of repetitive innovations integrated in the code – should be understood as Ricœur's dead metaphors.

References

Anvar, Leili, interviewer par Abdennour Bidar. 2015. "La poésie mystique." *Cultures d'Islam*. France Culture, 24 April. www.franceculture.fr/emissions/cultures-d-islam/la-poesie-mystique.

Arberry, Arthur John. 1961. *Tales from the Masnavi*. London: Allen and Unwin.
Benveniste, Émile. 1974. *Problèmes de linguistique générale*. Vol. 2. Paris: Gallimard.
Boileau, Nicolas. [1674] 1872. *L'Art poétique*. Vol. 1, in *Œuvres poétiques*, edited by Nicolas Boileau, 203–211. Paris: Imprimerie générale.
Cordonnier, Jean Louis. 1995. *Traduction et culture*. Paris: Didier.
Eco, Umberto. 1984. *Semiotics and the Philosophy of Language*. London: Macmillan.
Homāyi, Jalāleddin. 1367 [1988]. *Funun-e balāghat va ṣanā'āt-e adabi* [Rhetoric Techniques and Literary Devices]. Tehrān: Nashr-e Namā.
Jakobson, Roman. 1971. *Selected Writings II. Word and Language*. The Hague: Mouton.
Keshavarz, Fatemeh. [1998] 2004. *Reading Mystical Lyric: The Case of Jalal al-Din Rumi*. Columbia, SC: University of South Carolina Press.
Lewisohn, Leonard. 1989. "Shabistari's Garden of Mysteries: The Aesthetics and Hermeneutics of Sufi Poetry." *Temenos: A Review Devoted to the Arts of the Imagination* 10: 177–207.
Pinson, Jean-Claude. 1995. *Habiter en poète: essai sur la poésie contemporaine*. Seyssel: Champ Vallon.
Porter, Sir James. 1768. *Observations on the Religion, Law, Government, and Manners of the Turks*. London: J. Nourse, Bookseller to His Majesty.
Prandi, Michèle. 1992. *Grammaire philosophique des tropes*. Paris: Minuit.
Ricœur, Paul. 1975. *Métaphore vive*. Paris: Seuil.
Safavi, Seyed Ghahreman, and Simon Weightman. 2009. *Rumi's Mystical Design: Reading the Mathnawi, Book One*. Albany: State University of New York Press.
Shafi'i-Kadkani, Moḥammad Reẓā. 1350 [1971]. *Ṣovar-e khiyāl dar she'r-e pārsi* [The Forms of Imagination in Persian Poetry]. Tehrān: Enteshārāt-e Nil.
Shamisā, Sirus. 1380 [2001]. *Sabkshenāsi-ye she'r* [Versification and Poetic Genres]. 9th ed. Tehrān: Ferdows.
Steiner, George. 1975. *After Babel, Aspects of Language and Translation*. London: Oxford University Press.
Wellhausen, Julius. 1894. *Israelitische und jüdische Geschichte*. 2 vols. Berlin: Druck und Verlag von Georg Reimer.
Whinfield, Edward Henry. 1887. *Masnavi i ma'navi: The Spiritual Couplets of Mauláná Jalálu-'d-Dín Muhammed i Rúmí*. London: Trübner.
Williams, Alan. 2006. *Rumi, Spiritual Verses, The First Book of the Masnavi-ye Ma'navi*. London and New York: Penguin Classics.
Wilson, C. E. 1910. *The Masnavī, by Jalālu 'd-Dīn Rūmī. Book II*. London: Probsthain & Co.
Wittgenstein, Ludwig. 1922. *Tractatus Logico-Philosophicus*. London: Kegan Paul, Rench, Trubner & CO.

6 On the Politics of Reception

1 Beyond Language and Discourse

Throughout my presentation, I evoked the difficulties of translating Rumi. Challenges and obstacles were presented and examined in linguistic, discoursive semiotic, poetic, rhetoric, and hermeneutic perspectives. The modalities of the translative process employed by various English translators of Rumi to overcome these obstacles were also demonstrated by examples and excerpts from the corpus. At this juncture, I will adopt a more critical approach to evaluate these modalities from the burning and controversial standpoint of translation deontology. The ethics of translation was theorized by German idealists in their 19th-century translations of classical works and their treatises on translation. They fostered a revolutionary approach to translation that involved the abandon of classical tenets of readability and elegance for a move towards the glorification of foreignness. More recently, Henri Meschonnic and Antoine Berman advocated for a similar foreignizing approach, although the latter took the translator's subjectivity as the focal point of his reflections on translation. However, no theory of translation deontology can be considered independently from the sociopolitical and ideological drive behind any reception project. Translation, like any other cultural activity, is a corollary of the socioeconomic and political forces driving human societies. Both sociocultural and ethical perspectives are useful to form a thorough understanding of the nature and modalities of reception. Most ethical theories of translation attribute what they call the "distortion" of the original text by translation to the internal forces of the translator's subjectivity or the resistance of a culture to anything foreign. Sociolinguistic theories, on the other hand, adopt a more descriptive approach to explain the same phenomena with reference to overarching macrostructural forces outside both the text and the translator.

Accordingly, in the two last chapters of this book, I turn to some of the most influential theories of translation and intercultural communications to examine the reception of Rumi's work and thought from two major perspectives: first sociopolitical and then ethical. Here, I am opting to examine the reception of Rumi in the West not from a linguistic, textual semiotic or hermeneutic standpoint or to explain phenomena by pointing at a translator's personal choices.

DOI: 10.4324/9781003157960-7

These factors may all be well at play, but more importantly, it is beneficial to analyze the Western reception of Rumi in its actual reality, its successes and failures, throughout the past two and half centuries, in the broader context of the intercultural relations between two civilizational poles, or more precisely, the Anglo-Saxon-dominated Western culture and the Iranian civilization, or better still, the Persianate *narod*.[1] This instance of intercultural communication is also the point of contact between two worldviews, two *ethos*, two epistemological paradigms.

2 Sociocultural Aspects of Reception

2.1 Functionalist Theories of Translation

Functionalist theories of translation, based on the views of Russian formalists and structuralists, mark a major turning point within translation studies in several respects: they are target-oriented, interested in the target text and its function within the target cultural space; moreover, their approach is descriptive in the sense that they neither advocate nor criticize a specific way of translating but rather examine forces determining the characteristics of translation and the modalities of reception. Finally, they set the aim and the object of the study beyond the ST and the TT or the translator's subjectivity in an attempt to focus on a higher level, namely the set of systems constituting the reception space in its multiplicity of systems: linguistic, cultural, social, political, and economic.

2.1.1 Polysystem Theory

As from the second half of the 20th century, translation studies experienced an interesting change of paradigm, described as the "cultural and ideological turn" (Munday 2012, 197). Until then, mostly concerned with linguistic aspects of the translation, i.e., the technical dimension of the transfer of utterances into languages, the discipline turned its attention to external factors that have a bearing on translation. The philosophical approach to translation spurred by German idealists and their adepts such as Berman shifted the focus from the text to the translator's subjectivity, a trend that has recently taken a whole different dimension under the influence of cognitive sciences. Functional theories of translation and the School of Tel Aviv's polysystem theory redistributed the cards by offering a comprehensive picture of translation as part of a larger cultural and literary system. The theory of polysystems by Itmar Even-Zohar and Gideon Toury (1981) examines the stakes external to the text in the process of its reception, taking into account all the systemic data of the target cultural space in its linguistic, cultural, societal, political, and economic multiplicity. This semiotic super-system is called the polysystem (Even-Zohar 1990).[2] Typically structuralist and inspired by the views of Russian formalists Tynjanov and Ejxenbaum (*Ibid.*, 1–3), this theory offers a structural model of the historical and sociological functioning of culture and of literature. The centerpiece of the theory, which has served as the basis for so many others with a sociocritical vocation, is the concept of "system":

> The idea that semiotic phenomena, i.e., sign-governed human patterns of communication (such as culture, language, literature, society), could more adequately be understood and studied if regarded as systems rather than conglomerates of disparate elements has become one of the leading ideas of our time in most sciences of man. Thus, the positivistic collection of data, taken bona fide on empiricist grounds and analyzed on the basis of their material substance, has been replaced by a functional approach based on the analysis of relations. Viewing them as systems made it possible to hypothesize how the various semiotic aggregates operate.
> (Even-Zohar 1990, 9)

Each of these semiotic phenomena – language, literature, society – constitutes a system, i.e., a set of dynamic (nonstatic) relations. These systems stand in dynamic relations with each other that comprise a set of a higher level called a polysystem: "a multiple system, a system of various systems which intersect with each other and partly overlap, using concurrently different options, yet functioning as one structured whole, whose members are interdependent" (Even-Zohar 1990, 11). Inside each system as well as the polysystem, several concepts are defined: *stratum* – the level of importance of constituent elements, their *center* or *peripheral* position, the *heterogeneity* of the systems (their differences), their functionalism – the roles they assume, and the conflict of strata in a *dynamic hierarchy*. This hierarchy in the literary polysystem consists, for example, in the central or peripheral position of an innovative or conservative literary form. A central position establishes static (texts) or dynamic (literary model) canonicity of literary forms that is constantly disputed and in a permanent conflict. If a literary aesthetic model is at the center, it pushes others towards the periphery. Translated literature or simply translation, too, is considered as a system within the literary polysystem whose secondary or primary positionality varies according to given periods and social circumstances and is to be defined at each moment. Certain factors, forces, and formal occurrences are identified as components of the literary polysystem – and consequently of translation.[3]

This diagram based on Roman Jakobson's model of communication functions (see Chapter 2, section 1.4) shows the functioning of a literary work[4] – including

```
                    INSTITUTION [context]
                    REPERTOIRE [code]
PRODUCER [addresser] ------------------------- [addressee] CONSUMER
         (writer)                                          (reader)
                    MARKET [contact/channel]
                    PRODUCT [message]
```

Figure 6.1 Constituents of the polysystem

translated texts – in its quality as a commercial product regarded in an economic exchange. Here, the functional constituents of communication are replaced with economic actors. The *product* (text) is offered by the *producer* (author/translator) to the *consumer* (reader) in the *market* (the network of distribution that includes publishers and media owners). The literary *repertoire* with the various degrees of canonization of works and genres governs the creation and distribution of cultural products in the same way as the linguistic code rules the creation of discourse. However, the concept of *institution* as context seems somewhat contrived in this model insofar as the set of agents involved in a sociocultural activity can hardly be understood as the referential context of literary production.[5] In fact, it is hard to imagine that a *product*, albeit deeply influenced by the *institution*, is entirely determined by it in the same way as the content of the *message* is by the extralinguistic reference (context). In polysystem theory, which is better applicable to a socioeconomic analysis of reception than to a political one,[6] the central concept remains *repertoire* and not *institution*. Evan-Zohar uses Pierre Bourdieu's concept of *champ de production* in his description of *institution*. In Bourdieu's view, the champ de production can shape the habits and expectations of the reader-consumer.

> What 'makes famous' is not the Rastignacs of the provinces, as one may naively believe, such and such 'influential' person, such and such institution, journal, magazine, academia, cenacle, merchant, or publisher. It is not even all those called "the personalities of the world of arts and letters". It is the field of production as a system of objective relations between these agents or these institutions and a place of struggle for the monopoly of the power of consecration where the value of works and the belief in this value are continuously generated.
>
> (Bourdieu cited in Even-Zohar 1990, 38)

This description seems to correspond to the concept of *repertoire* rather than that of *institution*:

> "Repertoire" designates the aggregate of rules and materials which govern both the making and use of any given product. . . . If the most conspicuous manifestation of literature is considered to be "texts," then the literary repertoire is the aggregate of rules and items with which a specific text is produced and understood.
>
> (Even-Zohar 1990, 39–40)

Be that as it may, the key element of this theory that may apply to the process of reception is the position of given texts or genres in the repertoire. The canonicity of a product is defined by its relation to the center of the repertoire, i.e., its *primary* or *secondary* position. The text (static canon) or the literary model (dynamic canon) that is at the center of the repertoire constitutes the canon of the system that can be composed of elements deemed more or less conservative or innovative. According to the theory of the polysystem, translation generally occupies a secondary position in the literary repertoire, at the periphery of the literary polysystem of the target language-culture. There are three specific cases where translation holds a primary position: (1) when a literature is "young": French literature in the Renaissance, German Romantic literature, Hebrew literature in the 20th century; (2) the literary system is peripheral or weak in itself and is dominated by a foreign language-culture, for example, in case of colonial literature; and (3) the recognition of a "gap" or a "vacuum" in the system, following a radical change, such as a revolution, or simply in the historical absence of a specific literary form or a series of ideas: the advent of Romanticism in France after the French Revolution or the translation of works on psychoanalysis translated en masse from German into English or French. I postulate that the latter situation explains the various waves of translation of mystical poetry into English in the late 19th century or more recently.

2.1.2 Interference and Translation Norms

These situations aside, translation is a secondary literary activity. In its secondary status, it allows itself to be shaped by the conventional norms established by the literary forms and types dominating in the target polysystem. It even becomes a factor of conservatism by contributing to the consolidation of the central repertoire, the canon, of the target language-culture.[7]

> [Literary polysystem and] translated works do correlate in at least two ways: (a) in the way their source texts are selected by the target literature, the principles of selection never being uncorrelatable with the home co-systems of the target literature (to put it in the most cautious way); and (b) in the way they adopt specific norms, behaviors, and policies – in short, in their use of the literary repertoire – which results from their relations with the other home co-systems. These are not confined to the linguistic level only but are manifest on any selection level as well. Thus, translated literature may possess a repertoire of its own, which to a certain extent could even be exclusive to it.
> (Even-Zohar 1990, 46)

The relationship between two polysystems is established mainly through translation but is not restricted to it; there are also other forms of intertextuality like translation-imitation and adaptation. Goethe's *West-östlicher Divan* or Rückert's *Ghaselen* are examples of the latter. These relations whereby a certain literature A, a source literature, becomes a source of direct or indirect loan for a literature B, the target literature, is called *interference*. Evan-Zohar summarizes the modalities of interference as follows:

1 **General principles of interference**: 1.1. Literatures are never in non-interference. 1.2. Interference is mostly unilateral. 1.3. Literary interference is not necessarily linked with other interference on other levels between communities.

2   **Conditions for the emergence and occurrence of interference**: 2.1. Contacts will sooner or later generate interference if no resisting conditions arise. 2.2. A source literature is selected by prestige. 2.3. A source literature is selected by dominance. 2.4. Interference occurs when a system is in need of items unavailable within itself.
3   **Processes and procedures of interference**: 3.1. Contacts may take place with only one part of the target literature; they may then proceed to other parts. 3.2. An appropriated repertoire does not necessarily maintain source literature functions. 3.3. Appropriation tends to be simplified, regularized, schematized.

(Even-Zohar 1990, 59)

These rules, principles, and modes of interference form the cornerstone of the polysystem theory in terms of translation. As demonstrated later, most of these principles pertinently apply to the phenomenon of *Rumimania* given that the source repertoire has not preserved its original canonical function in the target polysystems, and the appropriation tends to distort the ST to match it to the standards and norms of the target polysystem. These last two processes of interference serve especially as the basis for the definition of a set of translation laws and standards by Evan-Zohar's successor, Gideon Toury, who offers a descriptive translation theory in an attempt to surpass a translation studies dominated until then by the linguistic paradigm of *equivalence* and *correspondence* – see Nida and Taber (1969) and Nida (1975).[8] Toury borrows from sociology the notion of *norm*, which he defines as the implementation of certain ideas or commonly shared values, with regard to what is good or bad, adequate or inadequate, in the form of practical instructions applicable to specific situations, and directives that show what is permitted or prohibited, banned or tolerated in this situation (Toury 1995, 55). Translation is an operation deeply governed by norms, imposed by the source culture or the target system.

Toury opposes *acceptable* translation, that which approaches the *initial norms* of the source polysystem, to *adequate* translation, that which respects the *initial norms* of the target polysystem. The characteristics and predispositions of translation (and not the distorting tendencies of translator, as Berman argues) are described in the light of the position, primary or secondary, of translation within the repertoire of the target polysystem. In addition to the initial *norms*, there are *primary norms* that govern the choice of source texts, or *translation policy*. For instance, *directness of translation* is a norm that determines the acceptability of indirect translations, carried out by passing through a third language. *Operational norms* relate to the requirement of completeness of the TT (*matricial norms*) and deletions, in addition to textual and linguistic norms pertaining to lexical, syntagmatic, and stylistic choices in the TT. Based on the empirical observation of these norms in motion in the TT, Toury seeks to identify "universals of translation" that he calls *laws*.[9] According to the *law of growing standardization*, "in translation source-text textemes tend to be converted into target-language (or target-culture) repertoremes," as a consequence of which, "textual relations obtaining in the original are often modified, sometimes to the point of being totally ignored, in favour of [more] habitual options offered by a target repertoire" (Toury 1995, 268). In other words, the discursive form tends to allow itself to be normalized to become compliant with the target operational norms, on the one hand, and the position of the text tends to differ from the target repertoire, on the other. Moreover, as a general rule, a text in primary position at the center of the source polysystem can be at the periphery of the target polysystem. The *law of interference* dictates, "In translation, phenomena pertaining to the make-up of the source text are transferred to the target text . . . the more the make-up of a text is taken as a factor in the formulation of its translation, the more the target text can be expected to show traces of interference (*Ibid.*, 275–276). This interference, which can take a *negative* or *positive* form, is met with *resistance* from target communities, who can show varying degrees of *tolerance*. The apparent contradiction of these opposing laws is resolved in a dialectical relationship determined by the position, status, and function of the TT in the target polysystem:

> The more peripheral this status, the more translation will accommodate itself to established models and repertoires. . . . tolerance of interference – and hence the endurance of its manifestation – tend to increase when translation is carried out from a 'major' or highly prestigious language/culture, especially if the target language/culture is 'minor', or 'weak' in any other sense.
>
> (Toury 1995, 271 & 278)

2.2 For a Typology of Reception[10]

It would be interesting to examine the applicability of the polysystem theory to the reception of Rumi. The position of Rumi's work within the target polysystems can reveal valuable information about the composition of the target polysystems and the initial norms to which the text was subjected, elucidating the origins of interferences or standardizations that texts have undergone in various eras. As mentioned in our Introduction, Rumi has been *directly* translated into English, French, German, Italian, Russian, Swedish, and, most recently, Spanish among European languages. Translations into other languages have been via English or French. The three major receiving languages, English, German, and French, are also the precursors of reception from Persian literature. Generally, these polysystems, along with Russian, are the ones with the highest mutual interference with Iran, although, quite surprisingly, a full translation of the *Masnavi* only came recently in Russian. English is the language with the largest number of translations, followed far behind by French and German.

An effective breakdown of the reception should be both diachronic and diatopic. Four major polysystems can be recognized in terms of the reception of Rumi in the West: the German polysystem, the French polysystem, the British polysystem, and the Anglo-American one. The English-speaking world is made up of geographic zones due to the cultural and chronological gap that separates the United Kingdom of the end of the 19th and the beginning of the 20th century from the North America of the second half of the 20th century. Later on, the convergence of cultural markets on both sides of the Atlantic on the one hand, and the advent of digital technology which dematerializes the space for the exchange of products – cultural products in particular – on the other hand, make it possible to assume an English-speaking globalized polysystem that unites North America with the rest of the English-speaking world (in Europe or Australia). Apart from the availability of multinational publishers like Penguin and Routledge active on both sides of the Atlantic, the access to English-language publications via the Internet through websites such as Amazon radically transforms the nature of polysystems. For all these reasons, it seems relevant to speak of a contemporary Anglo-American polysystem whose center of gravity is in North America nowadays. Figures 6.2 and 6.3 show a chronological breakdown of the reception in the major Western target polysystems with the longest history of reception.

Classic English Translations		Modern English Translations		
Orientalists (UK)	Specialists (UK)	Specialists	New Wave (US)	
			Professionnels	Amateurs
William Jones		*Chittick* (US)	Garbett (1956)	*Shiva*
Redhouse		*Lewis* (US)	Harvey	*Khalili*
Whinfield	Nicholson		Barks	
			Helminsky	*Homayounfar*
Wilson		Schimmel (US)	*Ergin*	*Mafi*
			Cowan	*Anvar (Iraj)*
	Arberry	*Mojaddedi* (UK)	Star	
			Saberi	*Maufroy*
			Gamard	*Houshmand*
		Williams (UK)	...	...
1794-1910	1898-1979	1984-2007	1988-2020	

Figure 6.2 Chronology of Rumi's reception in the Anglosphere[11]

French Translation				
Wallenbourg	Robin	Tchelebi	Tajadod	Jambet
Baudry				Vitray-Meyerovitch
Anvar				
1850-1900	1950-1980		1987-2020	
German Translation				
Hammer-Purgstall	Rückert	Schimmel	Engen	Hopfgartner
Höschle				
Platen Rosen	Rosenzweig		Bürgel	Maschajechi
Mezler				
1818-1927	1978-1995		1995-2020	

Figure 6.3 Chronology of Rumi's reception in other polysystems

These figures demonstrate the large number and diversity of translators in the Anglosphere followed by Germany, compared to France. Also, the chronological distribution of translations in the German and Anglo-Saxon polysystems are almost identical with a strong presence of classical translations, even stronger in the case of German, followed by a relatively long silence and then the phenomenal resurgence of translations as of the late 20th century and culmination in sheer bestselling status in the 21st century.

2.2.1 Classic Translations

I call "classic" any translation that appeared in the 19th or the first half of the 20th centuries. Classic translations include most of the translations made from the original text in all three polysystems. These texts appeared when translation, especially from Oriental languages, was in a secondary position in the British polysystem. However, contrary to Toury's theory, their peripheral position did not necessarily make them *acceptable*. As our examples show, most English translations are of relatively high quality even those in verse, such as Redhouse's. However, the sheer paradox are Nicholson's and Arberry's translations that are the epitome of *adequate* translation even compared to modern translations by academics. This may be due to the fact that these texts had a relatively small audience in the late Victorian and Edwardian eras and did not follow the general norms imposed by the institutions. In general, the influence of German Romanticism should not be forgotten. The demand for exotic literature and the discovery of Indo-European roots in the East had resulted in an unprecedented flood of translated literature from Persian and, to a lesser extent, from other languages of the Islamic world.

From a historical perspective and taking into consideration the diachronic variations of the language, classical translations can be considered to offer the most appropriate style given their perceived archaism and the fact that it matches Rumi's 13th-century Persian style of *khorāsāni* that also sounds archaic to modern Persian ears. Putting aside the lost translation of the *Masnavi* by Baudry, these translations exist only in German and English. I divide them into two categories:

A. ORIENTALIST TRANSLATIONS (19TH CENTURY)

Orientalists are all experts in Oriental languages and literatures without necessarily being academics. It was particularly after the undertaking of Hammer-Purgstall, Goethe, and Rückert in German that English speakers began to discover that there was a world of literary wealth beyond the borders of Europe. This was all the more striking that the British were very present in Muslim lands and South Asia as of the 18th century. After the publication of the translation of the *neynāme* in Sir Jones's anthology, there appeared a few anthologies that included a few verses by Rumi such as the ones compiled by Edward Henry Palmer and Luisa Stuart Costello and Emerson (in the United States). However, the publication of independent works was made possible by Redhouse (a specialist in the Ottoman world), followed by Whinfield, Wilson, and especially Nicholson, whose first translations were from the *Divan* ([1898] 2001).

B. CIRCLE OF CAMBRIDGE (20TH CENTURY)

Arberry succeeds to Nicholson in the Chair of Persian Literature in Cambridge. They embody the academic specialist of Rumi, whose translations are yet to be surpassed in comprehensiveness, accuracy, and adequacy. This is so despite some of Arberry's deviations in terms of second-degree deformation (see the next chapter) by Islamization of the discourse or despite Nicholson's superfluous archaisms and systematic deletions of "obscene" passages in submission to the norms of propriety in the Victorian polysystem. The irony of fate is that these translations are the most attacked, the most abused by English speakers, translators, and specialists as well, even though these critics all consider themselves indebted to these two specialists. Barks is not the only one who has the vocation to "free these verses from their cage" on Robert Bly's advice, referring to Arberry's translation of ghazals and quatrains (Barks 1995, 363); Alan Williams, too, no doubt in an attempt to promote his own British Academy–funded translation project of the *Masnavi*, describes Nicholson's edition "inaccessible," a "Victorian Gothic," or an imitation of the "King James Bible." As I discuss in the last chapter, the main virtue of Nicholson's approach consists precisely in not aiming for accessibility of translation but in encouraging the reader to seek the author, the very characteristic of a long-lasting quality translation. Few translators after these two specialists have succeeded in reaching this level of accuracy and ethics in translation, let alone exceeding them. New generations have often submitted to the expectations of the readership, to the norms of a market that requires translator to be *invisible* and the TT to be read like an original text in the TL. In consequence, these academic texts cannot be compared to more modern popularizing translations in terms of sales. Ironically, in the case of Rumi, the higher the quality of the translation, the higher the *resistance* of the target polysystem.

2.2.2 Modern Waves

Post-Arberry English translations are the most difficult to classify because of their scope, variety, and intent as well as the background and profile of the translators. I propose a classification based on the profile of the translators: on the one hand, specialists in Persian or literature and Rumi, on the other hand, professionals in Anglo-American literature, who worked either in collaboration with Persian speakers, or retranslated English translations, i.e., Nicholson and Arberry's texts, into English.

Even in French, this has been the case of Eva de Vitray-Meyerovitch, the Rumi specialist who has mistakenly come to be known as the French translator of Rumi (Sedaghat 2015). Her French translation in collaboration with a Persian speaker is actually a translation from Nicholson whom she imitates up to the microstructural level.[12] Other modern French translators, however, are all either Persian speakers or academic specialists of Persian literature and Sufism. In German too, the same pattern as in English is repeated. After a strong wave of classical translations, the re-emergence of translations occurred with Annemarie Schimmel, an uncontested specialist in Persian mystical literature who translates from Persian into both German and English. In the last decade, a Persian speaker and a number of academics have given rise to a popularizing wave, most probably under the influence of the American polysystem. Unlike in French where at least an indirect translation from Nicholson's version by Vitray-Meyerovitch has existed since the late 20th century, or in Russian where an academic collective of translators recently completed a full translation of the *Masnavi* (2007–2012), there was no complete German translation of the *Masnavi* since Georg Rosen's abridged versified version, entitled *Mesnewi* (1849/1913), until Otto Höschle's very recent edition in two volumes (2020) and (2021).[13]

A. THE POPULARIZING NEW WAVE

A wave of mostly *intralingual* translations/rewriting has had for its main objective making Rumi's poetry and thought more accessible and his translations more *readable* for a wider audience. Indeed, many of these publications are not technically translations but *hypertextual* activities called "versions." A number of these works (not all cited in our bibliography) consist of reproductions, imitations, or adaptations (Robert Duncan and Nazim Hikmat, among others). The boundaries between the various forms of these Rumi-inspired hypertextual products are all the more blurred since a single translator such as Colman Barks, Kabir Helminsky, and Nevit Ergin can have, under the same title, passages that range from an *acceptable* translation to what is more like an imitation. To be fair, as Lewis argues (Lewis 2007, 644–646), versions composed by individuals who do not have direct access to the Persian text cannot be considered translations but adaptations (in Berman's terms) or rewritings (in Henri Meschonnic's view). This does not prevent them from being useful in the translation process because it is actually to these *hypertexts* that Rumi owes his phenomenal popularity throughout the world. In short, one can claim that Rumi is known because he is Americanized. From a hermeneutic standpoint, furthermore, the majority of these translations have a naively romanticizing reading of mysticism and Sufi metaphysics, giving a profane account of Rumi's discourse. They regard mystical thought not necessarily as an antidote to Islam, as certain 19th-century orientalists would claim, but at least as an independent universalized religion of war. In fact, the question of Rumi's belonging to the Islamic world is minimized or simply absent in the paratext of these publications. They are hence often criticized by more specialized Rumi translators and commentators, especially those who are Muslim believers themselves, as superficial and disconnected from the reality of the text and the author.

There are two operation modes: either rewriting an already existing translation (usually by Arberry and Nicholson) while versifying and poetizing it or working in duo with a native speaker to translate directly from Persian: Persian speakers do the translating part and the English-speaking translator-poets act as the rewriters.

These are professionals of the target literary polysystem – academics (English literature), authors, translators from other languages of the world – which they do not actually speak. It is also possible to work on a translation from another language, notably Turkish as in the case of Nevit Ergin. The translating duos Barks-Moyen, Johnson/Barks-Ergin, Gamard-Farhadi, Lee-Banani, and Star-Shiva tend to break up after a few years of collaboration with the English-speaking actor working independently on his own translations and the Persian speakers doing the same, for instance Shahram Shiva, more or less successfully. The lower success rate for the Persian speakers can be explained by their secondary status in the literary polysystem and their limited access to power networks: publishers, media owners, etc.

B. SPECIALISTS' TRANSLATIONS

These are translations made by modern academics and specialists of Sufism, some of whom such as Chittick and Schimmel are Sufis themselves. Academics and experts of Rumi or publications about him generally follow a curve starting in the late 19th century and culminating in Nicholson's translation of the *Masnavi* and Arberry's translations of the *Divan*. Academic translation comes to a halt with these two stars for quite a long time. Translation of the *Masnavi* stopped for more than three quarters of a century to resume only with Mojaddedi and Williams in the UK. Translations of the *Divan* saw a rebound in the second half of the 20th century with Chittick and, recently, with Franklin Lewis in the US.

The market share is totally dominated by popularizing "versions" carried out either by Persian speakers or by Americans who did not even have access to the original text. These are literary translation-introductions made by poets and professionals and that have a very high degree of *acceptability* and compliance with the operational norms of the target polysystem. This may sound surprising since Rumi's texts can be considered to enjoy a central position in the repertoire of mystical literature in the English-speaking world and, according to Toury's law, when translation has a central position, it complies less with the operational norms such as readability. In this regard, the laws of Toury do not seem to properly apply to the reception of Rumi. One can argue, nevertheless, that the primary position held by Rumi's poetry in the English mystical literature thanks to the popularizing work of nonspecialists has resulted in the re-emergence and multiplication of *adequate* academic translations that are beginning to dominate the literary scene. This dominance is not in the number of copies, always largely exceeded by popularizing translations. It manifests itself rather in increasingly more awareness on the readers' side of the quality and accuracy of Rumi's translations. This positive development is ironically the result of a popularity that is owed to *acceptable*, and even "ethnocentric" as Berman would have said, translations of Rumi.

2.3 *Unequal Models of Reception in Target Polysystems*

There are incongruities in the reception of Rumi on two levels. On the one hand, it is unequal in terms of Rumi importance and position in the source polysystem compared to other important figures of Persian literature or Iranian philosophy. It is also heterogeneous, both quantitatively and qualitatively, with regard to the target polysystems. Rumi's thought in mystical philosophy as well as his poetic work undeniably hold a central position in Iran and the Persianate world. However, his importance is matched by other authors and thinkers like Ferdowsi, Hafez, Sa'di, Nezami, Khayyam, and other figures in Iran. Ferdowsi, whose epic "Shahnameh" is even larger than Rumi's entire work, can be deemed the father of modern Persian literature in the same way as Shakespeare for English, Dante for Italian, Cervantes for Castellan Spanish, and Martin Luther's Bible for High German. Hafez is perhaps the single most popular Persian author of all times for Iranians, and his *Divan* is present on any bookshelf and is even used for divination and fortune-telling. Sa'di is called *ostād-e soxan* [the Master of Speech] in Persian. Yet the number of (direct or indirect) translations and adaptation into any European language of the work of these authors, equal to Rumi in fame in their own country, is nowhere near that of Rumi's.

Furthermore, the importance of the reception in Western and non-Western polysystems, particularly in the Turkish-speaking world, from the second half of the 20th century on, seems to have contributed to the *repositioning* of Rumi within the source polysystem. Despite already occupying a central role throughout the history of Persian literature, Rumi seems to have further grown in popularity and awareness in Iran, especially after the revolution, with more and more events, conferences, and academic studies dedicated to his literary work and teachings. Even on the artistic scene, his poetry is increasingly used in both popular and classical musical performances, rivaling the mystical and lyrical poetry of Hafez, Sa'di, and Baba Taher, which dominated Iranian traditional music before. The singularity of Rumi's reception can be explained by recognizing two major factors: the punctual position of Rumi in the Western polysystems and the ideological values that could be considered to have motivated some institutions influencing the choice of texts to translate.

2.3.1 Rumimania *in the Anglosphere*

The English-speaking polysystem has the greatest number of translations, unmatched by any other language and culture in the world, at least since the beginning of the 20th century. Many Rumi translations in other languages, including French, are in fact indirect translations from English. This may be explained by the fact that the Anglosphere has become a prevalent polysystem in the world in general. Thanks to the status of English as the dominant language of commercial exchange and the geopolitical power of English-speaking nations, English has become the *de facto lingua franca* of the modern world with the largest amount of content production and translation both into and from it. Nevertheless, the higher frequency of Rumi translations in the Anglosphere cannot simply be explained by the dominance of this polysystem. Poetry translation is only a small part of translation in the English-speaking world (Venuti 2013, 173–174). In other words, it has a peripheral position in the general literary polysystem. The case of Rumi is therefore an exception rather than a rule. The phenomenon of *Rumimania* causes a polysystemic paradox in the US, where poetic translation has a peripheral position while mystical texts tend towards the center.

This paradox can be solved by understanding the composition of the English-speaking polysystem and, more precisely, the repertoire of the American literary and sociocultural polysystem. There are certain lacunae in this repertoire that have allowed for such a successful reception, whereas the absence of these vacuums in the French, German, or other European polysystems has led to far more limited interference of Persian mystical literature. More specifically, there exists a lacuna in the Anglo-Protestant literary and cultural repertoire that can be called the *theosophic-romantic* genre. This vacuum is increasingly sensed in the entire Western culture with the spread of the American lifestyle and the prevalence of the capitalist economic model in a monopolar world since the end of the 20th century. It is this gap in the canon of the target polysystems that has taken the translation of authors like Rumi out of the periphery and repositioned it at the center of literary activity, in the absence of local equivalents. On the other hand, this abundant translational activity has proliferated in a virtuous cycle of *intralingual* translations, whereby Nicholson's and Arberry's translations rather than a totally foreign text are retranslated from English into English.

Another polysystemic factor could be in relation to economic dynamics. "How any translator chooses to work on one poet, and not on others, is a mysterious thing," affirms Barks. Personal preferences and falling in love with Rumi aside, we can see how commercial interests could play a sizable part in choosing authors. It is difficult to ignore the function of the market and institutions of the American polysystem that have set the stage for a massive reception of exotic and (pseudo) spiritual literature. Along with New Age spiritualism, the interest in "Oriental" philosophies, yoga, and Zen meditation, Rumi has joined the center of the repertoire of mass cultural products. Rumi translations – academic circles aside – have become a mass consumer product on an industrial scale. The industrialization of love poetry, albeit of a spiritual and nonerotic nature, is part of a market trend in which all kinds of spirituality are in high demand. This demand has two sources: on the one hand, an audience seeking high-quality love poetry[14] and whose thirst is quelled by a *romanticized, de-Islamicized* version of Rumi; on the other hand, a deeply Christian society in a permanent quest for spirituality. Professionals of this microsystem are also spiritual Christians who see no problem in commercializing spirituality.

2.3.2 Lesser Appeal on the Continent

The growing interest in Rumi in the German, French, Italian, and Hispanic literary polysystems seems to be a modern phenomenon, as attested by the recent increase of publications in these languages. The most plausible hypothesis to explain this state of affairs is the impact of the Anglo-American polysystem and its craze for Rumi worldwide. This recent wave, however, is the exception that proves the rule that Rumi is less reputed as a mystical writer and is more obscure in these polysystems than in the Anglo-American world. The question is why reception has been considerably more limited in these continental European language-cultures than in the Anglophone world.

Historically speaking, the first point of contact between the French or the Germans with Rumi was with the Mevlevi whirling dervishes and Sufi brotherhoods, hence through the Ottoman polysystem. This might have partially altered the European field of interpretation, polluted by animosities towards, and historical hostilities against, the Turkish enemies. The didactic character of the *Masnavi* might also have had less appeal for continental Europeans of the Romantic era, compared to the works of Hafez, the master of Persian lyricism, who immediately won the hearts of the likes of Goethe (Lewis 2007, 566). The European repertoire of the Romantic era was less in need of mystical preachers than of Epicurean poets such as Khayyam. French academic circles had been relatively less interested in Rumi than in other Persian poets, such as Ferdowsi, Sa'di, and especially Hafez. In addition, the stronger interrelations between English-speaking and Iranian cultures can be explained by the more direct diplomatic relations between the two cultures as well as the politico-military presence of the British Empire in the Iranian world, and particularly in the British Empire's Indian colonies where the Persianate culture and the Persian language were systematically substituted by English under the British Raj.

There is little room for Sufi thought in the canon of the French polysystem founded on Catholicism and reformatted by contemporary *laïcité* and the ideals of *Les Lumières*. Neither Rumi's didactic *Masnavi* nor his passionate mystical lyricism can find a deep spiritual vacuum to fill in that particular polysystem. Many scholars like Arberry, Nicholson, Chittick, and Lewis explicitly state that Rumi does not have a system of thought like Ibn 'Arabi, coherent didactics like Sa'di, exquisite poetic images like Hafez, and elaborate metaphysics like Sohravardi, let alone a well-structured philosophy like Avicenna. In Europe, Rumi appears less as a thinker with original ideas than as a religious leader with prolix literary activity – a false image unfortunately shaped by the historical experiences of certain orientalists whose first contact with Rumi was through "whirling dervishes" in the Ottoman Empire. Initially, it was not philosophers like Louis Massignon or Henry Corbin who got interested in Rumi's work but historians of religions and poets. Moreover, notions such as theophany, mystical theosophy, theosophical metaphysics, and speculative theology, which characterize Rumi's thought and work, sound far less novel for the predominantly Catholic Europe of Saint Theresa of Avila and Meister Eckhart than for the Victorian intellectual space or North American society at grips with its debilitating materialism and capitalistic demons.

Rumi's poetical works enjoy a much greater prominence in the Anglo-American polysystem than in continental Europe because of the radical differences between the dynamics of the two cultural markets as well as their divergent horizons of expectations. The French market, for instance, regulated by state subsidies and dominated by a certain elite of professionals in the literary system, differs from the liberalized cultural market in North America characterized by more democratic and less elitist rules. Someone like Colman Barks, for instance, would never have survived in the French polysystem. Most (modern) French translators of Rumi come from a university or a specialized environment with a certain concept of adequacy, probably thanks to the awareness created by academics such as Berman and Meschonnic, who will be discussed in the next chapter. Moreover, the cultural market on the Continent does not have the same capacity to absorb foreign products as does the English-speaking market. There are more consumers and more producers (more Iranians with knowledge of English) in the Anglosphere than in Europe.

3 Ideological and Political Dimensions of Translation

3.1 Translation as Rewriting and Orientalism

As the polysystems theory shows, sociocultural and economic variables of the target cultural sphere shape the overarching structure of the reception acting upon transitions mainly by imposing patent or latent *norms*. Nevertheless, they are not the only factors that have a bearing on the quality of reception. There are other factors, such as the presence or the dominance of certain ideologies or political agendas at the specific moments of reception, that may affect or orient the translative choices as much as the quality and substance of the reception. These ideological orientations can particularly affect the level of resistance towards imported literature on the audience side. *Institutions* can shape the poetic and ideological canons of the target polysystem in order to determine the choice of translated content as well as the way translated content is *framed* and presented to the audience. The translator's cultural positionality – or in Bourdieu's words, *habitus* – can also determine the ideological turn the TT can take. Lawrence Venuti criticizes Toury's "scientific" observation of translation norms, affirming:

> Norms may be in the first instance linguistic or literary, but they will also include a diverse range of domestic values, beliefs, and social representations which carry ideological force in serving the interests of specific groups. And they are always housed in the social institutions where translations are produced and enlisted in cultural and political agendas.
> (Venuti 1998, 29)

Venuti's observation follows on André Lefevere's pivotal work on translation as both a political device and reflection of ideological orientation of target cultural sphere. Using the functional and descriptive scheme of the polysystems theory, Lefevere pinpoints the "very concrete factors" that govern the reception or rejection of work in a language-culture, namely, "issues such as power, ideology, institution and handling" (Lefevere 1992, 2). The central axis of his thesis is the notion of *rewriting*, close to Jean Genette's concept of *hypertext*, which designates any writing activity that is based on a previous work: translation, historiography, anthologization, criticism, and editing (*Ibid.*, 9). Rewriting is the device by which agents in positions of power govern the consumption habits of the cultural product for ends that are either ideological or poetic. Their motivation may be to reinforce, transform, or challenge the dominant *ideology* or *poetology* in a given polysystem. These two main aspects of the literary system are managed by two groups of agents: the *professionals* – translators, critics, academics, etc. – who determine the dominant *poetics* of the system, which is the equivalent of *repertoire* in the polysystem scheme, and the *patronage* – individuals holding political or economic power, circles of power such as publishers, media patrons, and owners, as well as institutions such as national education – who control and determine the *ideological* components of the system. *Professionals* manipulate the literary system from within, while the *patronage* does so from without. *Professionals* exercise their power through literary devices – genres, symbols, leitmotifs, narratologies, etc. – as well as the status of literary forms in the repertoire.

> A poetics can be said to consist of two components: one is an inventory of literary devices, genres, motifs, prototypical characters and situations, and symbols; the other a concept of what the role of literature is, or should be, in the social system as a whole. The latter concept is influential in the influential in the selection of themes that must be relevant to the social system.
>
> (Lefevere 1992, 27)

External manipulation is possible through three forms of influence: *ideological, economic*, and *statutory*. In other words, control is exercised by making ideological choices, allocating financial means, and using the balance of power that results from the status of the agents and stakeholders. Moreover, professionals depend on the financial means and communication networks that are in the possession of individuals or institutions constituting the *patronage*, which leads to the connivance between poetical choices – choice of texts, styles, or norms – and the ideological intent of the patronage. "While rewriting manipulates, and it is effective," argues Lefevere, "translation is the most obviously recognizable type of rewriting, and it is potentially the most influential because it is able to project the image of an author and/or a (series of) work(s) in another culture" (1992, 9). The main issue for the literary reception of a work through translation lies in the combination of ideological and poetological factors. Lefevere cites an excerpt from Edward Fitzgerald's letter about his translation of Khayyam[15] as "one of the most striking examples of the combination of ideological and poetological motivations/constraints" (Lefevere 1992, 8).

> In fact, Fitzgerald's *Rubayyat* is one of the most effective rewritings of the last century, and its influence makes itself felt deep into the present one. Ideologically Fitzgerald obviously thinks Persians inferior to their Victorian English counterparts, a frame of mind that allows him to rewrite them in a way in which he would have never dreamed of rewriting Homer, or Virgil. Poetologically, he thinks they should be made to read more like the dominant current in the poetry of his own time.
>
> (*Ibid.*)

It goes without saying that this attitude, at least on the ideological level, cannot be found in most academic translations of Rumi's work, such as Arberry's. Nevertheless, poetologically, Fitzgerald's approach bears uncanny resemblances to Redhouse's version and Sir William Jones's versified translation, which show little respect even for the semantic content of the original utterance in favor of an ennobling rhythm of the original text. One should never forget Wilson's or Whinfield's attitude to the perceived lack of coherence in Rumi's work. In the case of Nicholson, translation of *obscene* passages into Latin may constitute his *poetological* intentions to make the work conform to the literary norms of his era. However, one may wonder in Fitzgerald's arrogant boasting about how artfully he has managed to raise the quality of "these Persians' work" does not reveal something about his own complex of inferiority due to the inferior status of translators compared to *real* poets, as a result of the peripheral position of translation in the repertoire of the literary polysystem.

What is alarming in Fitzgerald's underlying ideology is not so much the expression of this purely ethnocentric mentality as the latency of such an approach in the translation of non-European literature. This well-disguised attitude manifests itself in a latent form in translations and versions of the American polysystem, with their popularizing, exoticizing, and above all, annexationist practices. As surprising as it may seem, similar poetological practices exist among Victorian Britons and contemporary Americans, which can be attributed to two unrelated facts about their respective polysystems: the *operational norms* for the former and the quest for financial profit for the latter. The 19th-century translators homogenized the text to make it conform to the moral criteria and the literary canon of their era, whereas American contemporary translators made the texts readable to meet the expectations of a flourishing market. Both cases expose the mixture of poetological and ideological norms recognized by Lefevere. These functions act upon translators' decisions both directly and indirectly, even unconsciously. The dominant ideology in the target polysystem has an undeliberate impact on the translator, which is reflected in his exegetical orientations and his linguistic or stylistic choices. The same forces act upon the readership, in a way to determine the failure or success of the reception of the foreign work. Lefevere remarks that a choice made under the influence of the ideological or poetological vectors almost always prevails over a choice dictated by linguistic or stylistic facts of the text.

> On every level of the translation process, it can be shown that, if linguistic considerations enter into conflict with considerations of an ideological and/or poetological nature, the latter tend to win out.
>
> (Lefevere 1992, 39)

As far as cultural interference between the West and what is commonly but vaguely called the East is concerned, it is difficult not to mention Edward Said's famous work *Orientalism* (1979). While Said's arguments are pertinent in certain areas of reception, especially the points of contact with the colonized Indian subcontinent and the Arabic-speaking world, they are mostly irrelevant to the framework of my criticism of ideologizing Rumi. In my demonstration, there is no question of Said's virulent criticisms about the incapacity of the West and orientalists to understand the complex dimensions of the "Orient." Mysticism is nothing new to Europe, whether in the antiquities in the form of Neoplatonism or in the Middle Ages with different mystical movements in Catholic and Orthodox Christianity. Neither is it the question of a harmonized political and ideological agenda to deliberately distort the image of the Orient and its culture. These presuppositions seem naïve for a number of reasons: first, focusing excessively on the Arab world taken as the embodiment of the "Orient," Said limits himself to a few extreme cases of uninformed and ethnocentric orientalists, which leads to a few hasty and generalized conclusions about a global and omnipresent desire of the West to inferiorize and humiliate the East. In fact, despite some value in his critical approach and some of his observations, Said's analyses are essentially restricted to the work of Anglo-Saxon orientalists on the Ottoman Empire and the British colonies and can by no means be generalized to vaguely sweeping notion of the East, which includes, at least in the popular culture, the Iranian, Turkic, and Vedic worlds. Nor can his conclusions be extrapolated to all orientalist research on the literature, civilization, and history of ideas of Asia. Also, his work should be put into perspective in a difficult geopolitical context in West Asia, where West-backed Israel successfully confronted and prevailed against Arab armies. Moreover, Said's proposals are at least not corroborated by the observations and findings of my research insofar as the evidence of annexionism and ethnocentrism in certain classical translations are more the consequence of *poetological* considerations than *ideological* manipulation. It would be extremely unfair and prejudicial to accuse Nicholson or Arberry of ethnocentrism or condescendence towards Iranian culture or mystical thought in Islam, given their dedication to the creation of source-oriented accurate translations.

3.2 The Geopolitics of Translating Rumi

There are several examples of how the patronage and professionals in the target polysystems play a significant role in the reception of Rumi's work, determining not only the choice of texts to be translated, but also the quality of translation.

3.2.1 Reception as a Political Indicator

The most interesting manifestation of the control of the patronage can be observed at the level of the number and choice of Rumi's texts that have been translated in English in the past one and a half centuries. This is about a latent and macrostructural influence of politics on reception reflected by the quantitative variations in the reception of Rumi in the English-speaking world. The chronological distribution of the publication of English translations in the past one and a half centuries follows an unstable curve that appears to be related to two main factors: the period and the profile of the translator. From the beginning and until the

1970s, almost all Rumi translators were orientalists and specialized scholars from the Iranian world. From the 1980s, a new group of amateurs neither specialized in Islamic studies nor learned in the Persian language and literature came into play to take center stage. The "Rumimania" craze Lewis mentions (Lewis 2007, 1–5) started mainly thanks to these amateur translators who either retranslated Rumi's poems from the versions of the two eminent specialists, Nicholson and Arberry, or worked in collaboration with a Persian speaker to understand the source text. The success of these popularizing translations, particularly in North America, pushed even more enthusiasts towards this enterprise. Among these nonspecialist or non-Persian-speaking translators, certain names come to mind: Colman Barks, Helminsky, Ergin, etc. These are English-speaking poets who have opened a niche market in the North American polysystem thanks to retranslations and adaptations that conform to the poetological standards of the target culture and are texts that "read well."

These publications entered a period of recession however at the turn of the 21st century in the aftermath of 9/11 and the emergence of Islamophobia in the United States. The market's enthusiasm for an author from the Muslim world declined, despite the wide gap that separates Rumi's thought from orthodox Islam and *a fortiori* from its extremist form. It should be noted, however, that this slowdown in the reception process of Rumi's work does not really concern translators who had already specialized in the field, whether academics or translators of best-sellers. Academics, such as Mojaddedi and Williams, do not let their projects be affected by market conditions, most probably because their translation projects often benefit from institutional funding. Popularizing translators for their part never intended to present Rumi as a Muslim mystical poet. Their priority was to underline the lyrical, even romantic aspect of Rumi's poetry and the universal dimensions of its philosophy. Figure 6.2 illustrates the chronological distribution of the works of the main translators of Rumi.

Publishers can affect reception in their choice of texts to be translated. The translations of Rumi's texts produced in the West reveal a clear preference for the mystical-didactic collection of the *Masnavi*. While there already exists a complete translation of the *Masnavi* into English by Nicholson, and its French version by Vitray-Meyerovitch, three partial translations (of Book I) in the middle of the 19th century, as well as two ongoing projects undertaken by Mojaddedi and Williams to retranslate the whole of this "Persian Koran," there is to date only the translation of a tiny part of the 35,000 mystical-lyrical ghazals of the *Divan*, the pinnacle of Rumi's poetic art. Do we owe the higher frequency of publication of the *Masnavi* to its stronger correspondence to the ideas the professionals of the target system have of a moderate Sufi master with a coherent system of thought? Are the bacchanalian images, the profane language, and the extravagant remarks of the *Divan*'s ghazals deemed by publishers too difficult to digest for a public more accustomed to the wisdom of the mystics of the East? The reception of Rumi is clearly under the influence of both the ideological norms of his source polysystem and the poetological norms of the target polysystem.

3.2.2 Translation and Nationalism

The systematic efforts of certain Turkish political or poetological institutions to annex the Persian poet to their Turkish bosom constitute a less insidious because more flagrant case of interference. Some Turkish-speaking translators have a secular Kemalist and nationalist ideological tendency that has long been part of the Turkish polysystem but has been reinforced by the arrival to power of Islamic conservatives. Their position is to idealize the opposition that exists between Rumi's Sufism and the dogmatic sharia of Islam without taking into account the broader context of Sufi metaphysics. Their aim is to associate the birth of Rumi's Sufi progressive ideas with the favorable context of intellectual development allegedly due to the religious tolerance and the good governance of the Seljuk sultanate of Rum, erroneously taken for the ancestor of present-day Turkey. These ideas are already expressed in the preface to the French translations by Tchelebi ([1950] 1984).

This historically caricatural point of view is also echoed by Turkish-American translator Nevit Ergin in the preface of their collection of Rumi poems bearing the ostentatious title *The Forbidden Rumi: The Suppressed Poems of Rumi on Love, Heresy, and Intoxication* (Ergin and Johnson 2006). The translators claim that the poems in question are antinomic and bacchanalian poems subject to censorship. Yet all the ghazals therein had already been published several times in all the Persian editions of the *Divan*. Ergin, not knowing Persian himself, translated the Turkish edition of the *Divan* by the Turkish translator Gölpinarli. Ergin also mentions the financing of his project by the Turkish government, financing which had allegedly been cut to prevent him from publishing these "forbidden poems." The highly questionable conclusion that Ergin draws is that there is a conspiracy to censor Rumi. He then praises the tolerance of the Turkish cultural community of Konya who welcomed Rumi with open arms, unlike his Persian native land! The anachronism of Ergin's myth and his distortion of historical facts seem all the more ludicrous that the Turkish nation-state did not even exist at the time of Rumi's immigration to Konya – or Iconium, as the local Greek-speaking majority population called it. Konya was, in fact, a multiethnic and multilingual city recently conquered by Muslim Turks, where the political and intellectual elite were Persian speakers and the newly settled warriors and tribesmen spoke various Oghuz dialects. In Ergin's words:

> Rumi let go of the precepts of formal religion, insisting instead that only a complete personal dissolving into the larger energies of God can provide the satisfaction that the heart so desperately seeks. It is a testament to how well-loved Rumi was in his adopted community of Konya, Turkey, that he encountered no reprisals for pronouncements that would certainly have gotten him into very hot water indeed had they been uttered instead in present day Iran or in Afghanistan under the Taliban. . . . (Ergin and Johnson 2006, 3–4) . . . The second thing to know about these poems is the story of intrigue that has kept them from finding their way to their audience in the West.
>
> (*Ibid.*, 5)

A glance at Nicholson's and Arberry's versions, where these poems were previously published, easily falsifies Ergin's claims. Elsewhere, the translator rashly praises Rumi's religious eclecticism: "While Rumi remained a devout Muslim throughout his life, he was nonetheless a beacon to all people, regardless of the religious tradition into which they had been born" (*Ibid.*, 6). Yet the question of Rumi's religious convictions is far too complex to be summarized and judged in such a hasty manner. Rumi's own words – throughout his poetry and discourses – about his religion are at best paradoxical and contradictory. Furthermore, the idea of being "liberal while remaining Muslim" is the hallmark of the present Islamic-conservative political discourse in a Turkey dominated by Muslim Brotherhood–inspired Erdoganism. Ergin's *rewriting* project seems to be in line with the general political agenda of Turkish revisionism, insofar as it appropriates the Persian poet, on the one hand, and promotes his presumed intellectual openness as the innate traits of a nation that did not even exist in Rumi's time period.

This ideology of annexation promulgated by nationalist policies is also denounced by Franklin Lewis who mentions a tourist guide, entitled *Mevlana Jelaleddin Rumi*, published on the initiative of the Turkish Ministry of Culture by a person named Önder:

> This book published by [the] Turkish Ministry of Culture, displays an extremely exuberant ignorance, or an ethnocentric agenda. In the introduction, Önder refers to Rumi as "the great Turkish mystic" and "a great Turkish intellectual." . . . In any case, we can forgive the linguistic chauvinism of poets and authors who believe their language to be the best since Babel, but Önder must surely know that Rumi wrote and spoke Persian. Therefore, we can only surmise that his cultural jingoism represents a conscious effort to rob Rumi of his Persian and Iranian heritage, and claim him for Turkish literature, ethnicity and nationalism.
>
> (Lewis 2007, 548–549)

The cases cited exemplify the phenomenon that Lefevere calls "rewriting," with translation occupying the central place. These are manipulations that often result from the bad faith of patrons who finance translation projects, and of (pseudo) professionals such as translators and publishers who undertake the task. The result is the exploitation of the work of a world-famous figure to advance the political interests of particular groups and the promotion of the soft power of a young nation in search of fame.

3.3 Ideological Distortion of Rumi

3.3.1 Rumi and Antisemitism

The political context of the host polysystem can have a negative impact on reception of a work despite the neutrality of its translator. The prose translation of some of the *Masnavi*'s tales by Arberry in post-war Britain was a case at hand.

The mystical discourse was poorly received by a readership whose field of interpretation had been contaminated by a toxic historical-political climate. Despite the work's rather positive reception in intellectual circles, some readers accused Rumi and his translator of anti-Semitism because of the content of one of the stories in Book I entitled "The Jewish King Who Killed the Christians" (Arberry 1961, 31–39).

The protagonist, a Jewish king, massacres Christians by sowing discord in their community and deepening their religious differences with the help of his undercover agents. The allegorical character of the story is all the more evident that Rumi's narrative, like the vast majority of the *Masnavi*'s stories, are not based on historical facts. They are fictions rooted either in Vedic, Semitic, or Iranian folklore – before and after the Muslim invasion – or in the pure imagination of the author. Besides, the image of Judaism is generally far from negative in the work of Rumi, where great figures of the Old Testament such as Moses are largely featured. The target of Rumi's criticisms are the religious and sectarian disputes that deviate the faithful from the path of divine truth. Rumi does not attack a specific religion or community. If there is an attack, it is against sectarianism and interfaith competition such as exist between the Sufi brotherhoods themselves, hence the self-critical nature of the text. Evil in the story in question does not stem from the manipulations of the Jewish king but from the blindness of the Christian disciples who submit to the authority of their so-called spiritual leaders at the expense of an individual and internalized quest for truth. Rumi's allegory aims at the practices of sects and Sufi brotherhoods.

Faced with these accusations of anti-Semitism, the result of a hasty reading and a faulty interpretation, the translator was obliged to explain the context of the genesis of the original work and the aim of its author. Indeed, this anecdote shows not a deformation of speech by the translator nor the interference of the translator in the field of indication of the message, but the variation of the field of interpretation of the readers, upset by political issues specific to their personal historical context, namely that of the reception, contaminated by a hypersensitivity to anti-Semitic propaganda and to the tragedies of the war in Europe.

3.3.2 Mysticism: The Quintessence of Islam

Throughout my study, and more specifically in the discussion about gender in the first chapter and of the profane imagery of Sufi poetry in Chapter 5, I have drawn attention to the existence of an ideology that considers mystical thought in the Islamic world as a branch of Islamic theology rather than as independent metaphysics. The influence of this ideology manifests itself in both the text and the paratext. Examples 1.3 to 1.6 show, for instance, how a certain worldview caused translators to make deforming choices in the translation of the Persian neutral gender. Other examples show how most translators use capital letters for all anaphoric references to the object of love, whom they unequivocally take to be God. Rumi's poetic imagery, vested in *non-dit*, undergoes an almost total destruction in most translations, thus showcasing flagrant distortions of the text under the effect of ideological and aesthetic standards imposed by the target polysystems. The degree of these deformations, however, varies over time, thus possibly reflecting changes in the ideological and poetological tendencies of each polysystem over time. In the Victorian era in particular, a conflict of interpretation was caused by an ideological principle originating from the source polysystem according to which erotic images are incompatible with a mystical text supposedly belonging to the religious repertoire. This dogmatic vision does not seem to have guided the choice of the orientalist, Redhouse: he was not afraid to feminize "the beloved" of the poet.

As I will discuss in Chapter 7 on the ethics of translation, the more insidious form of distortion is that of second degree, which takes shape not in the text but in its margins. Just as the example of Nevit Ergin shows (in the last section), the margin of the TT, i.e., the preface, footnotes, translator's note, etc., is a propitious space for orienting the reader's interpretation of the text. Information provided in the translative *paratext* can only interfere with the reader's field of interpretation (see Chapter 5). Rumi translators have often used this space to exercise their ideological influence through their exegetic comments. A convincing case of this type of ideological distortion manifests itself in a process referred to as the Islamization of Rumi's mystical discourse. It consists of reconstructing – or rewriting – the greatly deteriorated image of Islam in the West by presenting the figure of Rumi, his poetry, and his thought as the authentic representation of this religion. This phenomenon is illustrated, among others, in the preface of the anthology translated by the French scholar Leili Anvar, whose first lines insist on the Koranic origins of Sufism:

> "I was a hidden treasure, I wanted to be known; this is why I created the creatures so that they know me." It is in these terms that one of the religious traditions of Islam makes God speak. . . . The entire created universe is therefore the Book of God where everyone can read the splendor of the divine attributes. The Quran itself and all the sacred and spiritual texts are but the reflecting mirrors of this great Book of divine realities.
>
> (Anvar 2011, 7)

Several modern orientalists of Sufism defend the idea that the real origins of mystic metaphysics in the Islamic world are found within the teachings of Islam, a thesis refuted out of hand by many older orientalists (see Introduction and Chapter 5). The latter see mysticism rather as the vestiges of a tacit agreement between the Sufis and the religious authorities, a sort of *modus vivendi* within the Muslim world that has allowed mystical thought to survive there. It is very interesting to note this Islamizing attitude among many translators who themselves adhere to Sufi brotherhoods. The keystone of the argument of the supporters of the Islamizing thesis is the belonging of the Sufis to the bosom of the Muslim world, a belonging supported by numerous references in Rumi's work to the Koran. Yet the eclecticism and universality of Rumi's message defy any attempt at hasty classification.

Indeed, these intellectuals can give credit to Islam for a spiritual phenomenon that existed, at best, on the fringes of the Islamic theological tradition and, at worst, in direct opposition to its literalist dogma. Rumi's mysticism is a theosophy whose epistemological contours only take shape by seeking its origins in philosophical traditions such as Neoplatonism and Vedism. The references, in the work of Rumi or of other (supposedly) Muslim mystics, to Koranic verses and stories or to prophetic traditions do not entail their pure and simple adherence to the religious dogma of their time; their use simply reflects the historical context in which these thinkers lived, taught, and wrote. This thematic presence is more likely the recycling of all the oral and written traditions common to the three religions of the Book. After all, doesn't the Koran itself take up a large number of biblical stories to reshape them as it sees fit? Many of Rumi's so-called Koranic references may as well have been drawn from pre-Islamic sources as they sometimes favor the biblical version of the accounts at the expense of the Koranic narrative. Trying to pass off Rumi as a typical Muslim theologian is either to betray the very reality of his work or to caricature Islam. The reconciliatory attitude of these Islamizing orientalists in the face of the interfaith conflicts of our times is certainly commendable, but the distorting repercussions of their act on the source text suggest the adage: "The road to hell is paved with good intentions."

Notes

1 In the Russian political philosopher Alexander Dugan's view, народ [people] is defined as an intermediary stage between *ethnos* and nation (see Dugin (2018) and Dugin (2019)). For Dugin, *ethnos* or ethnic society is the primordial form of society, "a simple society, organically (naturally) associated with a territory and bound together by common mores, customs, and a symbolic system" (Millerman 2021, n.10). Unrelated to race, ethnos is concrete and particular, while its first derivative, *narod*, is plural, differentiated and significantly more complex. *Narod* is neither a nation nor civil society, whose subsequent stages of historic evolution as nation is associated with a state and country with boundaries. *Narod* is the origin of state, religion, and civilization and is incarnated in them (Dugin 2019, 2.I). The concept of Persianate culture or, as I argue, the Greater Iran, should be understood in terms of *narod*, people with more or less shared linguistic framework, cultural practices, and particularly, spiritual values belonging to different nations regardless of race.
2 See also Even-Zohar's "The Position of Translated Literature Within the Literary Polysystem" in Venuti ([2000] 2012).
3 This is similar to French sociologist Pierre Bourdieu's concept of *champs littéraire*, defined as "a network, or a configuration of objective relations between positions. These positions are objectively defined in their existence and in the determinations that they impose on their occupants, agents, or institutions, by their actual and potential situation (*situs*) in the distributional structure of different kinds of power (or of capital) whose possession commands access to the specific profits that are at stake in the field, and at the same time, by their objective relations to other positions (domination, subordination, homologies, etc.)" (Bourdieu et Wacquant 1992, 72–73).
4 By extension, this model is applied not only to the literary system of the polysystem, but also to any semiotically structured cultural phenomenon and artistic activity.
5 Institution is defined as "at least in part of the producers, critics (in whatever form), publishing houses, periodicals, clubs, groups of writers, government bodies (like ministerial

offices and academies), educational institutions (schools of whatever level, including universities), the mass media in all its facets, and more" (Even-Zohar 1990, 37).
6 In this respect, the model proposed by André Lefevere (see the following section) is best applicable to cultural and hypertextual activities. Pierre Bourdieu, and Alain Badiou's works on sociocriticism of language and culture are of utmost importance as well; nonetheless, they are not a part of my methodology for two reasons: the political orientation of their thought and the nature of their respective disciplines (sociology and philosophy), which makes them less relevant to my analysis of a case of intercultural communication through translation.
7 Translation, in this usual case, becomes one more tool to comfort convention in the dominant aesthetics of the Same at the expense of the Other. This is what Henri Meschonnic calls translation-annexation (see Chapter 7, section 3).
8 Two texts to be cited: *Descriptive Translation Studies and Beyond* was revised and republished by Toury in 1995. Its short version appears as "The Nature and Role of Norms in Literary Translation," in Venuti ([2000] 2012, 205–218).
9 This seemingly excessive scientific ambition in calling these repetitive patterns "laws" has been sharply criticized by most translation scholars.
10 For the full version of this section, see Sedaghat (2015, 368–383).
11 Only important translators, either academics, specialists, or the ones with multiple publications, are cited here. Translators in italics have published in the US and are American. The only exception is Mojaddedi, who is Afghan-British but published in the US.
12 A clue is her translations of so-called obscene language into Latin (see example 2.12).
13 I have not reviewed this German translation and cannot confirm whether it is a direct translation from Persian or an indirect translation from an English version of the *Masnavi*. According to his biobibliography, Otto Höschle is an author and playwright who studied English, German, and Islamic Studies. Given that he is not an academic or a specialist of Persian literature, it is highly likely that his translation, like Vitray-Meyerovitch's, is based on Nicholson's version, the only existent complete English translation of the *Masnavi*.
14 As opposed to cheap eroticism ubiquitous in the daily content of Western mass media.
15 Here is Fitzgerald's epigraph: "it is an amusement for me to take what Liberties I like with these Persians, who (as I think) are not Poets enough to frighten one from such excursions, and who really do want a little Art to shape them" (Lefevere 1992, 1).

References

Anvar, Leili. 2011. *Rûmî La religion de l'amour*. Paris: Éditions Points.
Arberry, Arthur John. 1961. *Tales from the Masnavi*. London: Allen and Unwin.
Barks, Coleman. 1995. *The Essential Rumi*. New York: Harper Collins.
Bourdieu, Pierre, and Loïc Wacquant. 1992. *Réponse, Pour une anthropologie réflexive*. Paris: Seuil.
Dugin, Alexander. 2018. *Ethnos and Society*. London: Arktos.
Dugin, Alexander. 2019. *Ethnosociology: The Foundations*. London: Arktos.
Ergin, Nevit Oguz, and Will Johnson. 2006. *The Forbidden Rumi: The Suppressed Poems of Rumi on Love, Heresy, and Intoxication*. Rochester, VT: Inner Traditions.
Even-Zohar, Itmar. 1990. *Polysystem Studies*. Tel Aviv: Porter Institute for Poetics and Semiotics, Tel Aviv University.
Even-Zohar, Itmar, and Gideon Toury. 1981. *Translation Theory and Intercultural Relations*. Tel Aviv: Porter Institute for Poetics and Semiotics, Tel Aviv University.
Lefevere, André. 1992. *Translation, Rewriting, and the Manipulation of the Literary Frame*. London: Routledge.

Lewis, Frankin D. 2007. *Rumi Past and Present, East and West: The Life, Teachings, and Poetry of Jalal al-Din Rumi.* Oxford: Oneworld.

Millerman, Michael. 2021. "The Ethnosociological and Existential Dimensions of Alexander Dugin's Populism." *Katehon.* https://katehon.com/en/article/ethnosociological-and-existential-dimensions-alexander-dugins-populism.

Nicholson, Reynold Alleyne. [1898] 2001. *Selected Poems From the Dīvāni Shamsi Tabrīz.* Bethesda, MD: Ibex Publishers.

Nida, Eugene. 1975. *Language, Structure and Translation.* Stanford, CA: Stanford University Press.

Nida, Eugene, and Charles Taber. 1969. *The Theory and Practice of Translation.* Leiden: Brill.

Said, Edward W. 1979. *Orientalism.* New York: Vintage Books Random House.

Sedaghat, Amir. 2015. *Le soufisme de Roumi reçu et perçu dans les mondes anglophone et francophone: étude des traductions anglaises et françaises.* Paris: Université Sorbonne Paris Cité. https://tel.archives-ouvertes.fr/tel-01579400.

Toury, Gideon. 1995. *Descriptive Translation Studies and Beyond.* Amsterdam and Philadelphia: John Benjamins.

Venuti, Lawrence. 1998. *The Scandals of Translation.* London: Routledge.

Venuti, Lawrence. [2000] 2012. *The Translation Studies Reader.* Edited by Lawrence Venuti. London: Routledge.

Venuti, Lawrence. 2013. *Translation Changes Everything: Theory and Practice.* London: Routledge.

7 Translation as an Ethical Locus

1 The Aim of Translation

This last chapter discusses the reception phenomenon from an ethical perspective, showing how translation norms of the target polysystem and translators' tendencies, whether of a personal, polysystemic, ideological, or political nature, act upon the text and the paratext of translation and result in deformation of the discourse. The chapter includes a critical discussion on the never-ending conflict between the adherents of source-oriented and those of target-oriented translation and its relevance to the translation of mystical Persian poetry in general and Rumi's work in particular.

Deformation, be it due to a translator's unconscious subjectivity, the corollary of the dominant ideology or under the influence of the TT's polysystemic forces, more often than not boils down to a question of respect. A translator's adherence to the ST is related to the respect the text commands. Even the most target-oriented classical translators show reverence for the Bible. Saint Jerome uses the metaphor of translated text as foreign soldiers bound as captives in the target language (TL) to illustrate the predicament of translation.

Thanks to two French thinkers, Henri Meschonnic (*Pour la poétique I* 1970b)/(*Pour la poétique II. Epistémologie de l'écriture. Poétique de la traduction* 1973)/(*Poétique du traduire* 1999) and Antoine Berman (*L'épreuve de l'étranger, Culture et traduction dans l'Allemagne romantique* 1984)/(*Pour une critique des traductions: John Donne* 1995)/(*La traduction et la lettre ou l'auberge du lointain* 1999), translation studies underwent a theoretical turning point. translation studies before Meschonnic and Berman were dominated by linguistics and prescriptive theories of translation at the origin of which were linguists such as Eugene Nida. Their main principles were rooted in the theory of communication focused on the reception of the translation and respect for the idiomatic and stylistic norms of the target language. These theorists advocated the clarity and readability of the translated text above all. Suddenly the values of transparency and invisibility of translation, long favored by literary critics and corroborated by linguistics, were called into question by Meschonnic's poetic project and Berman's ethical project, based not only on the theoretical thought of Romantic translators or Walter Benjamin's in *The Task of the Translator* ([1913] 2004), but also on that of Saint

DOI: 10.4324/9781003157960-8

Jerome who believed in the literalist translation of sacred texts. Foreign texts were henceforth treated as sacred and respected in their materiality, not only in their pragmatic functionality. The end task of translation became, therefore, to respect the foreignness of a text up to the finest grains of its infradiscoursive purport. With the Hebraist Meschonnic, this view of translation gained a mystical, almost religious, dimension.

1.1 The Poetics of Translating

Poetics scholar, essayist, and French translator of the Pentateuch (*Les Cinq Rouleaux* 1970a), Henri Meschonnic is a precursor of shifting theoretical considerations on the source text. His views on *rhythm* are, more than any Western thinker's, pertinently relevant to any epistemological reflection on classical Persian poetry, given their focus on the modes of significance of Semitic languages. Meschonnic's meticulous work on the role of rhythm in the significance of sacred texts and their translation into European languages is applicable to the translation of mystical poetry and its hybrid semiotic system. His poetic project unfolds in a series of essays called *Pour la poétique I–V* (1970b–1978), in which he redefines concepts of *poétique*, *discours*, and *rythme*. Meschonnic's poetics are not a theoretical study of poetry or even of literature in general. They provide even broader notions than Jakobson's poetic function. His poetics are "an epistemology of writing," a general theory of language, and a "historical anthropology of language" (1973). Rhythm is defined as the materiality of the discourse, in its musical harmony and phonetic incarnation. Rooted in the Semitic notion of the *letter*,[1] one of the hallmarks of the general theory of language is Meschonnic's categorical rejection of the semiotic *duality* or *discontinuity* of the sign, divided into expression or *letter* on the one hand, and content, meaning or spirit, on the other.[2]

This conception has crucial consequences for translation. In a highly controversial and sweeping generalization, Meschonnic rejects the validity of all translations of the Hebrew Bible into any Indo-European language since the *Vulgate*, as translators have all been inattentive to the central importance of *rhythm* in the Hebrew and Aramaic texts of the *Tanakh*. This founding act of translation in Western civilization having been imbibed in such a primordial error, the entire millennial monument of translation was worthless. Translation in Europe had been an act of *annexation* since the translation of the Old Testament had been the annexation of a text founded upon rhythm by a Hellenistic tradition rooted in the duality of sign whereby the spirit is prioritized over the letter. The aim of Meschonnic's *Poétique du traduire* was then *décentrement*, i.e., escaping from the core of an ethnocentric culture imprisoned in its own worldview by way a new epistemology of writing (Meschonnic 1999). Meschonnic's ambition was very broad: he proposed a general theory of writing centered on rhythm. By calling into question the notion of the *discontinuity* of the sign, Meschonnic saw the need for a radical change in notions such as *transparency* or *fidelity*, or source- or target-oriented translation. The *inseparability* of form and content manifests itself best in poetic *significance*, where the vehicle of meaning is *rhythm*.[3] The place of translation in the general theory of language is primordial, contrary to its ancillary status within literature, as the polysystem theory suggests. "Translating a text is situated in the practice and the theory of texts, which are themselves situated in a *translinguistic* theory of enunciation" (Meschonnic 1973, 306). Meschonnic's poetic project consisted in a *translinguistic* creation of discourse.[4] Translation was no longer to be regarded as the "transportation of the source text into a target literature or, conversely, the transport of the target reader into the source text" (1973, 313), but as the establishment of a "textual relationship between two texts in two language-cultures up to the linguistic structure of the language, this linguistic structure being of value in the system of the text" (*Ibid.*, 308). The transposition of the infradiscourse and the recreation of the discourse in its very materiality in the TL were precisely what Meschonnic calls *décentrement* (decentering), the absence of this relationship constituting *annexation*:

> Annexation is the obliteration of this rapport, the illusion of naturalness, the *as-if*, as if a text in the source language were written in the target language, disregarding the differences of culture, epoch, linguistic structure. A text is *at distance*: we either show it, or we hide it.
>
> (Meschonnic 1973, 308)

The central element of discourse is *rhythm*, and it is what counts above all, above the stylistic or even syntactic constraints of any given language. *Rhythm* is the way writing (or speaking) subjects organize their discourse by the linguistic structuring of the text. Discourse is a transcendent reality in relation to language in that the text, the embodiment of the relationship between subject and history, can be realized translinguistically manifested, at any given moment, in the structure specific to a language, the structure that composes its *value*.[5] Translation must then be an "interpoetic relationship between value and meaning, structuring of a subjectivity and history, and no longer meaning" (1973, 314). In other words, translation's aim is to reestablish the relationship between the author's discoursive form and the language, his discourse and the code, and not the meaning of the utterance. "Translating a text is not translating language, Meschonnic argues, but translating a text in its own language, which is a text by its language, the language itself being by the text" (1973, 312).

The notion of history is of major importance insofar as a *text* is a connection between the subject (an author's subjectivity) and history (his/her language and culture), and it is for this reason that the translation must be a *text*, homogeneous with the source text, and not one reflecting the norms of the target language. What matters is to translate the text as a text *in* the TL that recreates the structures of the source text and that give it its *value*. The translation that aims at a text "in its language" is called a *translation-text* as opposed to a *translation-introduction* that only accounts for the meaning of the text and not for its value. To put this in perspective, the structure of Rumi's discourse, in its peculiar relation to the Persian language, in its vulgarity for instance, establishes its value. It is this value that must be preserved in the TT by reestablishing the same peculiarity at the expense of the stylistic, even syntactic and idiomatic, characteristics of the target language. Our examples all through this essay show how far the translations or Rumi's poetry have been from this ideal.

Meschonnic briefly formulates the characteristics of the *translation-text* (1973, 315–316), albeit much less systematically than Berman's analytics, discussed later. Meschonnic points out the dominance of certain translation practices exercised by translators of poetry and prose that result in the distortion of the text. These distorting practices are, among others, poetization or *literarization*, rewriting, and the domination of an *aestheticizing* ideology or literary elegance, "which is marked by a practice of deletions (repetitions for example), additions, displacement, transformations, according to a ready-made idea of language and literature" (*Ibid.*, 315).

1.2 Translation Analytics

Antoine Berman, perhaps the most influential translation theorist, argued ten years after Meschonnic in favor of source-oriented translation but in a more systematic and productive way. His translation analytics had an enduring impact on the ethical reflections on translation. In the chapter "Le projet pour une critique productive" (Berman 1995, 34–63), he examines two strong analytic theories in translation, that of Meschonnic's "engaged analyses" and the polysystem theory's "sociocritically oriented descriptive analyses," pointing out the lacunae of each before proposing his own project. As far as Meschonnic is concerned, Berman objects to "certain stereotypes of the poetician's writing," to the "aggressive orientation" he remains a "prisoner" of, and the militant negativity with which he blacklists translations that "mistreat" original texts. Berman is harsher against the "mechanicity" of the polysystem theorists' descriptive analyses that minimize the role of the translators and their responsibility as the principal agents of the translating operation. With the disempowering of the "sujets traduisants" and their choices by an "objectively" descriptive theory, translation is reduced to a simple social behavior conforming to the norms. Berman further condemns the resurgence, behind some "scientific" mask, of an old tradition of relegating translation to a peripheral and epigonal position in the polysystem. The major failing of functionalist theories, as identified by Berman, lies in their limited scope and their refutability by examples contradicting their alleged scientific laws. Berman also criticizes the blindness of these theories to the "uniqueness of History while sociologizing historicity" (Berman 1995, 54).[6] Berman's main objection to polysystem theory is its attribution of a secondary position to translation and its latent desire to justify target-oriented *deformations* by forces imposed on translators from outside. Berman argues that this approach goes against the historical fact that translation is a central pillar of Western culture (*Ibid.*, 58–59). Toury's target-oriented vocation is only an attempt to "justify" this ethnocentric way of translating which goes against the main task of "true" translation, namely, to reveal the "truth" of the text.[7]

Berman proposes his own analytics of translation based on the axiom that "translation is translation-of-the-letter," that is to say, the translation of a text is only the translation of "the text as it is *letter*" (Berman 1999, 25). He theorizes a system of *déformant* [deforming/distorting] forces and tendencies inevitably at work in all translating operations that translators must be made aware and wary of so as to avoid them. This essentially negative approach is followed by positive propositions for an "ethics of translation." In this approach, Berman contrasts the "ethnocentric" translation with the "ethical" translation and *hypertextual* translation to poetic translation (*Ibid.*). The primary aim of translation, according to Berman, can be summed up by a key theoretical concept, that of the "ethical translation," embodied in its most sublime form in the "great translations" of German idealists such as Hölderlin, Humboldt, and Schlegel, who prepared the ground for a Hegelian project of *Bildung*. Translation, according to them, can only be beneficial for the target language-culture if there is an opening of the *Self* towards the *Other*, to accept it and absorb it in its otherness; *foreignness* must, therefore, be the purpose of translating. This attitude can be summed up in Schleiermacher's formula, made famous by Berman: "to bring the reader to the author" and not "the author to the reader" (Berman 1984, 15).

> Any culture resists translation, even if it essentially needs it. The very *aim* of translation – to open a certain relation to the Other at the level of writing, to fertilize the Self through the mediation of the Foreign – collides head-on with the ethnocentric structure of any culture, this narcissism whereby any society likes to be a pure and unmixed Whole.
>
> (Berman 1984, 16)

This conflict between the "reductive forces" of a culture on the one hand, and the desire to open up translation on the other, has as its corollary the appearance of a kind of translation which can be qualified as ethnocentric; one which, taking into account the need for the enrichment of culture, sets out to conquer other cultures without integrating them into its own but by assimilating it. This is precisely what Berman calls a bad translation: "the translation which, generally under the guise of transmissibility, operates a systematic negation of the strangeness of the foreign work" (1984, 17). These types of translations constitute an important part of the existing translations of Rumi, especially the more recent ones, but also some of the oldest. They violate the ethics of translation based on fidelity and accuracy, two Grundwörter (big words) that refer "to a certain behavior of man vis-à-vis himself, others, the world and existence. As well, of course, with regard to the texts. . . . The ethical act consists in recognizing and receiving the Other as Other (Berman 1999, 74). This fidelity to the otherness of the Stranger and to the novelty brought by the Other within the language of the Same has a "carnal" form which is represented by the "letter":

> Now, just as the Foreigner is a carnal being, tangible in the multiplicity of its concrete signs of strangeness, so the work is a carnal, tangible, living reality at the level of language. . . . The ethical aim of translating, precisely because it proposes to welcome the Stranger in his carnal corporeality, can only be attached to the letter of the work. If the form of the aim is fidelity, it must be

said that there is fidelity – in all domains – only to the letter. Being "faithful" to a contract means respecting its terms, not the "spirit" of the contract. To be faithful to the "spirit" of a text is a contradiction in terms.

(Berman 1999, 76–77)

The notion of literality, in Berman's view, does not, however, correspond to the traditional concept of literal translation. Rather, it is about the "attachment to the letter" where the discursive form constitutes a deviation from the discursive norm within the source language, a deviation which gives rise to what Eco calls *ratio difficilis*. Faithfulness to the letter makes sense when the form is responsible for part of the utterance's meaning, that which Folkart calls translation-practice.[8] It is a re-enunciation that remanifests in the TT the remotivation of the expression plane by the content-plane and recovers the discursive form of the original utterance down to its infradiscoursive structure, even if this practice leads to a counter-idiomatic utterance in the target system. This is the deep substance of Berman's literalism. By no means is it equivalent to literal blind translation.

2 Target-Oriented Positions

2.1 Source or Target: A Perpetual Conflict

Despite all the theoretical developments and epistemological shifts in translation studies, the unresolved conundrum remains over a rather simple tension between target-oriented and source-oriented tendencies in translation. This never-ending debate took a sharp turn in the West with German idealists who extended a position that applied only to the translation of Holy Scriptures to apply to all literary texts where the discursive forms are at least as important as the reference. In modern times, this theoretical debate continued between the tenants of *foreignizing* translations represented by the likes of Antoine Berman, Henri Meschonnic, and the Russian author Nabokov, on the one hand, and the representatives of *fluent* and *transparent* translations with *equivalent* discursive effects rather than equivalent discursive forms on the other. The latter group deploy an army of scientific arguments, from linguistics to semiotics, from sociology to hermeneutics, to defend an old philosophical tradition that places *spirit* above *letter* and the purity of language over the disturbing presence of the foreign. Some of the gatekeepers of this old and well-established millennial tradition are Georges Mounin, Eugene Nida, Jean-René Ladmiral, Ezra Pound, Barbara Folkart, and, in a sense, Lawrence Venuti.[9] These two antagonistic tendencies were already recognized by Friedrich Schleiermacher in his *Über die verschiedenen Methoden des Übersetzens*:

> In my opinion, there are only two possibilities. Either the translator leaves the writer in peace as much as possible and moves the reader toward him; or he leaves the reader in peace as much as possible and moves the writer toward him.

(Venuti [2000] 2012, 49)

248 *Translation as an Ethical Locus*

German Romantics opted clearly for the former approach, i.e., bringing the reader to the writer. In the end, however, this *foreignizing* revolution did not altered translation practices much: they are still largely dominated by principles of aesthetic reception and characterized by a preference for transparency and readability over form and even semantic content. Rumi's translators too, overwhelmingly, were no exception to this rule. This dominant approach, according to Meschonnic, has had the upper hand over any other theoretical adventure throughout the history of translation and reached its apogee with French classicism with its aesthetic doctrine of good taste and strict precepts of clarity and consistency. In the 20th century, linguists like the American Eugene Nida (1964)/(1975)/(Nida and Taber 1969) with his insistence on *dynamic equivalence*, French Georges Mounin (*Les problèmes théoriques de la traduction* 1976)/(*Les Belles infidèles* [1955] 1994), with his notion of *transparency* and, later on, French philosopher Jean-René Ladmiral (2014) are some of the major proponents of target-oriented translation and its aesthetic of clarity and distinctness. George Mounin analyzes translation as an act of communication: as such, what matters most is the reception of the text in the TL and culture. He recognizes three important gaps that translation must overcome in order to bring the ST closer to the TT: a linguistic gap between the translated and translating languages, the historical discrepancy between the source and target texts, and the cultural divergence between source and target communities. He reformulates Schleiermacher's dichotomy, recognizing two opposing approaches among translators with two end results: a translated text which gives the impression of having been originally written in the TL and one which constantly reminds the reader that this is a translation.

> there are several types of translation, legitimate according to the texts. At first, two major classes emerge. Either, for the translator, [the goal is] to translate in such a way that the text, literally francized, without a strangeness of language, always seems to have been directly thought out and then written in French – that is, in a way, to realize the ambition of the *Belles infidèles*[10] without their unfaithfulness, which is at the origin of a first class of translations.
>
> Or else, to produce text by translating the exotic impression of reading the text in the original forms (semantic, morphological, stylistic) of the foreign language – so that the reader never forgets for a single moment that he is reading in French a text which was first thought out and then written in such and such foreign language: the second class of translators.
>
> (Mounin 1976, 110)

Mounin uses the metaphor of "transparent glass" for the first class as opposed to "colored glass" for the second, with both containing the meaning of the original text. He then opts for the first class for the translation of literary works, following the example of Cicero and French classicists. This distinction is rejected by Meschonnic's or Berman's ethical theory. For these two thinkers, there are only *good* or *bad* translations. To believe like Meschonnic and Berman that there exist two equally valid classes of translation gives legitimacy to what they consider linguistic and cultural *ethnocentrism* and *annexationism*.

Jean René Ladmiral evokes the same dichotomy in his *Sourcier ou cibliste* [Source-oriented or Target-oriented] (2014). Like Meschonnic, he is critical of the positivist and empiricist approaches of modern normative linguistics, which he finds reductive and blind to the real problems of translation. However, Ladmiral is a fervent defender of target-oriented translation and a fierce critic of source-oriented advocates. He finds in the literalist practices of source-oriented advocates a disconnection from reality and a confinement in theoretical concepts that have no connection with reality. For Ladmiral, the sterility of the literalist approach lies precisely in its excessive subjectivity in relation to a theoretical and idealistic definition of *fidelity*. According to Ladmiral, faithfulness to the ST is strongly called into question by the destruction of the "semiotic meaning" of the utterance when translators stick to the form of the original letter in the target language. Literalism, according to Ladmiral, is not fidelity to the original text because it renders it devoid of denotative and connotative semantic content. The main criticisms of target-oriented advocates against literalists like Meschonnic consist in denying the very possibility of literalism in translation. Ladmiral compares literal translation to a sexual relationship, emphasizing that it is only authorized and legitimate when there is consent, i.e., the "possibility" of use in the target language. When literalist translators set out to create a structure that is impossible in their own language, they are actually "violating" it (Ladmiral 2014, 23–27). In a semiotic approach, Ladmiral likens literalism to the process of transcoding, which is not equal to translating because language is not limited, as Benveniste shows, to a semiotic significance on the paradigmatic axis; the semantic mode of significance exists and is realized on the syntagmatic axis. In other words, Ladmiral takes up Benveniste's emphasis on the semantic structure of the connotations and specifies that the "semiotic meaning" is not equal to the sum of its denotative constituents in the first degree. He proposes the notion of *dissimilation* with the aim of "compensating" connotations characterizing any text:

> Translator should be authorized or even encouraged to "dissimilate" (or, we could say, to "throw the weight further"), that is to move away from the source-connotator, in order to choose a target-connotator which does not "resemble" it on the level of the signifier but indeed connotes the same signified.
>
> (2014, 190)

Ladmiral's understanding of literalism, however, seems somewhat caricatural. As Folkart recognizes, literalism is an attempt to recover the infradiscoursive structure of the utterance in re-enunciation. What takes precedence in ethical translation is to make translation visible by highlighting the foreign in its foreignness, i.e., the foreignness in its enunciation. This approach is hardly intended to transpose the source text word for word into the target language, as Ladmiral seems to suggest.

2.2 The Hermeneutic Model

The most recent criticism of literalism in translation is from an unusual suspect, the main introducer of Antoine Berman's theories in North America, Lawrence Venuti. The evolution of Venuti's thought is impressive, from his fierce criticism of the paradigm of TT *readability* and the translator's effacement from the scene (*The Translator's Invisibility: A History of Translation* [1995] 2008)/(*The Scandals of Translation* 1998) to his proposed hermeneutic model in later work (2013) whereby he seems sympathetic to the idea of justifying adaptations and free translations – which he calls "versions" – at least in poetry translation. In his preliminary work, Venuti departs from the ethic theories of translation to denounce the situation of translators in the Anglo-American cultural sphere, which he calls *invisibility* and describes as follows:

> A translated text, whether prose or poetry, fiction or nonfiction, is judged acceptable by most publishers, reviewers, and readers when it reads fluently, when the absence of any linguistic or stylistic peculiarities makes it seem transparent, giving the appearance that it reflects the foreign writer's personality or intention or the essential meaning of the foreign text – the appearance, in other words, that the translation is not in fact a translation, but the "original." The illusion of transparency is an effect of fluent discourse, of the translator's effort to insure easy readability by adhering to current usage, maintaining continuous syntax, fixing a precise meaning.
>
> (Venuti [1995] 2008, 1)

Inspired by Berman's dichotomy of the *étrangéisant* versus *homogénéisant* translation, Venuti distinguishes two practices in translation: *domestication* and *foreignization*, which reflect Schleiermacher's distinction between translations that "leave the reader in peace and move the author toward him" and those which "send the reader abroad towards the author" (Venuti [2000] 2012, 43–63). This dichotomy forms the two poles of a continuum on the ethical level that corresponds, on a discursive level, to the opposition between *fluency* (transparent readability of the TT) and *resistance* to the target linguistic and stylistic norms. Just as Schleiermacher did in the context of the German construction of *Bildung*, Venuti advocates in favor of foreignizing practices, albeit not as a general philosophical approach to translation but rather as a militant act. For Venuti, foreignization is:

> a strategic cultural intervention in the current state of world affairs, pitched against the hegemonic English-language nations and the unequal cultural exchanges in which they engage their global others. Foreignizing translation in English can be a form of resistance against ethnocentrism and racism, cultural narcissism and imperialism, in the interests of democratic geopolitical relations.
>
> (1995, 20)

However, for Venuti, foreignization neither necessarily leads to literal translation nor does it have the metaphysical dimensions that exist in Walter Benjamin's view or French ethical theories of translation. Foreignization is not necessarily the ultimate aim of translation and the true task of the translator. In Venuti's view, objectivity is a myth and translation, be it foreignizing or domesticating, cannot be devoid of cultural values and ideological motivations. This gives his ethical position an apparent paradoxical dimension when it comes to the recognition of adaptation. Foreignizing translations are actually as vested in an ideological value as domesticating ones since foreignizing is an act of resistance and domestication an act of control. In fact, for Venuti an ethical position in translation is unrelated to the TT's literal proximity to the ST, but rather to the TT's defiance towards the target system's norms and values. In consequence, the mere choice of a minority text, which he calls *minoritization* (Venuti 1998, 13–20) constitutes an act of foreignization, and this regardless of the literality or semantic proximity of the translated text to the ST. Venuti's translative militantism in conjunction with his textual deconstructionism leads to a paradoxical attitude towards the ethical obligation of semantic correspondence between ST and TT.

Venuti's way of resolving this paradox is a hermeneutic model of translation ethics discussed in *Translation Changes Everything: Theory and Practice* (2013), where he proposes the radical idea that "we must abandon the instrumental model of translation, the notion that a translation reproduces or transfers an invariant that is contained in or caused by the source text, whether its form, its meaning, or its effect" (Venuti 2013, 178). Since all "second-degree" production of text, including translation, imitation, version, anthology, adaption, etc. primarily involves an act interpretation, first by the *rewriter* and then by the reader of the secondary text, the question of translation should be understood "on the basis of a hermeneutic model" (*Ibid.*, 179). For Venuti, more important than establishing a formal and semantic correspondence between ST and TT is the interpretative act itself, which is always determined by the exigencies and circumstances of the target culture. In other words, since interpretation can vary according to space-time's fluctuating nature, there is no fixed content or even form to be adhered to in the target text, and various translations with varying degrees of formal or semantic correspondence are possible and valid.

> Translation should be seen as interpretation because it is radically decontextualizing. The structural differences between languages, even between languages that bear significant lexical and syntactical resemblances based on shared etymologies or a history of mutual borrowing or analogous formal features like inflections, require the translator variously to dismantle, rearrange, and finally displace the chain of signifiers that make up the source text.
> (2013, 180)

Venuti explains that in all acts of interlingual transposition, "three source-language contexts" that are "constitutive" of the ST are irremediably lost: the first is the *intratextual* context, that is the network of "linguistic patterns and discoursive structures." Next are the *intertextual* relations of the ST to the pre-existing texts and *interdiscoursive* relations to the pre-existing forms and themes, which constitute the significance of the text for the source language readers who have been exposed to them. The third are the *intersemiotic* and metatextual contexts of the reception, "the various media through which the source text continues to accrue significance when it begins to circulate in its originary culture" (*Ibid.*). Venuti's description is pertinently comparable to our discussion of the differential between the two fields of indication and interpretation in the previous chapter. There is always an irreparable mingling of the forces and elements of the field of interpretation with any act of *re-enunciation*. Venuti rules out any possible equivalent effect between ST and TT, as the reader of a translation "can never experience it with a response that is equivalent or even comparable to the response with which the source-language reader experiences the source text" (*Ibid.*). By the same token, the translator's response to the text, i.e., his interpretation, takes place in and is affected by "a cultural situation" with specific values, beliefs, representations, and groups of power. The translator's understanding and interpretation of the text varies insofar as the interdiscoursive, intertextual, and intersemiotic relations between the text and its pre-existing texts constantly change. Venuti refers to Derrida's concept of *différance* (*Difference in translation* 1985) and iterability to explain how "the change in meaning that can occur with a change in context" condemns translation to be ineluctably different from its source text because it is recontextualization.

> Every interpretation is fundamentally evaluative insofar as it rests on the implicit judgment that a text is worth interpreting, not only in commentary but also through translation or adaptation . . .
> The evaluation must be shifted to a different level that seems to me properly ethical: in inscribing an interpretation in the source text, a translation or adaptation can stake out an ethical position and thereby serve an ideological function in relation to competing interpretations.
> (Venuti 2013, 183–184)

Any interpretation is valid as long as it explicitly states so by means of meta-translative and exegetic commentaries. Insofar as these numerous possible interpretations are different, translations could only be different and plural. In essence, since the translated text can never be interpreted and understood in the same way as the source text and since any interpretation brings in a new perspective and enriches the source text by viewing it in a different light, then no formal equivalence is ever fathomable or necessary. In fact, in Venuti's ethics of translation, imposing a particular norm on translation, designating a fixed "truth" to the source text and forcing that truth upon the translator is considered totalizing and unethical. Venuti evokes Alain Badiou's conception of a "truth-based ethics" according to which truth is an investigative process spurred by an event that "brings to pass 'something other' than the situation" defined by "opinions" and "instituted knowledges" (cited in Venuti 2013, 184). Such an event locates a "void" in the situation or the institution and pushes the truth-seeking investigating subject to violate the established and circulating knowledges. Such search for truth "reworks" the encyclopedia "from which opinions, communications and sociality draw their meaning." Truth is specific to the situation and never definitive. No universal or transcendent dimension can be established for it. Truth is based on an "unnameable," an element that stands outside its conceptual grasp and, as such, it should not "assert power that is exclusionary or repressive and totalizing." This truth process is good whereas a *bad* process seeks to appoint a "substance" instead of a "void" to the situation, thus creating a "simulacrum of truth" related to the "the absolute particularity of a community" excluding certain individuals while accepting some others. Venuti's application of this concept to translation ethics is quite discomforting as he denies any such exclusionary truth for the ST.

> A translation, then, might be evaluated according to its impact, potential or real, on cultural and social institutions in the receiving situation, according to whether it challenges the styles, genres, and discourses that have gained institutional authority, according to whether it stimulates innovative thinking, research, and writing. The bad in translation is "the desire to name at any price" (Badiou 2008, 127), imposing cultural norms that seek to master cognitively and thereby deny the singularity that stands beyond them, excluding the alternative set of interpretants that enable a different translation, a different interpretation. Hence a translation, including a poet's version, should not be faulted merely for exhibiting features that are commonly called unethical: wholesale manipulation of the source text, ignorance of the source language, even plagiarism of other translations. We should instead examine the cultural and social conditions of the translation, considering whether its interpretants initiate an event, creating new knowledges and values by supplying a lack that they indicate in those that are currently dominant in the receiving situation.
>
> (Venuti 2013, 185)

3 The Analytics of Rumi Translations

At least in the case of translating Rumi, I oppose Venuti's view on ethical translation just as the rest of target-oriented arguments mentioned earlier. My main argument relies on a theory of *discoursive distortion* that demonstrates how translators' liberties regarding the recreation of the semantic content and discoursive forms of Rumi's mystical text cause detrimental losses to its integrity, and this with little or no obvious gains.

3.1 *Deforming Tendencies*

Berman's negative analytics consist in identifying distorting tendencies in the translation of prose, which "form a systematic whole, the end of which is the destruction, no less systematic, of the letter of the original, for the sole benefit of 'meaning' and 'beautiful form.'" These practices, which can be both conscious and unconscious, take place above all on the level of lexicon and syntax. Berman recognizes 12 deforming tendencies in translation: rationalization, clarification, expansion, ennoblement, qualitative impoverishment, quantitative impoverishment, the destruction of rhythms, the destruction of underlying networks of signification, the destruction of linguistic patterns, the destruction of vernacular network or their exoticization, the destruction of expressions and idioms, and the effacement of the superimposition of languages (Berman 1995, 52–68).

Although Berman's deforming tendencies primarily concern prose translations, they can also easily be applied to Rumi's poems insofar as certain properties of prose also exist within poetry, and even in a more significant way. I referred to some of these distorting tendencies in the examples examined in this study.[11] Some of my findings about the nature and statistical distribution of such tendencies among Rumi translators can be summarily formulated as follows:

1 No translator of Rumi has been immune to distorting tendencies, including the most literalist ones like Nicholson, Arberry, and Williams. Nonetheless, distorting tendencies are significantly more recurrent among translators with a nonacademic profile.
2 The forces of deformation weigh more heavily in French than in English, probably due to the French language's more rigid syntax and its more rationalizing stylistic disposition in comparison with the paratactic, lexicological, and stylistic flexibility of English. This can be extrapolated to any other TL with similar syntactic and stylistic characteristics such as Romance languages and German, where the presence of grammatical gender, for instance, can inevitably lead to rationalization and clarification. On the contrary, the tendency towards destruction of idioms and linguistic patterns is less conspicuous in Romance languages and German, where certain structures such as verbal compounds resemble those of Persian. Also, the flexibility of German syntax, in terms of word order for instance, allows for a better recreation of Persian syntax.
3 The greater the translation task quantitatively, the lesser the quality of the translation, including in terms of deforming tendencies and this, despite his/her literalist approach. This is notably the case of Vitray-Meyerovitch in comparison to other less ambitious French translators. However, such a correlation is less likely to be observed in English classical translations, i.e., in the case of Nicholson.
4 In the English polysystem, the more recent the translations are, the higher the probability of deformation, annexationism, and ethnocentrism. The exception are the translations published by specialists and academic translations.

The last claim refers primarily to translations by Barks, Helminsky, Star, Harvey, Khalili, Shiva, and especially Ergin, who have largely exceeded the limits of deforming tendencies. They are closer to translation-introductions in Meschonnic's term, hypertextual translations in Berman's, or "poet's versions" in Venuti's (2013, 174). The omnipresence of subjective practices of deletion, addition, displacement, transformation, and textual mutilation in these hypertextual activities evoke other types of *rewriting* more than translation: adaptations, imitations, or even pastiches, regardless of whether the translator masters the source language. However, the ethical issues arise when most of these translators do not explicitly mention the nature of their work. From a literary perspective, the presence of these *ultra-deforming* practices[12] does not appear to bring in any major aesthetic assets to the discourse. It is, for example, very difficult to note the slightest gain in the numerous English reproductions of the *Neynāme* or of ghazal 2214 – which has the greatest number of English translations. Versions by Barks, Shiva, Helminsky, Schimmel, and Ergin have recovered neither the original rhythm nor any rhyme. However, these free translations have succeeded in moving considerably away from the original content in destroying the original discursive form and underlying networks of meaning, and in impoverishing the text qualitatively and quantitatively.

3.2   Second-Degree Deformation

Domestication, or "the failure of the translation" (Berman 1984, 297), is above all the result of what Venuti calls the value-driven nature of sociocultural frameworks. Values are not only determined by the economic and cultural norms imposed by the target institutions but, most importantly, by the dominant ideology of both source and target polysystems. Regardless of the causes and origins of deformation, it does not occur only at the level of the utterance or of the body of the translated text, but also *around* it, namely, in any textual or nontextual activities related to the translated text: from the choice of text, the translator's commentaries and titles to the editor's decisions about typography, illustrations, and design, to academic reviews, advertisement, interviews, etc. The deforming forces that apply to this area of the reception do not act upon the utterance but on its *secondary* field of interpretation, i.e., to the reader of the TT's field of interpretation. While the semantic content of the message, or even its discursive content, may remain intact, the field of interpretation of the message can be *altered* or *contaminated* by elements and forces that existed neither in the primary field of indication nor in the primary field of interpretation of the ST. The forces only start to appear in the secondary field of indication, that of the TT, and are reinforced and augmented in the secondary field of interpretation of the message. These forces act on secondary fields. In consequence, I call this facet of deformation *second degree*.

3.2.1   The Translational Paratext

Second-degree deformation occurs thanks to a panoply of *paratextual* devices found in the *peritext* as well as in the *epitext*. In *Seuils* [Thresholds] (1987), Gérard Genette defines *paratext* as the elements that are found on the periphery of the text and are related to it in some way. These elements are divided into two categories: the paratext directly attached to the text is called the *peritext*. It includes, among other elements, footnotes, prefaces, afterwords, introductions, titles, and various types of text commentaries published with, or separately from, the text. The *epitext* relates to what is published separately: interviews, reviews, editorial notes, critiques, etc. In rewriting practices, we can imagine other paratextual elements such as the choice of texts to be translated, their organization, their positioning in relation to each other, their manipulation, and the recreation of their context. In fact, translation itself is paratextual in nature. Genette considers translation as a type of *transtextuality* or "textual transcendence" of the original text (*Palimpsestes: La littérature au second degré* 1982, 7–8). In other words, translation paratext is paratext of the paratext, a second-degree paratext, impacted by deforming forces.

The *transtextual* paratext also has certain *immaterial* elements in addition to the usual paratext. Perhaps the most important component of this immaterial paratext is the choice of the text to translate. The other element is *text sequencing*, i.e., the sequence in which individual poems are presented in an anthology. The choice of the passage to be translated is complemented by the choice of the place where it appears. Together, these choices contribute to the *framing* of the message, which can hold certain ideological or cultural values. Given the sheer size of Rumi's work, most translators have published anthologies with all the freedom to select the location of the poems and excerpts in relation to each other in the organizational scheme of their works. The interpretation of the message is then altered by the recontextualization of the poems. This type of decontextualization constitutes a deforming tendency as it shatters the textual system and breaks the underlying networks of meaning in the discourse. This recontextualization furthermore presents a second-degree deformation affecting the secondary field of interpretation, for instance by associating poems with similar themes to create a particular value.

This is the case with Barks, among others. His translation of an excerpt of the *Neynāme* in his anthology *Essential Rumi* appears in Chapter 3, entitled "Emptiness and Silence: The Night Air" (Barks 1995, 17–32). The preface of each themed chapter plays an important role in guiding the reader towards a specific interpretative angle. The poems in this chapter should all be understood as sharing a common theme of "silence." In the chapter's preface, immediately before the excerpt from the *Neynāme* entitled "The Reed Flute Song" following Nicholson's model, Barks places the focus on the question of language and silence, excluding other interpretative possibilities in the prelude of *Ney*:

> [Rumi] gives the poetry to its true authorship [Shams], including the emptiness *after* as part of the poem. . . . Rumi is less interested in language, more attuned to the sources of it. . . . Words are not important in themselves, but as resonators for a center. Rumi has a whole theory of language based on the reed flute (ney). Beneath everything we say, and within each note of the reed flute, lies a nostalgia for the reed bed. Language and music are possible only

because we're empty, hollow, and separated from the source. All language is a longing for home.

(Barks 1995, 17)

The chapter contains four other passages from the *Masnavi*, seven ghazals and two quatrains. The succession of poems is not without interest. The first text is a version based on the first 18 lines of the *Neynāme*. The couplets are all mingled. Certain couplets are omitted, or their content appears in other couplets. A single couplet can give rise to several lines in Barks's translation or, conversely, some couplets disappear completely (l.3 for example). This passage is followed by a ghazal entitled by Barks "A Thirsty Fish" to expand on the allegory of fish mentioned in line 17 of the *Neynāme*. He uses the last line about the poet's repentance for writing poetry to link this theme to another ghazal called "Enough Words." Barks's recontextualization creates an arbitrary order based on similarities of themes that he finds here and there in the poems, themes that have no logical connection and that only make sense in the context of their respective poems. Regardless of the accuracy of Barks's points, this manipulation of the transtextual paratext has a deep impact on the reader's understanding of an otherwise mute text.

3.2.2 Titling

While tales of the *Masnavi* bear a summarizing title, poems of the *Divan* do not have any title. Adding titles to these poems associates them with semantic content that is absent from the original text. New elements doubtless alter the secondary field of interpretation, especially if the translator does not explicitly mention the source of addition. Two types of titling practices can be recognized among Rumi translators: the first affects the title of the published work and the second relates to individual poems. The first category can in turn be divided into two groups: neutral titles are the literal translations of the main work, Tajadod's *Le livre de Chams de Tabriz*, Nicholson's *Selected Poems From the Dīvāni Shamsi Tabrīzi*, or Arberry's *The Ruba'iyat of Jalal al-Din Rumi*. However, there exist arbitrarily chosen titles by the translator or editor, representing the content under a particular light, and giving it a particular contextual value: Vitray-Meyerovitch's *Mathnawî: la quête de l'absolu*, Shiva's *Rendering the Veil*, Barks's *Rumi: Bridge to the Soul*. Shaping the reader's first impression about the work and making a commercial appeal on the bookstore shelf, the title given to a translation implicitly announces its content. For example, the translation of Leili Anvar's *Rûmî la Religion de l'amour* automatically classifies the text as religious or theological. It also shows her position from the outset: Rumi's thought is the love-centered nondogmatic version of Islam.

As for inventing titles for poems, their very existence is a distorting tendency insofar as even if they are perfectly neutral, they highlight a specific aspect of the content to the detriment of others, while no such a choice was made by the author. For instance, *Song of the Reed* (by Nicholson and Helminsky) restricts the Prelude of the *Ney* to a specific idea. The most striking example is ghazal 2039 that is given the following titles obviously based on a legend relayed by Aflaki, Rumi's hagiographer, according to whom the poem was composed by Rumi on his deathbed: Helminsky entitles it "On the Deathbed" and Tajadod "DERNIER POÈME." While there is absolutely no textual evidence to support Aflaki's claim, readers of the TT, unlike readers of the ST, are deprived of their freedom of interpretation and are led to believe that these are the final words of a dying Rumi.

3.2.3 The Translator's Commentary

Subject of heated debate in translation studies, translator's notes and commentary are the most important locus in translational paratext. In the form of footnotes, endnotes, forewords, introductions, and afterwords, translator's comments and notes can be about the semantic content, the process of translation, or the circumstances of the creation of the work, such as the author's biographical data or the historical setting. They are a major source of additional elements to the field of interpretation, thus they are a double-edged sword, as they are both dangerous and essential to a foreignizing translation and instructive translation. What distinguishes essential notes and comments from *second-degree deformation* is their nature, whether they are *meta*-translational notes or *exegetical* comments.

Meta notes deal with problems of translation and inform the reader about the difficulties, potential losses, or inevitable deformations due to the translating process. *Exegetical* notes are to help the reader better understand the content of the translated text. There are two types of exegetical notes: *factual* and *interpretative*. Factual notes stick to the historical and cultural facts about the genesis of the text, usually with proper references and citations, and are devoid of value judgments. *Interpretative* comments, on the contrary, convey the translator's own points on view without acknowledging them as such. These are the notes that interpret the text for the reader in the manner of a psychologist or historian. The traditional distinction was clearly pointed out by Wilhelm Dilthey in *Die geistige Welt* (cited in Ricœur (1986, 154–163)), who differentiated *explanation* and *understanding* as two sides of hermeneutics. Explanation is pursued by the natural sciences whereas understanding is the subject of psychology and history. Factual and *meta* notes are not only acceptable but indispensable for a translation that seeks to be an *education to the foreign*, as Berman puts it. Interpretative translator's notes, however, are the single most important sources of *second-degree deformation* in the translation of mystical discourses insofar as such texts are, by essence, meant to be ambivalent and metasemic in such a way as to provide unlimited interpretations of their message. Any attempt by the translator, therefore, to orient the readers' understanding of an otherwise multifaceted text constitutes a distortion since the intervention is reductionist, restrictive, and impoverishing to the message.

If commentary and translation are both likely to pose ethical problems, it is because they are in an intertextual relationship that sometimes makes them inseparable. They share undeniable similarities. Both follow an original text to which they are linked by a relationship of *secondarity* giving rise to an ethical obligation. Both are the continuation of the text, its extension, its survival. What viscerally connects these two practices is the work of interpretation done by the translator: understanding in order to *translate* or understanding in order to *explain*. What separates them is indeed the place of interpretation, hidden and preliminary in the translation, apparent and explicit in the commentary. If the interpretation is prior to the translation while not allowing itself to be seen by the reader, it is at the center of the commentary, the purpose of which is to explain. Explicitation is not and should not be the aim of translation. It is not up to the translation to interpret the work for the reader. Translators should not impose their own exegesis on the reader. If the ST is hard to decipher for the ST reader, it must remain so in its translation. The original work, being the manifestation of a world, must be remanifested as it is without delimiting its facets. Translators who enrich the field of interpretation of the text, not by "indicative elements" of the text but by directing comprehension, deprive the reader of a freedom of thought which the reader of the original text enjoys.

The boundaries between translation and *interpretative* commentary are probably nowhere else as blurred as in the translations of Sufi poetry. This is due, one the one hand, to the discoursive and hermeneutical particularities of mystical poetry and, on the other hand, to the profile of its translators, often orientalists, and usually endowed with an Islamizing reading grid. Most of these translators have not been able to distance themselves from their role as expert commentators from their role as translators. This has caused tremendous harm to Rumi's reception in the West since his texts are not often transmitted to the Western reader without interference from these experts' exegeses, and this regardless of what specific ideological orientation or institutional agenda may motivate them.

Among most Rumi translators, the preferred device for presenting meta-translational commentaries seems to be the introduction or preface preceding the translated text. Translator's notes alongside the text itself in order to offer exegetical commentaries are more common among more recent translators. Nicholson's methodology, for instance, consists in using notes as footnotes and endnotes, the former usually meta-translational and the latter often of an exegetical type but usually factual and offering intertextual references (Koran, hadith, etc.). This practice shows Nicholson's high awareness of the problem. Nicholson kept his detailed commentaries on the *Masnavi* well separated from the actual body of the text and actually published in separate volumes, thus giving the reader the freedom to confront the text at first hand without consulting Nicholson's commentary and therefore without his field of interpretation being contaminated by clues provided by a third party. This same practice was taken up by Arberry in all his translations as well as by Lewis, Mojaddedi, and Williams among others. On the contrary, Gamard's heavily annotated version of the *robāʿis* represents a peculiar case of intermingling of translation and commentary.

260 *Translation as an Ethical Locus*

3.2.4 On the Textual Margins

The translational epitext comprises everything that surrounds the text in an intertextual relationship external to the work. Many Rumi translators are also authors of critical works and commentaries on Rumi, Sufism, Islam, Persian literature, etc. Nicholson's last three volumes of the *Masnavi* are dedicated to his commentary, which constitutes a translational epitext. His anthology of ghazals, for instance, is where he expounds about the Neoplatonic origins of Sufism. There are also translators whose translation is only part of a more global enterprise of pedagogical commentary. Chittick's translation (1984) is in fact the peritext of his theoretical work on Rumi. He uses his translations of sporadic verses to support his often Islamizing views about various aspects of Rumi's work.[13] More recently in French, Leili Anvar has followed the same model. She has lately published several books and had numerous interviews and lectures on Sufism, in addition to her small, but high-quality, French anthology of Rumi. Translation is above all an educational tool for these translators. The problem of such projects is that often singled out verses are recontextualized in a general discourse to support a certain argument. Anvar, for example, in the ideological wake of Vitray-Meyerovitch, is a fervent defender of resituating the poet within the framework of an Islamic tradition by placing the Koran at the main source of the poet's inspiration, and this in a very comprehensive perspective extrapolated to all Sufi poets.

4 For an Ethics of Translating Rumi

4.1 Discoursive Distortion in Translation

I use the term *discoursive distortion* to refer to the entire phenomenon of substantial, qualitative and quantitative, avoidable or unavoidable, modification suffered by the discourse in the process of its transposition. The translator-rewriter grasps the text and re-enunciates it in a target language-culture recreating a maximum of discoursive structures and maintaining a maximum of semantic content and structure, all the while influenced and affected by multiple circumstantial realities. These realities include the translator's personal aesthetic and ideological orientations, institutions' legitimate and illegitimate pressures, and the composition of the fields of interpretation at any given moment of reception. The term "discourse" here is understood not only in its pure linguistic sense but, in general, as the totality of the semiotic facts (relations, units, operations, etc.) located on any syntagmatic axis belonging to any media. In this sense, discourse is the product of the semiotization of reality, and translation the process of *resemiotization*. Distortion should not necessarily be understood as a premeditated and deliberate act of changing a discoursive form or substance for specific purposes and motivated by specific agendas, although this is its main mode of functioning. Distortion can simply occur because of the differential between (primary and/or secondary) fields of indication and interpretation of the discourse due to decontextualization and subsequent recontextualization of texts as in any process of rewriting. The expression *discoursive distortion* in translation should not be associated with any pejorative connotation, accusatorial tone, or sense of culpability on the translator's side insofar as discoursive phenomenon can only be partially attributed to a translator's ideological tendencies or the target polysystem's ethnocentric predisposition. The acting forces that lead to discoursive distortion are multiple and most often natural and hence inevitable. They are not exclusive to interlingual translation but affect all types of translation, including intralingual and intersemiotic – i.e., rewritings and adaptations – even to all forms of human communication. Discoursive distortion in translation should, above all, be understood in the same context as what mystics consider to be the inaptitude human language to express thought and truth. It is, in fact, a variant of our epistemological deficiency in *semiotizing* the extrasemiotic world.[14] Noumena can only be *understood*, or *translated* as phenomena, according to George Steiner, since that is the way reality appears to the subject. This is also the basic idea of the process of semiotization, which consists in using *a priori* categories to shape reality into a discourse with functionally related expression and content planes. The immediate access to reality is only possible in a mystical context where truth is revealed to the mystic. In the realm of ordinary mortals that we are, the imperfect process of semiotization and resemiotization is the only possibility of understanding and communicating.

Nevertheless, the unreachability of an ideal does not dispense the moral imperative to make attempts to reach it. The insufficiency of human language has not thwarted Rumi from composing over 120,000 verses. The inevitability of discoursive distortion in translation should not justify passivity in rendering an ethical translation. Detrimental effects of natural phenomena cannot be ignored under the pretext that they are "natural." There are a myriad of natural phenomena that are faced, combatted, or evaded by humans at all costs even if their eradication is impossible. From a living creature's standpoint, avoiding death or physical pain is regarded as an ultimate goal, no matter how natural its cause may be. By the same token, no epistemological defeatism can justify discoursive distortion just because the ST can never be recreated and grasped as such in a different language, time, and circumstances. This is the core of the argument against the target-oriented creative approach in literary translation.

The goal here is not to propose a final solution to the source-orientation or target-orientation dialectic, a dichotomy perfectly relevant today, according to Ladmiral, Mounin, and other advocates of transparency and fluency in translation, yet considered outdated by Meschonnic, Berman, and partisans of translation ethics who only believe in a continuum on both extremities of which are placed *good* and *bad* translation, foreignizing or homogenizing translation, annexationism or *décentrement*. No matter how hard these theorists argue for an overcoming of this dialectic, by transposing the debate in an ethical context like Berman and Meschonnic or a discoursive linguistic theoretical framework like Folkart, it is undeniable that there remains a certain polarity in the continuum of translational tendencies upon which translators should position themselves from time to time, regardless of what the continuum is called. Translation choices are above all a function of the nature of the ST: it is the nature of the text that should determine the translator's position on the continuum of Nida's dynamic-formal correspondence, Toury's acceptability-adequation, Folkart's transitive-practical translation, Meschonnic's annexation-decentering, and Berman's hypertextual-poetic or ethnocentric-ethical translation. Whether one is good and the other bad is determined by specific circumstances of reception and ST. The ethical choice is made occasionally, punctually, situationally, and not critically. A financial article, with varying degrees of poeticity and literality,[15] should not be translated with the same level of literality as a Japanese haiku.

As far as the practice of Rumi's translators is concerned, I put forth critical views that only relate punctually to a specific text, or at most to the translation of classical Persian poetry. The best and most valid approach to translating Rumi's poetry should be a discomfortingly literalist, foreignizing approach with ample meta and factual exegetical notes to educate the TL reader about the complexity and (inter- and intralingual) untranslatability of the source discourse. My argument has two major facets: pragmatic, referring to the impossibility of any dynamic equivalence in target languages, and philosophical, consisting in demonstrating the ethical paradox of the denial of innovation.

Pragmatically speaking, a functionalist recreationist approach to translate Persian classical poetry is simply not worth the high price in terms of the loss of semantic content and expressive form. The re-creation of a dynamic equivalence always comes with a more or less high price tag. Dynamic correspondence in the form of expression and content was shown to be merely impossible in any European target language. No matter how serious a Rumi specialist's hermeneutic effort, the hermetic character of mystical poetic discourse is such that the elusive meaning can often not be determined with certainty. Consequently, the best way to preserve the semantic haziness of the original discourse is by preserving its expressive form, no matter how disconcerting it sounds in the target system. In other words, because the *spirit* is neither accessible nor retrievable, at least the *letter* must be preserved. The omnipresence of *ratio difficilis* means that no expression plane exists in the source language to correspond to the given content plane. How then can one claim that an equivalent expression plane can be found in the target linguistic and cultural systems? How can an equivalent linguistic discourse be created in the TL when the original discourse is not even exclusively linguistic but a hybrid multisemiotic utterance? The "compensation" of "semiotic meaning," proposed by Ladmiral, is simply impossible since the semantic content is simply not contained in a linear linguistic utterance. When there is no isomorphism between the units of denotation in source and target languages, there is *a fortiori* no equivalence between the connotative sums that depend on them. When the connotative content of the utterance remains so difficult to recreate by discursive means in the target language, it is best to give up its compensation to the detriment of the formal materiality of the original discourse and resort to explanatory notes to minimize potential confusion in reading. Abandoning the infradiscursive forms of classical poetry in favor of establishing an equivalent semantic content that is not even wholesomely available in the source language means making great sacrifices for little gain.

4.2 The Aporia of the Annexationist Position

The philosophical facet of my argument proposes two perspectives: aesthetic and ethical. Mounin's ideal of *les belles infidèles* without *infidélité* can be challenged by the fact that beauty is not only created by way of conformity to a pre-established aesthetic canon but also by way of innovation. Is aesthesis necessarily a corollary of the reproduction of a certain pre-established canon that governs the notion of beauty or does a facet of the creation of beauty relate to novelty? What is the place of innovation in aesthetics? From an ethical standpoint, one can wonder why one should turn to a foreign artefact in search of aesthetic pleasure, while domestic counterparts are there to satisfy. If the *sine qua non* condition of aesthetic pleasure is absolute familiarity, then what is the point of translating *unfamiliar* works to one's language? If we take the Foreigner for its exoticism within its culture while throwing away its disturbing side, does such practice of expropriating the foreign property still mean openness? What would be the point of such a practice? If the objective sought is the enrichment of a one's culture, the goal is completely missed. If the point was to expose oneself to new worldview, new horizons, one may wonder how successful the project undertaken by Colman Barks or many other popularizers has been.

These reflections reveal the internal aporia of the target-oriented position in literary and poetry translation. This aporia of the annexationist perspective can best be described by its inherent hypocrisy and schizophrenia. I can even use the term *schizophrenic hypocrisy* to qualify the concept of "transparent translation" or that of "dynamic equivalence" in literary translation. Hypocrisy is not evoked in a pejorative way but in the etymological sense of the term: "acting," "mimicry," and "concealment." Schizophrenia too, is denoted by its etymology: *skhizein* [to split, to separate] and *phrên* [spirit],[16] meaning a fission of spirit between antagonistic and ambiguous forces. *Schizophrenic hypocrisy* refers to the desire to conceal the disturbing part of the Other to serve the Self with the intention of opening up to the novelty of the Other.

Ladmiral praises the idea of hypocrisy as the best target-oriented strategy, citing Efim Etkind who gives the example of numerous diminutives in Russian "which are untranslatable into French." Etkind recommends that they not be translated as such: "what must be translated, in this case, are not the diminutives themselves but the tenderness of which they are the signifier" (Ladmiral 2014, 23). I respond to this position by a rhetorical question: why should the TL reader even go to a Russian work with its queerly numerous diminutives to begin with if he finds this way of expressing tenderness disturbing? If the purpose of seeking aesthetic pleasure *elsewhere* is not distance from the conventions and exposure of oneself to *other* ways of being, then there is no point in reading translations of literary works. The very aim of translation is to broaden one's intellectual horizon by reaching out to the Other, to discover what lies within, in order to enrich one's worldview of the Self. Therefore, *concealing* baroque ways of expressing tenderness is a form of hypocrisy. And is not the desire to discover the Other in its otherness while dissimulating its strangeness under the "veil" of Self a typical symptom of schizophrenia? A highly "readable" translation of Rumi's work is "hypocrisy" in that it only *mimics* a foreign discourse, with a simulacrum of novelty. It is a window displaying an exotic Other with an illusion of the Foreign. The transparency in translating Rumi's poetry is also schizophrenic because it exposes an inner conflict at the depth of the collective subconscious of the target culture that is torn between desire for the Other and its rejection, the will to enrich itself through foreign cultures and the need to be comforted by forms and ideas that are familiar.

4.3 The Hermeneutic Model: A False Resolution

A case can be made against the position of dynamic equivalence proposed by Nida against the concept of translator's subjectivity and the emotional movement Folkart supports and that is reaffirmed by Venuti's hermeneutic model based on the *positional* validity of such theories: they are inapplicable and irrelevant to the translation of Persian poetry. Like in many other instances, the root of the problem is found in the Western paradigm that prevails in the epistemology of human sciences in the world. The great majority of theories in translation studies, too, are based on empirical evidence retrieved from quantitatively diverse but qualitatively limited homogeneous phenomena. Venuti, for instance, gives several examples of Latin translations from the Greek (2013, 178–179) to make a point about his hermeneutic model of translation ethics. Yet it goes without saying how close these code systems are and how irrelevant this demonstration could be when applied to language like Chinese, Arabic, or Persian. Translating Portuguese poetry into Spanish cannot be of the same order of difficulty, does not represent the same challenges, and should not be analyzed with the same methods as translating a tonal language like Chinese into English. Advocates of dynamic correspondence or of translation-recreation for poetry may have a valid point with regard to translation between similar languages. However, such approaches can only be detrimental to the translation of Persian classical poetry, a hybrid semiotic constellation, with rhythm constituting its central core. If the amount of loss could be measurable and put in a quantitative perspective,[17] then the ratio of loss in the English translation of Saint John Perse or Baudelaire to that of a Rumi ghazal should be written in exponentials. If sacrificing some semantic and lexical content can lead to the construction of the rhyme and rhythm and forms, then it may be worth doing so. When this sacrifice cannot possibly serve any purpose, then it is pointless.

The criticism against Venuti's hermeneutic model of translation ethics is of a logical order. According to Venuti, since no text is formally and contextually translatable, and because new interpretations view the ST in new perspectives, then any target text should be considered a valid interpretation of the source text, even poetic versions semantically far from the original, as long as they open up new foreignizing horizons. The fundamental flaw in this argument is that no formal equivalence with the extralinguistic reality is ever possible even in the original semiotization of the world when the ST was created. In Venuti's postmodern worldview, since the recreation of the text is always associated with alteration, then all new target texts have a life valid in its own right. Since there is no absolute truth, the source text cannot be deemed to hold the absolute reality of its own being. If even the author himself cannot be fully aware of what he meant to express, then why should the translator be bound by his faithfulness to either the letter or the spirit of the ST? In the extreme form of Venuti's postmodern logic, if there could be a well-created version of Rumi's poetry, regardless of its relation to the original text, it would be as valid as a literal translation, only because the discourse of Rumi was created in ambiguity, in *non-dit*, and hence it is open to interpretation. In this postmodern relativism, there is no place for absolute reality, only for alternative interpretations. Neither the source text nor the author has the monopoly of truth conveyed by the sign. No particular sign object can be definitively determined for the poetic utterance. While it may be an interesting epistemic paradigm with rich imaginative and creative potential, its actual application to real life seems unfeasible. Let us imagine a judge refusing to convict a suspect despite material evidence only because there could be endless interpretations of evidence depending on the observer's standpoint. While such scenarios may sound ludicrous in a judiciary context, advocates of postmodern hermeneutics do not shy away from applying them to literary texts.

Venuti's postmodern argumentation can be contested at various levels. Firstly, the absence of absolute truth does not mean the absence of relative truth that can serve as the reference, and the reference of translation is the source text. In phenomenological terms, according to Husserl's formulation of intentionality, every understanding is the understanding of something. Translation too, is always the translation of a text. Semiotic forms are defined as relations or nonmathematical functions. In any function, there is a *domain of validity*. The domain of validity for the translation is the source text. The second point is about the failure of postmodern hermeneutics to recognize one of the most elementary concepts of modal logic: the difference between plurality and totality. If we accept that a text – especially a mystical poetic text – is open to interpretation, that its meaning is not fixed, and that the possibilities of interpretation are not unique, the conclusion is that there are *several* possible interpretations. Yet *several* does not mean *all*. *All* interpretations cannot be equally worthwhile. Venuti questions the communicative function of a poetic utterance, citing Badiou:

> "The poem," argues Alain Badiou, "does not consist in communication" because it performs two operations: a "subtraction" from "objective reality," whereby the poem "declares its own universe" and "utters being, or the idea, at the very point where the object has vanished," and a "dissemination" which "aims to dissolve the object through an infinite metaphorical distribution," so that "no sooner is it mentioned than the object migrates elsewhere within meaning" through "an excessive equivalence to other objects."
>
> (Venuti 2013, 174)

In other words, the sign object of the poetic sign is ever elusive. However, even if we accept that poetry is not a form of communication – which is highly debatable[18] – we still cannot generalize that assumption to the translation of poetry. The translation of poetry is indeed an act of communication, part of a general process of intercultural and interlingual communication. As in all instances of communication, there needs to be a code that both counterparts adhere to; otherwise, no communication is possible.

The aporia of translation-recreation and poet-translators like Don Peterson, also cited by Venuti, is that their intention to recreate the general spirit of the poetic discourse defeats their purpose of offering indefinite rebirths to the text. Their versions destroy the infinity of the original poem when they bind its "general spirit" by naming their version a translation. "The only defensible fidelity is to the entirely subjective quality of 'spirit' or 'vision,' rather than to literal meaning," argues Paterson (cited in Venuti 2013, 179). Except that there is no guarantee that the presumed spirit of the original text is what the poet-translator, who may not even know the source language, has discerned and salvaged in his poetic version. The subjectivity of poet-translators is the reference for the reconstitution of the presumed spirit. The ethical conundrum resurfaces when we consider that the TL reader may not even be aware of this creative spirit-hunting process.

Venuti argues that due to the recontextualization of the text by translation, the TT can never have the same effect and cannot be interpreted in the same way as the ST, no matter how literal the translation is; therefore, the quality of translation should not be judged based on its proximity to the ST. This sounds like an *all-or-none* totalitarian fallacy, according to which because absolute perfection is impossible, then no attempt should be made to go in its direction. This nihilistic approach poses fundamental ethical problems insofar as it can be applied to any human action. Like any other human behavior, the act of communication, including interlingual and intercultural communication, is inherently approximative. The final goal of attaining perfection is unattainable but approachable. I propose the notion of the *asymptotic movement* as the ideal goal of an ethical translation. No translation can be perfect, but many translations can approach perfection like an asymptotic curve to a direct line. The concept of the asymptote is a basic geometrical concept. Curves can approach a point or a line without reaching it, or rather, they can only meet in infinity. Again, in mathematical terms, a given point on the curve of a function can be approached from different directions without an immediate point of contact. In differential calculus, the quantity of Y when the input of X approaches a specific point, like zero, can be calculated in a secondary equation called the *limit of the function*. I use this model by analogy to describe what an ideal translation should be. While untranslatability is an undeniable state of the affairs, and the formal equivalence between the source and target texts is virtually impossible, the objective of an ethical translation remains to *tend towards* the ideal situation whereby the text remains unchanged in its semantic content and discoursive infrastructure, as well as its effect on the reader and stylistic aesthetics. If sacrifices are to be made and losses inevitable, the preservation of the semantic content in its literal materiality must be the absolute priority.

Notes

1 In the Hebraic philological tradition, the *letter* of a word is superior to its spirit. The fundamental argument is that the spirit is ephemeral contrary to the letter, immutable in substance. The semantic content can change insofar as the field of interpretation varies according to circumstances. The primacy of the *letter* takes metaphysical and spiritual magnitude in the Kabbalah as it finds religious dimensions in the Talmud. The primordial materiality of the letter has its roots in the Hebraic account of creation in תִּישָׁאךְבּ [*Genesis*] where phenomena are created by God *calling* their names (Genesis, 1:3–1:10): "And God said: 'Let there be light.' And there was light." It is the letter of *light* when pronounced by God that actually turns into light. There is, therefore, no substantial differentiation between the signified and the signifier of *light*.
2 Contrary to Meschonnic's view, the duality of the sign does not necessarily mean its discontinuity. Meschonnic refers to the Hellenic concept of separation of form and content and rejects modern structural semiotics. In Hjelmslev's model, for instance, the expression and content planes are by no means discontinuous but in a mutual relation that constitutes the sign's function.
3 See my demonstration in Chapter 3.
4 This can only evoke Walter Benjamin's view on the *task of the translator*, which consists in reaching an idealized super-language that is placed somewhere far and beyond natural languages. I compare the idea of a transcendent *perfect* language as the ultimate aim of transiting to Rumi's, and other mystics', quest for a semiotic system that surpasses the constraints and insufficiencies of human language.
5 By *value*, Meschonnic means the structuring of the discourse in the given language, and by *signification*, the intention of the author. This is akin to the concept of *discoursive structure* and *reference* in structural semiotics.
6 Berman argues, "the statement that when translated literature occupies a secondary position, the translator submits to the norms of 'acceptability' may occasionally be true. But in the case of 16th century France, the reverse relationship takes place: translation clearly occupies the center of the polysystem, but it does not prevent most translations of this period from going in the direction of acceptability." By the same token, Nicholson's translations of ghazals should be considered *adequate* rather than *acceptable* in the sense that they do not meet the operational norms of stylistics in the Victorian polysystems; they are literal and full of loanwords. This happened when translation was not at the center of the English polysystem and Persian was not a dominant language or in a position of power.
7 Toury's "scientific" descriptive model finds its strongest critic in the English-speaking world in Lawrence Venuti. Venuti contests the benefits of "value-free" norms and laws of translation, which he thinks, will prevent Translation Studies from exercising self-criticism (*The Scandals of Translation* 1998) As Venuti argues, neither translation nor scholarly reviews of translation can be free of orientation by certain ideological values the individual adheres to. The data collected in linguistic and stylistic observations "can only be interpreted in a cultural theory" since translation cannot be detached of the cultural values that weigh on translators' choices.
8 "The term 'translation-practice' emphasizes the inventiveness that the re-enunciator must demonstrate, similar to that of the enunciator" (Folkart 1991, 456).
9 Dryden, Paterson, and Bly are some of the fervent advocates of poets' versions or the translation-recreation movement.
10 By *Belles infidèles* [the unfaithful beautiful], which is also one of his famous titles (Mounin [1955] 1994), Mounin means translations that are stylistically elegant in the TL but are semantically distant from the original text.
11 I have previously conducted a detailed analysis of deforming tendencies in Rumi's French and English translations. See Sedaghat (2015, 282–296).

12 I create the term following Ladmiral's neologism, *ultra-target-oriented*, which refers to "translators who correct a text in the name of their best knowledge they pretend to have of the *realia* which the author would have misrepresented" (Ladmiral 2014, 15).
13 Schimmel (2011) has a similar approach.
14 This is the hallmark of Cassirer's semiotic theory that he calls "the philosophy of symbolic forms," which is essentially rooted in Kant's phenomenology. See Rastier (2017, 2–5).
15 There is no doubt that even in a technical text with a mainly informative function, there may be a myriad of live and institutionalized tropes and other figures of speech to have a specific effect on the reader.
16 Both roots are Indo-European with Persian equivalents of *shekaft* [fission/split] and *faravashi* [guardian spirit in Mazdeism].
17 I strongly recommend such quantification, as it is necessary for the sake of understanding a problem. We resort to quantification and mathematical modelling methods all the time to explain phenomena, but little research has been made to apply such models to textual phenomena like translation.
18 Given the widespread use of verse for narrative texts in various world literatures, the *Masnavi* being one of them.

References

Barks, Coleman. 1995. *The Essential Rumi*. New York: Harper Collins.
Benjamin, Walter. [1913] 2004. "The Task of the Translator." In *Walter Benjamin: Selected Writings, Volume 1: 1913–1926*, by Walter Benjamin, edited by Marcus Bullock and Michael Jennings. Boston: Harvard University Press.
Berman, Antoine. 1984. *L'épreuve de l'étranger, Culture et traduction dans l'Allemagne romantique*. Paris: Gallimard.
Berman, Antoine. 1995. *Pour une critique des traductions: John Donne*. Paris: Gallimard.
Berman, Antoine. 1999. *La traduction et la lettre ou l'auberge du lointain*. Paris: Seuil.
Chittick, William. 1984. *The Sufi Path of Love: The Spiritual Teachings of Rumi*. Albany: University of New York Press.
Derrida, Jacques. 1985. *Difference in Translation*. "Les tours de Babel". New York: Éditions Joseph Graham, Cornell University Press.
Folkart, Barbara. 1991. *Le conflit des énonciations: traduction et discours rapporté*. Montréal: Balzac.
Genette, Gérard. 1982. *Palimpsestes: La littérature au second degré*. Paris: Seuil.
Genette, Gérard. 1987. *Seuils*. Paris: Éditions du Seuil.
Ladmiral, Jean René. 2014. *Sourcier ou cibliste*. Paris: Les Belles Lettres.
Meschonnic, Henri. 1970a. *Les Cinq Rouleaux*. Paris: Gallimard.
Meschonnic, Henri. 1970b. *Pour la poétique I*. Paris: Gallimard.
Meschonnic, Henri. 1973. *Pour la poétique II. Epistémologie de l'écriture. Poétique de la traduction*. Paris: Gallimard.
Meschonnic, Henri. 1978. *Pour la poétique V*. Paris: Gallimard.
Meschonnic, Henri. 1999. *Poétique du traduire*. Paris: Verdier.
Mounin, Georges. 1976. *Les problèmes théoriques de la traduction*. Paris: Gallimard.
Mounin, Georges. [1955] 1994. *Les Belles infidèles*. Lille: Presses Universitaires de Lille.
Nida, Eugene. 1964. *Toward a Science of Translating: With Special Reference to Principles and Procedures Involved in Bible Translating*. Leiden: Brill.
Nida, Eugene. 1975. *Language, Structure and Translation*. Stanford, CA: Stanford University Press.

Nida, Eugene, and Charles Taber. 1969. *The Theory and Practice of Translation*. Leiden: Brill.
Rastier, François. 2017. "Cassirer et la création du structuralisme." *Texto! Textes et cultures* XXII, n° 4.
Ricœur, Paul. 1986. *Du texte à l'action*. Paris: Seuil.
Schimmel, Annemarie. 2011. *Mystical Dimensions of Islam*. Chapel Hill: University of North Carolina Press.
Sedaghat, Amir. 2015. *Le soufisme de Roumi reçu et perçu dans les mondes anglophone et francophone: étude des traductions anglaises et françaises*. Paris: Université Sorbonne Paris Cité. https://tel.archives-ouvertes.fr/tel-01579400.
Venuti, Lawrence. 1998. *The Scandals of Translation*. London: Routledge.
Venuti, Lawrence. [1995] 2008. *The Translator's Invisibility: A History of Translation*. Edited by Lawrence Venuti. London: Routledge.
Venuti, Lawrence. [2000] 2012. *The Translation Studies Reader*. Edited by Lawrence Venuti. London: Routledge.
Venuti, Lawrence. 2013. *Translation Changes Everything: Theory and Practice*. London: Routledge.

Conclusion

Translation as a Communication Paradigm

Translation of Rumi's poetic work and philosophical thought in the West constitutes an unmatched case study in which the patent and latent aspects of an important paradigm of transcultural communications between Western Christian civilizations and Islamic civilizations in general, and the Iranian part of Islamic civilizations in particular, are revealed. If translation in general brings to light fundamental linguistic problems that can then be extrapolated to higher cultural and civilizational levels, translation of Rumi in particular is all the more enlightening because of its particularities. The technical complexity of the task, the hermeneutic dimensions of Rumi's mystical texts, Rumi's central place in the source and target polysystems, and the hermeneutically conflictual position of mysticism within the Islamic ideological canon makes this case study of particular interest. I saw how the distance separating the Persian linguistic system and target languages, namely in terms of determination and gender, is significant enough to complicate the transfer of mystical discourse. As I tried to demonstrate, the sophisticated rhetoric and poetic tools that Rumi uses to create a whole code system of communication of his own are such that translation of his verse becomes far more approximate than average verse translation. The ineffable referent of poetic utterances can only be hinted at, and the depth of its multiple semiotic layers, some of which are non-linguistic, can only be acknowledged and sensed, rather than fully understood and interpreted like the referent of a regular discourse. The role of music as a second layer of semiosis makes the expression plane of the utterances at least as important as their content plane in an act of *ratio difficilis*.

The innate and intentional ambiguity of Rumi's text, his resort to mystical symbolism, as well as his use of live metaphor omnipresent throughout his entire textual monument put it on par with Sacred Scriptures in terms of hermeneutical complexity. In this respect, any attempt to translate Rumi's verse implies adopting an ideological stance. It is in this sense that all paratextual activity, be it interlingual or intralingual, around Rumi's text reveals the underlying ideological tendencies of the active agents. Thus, foreign language offshoots of the source text, its afterlife after the author's death, as modern literary criticism puts it – from the choice of texts to the choice of titles, from the forewords and the epilogues to the footnotes, up to the slightest lexical or syntactic choice – can inform on translators'/rewriters' conscious or unconscious attitudes. At sociocultural levels, Rumi's phenomenon is unique in its genre. No Persian text, nor possibly any other foreign text, has ever been translated into English to this extent, i.e., as often and as broadly as Rumi's. Interpreting mere statistic and historic data on these translations offers insight into the conditions of reception in the target polysystems.

In this monography, I offered my interpretation of the presented data. Despite adopting a principally descriptive approach in textual and discoursive analyses, I did not hesitate to present prescriptive judgments on the quality of certain translation practices. It goes without saying that some of my conclusions are debatable. My stance on the ethics of translation especially might not be shared by those scholars who consider translation as the *contingent* continuation of the work under different, equally valuable avatars, hence bound by no *necessary* link to the original. However, the main purpose of this essay is to create a new field of reflection, rather than to present a repertoire of Rumi translations, judge them based on their mistakes, or advise on the right or wrong attitudes of a Rumi translator. Through my examination of one of the most emblematic cases of transcultural communication, we were able to see the common errors, possible shortcomings, and beneficial results of such communication. We were also able to observe how translation norms indicate the ideological, social, political, and economic conditions of the reception. The precision and accuracy of some early English translators seem striking in comparison to the light-hearted attitude of certain modern rewriters whose work occasionally lacks proper referencing to the source text. At the same time, it is important to highlight the elegance, readability, and appeal of certain modern translations carried out by well-versed scholars. Even those publishers and poets who have offered adaptations, versions, and (excessively) free translations have undeniable use and benefit, despite their inaccuracy and commercial pragmatism. It is all the more true since without these popularizers, Rumi would probably never have enjoyed such stature in world literature and his message would never have been spread to the extent it has.

Untranslatability or Asymptotic Translation?

Inspired by his Hebraist education, Henri Meschonnic demonstrated well that the poetic signifying mode surpasses the traditional content-form dichotomy. I argued that this is all the more so in the case of Persian classical poetry. The translation of mystical poetry of this type, just as that of sacred texts, presents a challenge of an extraordinary dimension. I described how Rumi's verse transcends the border separating the *letter* from *spirit* of the text, the *expression* from *content planes* of the sign, making it virtually impossible to recreate not only the expressive infradiscoursive structure but also the semantic structure of the discourse in any target language. Mystical poetry epitomizes the nature of *ratio difficilis*, that is the semiosis of new meaning by creating new signs currently absent in the code system. The author has to create new expression forms and substances to express the novel content. The nature of the newly created sign is such that the internal structure of the expression and content planes are similar. In other words, signifier and signified become undistinguishable. Where the spirit is inseparable from the letter, the internal structure of the discourse in one language, hence its meaning, can definitely not be remanifested in another verbal system. This situation is tantamount to a practical state of untranslatability. The degree of untranslatability, however, varies according to the degree of *literarity*, or as Meschonnic argues, poeticity, i.e., the presence and place of rhythm in the text. My analysis attempted to show how untranslatability is of a different order of magnitude in Rumi's poetic discourse.

The argument against untranslatability, on the other hand, is best formulated by Jakobson's purely linguistic – and not discoursive – standpoint, according to which, "languages differ from what they *must* say and not by what they *can* say" (1971, 261); that is, any given language can express anything that can be expressed by another language in its own ways. In this perspective, all target languages should technically be able to recreate the content of Rumi's message, if not by recreating the same or similar discursive forms, at least in their own pragmatically equivalent forms. The problem of mystical poetry, however, is that it does not necessarily seek to *say* a message. According to mystics like Rumi, not everything is meant or deemed to be *said*. The esoteric character of the message is such that its deepest layer is *not said*, because the author either should not or cannot say it. The nature of esoteric truth or the experience of such truth are simply *ineffable*. The conundrum lies precisely here: how can one translate something that is not said or cannot be said? Perhaps in the same way as the author expressed the transcendent, by transcending the boundaries of language itself? And if the boundaries of the target system are to be surpassed, how can the target text be still understandable?

Yet translation exists, against all odds. In fact, Rumi translations not only exist but are abundant. The case of Rumi shows how translation lies at the core of a conflictual zone where the translator is constantly divided between opposing sentiments of joy and sorrow, the joy of a gain and the sorrow for a loss. Just as Rumi's internal urge to express the ineffable pushed him to compose tens of thousands of verses while constantly decrying the ineptitude of human language, Rumi translators could not resist the urge to share the wealth and depth of his message with their respective readers while understanding the essential limits of their feat. This is a manifestation of the dialectic specific to translation mentioned by Paul Ricœur in his *Défi et bonheur de la traduction*. The difficulties of the task are enormous, the challenges serious, and the losses inevitable and numerous, but the happiness of "inhabiting the language of the other" and "the pleasure of receiving at home, in one's own home, the word of the Foreign" (Ricœur 2004, 20–21) must have been even stronger with Rumi translators. The absence of a fixed and clear message, the fluidity of Rumi's intention, his unconventional utilization of language, his ventures beyond the limits of language and semiotic systems, in short, that which characterizes the very essence of Rumi's gnostic discourse constitutes a fertile ground for the realization of the transcendental mission of translation in Walter Benjamin's view: to make the text live beyond its lifetime and beyond the language in which it is conceived in a quest for the ideal language. It is so because literary works are neither frozen nor dead. They live on in other linguistic forms, other cultural systems, and in other minds, thanks to translation. It is indeed this continuation of the life of the work, this survival of the text in a foreign home, this resurrection of the reported speech in a new linguistic universe that will eventually reveal what Berman calls the "truth" of the text. This is what Walter Benjamin calls "the task of the translator." It is probably this quest for a transcendent truth that shaped this "drive to translate" – as Ricœur called it (2004, 8) – common to all translators.

The conflictual tension between the "impossibility" of translation and the "urge" to translate – whether by necessity or because of the translator's internal drive to share a treasure trove – finds its resolution in the realization of a compromise. As Victor Hugo said, "science is asymptotic of truth. It constantly approaches and never touches it," (Hugo 1864, 151); the perfect translation can only be *asymptotic* of the text. Translation as asymptote describes a situation where the target text approaches the source text but only reaches it in the infinity, just like a geometric asymptote to a direct line. Translation can become close to the source as much as possible while an infinitesimally small distance separates them forever. That is how the dialectic of success and sorrow, the quest for truth and the despair of untranslatability, culminates in a synthesis. This is the zenith of achievement in the task of the translator who just like Rumi seeks and expresses the truth by all means at his disposal while still lamenting his separation from it. Such strong translations of Rumi's poetry are rare but do exist at least in English, for instance some of Arberry's translations of quatrains and certain ghazals, Nicholson's version of ghazals, and more recently Lewis's rendering of a selection of the *Divan* among others. What is common among these translators is their absolute commitment to the ideal of foreignizing and didactic translation whereby they endeavor to bring the reader to the author while recreating as best as possible Rumi's heterogenic discourse structure.

Ethical Translation

The literalist approach to translation, as prescribed for the translation of Holy Scripture by Saint Jerome, has suffered multiple attacks from different directions: from linguists who saw translation as a technical operation of transfer of the utterance from one code system to another; from descriptive theorists who passively observed and actively justified how polysystems impose their norms and rules on translation to the detriment of the source text; and more recently from philosophers who, under the influence of a relativism inherited from postmodern deconstructionists, impose a translation hermeneutics that places the target text in discontinuity vis-à-vis the source text, refuting the existence of any original intention of the author or fixed initial referent for the text, thus crediting all kinds of rewriting with some degree of truth.

No set of prescriptions as to how to translate classical mystic poetry exists. Yet my analysis of the various waves of translations of Rumi presented conclusive evidence that certain tendencies should be avoided for the sake of a somewhat ethical and respectful rendering of the original text. In other words, while it is futile to set out a unique framework of definition of a *good* translation, one can at least describe what a *bad* translation may be. No single formula can indicate a universally valid solution as to how to translate poetry, but some positional theory of *adequacy* can be sketched to be applied to specific contexts and for specific purposes. In the case of Rumi's verse, for instance, a prescriptive theory of translation can be of an ethical nature rather than a technical one. On that note, this book explored a large array of scholarly stances on the ethics of translation and their pertinence to the translation of mystical poetry before presenting my unequivocal position: translation of Rumi's verse can only serve a purpose when it is foreignizing and literalist, at the cost of diminished readability.

The argument is simple but multifaceted. From a technical standpoint, the choice of a formal correspondence seems more reasonable than that of a dynamic equivalence. Since there is no way to recreate even minimally either rhythm, or rhyme, or formal figures of speech, or any other discursive structure that constitutes the musicality of the verse in Persian classical prosody, what is the point of attempting to versify, embellish, or poeticize an otherwise prosaic plain target text? Any such attempt inevitably leads to the alteration and loss of the semantic content with no direct or indirect gain whatsoever. The translation-recreation trend to which many modern American translators seem to adhere may be valid in many imaginable contexts, yet as far as Persian classical poetry is concerned, it seems to offer no tangible gain in exchange for a tremendous loss on the content side. Insofar as a dynamic equivalence is not possible in the translation of such poetry, the only justifiable approach appears to be the literalist one, even if the result may be deemed tedious to read. After all, if the target reader's main purpose is to be entertained by familiarity, what is the point of choosing a 13th-century Sufi poet to read? A text stripped of its disturbing *otherness*, shocking difference, and sheer strangeness is but an illusion of the experience of the foreign. Translation of Rumi can only be faithful to the *letter* and not to the *meaning* of the utterance insofar as the latter is designed to remain elusive as much for the Persian reader as for the foreign one.

In a hermeneutic perspective, an ethical translation of Rumi should remain as mute as the text itself when it comes to what is not *said*. While explicative and metalinguistic notes are the inseparable part of any translation project as education about the *foreign*, any attempt to interpret an otherwise obtuse text is a form of distortion. Ethical translations avoid clarification since clarifying the ambiguity of the message, making explicit what is inherently implicit, fixing the meaning of an utterance whereas it was destined to be fluid is tantamount to an infringement of the essential property of the text. This principle applies all the better to the translation of mystical poetry since it incarnates live metaphor, that which eternally resides in ambiguity, trapped in a never-ending ontological dialectic of what is meant and what is not meant. Any attempt to assign a fixed meaning to such discourse causes its destruction. Yet among all deforming tendencies, the strongest distorting force observed in the reception of Rumi is that of clarification either directly in the text or indirectly in the paratext. Second-degree deformation of the communication process under the ideological influence exerted by translators themselves or the translation norms proves to be both strong and insidious because it takes place in all discretion, i.e., not only through linguistic choices but on the margin of the text: in the choice of texts, in introductory notes and exegetic comments.

New Notions and Neologisms

In the course of this study, new notions were brought up which sometimes needed the introduction of certain neologisms. In the discursive linguistic analysis, I calqued the terms *sufiolect* and *rumiolect* as discoursive subsystems within the general code system of the Persian language. Sufiolect and rumiolect are akin to idiolects specific to mystic poetry and Rumi's use of language. In this particular technolect, terms have *ad hoc* semantic values, syntax may be compromised, and, most importantly, the general organizational cohesion of the text is altered for the sake of mystic teachings. These linguistic variations constitute novel communication codes ruled by a new epistemological paradigm. Rumi's use of deviation from the established code constitutes the perfect example of *ratio difficilis* insofar as it enriches the Persian language code. Nonetheless, his desire to surpass the boundaries of linguistic code not being fulfilled, Rumi resorts to other semiotic systems, like music, to semiotize the *insemiotizable*.

The semiotic analysis of Persian versification and Rumi's poetics lead to the introduction of terms such as *semiotic hybridization* and *hybrid connotative systems*. A hybrid sign is one whose expression plan consists not only of entire signs of the same semiotic system, but also of signs or elements thereof governed by other semiotic systems. The paragon of such systems is the highly musical Persian classical poetry, reaching its zenith of rhythm and harmony in Rumi's ghazals, where verses cannot be considered only as linguistic utterances but must also be understood as musical phrases. The semantic content of such utterances is semiotized not only by their verbal component, but also by the combination of language and music. The semantic content of such hybrid signs is not equal to the sum of the content planes of each of its constituents: it surpasses it. The raison d'être of these hybrid signs is to transcend the existing regular semiosis.

In the ethics of translation, I relied on the hermeneutics of tropes, German idealists' view on translation, and Antoine Berman's theory of deforming tendencies to introduce the notion of *second-degree deformation*. This corresponds to a 13th deforming tendency particularly present in the translation of metaphorically charged texts, such as mystic poetry, caused by the paratextual indices offered by translators, who are often bound to play the role of commentators. Such exegetic interventions by translators/commentators can only restrict the messages of mystic discourse that are by nature fluid and open to interpretation. Second-degree deformation can exist despite translators and as a result of their unconscious ideological tendencies. On the other hand, such subtle deformation may be the direct result of translators' deliberate intervention in favor of certain editorial politics or ideological tendencies.

Principal Findings and Future Prospects

In a nutshell, a few major points can be highlighted as the conclusions drawn in this research monography. *Primo*, the difficulty of translating Rumi's poetry greatly exceeds the degree of complexity associated with the translation of literary texts between Western languages and cultures, given the cultural and epistemic distance separating the source and target linguistic communities as well as the structural characteristics of the source text. *Segundo*, despite these difficulties, speaking of the untranslatable nature of Persian poetry or of mystical poetry constitutes a logical paradox within the framework of a theory of translation. Numerous successful asymptotic translations in English, French, and German demonstrate how mystical poetry can continue to live in a linguistic home. This new life is by no means disconnected from the original content but closely related to it. *Tertio*, given the hybrid character of the signifying mode in Rumi's poetic discourse, literalism in translation is necessary but not enough to make the discoursive structure of the source text resurface in the target text. Indeed, the quality of translation is a direct corollary of the effort spent on crafting the stylistic sophistication of the target text. However, the inevitable loss should be indicated to the reader by means of metalinguistic translator notes. As such, the more verbose translators seem to be the less inclined to produce high-quality translations.

Quarto, the deforming tendencies are manifested in all English translations albeit to varying degrees. In general, academic and classical translations can be qualified as more foreignizing than the majority of modern translations that are popularizing and *annexionist*. The level of distortion is a corollary of several factors, such as the ideological profile of the translator, translation norms imposed by the target polysystem, and the sociopolitical circumstances of reception in both source and target cultural spheres. *Quinto*, Rumi's work simultaneously owes a great debt to and is victim of an extraordinary infatuation of the English-speaking North American polysystem for his work and philosophy. The rare phenomenon of intercultural relations called *Rumimania* has given a visibility to a great figure of Iranian mysticism and Persian poetry not only in the English world but also in other Western cultures thanks to the heavy influence of American culture on them. This same phenomenon should be considered responsible for varying degrees of distortion of Rumi's thought and work due to the popularizing and commercializing rationales, oversimplifying a philosophy of tremendous complexity, reducing it, in certain contexts, to a product of spiritual consumption.

It is my hope that these findings contribute to the future advancement of the theory of translation on the one hand, and Iranian and Rumi Studies on the other, in a number of ways. For instance, the semiotic approach to the theory of poetic translation helped demonstrate how the musicality of Persian classical poetry should be regarded as an extra semiotic layer of utterance, causing a challenge of a whole different magnitude to translation. This problematic could be further explored at two levels. At a practical level, one can make an attempt to broaden the scopes of didactic foreignizing translation by accompanying the target text with other nonverbal components of the text. For instance, certain translations of Rumi could be associated with audio files in which the reader can listen to the recitation or musical compositions of verses in the original language, letting the audience appreciate the musical component of Rumi's semiosis. At an epistemological level and in the light of a theory of intersemiotic translation, there is room for the development of a theory of intersemiotic transcultural communication that can explore how various forms of art are related within a cultural zone and among various civilizations. This new branch of cultural anthropology, which one may call "comparative semiotics," involves all aspects of intercultural communication through all systems of meaning and expression as well as their interrelations.

Another question raised by this book with strong prospect of further development is the role of polysystemic conditions in the creation of reception norms. The remarkable appeal of Rumi to English-speaking North America, showcased by his bestselling status for decades, is explained as a multidimensional sociocultural phenomenon rooted, among other factors, in the belief systems, economic dynamics, and ideological tendencies in the target culture. This approach can constitute a methodological paradigm applicable to the analysis of other similar phenomena: the reception of Rumi in Eastern languages, the reception of other figures like Rumi in the West, or in general, the reception of other non-Western systems of thought in modern Western cultures. This last question can be exemplified by the rampant popularity of Eastern and Vedic spiritualities in various Christian cultures, especially in the US. It is also noteworthy to study the role of the American culture in the genesis of such phenomena in the rest of the Western world and beyond.

The concept of the second-degree deformation, as part of a general ethical theory of translation, can also be extrapolated to larger scales and higher levels of transcultural communication. One can imagine how the mediators of all forms of intercultural communications can deliberately or unconsciously orient the understanding of the target society to a foreign culture. It is ultimately this reception of various cultural products that shape one's representation of foreign cultures. It is, therefore, particularly beneficial to study the effects of the circumstantial variables of various instances of the reception, or lack thereof, in the West of other Islamic or Iranian cultural products. One example of this could be the whole set of Shia rituals, literature, and art around the myth of Ashura. In the present academic state of affairs, Shiism and the Shia civilization remain greatly understudied compared to other branches of Islam and their cultural products. This topic can be all the more interesting since the representation of Shia culture could only have suffered the deformation caused by the current confrontation between the West and Iran in West Asia.

References

Hugo, Victor. 1864. *William Shakespeare*. Paris: A. Lacroix, Verboeckhoven et Cie, Éditeurs.
Jakobson, Roman. 1971. *Selected Writings II. Word and Language*. The Hague: Mouton.
Ricœur, Paul. 2004. *Sur la traduction*. Paris: Bayard.

Bibliography

1 Primary Sources

A Original Persian Texts

Aflāki, Shamsoddin Ahmad. 1362 [1983]. *Manāqeb alārefin*. Edited by Tahsin Yaziji. Tehrān: Donyāye ketāb.
Aṭṭār Neyshāburi, Sheykh Farideddin. 1381 [2002]. *Divān-e Attār-e Neyshāburi*. Edited by Badi'ozzamān Foruzānfar. 4th ed. Tehrān: Negāh.
Bahā'e Valad, Mohammad ebn Hosein. 1352 [1973]. *Ma'āref*. Edited by Badi'ozzamān Foruzānfar. Tehrān: Ṭahuri.
Balkhi (Rumi), Mowlānā Jalāleddin Mohammad. 1345 [1966]. *Kolliāt-e Shams-e Tabrizi* [Divan of Shams of Tabriz]. Edited by Badi'ozzamān Foruzānfar. Tehrān: Enteshārāt-e daneshgāh-e Tehrān.
Balkhi (Rumi), Mowlānā Jalāleddin Mohammad. 1362 [1983]. *Maṣnavi-e ma'navi, bar asās-e noskhe-ye Lāyden* [Based on the Leiden Version]. Edited by Reynold Alleyne Nicholson. Tehrān: Amir-Kabir.
Balkhi (Rumi), Mowlānā Jalāleddin Mohammad. 1379 [2000]. *Maktubāt*. Edited by Javād Salmānizāde. Tehrān: Eqbāl.
Balkhi (Rumi), Mowlānā Jalāleddin Mohammad. 1330/1385 [1951/2006]. *Fihe mā fih*. Edited by Badi'ozzamān Foruzānfar. Tehrān: Dāneshgāh-e Tehrān.
Ḥāfeẓ Shirāzi, Xwāje Shamseddin Moḥammad. 1374 [1995]. *Divān*. Edited by Bahāoddin Khorramshāhi. Tehrān: Enteshārāt-e Khārazmi.
Sa'di Shirāzi, Moslehoddin. 1363 [1984]. *Kolliyāt-e Sa'di* [The Complete Works of Sa'di]. Edited by Mohammad-Ali Forughi. 4th ed. Tehrān: Enteshārāt-e Amirkabir.
Sanāyi Ghaznavi, Abolmajd Majdud ebn-e Adam. 1383 [2002]. *Hadiqat ol-Haqiqah va Shari'at ol-Tariqah*. Edited by Mohammad Taghi Modarres Raẓavi. Tehrān: Markaz-e Nashr-e Daneshgāhi.
Sepahsālār, Fereydun ebn Mohammad. 1323 [1944]. *Resāle dar ahvāl e Mowlānā Jalāleddin*. Edited by Sa'id Nafisi. Tehrān: Ketābxāne ye Eqbāl.
Solṭān Valad Bahāeddin, Mohammad ebn Mohammad. 1376 [1997]. *Valadnāme*. Edited by Homāyi Jalāleddin. Tehrān: Enteshārāt-e Homā.
Tabrizi, Shamseddin Mohammad. 2536/1356 [1977]. *Maqālāt, Bā moqaddame va tanqih va ta'liq*. Edited by Mohammad Ali Movahhed. Tehrān: Mo'assese ye Elmi e Daneshgāh e San'ati e Āriāmehr.

B English Translations

a Masnavi-ye Ma'navi

Arberry, Arthur John. 1961. *Tales from the Masnavi*. London: Allen and Unwin.
Arberry, Arthur John. 1963. *More Tales from the Masnavi*. London: Allen and Unwin.
Gupta, Madan Gopal. 1990. *Maulana Rum's Masnawi Translation and Commentary*. Vols I–VI. Agra and New Delhi: MG Publishers, Huma Books Inc.
Jones, Sir William. 1993. *The Collected Works of Sir William Jones*. Edited by Garland Cannon. Vol. 4, 230–231. New York: New York University Press.
Mojaddedi, Jawid. 2004–2022. *The Masnavi, Book I–V*. Oxford and New York: Oxford University Press.
Nicholson, Reynold Alleyne. [1926] 1990. *The Mathnawi of Jalálu'ddín Rúmí*. 8 vols. Cambridge: The Trustees of the E.J.W. Gibb Memorial.
Nicholson, Reynold Alleyne. [1926] 1995. *Tales of Mystic Meaning: Selections from the Mathnawi of Jalal-Ud-Din Rumi*. London: Oneworld Pubns Ltd.
Redhouse, James W. 1881. *The Mesnevī (usually known as the Mesnevīyi sherīf, or holy Mesnevī) of Mevlānā (our Lord) Jelālu-d-Dīn, Muhammed, er-Rūmī*. London: Trübner & Co.
Türkmen, Erkan. 1992. *The Essence of Rumi's Masnevi*. Konya: Eris Booksellers.
Türkmen, Erkan. 1996. *A Bouquet of Rumi's Versified Poems*. Konya: Konya ve Mulhekati.
Whinfield, Edward Henry. 1887. *Masnavi i ma'navi: The Spiritual Couplets of Mauláná Jalálu-'d-Dín Muhammed i Rúmí*. London: Trübner,
Williams, Alan. 2006. *Rumi, Spiritual Verses, The First Book of the Masnavi-ye Ma'navi*. London and New York: Penguin Classics.
Williams, Alan. 2020. *The Masnavi of Rumi, Book One-Two: A New English Translation with Explanatory Notes*. London: I.B. Tauris.
Wilson, C. E. 1910. *The Masnavī, by Jalālu'd-Dīn Rūmī. Book II*. London: Probsthain & Co.
Yildiz, Harun. 2007. *Selections from Mathnawi of Rūmī*. Konya: Rumî Publishing House.

b Divān-e Shams-e Tabrizi Ghazals

Anvar, Iraj. 2002. *Divan-I Shams-I Tabriz: Forty-Eight Ghazals*. The Hague: Semar Publishers.
Anvar, Iraj. 2008. *Shams-e Parandeh (Shams the Bird): Forty-Eight Ghazals from the Divan of Shams of Tabriz*. Maharashtra, India: Nazar Publications.
Anvar, Iraj, and Anne Twitty. 2008. *Say Nothing: Poems of Jalal al-Din Rumi in Persian and English (English and Farsi Edition)*. Sandpoint, ID: Morning Light Press.
Arberry, Arthur John. [1968] 1991. *Mystical Poems of Rumi 1*. Foreword by Ehsan Yarshater. Chicago: University of Chicago Press.
Cowan, James. 1992. *Where Two Oceans Meet: A Selection of Odes from the Divan of Shems of Tabriz*. Shaftesbury: Element.
Cowan, James. 1997. *Rumi's Divan of Shems of Tabriz: Selected Odes*. Rockport, MA, Shaftesbury, Dorset Element Books.
Ergin, Nevit Oguz. 1992. *Crazy as We Are: Selected Rubais from Divan-Kebir*. Prescott, AZ: Hohm Pr.
Ergin, Nevit Oguz. 1995–2003. *Divan-i Kebir*. Royal Oak, MI: Society for Understanding Mevlana and Echo Publications. Complete English Translation, 22 volumes, 5600 pages.

Garbett, Colin. 1956. *Sun of Tabriz: A Lyrical Introduction to Higher Metaphysics*. Cape Town: R. Beerman.
Hastie, William.1903. *The Festival of Spring from the Diván of Jeláleddin: Rendered in English Gazels after Rückert's Versions*. Glasgow: James MacLehose.
Nicholson, Reynold Alleyne. [1898] 2001. *Selected Poems From the Dīvāni Shamsi Tabrīz*. London: Routledge and Cambridge: Cambridge University Press.

ROBĀ'I (QUATRAINS)

Arberry, Arthur John. 1949. *The Ruba'iyat of Jalal al-Din Rumi, Select Translations into English Verse*. London: Emery Walker.
Ergin, Nevit Oguz, and Johnson Will. 2007. *The Rubais of Rumi: Insane with Love*. Rochester, VT: Inner Traditions Bear and Company.
Gamard, Ibrahim W., and Rawan Farhadi. 2008. *The Quatrains of Rūmī: Ruba'iyat- Jalaluddin Muhammad Balkhī-Rūmī*. San Rafael, CA: Sufi Dari Books.
Houshmand, Zara. 2020. *Moon and Sun: A Selection of the Rubaiyat of Molana Jalal al-Din Rumi*. San Francisco: Amrevan Books.
Lee, Anthony A., and Amin Banani. 2014. *RUMI – 53 Secrets from the Tavern of Love: Poems from the Rubiayat of Mevlana Rumi*. Ashland, OR: White Cloud Press, Bilingual edition.
Moyne, John, and Coleman Barks. 2001. *Unseen Rain: Quatrains of Rumi*. Boston: Shambhala.
Shiva, Shahram. 2000. *Rumi – Thief of Sleep: 180 Quatrains from the Persian*. Prescott, AZ: Hohm Press.

PROSE TRANSLATIONS

Arberry, Arthur John. 1995. *Discourses of Rumi*. London: Routledge.
Marman, Doug. 2010. *It Is What It Is: The Personal Discourses of Rumi*. Ridgefield, WA: Spiritual Dialogues Project.
Thackston, Wheeler McIntosh. 1994. *Signs of the Unseen: The Discourses of Jalaluddin Rumi*. Putney, VT: Threshold Books.

c Mixed Sources

Barks, Coleman. 1988. *Rumi: We Are Three: New Rumi Poems*. Athens, GA: Maypop.
Barks, Coleman. 1988. *This Longing: Poetry, Teaching Stories and Letters of Rumi*. Boston: Shambhala.
Barks, Coleman. 1990. *Delicious Laughter: Rambunctious Teaching Stories from the Mathnawi of Jelaluddin Rumi*. Athens, GA: Maypop.
Barks, Coleman. 1992. *Rumi: One-Handed Basket Weaving: Poems on the Theme of Work*. Athens, GA: Maypop.
Barks, Coleman. 1993. *Rumi Birdsong: Fifty-Three Short Poems*. Athens, GA: Maypop.
Barks, Coleman. 1995. *The Essential Rumi*. New York: Harper Collins.
Barks, Coleman. 1997. *The Illuminated Rumi*. New York: Broadway Books.
Barks, Coleman. 1998. *Heartwood: Meditations on Southern Oaks*. New York: Bulfinch (Little Brown).
Barks, Coleman. 2002. *The Soul of Rumi: A New Collection of Ecstatic Poems*. New York: HarperOne.

Barks, Coleman. [2003] 2005. *Rumi: The Book of Love: Poems of Ecstasy and Longing*. New York: HarperOne.
Barks, Coleman. 2006. *A Year with Rumi: Daily Readings*. New York: HarperOne.
Barks, Coleman. 2007. *Rumi: Bridge to the Soul: Journeys into the Music and Silence of the Heart*. San Francisco: Harper.
Barks, Coleman. 2010. *Rumi: The Big Red Book: The Great Masterpiece Celebrating Mystical Love and Friendship*. New York, HarperOne, Reprint edition.
Barks, Coleman. 2014. *Rumi: Soul Fury: Rumi and Shams Tabriz on Friendship*. New York: HarperOne.
Barks, Coleman, and Arthur John Arberry. 1990. *Like This: Rumi, Versions*. Athens, GA: Maypop.
Barks, Coleman, and John Moyne. 1994. *Say I Am You: Poetry Interspersed with Stories of Rumi and Shams*. Athens, GA: Maypop.
Barks, Coleman, and John Moyne. 1998. *Lion of the Heart*. London: Arkana.
Barks, Coleman, and John Moyne. 1998. *Whoever Brought Me Here Will Have to Take Me Home*. London: Arkana.
Barks, Coleman, and John Moyne. 1999. *Open Secret: Versions of Rumi*. Boston: Shambhala.
Barks, Coleman, and John Moyne. 2004. *The Essence of Rumi, New Expanded Edition*. New York: HarperOne.
Barks, Coleman, and John Moyne. 2005. *The Drowned Book: Ecstatic and Earthy Reflections of Bahauddin, the Father of Rumi*. Translation of *Ma'āref* of Baha'oddin Valad. New York: HarperOne.
Barks, Coleman, and Nevit Oguz Ergin. 2009. *Tales of a Modern Sufi: The Invisible Fence of Reality and Other Stories*. Rochester, VT: Inner Traditions.
Bilkan, Ali Fuat. 2008. *Tales from Rumi*. Somerset, NJ: Tughra Books.
Bly, Robert. 1981. *Night and Sleep*. Illustrator: Shumaker Rita. Somerville, MA: Yellow Moon Press.
Bly, Robert. 2004. *The Winged Energy of Delight: Selected Translations*. New York, Harper.
Chittick, William. 1984. *The Sufi Path of Love: The Spiritual Teachings of Rumi*. Albany: University of New York Press.
Chittick, William. 2004. *Me and Rumi, The Autobiography of Shams-I Tabrizi*. Louisville, KY: Fons Vitae.
Chopra, Deepak. 1998. *The Love Poems of Rumi*. Edinburgh: Harmony.
Dhondy, Farrukh. 2011. *Rumi: A New Translation*. New York: Harper Collins.
Dhondy, Farrukh. 2013. *Rumi: A New Translation of Selected Poems*. New York: Arcade Publishing.
Dunn, Philip, Manuela Dunn, and R. A. Nicholson. 2010. *The Illustrated Rumi: A Treasury of Wisdom from the Poet of the Soul*. New York: HarperOne.
Ergin, Nevit Oguz. 1993. *Magnificent One: Selected New Verses from Divan-I Kebir*. Burdett, NY: Larson Publications.
Ergin, Nevit Oguz. 1997. *A Rose Garden: Selections from Meter I of Divan-I Kebir of Rumi*. Royal Oak, MI: Echo Publications.
Ergin, Nevit Oguz, and Colman Barks. 2009. *Tales of a Modern Sufi: The Invisible Fence of Reality and Other Stories*. Rochester, VT: Inner Traditions.
Ergin, Nevit Oguz, and Will Johnson. 2006. *The Forbidden Rumi: The Suppressed Poems of Rumi on Love, Heresy, and Intoxication*. Rochester, VT: Inner Traditions.
Freke, Timothy. 2003. *Rumi Wisdom: Daily Teachings from the Great Sufi Master*. New York: Sterling.

Gamard, Ibrahim. 2004. *Rumi and Islam: Selections from His Stories, Poems, and Discourses Annotated & Explained.* Nashville, TN: Skylight Paths Publishing.
Garemani, Homa A. 2014. *Rumi's Banquet of Love.* North Charleston, SC: CreateSpace Independent Publishing Platform.
Harvey, Andrew. 1988. *Love's Fire: Re-creations of Rumi.* London: Jonathan Cape.
Harvey, Andrew. 1989. *Speaking Flame.* Ithaca, NY: Meeramma Publications.
Harvey, Andrew. 1996. *Love's Glory: Re-creations of Rumi.* Berkeley, CA: North Atlantic Books.
Harvey, Andrew. 1997. *How Could the Soul Not Take Flight: For Double Choir.* London: Faber Music.
Harvey, Andrew. 1999. *Teachings of Rumi.* Boston: Shambhala.
Harvey, Andrew. 2000. *The Way of Passion: A Celebration of Rumi.* New York: Tarcher.
Harvey, Andrew. 2004. *Light Upon Light, Inspirations from Rumi.* New York: Tarcher.
Helminski, Camille, and Refik Algan. 2008. *Rumi's Sun: The Teachings of Shams of Tabriz.* Sandpoint, ID: Morning Light Press.
Helminski, Kabir. 2000. *Love Is a Stranger: Selected Lyric Poetry.* Boston and London: Shambhala.
Helminski, Kabir. 2000. *The Rumi Collection an Anthology of Translations of Mevlāna Jalāluddin Rumi.* Edited by Andrew Harvey. Boston: Shambhala.
Helminski, Kabir. 2001. *The Pocket Rumi Reader.* Boston and London: Shambhala,
Helminski, Kabir. 2010. *Love's Ripening: Rumi on the Heart's Journey.* Boston and London: Shambhala.
Helminski, Kabir. 2011. *The Knowing Heart: A Sufi Path of Transformation.* Boston: Shambhala.
Helminski, Kabir Edmund, and Camille Adams. 2000. *Jewels of Remembrance: A Daybook of Spiritual Guidance Containing 365 Selections from the Wisdom of Mevlana Jalaluddin.* Boston: Shambhala.
Helminski, Kabir Edmund, and Camille Helminski. 2011. *The Rumi Daybook.* Boston: Shambhala.
Homayounfar, Kambiz. 2007. *Love Mad: Poems of Rumi.* Leicester: Troubador Publishing.
Khalili, Nader. 1994. *Rumi, Fountain of Fire.* Hesperia, CA: Cal-Earth.
Khalili, Nader. 2001. *Rumi, Dancing the Flame.* Hesperia, CA: Cal-Earth.
Khalili, Nader. 2020. *The Friendship Poems of Rumi.* New York: Wellfleet Press.
Khalili, Nader. 2020. *The Love Poems of Rumi.* New York: Wellfleet Press.
Khalili, Nader. 2020. *The Spiritual Poems of Rumi.* New York: Quarto Publishing.
Khosla, Krisha. 1996. *Rumi Speaks Through Sufi Tales.* Chicago: Kazi Publications, Inc.
Ladinsky, Daniel. 2012. *The Purity of Desire: 100 Poems of Rumi.* New York: Penguin Books.
Lewis, Franklin D. 2007. *Rumi Past and Present, East and West: The Life, Teachings, and Poetry of Jalal al-Din Rumi.* Oxford: Oneworld.
Lewis, Franklin D. 2008. *Swallowing the Sun.* Oxford: Oneworld.
Lewis, Franklin D. 2009. *Mystical Poems of Rumi.* Chicago: University of Chicago Press.
Mafi, Maryam. 2000. *Rumi: Whispers of the Beloved.* London: Thorsons.
Mafi, Maryam. 2004. *Rumi: Gardens of the Beloved.* London: Element Books Ltd.
Mafi, Maryam, and Azima Melita Kolin. 2001. *Rumi: Hidden Music.* London: Thorsons.
Mafi, Maryam, and Azima Melita Kolin. 2012. *Rumi's Little Book of Life: The Garden of the Soul, the Heart, and the Spirit.* Newburyport, MA: Hampton Roads Publishing.
Mafi, Maryam, and Azima Melita Kolin. 2014. *Rumi, Day by Day.* Newburyport, MA: Hampton Roads Publishing.

Mafi, Maryam, and Azima Melita Kolin. 2014. *Rumi's Little Book of Love: 150 Poems That Speak to the Heart.* San Antonio, TX: Hierophant Publishing.
Marman, Doug, Farzad Khalvati, and Mitra Shafaei. 2019. *The Hidden Teachings of Rumi.* Ridgefield, WA: Spiritual Dialogues Project.
Maufroy, Muriel. 1997. *Breathing Truth, Quotations from Jalaluddin Rumi.* London: Sanyar Press.
Niazi, Negar, and G. John Oster. 2013. *Rumi's Fables.* North Charleston, SC: CreateSpace Independent Publishing Platform.
Saberi, Reza. 2000. *A Thousand Years of Persian Rubáiyát: An Anthology of Quatrains from the Tenth to the Twentieth Century Along with the Original Persian.* Bethesda, MD: Ibex Publishers.
Schimmel, Annemarie. 1996. *Look! This is Love.* Boston: Shambhala.
Scholey, Arthur. 2002. *The Paragon Parrot: And Other Inspirational Tales of Wisdom.* London: Watkins Publishing Limited.
Sener, Evren. 2013. *Tales from Masnavi of Rumi.* North Charleston, SC: CreateSpace Independent Publishing Platform.
Shams, Rasoul. 2012. *Rumi: The Art of Loving.* Salt Lake City, UT: Rumi Poetry Club.
Shiva, Shahram. 1995. *Rending the Veil: Literal and Poetic Translations of Rumi.* Chino Valley, AZ: Hohm Press.
Shiva, Shahram. 1999. *Hush, Don't Say Anything to God: Passionate Poems of Rumi.* Fremont, CA: Jain Pub Co.
Shiva, Shahram. 2000. *Rumi – Thief of Sleep: 180 Quatrains from the Persian.* Chino Valley, AZ: Hohm Press.
Shiva, Shahram, and Jonathan Star. 1992. *A Garden Beyond Paradise: The Mystical Poetry of Rumi.* New York: Bantam Books.
Solahuddin, Edwin. 2013. *A Spiritual Journey to the Land of Love: 40 Love Poems of Jalaluddin Rumi.* Kindle edition. Rawalpindi: Al Mizan Foundation.
Star, Jonathan. 2008. *Rumi: In the Arms of the Beloved,* Série Cornerstone Editions. New York: Tarcher.
Zavosh, Hamid. 2003. *Rumi and Friends: Speak with the Music of Poetry to Stressed-Out Souls Across the Centuries.* Bloomington, IN: iUniverse, Inc.

d English Anthologies

Arberry, Arthur John. 1964. *Persian Poems: An Anthology of Verse Translations.* New York: Dutton.
Arberry, Arthur John. 1983. *Immortal Rose: An Anthology of Persian Lyrics.* London: Luzac.
Bowen, J. C. E. 1948. *Poems from the Persian.* London: Blackwell.
Browne, Edward Granville. 1927. *A Persian Anthology: Being Translations From the Persian.* London: E. Benn.
Castello, Louisa Stuart. 1845. *The Rose Garden of Persia.* London: Longmans.
Dole, Nathan Haskell. 1901. *Flowers from Persian Poets.* New York: Thomas Crowell.
Emerson, Ralph Waldo. 1867. *May Day.* London: George Routledge and Sons edition.
Jackson, A. V. W., and Charles Dudley Warner, eds. 1896. *The Library of the World's Best Litterature: Ancient and Modern.* 32 vols. New York: Peale.
Nicholson, Reynold Alleyne. 1950. *Rûmî: Poet and Mystic, 1207–1273: Selections from His Writings.* London: George Allen and Unwin.
Nicholson, Reynold Alleyne. 2000. *A Rumi Anthology: Rumi: Poet and Mystic Tales of Mystic Meaning.* Oxford: Oneworld.

Palmer, Edward Henry. 1877. *The Song of the Reed and Other Pieces*. London: Trubner.
Robinson, Samuel. [1883] 1976. *Persian Poetry for English Readers*. Tehran: Imperial Organization for Social Services.
Van Doren, Mark. 1928. *Anthology of World Poetry*. New York: Literary Guild of America.

e   Translations of other Persian Texts

Attār Neyshāburi, Sheykh Farideddin. [1954] 1961. *The Conference of the Birds – Mantiq Ut-Tair*. English Translation by Charles Stanley Nott. London: Routledge.

C   French Translations

a   Masnavi-ye Ma'navi

Baudry, F. 1857. "Moïse et le chevrier." *Magasin Pittoresque*. Paris, p. 242.
Ibrahim-Ouali, Lila, and Bahman Namvar-Motlag. 2001. *Sagesses et malices de la Perse, contes du "Masnavi"*. Paris: Albin Michel.
Kudsi, Ahmed Erguner, and Pierre Maniez. 1988. *Le Mesnevi, 150 contes soufis*. Paris: Albin Michel.
Vitray-Meyerovitch, Eva de, and Djamchid Mortazavi. 1990. *Mathnawî: la quête de l'absolu*. Monaco: Édition du Rocher.

b   Divān-e Shams-e Tabrizi

Jambet, Christian. 1999. *Soleil du réel: poèmes d'amour mystique*. Traduit du persan et présentation. Paris: Imprimerie nationale.
Robin, Pierre. 1955. "Quatorze Qazals." *Cahiers du Sud*, n°4. Paris.
Tajadod, Mahin, Nahal Tajadod, and Jean Claude Carrière. 1993. *Le livre de Chams de Tabriz, cent poèmes par Mowlānā Djalāl-od-din Mohammad Balkhi (Roumi)*. Paris: Gallimard.
Tajadod, Nahal, and Jean Claude Carrière. 2020. *Cette lumière est mon désir: Le Livre de Shams de Tabrîz*. Paris: Gallimard.
Tchelebi, Assaf Hālet. [1950] 1984. *Roubā'yāt, traduits du persan*. Paris: Librarie d'Amérique et d'Orient Adrien-Maisonneuve.
Vitray-Meyerovitch, Eva de, and Mohammad Mokri. 2003. *Odes mystiques (Dîvān-e Shams-e Tabrîzî)*. Traduction du persan avec des notes. Paris: Seuil, Éditions UNESCO.
Vitray-Meyerovitch, Eva de, and Djamchid Mortazavi. 1987. *Rubāi'yāt (extraits)*. Traduit du persan. Paris: Albin Michel.
Vitray-Meyerovitch, Eva de, and Djamchid Mortazavi. 2000. *Les quatrains de Rûmî*. Paris: Albin Michel.
Wojciech, Skalmowski. 1992. "Sept ghazals de Rumi." *Orientalia Lovaniensia Periodica*. Vol. 22, 169–183, 1991, *Abstracta Iranica XV*. Téhéran: Institut français de recherche.

c   Mixed Sources

Anvar, Leili. 2011. *Rûmî La religion de l'amour*. Paris: Éditions Points.
Fouladvand, Marjan. 2005. *Le marchand et le perroquet*. Paris: Éditions Syros.
Koraichi, Rachid. 2002. *Rûmî: Le Miroir Infini*. Paris: Éditions Alternatives.

Mabey, Juliet, and Gérard Leconte. 2003. *Rûmî: la sagesse des derviches tourneurs*. Paris: Véga.
Massé, Henri. 1949. *Anthologie persane*. Paris: Payot.
Massé, Henri. 1964. *Anthologie de la poésie persane*. Edited by Zabihollah Safa, 207–221. Paris: Gallimard.
Metoui, Lassaâd. 2005. *Amour: ta blessure dans mes veines*. Paris: Jean-Claude Lattès.
Metoui, Lassaâd. 2006. *Les couleurs de l'amour*. Paris: Éditions Dervy.
Moussawy, Salah. 2002. *Le Calligraphe et le Derviche*. Paris: Éditions Bachari.
Vitray-Meyerovitch, Eva de. 1990. *Lettres*. Paris: Édition Jules Renard.
Vitray-Meyerovitch, Eva de. 1997. *Le Livre du dedans (Fîhi-mā-fîhi)*. Paris: Albin Michel.

D German

Bürgel, Johann Christoph. 1992. *Dschalaluddin Rumi: Traumbild des Herzens – Hundert Vierzeiler*. Zürich: Manesse Bücherei.
Engen, Christoph. 2009. *Die Musik, die wir sind*. Freiburg: Arbor Verlag.
Engen, Christoph. 2015. *Das Eine Lied*. Freiburg: Arbor Verlag.
Engen, Christoph. 2015. *Durchwachte Nacht*. Freiburg: Arbor Verlag.
Ghazanfari, Ali. 2009. *Ǧalāl-ad-Dīn Rūmī: Gipfel der Liebe. Ausgewählte Vierzeiler von Rumi; persisch-deutsch*. Zweisprachige Ausgabe, Leipzig: Engelsdorfer Verlag.
Hammer-Purgstall, Joseph von. 1818. *Geschichte der schönen Redekünste Persiens*. Wien: Heubner und Volke.
Hopfgartner, Herbert. 2007. "Horch mit dem Ohr der Seele den zahllosen Tönen. Musikalische Notizen über den Mystiker Dschelaleddin Rumi." In *Talk Together*. Issue 21. Salzburg.
Höschle, Otto von. 2020. *Masnawi – Gesamtausgabe in zwei Bänden. Erster Band: Buch I–III*. Vollständiger Text aus dem Persischen in deutsche Blankverse übersetzt. Xanten: Chalice.
Höschle, Otto von. 2021. *Masnawi – Gesamtausgabe in zwei Bänden: Zweiter Band: Buch IV–VI*. Vollständiger Text aus dem Persischen in deutsche Blankverse übersetzt. Xanten: Chalice.
Leviculus. 2018. *Rumi 33 Perlen aus dem Ozean der Liebe: Gedichte*. Independently Published.
Maschajechi, Reza. 2004. *Liebesmystik: Gedichte aus dem Diwan*. Weitra: Verlag Bibliothek der Provinz.
Maschajechi, Reza. 2010. *Das Lied der Flöte, Zweisprachige Ausgabe der 51 Verse des Inhaltsverzeichnisses des Mathnawi, mit Rezitation*. Herausgegeben mit einem Begleitwort von Uta Kutter. Stuttgart: Akademie für Gesprochenes Wort.
Melzer, Uto von. 1994. *Nie ist wer liebt allein: Mystische Liebeslieder aus dem Diwan-i Šams*. Edited by N. Rastegar, revised by Monika Huttenstrasser, with Persian text and the translations of Vincenz von Rosenzweig (1791–1865). Graz: Studienbücher zur persischen Dichtung.
Melzer, Uto von. 1999. *Mondenschöner, schlafe nicht: Rubaʿiyat – 102 Mystische Vierzeiler*. Edited by N. Rastegar, revised and supplemented by Monika Huttenstrasser. Graz: Studienbücher zur persischen Dichtung.
Platen, August Graf von. 1821. *Ghaselen*. Leipzig: C. Heyder.
Rosen, Gerog. 1849. *Mesnewi oder Doppelverse des Scheich Mewlana Dschelal-ed-din Rumi, aus dem Persischen übertragen von Georg Rosen*. Leipzig: Fr. Chr. Wilh. Vogel.

Rosenzweig, Vincenz von. [1838] 2017. *Gedichte des Sams aus Täbris: Eine Auswahl.* Berlin: Hofenberg.
Rückert, Friedrich. 1822. *Östliche Rosen.* Leipzig: F.M. Brodhaus.
Rückert, Friedrich. 1927. *Mytische Ghaselen nach Dschelaleddin Rumi der Perser.* Hamburg: Lerchenfeld.
Schimmel, Annemarie. [1978] 2003. *Rumi: Ich bin Wind und du bist Feuer. Leben und Werk des großen Mystikers.* Munichen: Hugendubel.
Schimmel, Annemarie. 1986. *Aus dem Diwan.* Ditzingen: Reclams Universal Library.
Schimmel, Annemarie. 1988. *Von Allem und vom Einen.* München: Hugendubel Verlag.
Schimmel, Annemarie. 1993. *Sieh! Das ist Liebe: Gedichte: Rumi.* Basel: Sphinx.

E Italian

Arena, Leonardo Vittorio, ed. 1993. *Il canto del derviscio. Parabole della sapienza sufi.* Raccolta di storie **tratte** dal Masnavi. Milano: Mondadori.
Bausani, Alessandro. 1980. *Poesie mistiche.* Introduzione, traduzione, antologia critica e note. Milano: Rizzoli.
Fiorentini, Giorgio. 2000. *L'amore è uno straniero.* Roma: Astrolabio Ubaldini.
Fiorentini, Giorgio. 2015. *Divan (Divan-e Sams-e Tabrizi).* Torino: Psiche.
Foti, Sergio. 1995. *L'Essenza del Reale. Fîhi mā fîhi (C'è quel che c'è),* traduzione dal persiano, introduzione e note, revisione di Gianpaolo Fiorentini. Torino: Libreria Editrice Psiche.
Helminski, Kabir Hedmund. 2000. *L'amore è uno straniero poesie scelte*, traduzioni e revisione. Traduzione in **italiano** di Gianpaolo Fiorentini. Roma: Ubaldini Editore.
Jevolella, Massimo, ed. 1995. *Racconti sufi.* Traduzione dal francese di Barbara Brevi. Como: Red.
Mandel Khàn, Gabriele, e Cerati Mandel. 2006. *Mathnawì. Il poema del misticismo universal.* 6 vols., traduzione in **italiano**. Milano: Bompiani.
Pellò, Stefano. 2020. *Settecento sipari del cuore.* Milano: Ponte alle Grazie.
Schenardi, R. 2013. *Il libro delle profondità interiori.* Milano: Luni Editrice.

F Spanish

Arus, Esteve Serra. 2015. *Cuentos Del Mathnawi.* Palma de Mallorca: Olañeta.
Janés, Clara, y Ahmad Taheri. 2006. *El corazon del fuego: poemas sufies.* Malaga: Adamaramada Ediciones.
Janés, Clara, y Ahmad Taheri. 2015. *Rubayat.* Madrid: Alianza Editorial.
Lizandra, Alberto Manzano, y María Marrades Tattarachi. 2020. *El Masnavi: Las enseñanzas de Yalaluddîn Rumi.* Selection de textos de E. H. Whinfield. Barcelona: Blume.
Menzano, Alberto. 1997. *Poemas Sufies.* Madrid: Hiperión.
Piruz, Mahmud, y José María Bermejo. 2010. *Luz del Alma: Selección de poemas de Rumi.* Madrid: Gaia Ediciones.
Random, Michel. 2006. *Rumi. El conocimiento y el secreto.* México: Fondo de Cultura Económica.
Star, Jonathan. 2005. *Un jardín más allá del paraíso, poemas de amor de Rumi.* Traducido en español por Vandita Martin Fernandez. Madrid: Mandala Ediciones.
Star, Jonathan. 2011. *En Brazos Del Amado.* Traducido en español por Alfonso Colodrón. Madrid: Edaf.

G Russian

Akimushkina, O. F., Yu. A. Ioannesyan, B. V. Norik, A. A. Khismatulin, O. M. Yastrebova, O. Osmanova, L. G. Lakhuti, et al. Obshh. red. A. A. Khismatulina. 2007–2012. *Masnavi-ji Ma'navi "Pojema o skrytom smysle". V shesti daftarah (prozaicheskij perevod)* [Masnavi-yi Ma'navi Poem about the Hidden Meaning in Six Daftars (Prosaic Translation)]. Sankt-Peterburg: Peterburgskoe Vostokovedenie.
Grebnev, Naum. 1986. *Pojema o skrytom smysle: Izbrannye pritchi* [Poems of the Hidden Meaning: Selected Parables]. Glavnaja redakcija vostochnoj literatury izdatel'stva. Moskva: Nauka.
Grebnev, Naum. 2005. *Istiny: izrechenija persidskih i tadzhikskih narodov* [Truths: Sayings of the Persian and Tajik Peoples, Their Poets and Sages]. Sankt-Peterburg: Azbuka-Klassika.
Grebnev, Naum. 2005. *Persidskaja klassika pory rascveta* [A Persian Classic of the Heyday]. V sostave sbornika: Rumi. Pojema o skrytom smysle. Moskva: Pushkinskaja biblioteka: AST.
Derzhavin, V., A. Kochetkov, Y. Neyman, R. Moran, T. Streshneva, K. Arsenyeva, I. Selvinsky, E. Dunaevsky, S. Lipkin, G. Plisetsky, V. Levik, O. Rumer, et al. *Irano-tadzhikskaja pojezija* [Iranian and Tajik Poetry]. 1974. Biblioteka Vsemirnoj Literatury. Serija pervaja, tom 21. Moskva: Izdatel'stvo "Khudozhestvennaja literatura". 127–186.
Korogly, Kh. G. 1991. *Klassicheskaja vostochnaja pojezija: Antologija/Sost* [Classical Oriental Poetry: Anthology]. Predisl., vvedenie, glossarij, komment, 293–319. Moskva: Vyssh. shk.
Shhedrovickogo, D. V., and M. Oklik. 2009. *Doroga prevrashhenij: sufijskie pritchi* [The Road of Transformation: Sufi Parables]. Moskva: Oklik.
Stepanyants, M. 1995. *Rumi v russkih perevodah Chittik U. V poiskah skrytogo smysla. Duhovnoe uchenie* [Rumi in Russian Translation: William Chittick's in Search of Hidden Meaning, Sufi Way of Love, Spiritual Teaching of Rumi]. Moskva: Ladomir.
Vasilievich, Derzhavin Vladimir, translator. 1998. *Gazeli Pritchi* [Gazelles, Proverbs]. Dushanbe: Adib.

H Non-European Languages

Gölpinarli, AbdÏbāki. 1957–1960. *Dîvān-i Kebîr: [Yazan] Mevlānā Celāleddin. Hazirhyan.* Istanbul: Remzi Kitabevi.
Gölpinarli, AbdÏbāki. 1963. *Mevlānā Celāleddin Mektuplar*. Istanbul: Inkılap Kitabevi.
Gölpinarli, AbdÏbāki. 1983. *Mesnevî Tercemesi ve SHerhi*. Cilt. I–VI. Istanbul: Inkılap Yayınevi.

2 Secondary Sources

Ahmadnezhād, Kāmil, and Shiva Kamāli Aṣl. 1385 [2006]. *'Arūẓ va qāfiye* [Rhythm and Rhyme]. Tehrān: Āyij.
Allerton, D. J. 1982. *Valency and the English Verb*. London: Academic Press.
Amir-Moezzi, Mohammad Ali. 2009. *The Spirituality of Shi'i Islam: Beliefs and Practices*. London: I. B. Tauris.
Amossy, Ruth. 2001. "D'une culture à l'autre: réflexion sur la transposition des clichés et des stéréotypes." *Palimpsestes, Le cliché en traduction*, n°13.
Anvar, Leili. 2015. "La poésie mystique" interview with Leili Anvar by Abdennour Bidar, *Cultures d'Islam*, Radio France Culture, April 24, 2015. www.franceculture.fr/emissions/cultures-d-islam/la-poesie-mystique

Arberry, Arthur John. 1956. *Classical Persian Literature*. London: George Alien and Unwin Ltd.
Asatrian, Garnik. 2010. *Etymological Dictionary of Persian*. Leiden Indo-European Etymological Dictionary Series. Leiden: Brill Academic Publishers.
Bacry, Patrick. 1992. *Les figures de style: et autres procédés stylistiques*. "Collection Sujets". Paris: Belin.
Baker, Mona et al. [1998] 2009. *Routledge Encyclopedia of Translation Studies*. London: Routledge.
Baldrick, Chris. 2008. *Oxford Dictionary of Literary Terms*. New York: Oxford University Press.
Barthes, Roland. 1957. *Mythologies*. Paris: Seuil.
Barthes, Roland. 1967. *Système de la mode*. Paris: Seuil.
Bassnett, Susan. 2002. *Translation Studies*. London and New York: Routledge.
Bassnett, Susan, and André Lefevere.1998. *Constructing Cultures: Essays on Literary Translation*. Clevedon and Philadelphia: Multilingual Matters.
Benjamin, Walter. [1913] 2004. "The Task of the Translator." In *Walter Benjamin: Selected Writings, Volume 1: 1913–1926*, edited by Marcus Bullock and Michael Jennings. Boston: Harvard University Press.
Benveniste, Émile. 1966. *Problèmes de linguistique générale*. Vol. 1. Paris: Gallimard.
Benveniste, Émile. 1974. *Problèmes de linguistique générale*. Vol. 2. Paris: Gallimard.
Berman, Antoine. 1984. *L'épreuve de l'étranger, Culture et traduction dans l'Allemagne romantique*. Paris: Gallimard.
Berman, Antoine. 1995. *Pour une critique des traductions: John Donne*. Paris: Gallimard.
Berman, Antoine. 1999. *La traduction et la lettre ou l'auberge du lointain*. Paris: Seuil.
Boileau, Nicolas. [1674] 1872. "L'Art poétique." In *Œuvres poétiques*. Vol. 1, 203–211. Paris: Imprimerie générale.
Browne, Edward Granville. [1906–1908] 1997. *A Literary History of Persia*. 4 vols. Cambridge: Ibex Pub.
Bühler, Karl. [1934] 2011. *The Theory of Language: The Representational Function of Language (Sprachtheorie)*. Translated by Donald Fraser Goodwin. Amsterdam: John Benjamin's Publishing Company.
Chomsky, Noam. [1965] 1969. *Aspects of the Theory of Syntax*. Cambridge, MA: M.I.T. Press.
Christensen, Arthur Emanuel. 1970. *Études sur le persan contemporain*. Copenhague: Munksgaard.
Chuquet, Hélène, and Michel Paillard. 1987. *Approche linguistique des problèmes de traduction. Anglais-français*. Gap/Paris: Ophrys.
Cicero, Marcus Tullius. 1960. *De inventione. De optimo genere oratorum. Topica*. Translated by Harry Mortimer Hubbell. Cambridge, MA: Harvard University Press.
Corbin, Henry. 1389 [2008]. *Farhang-e estelāhāt-e falsafi-'erfāni, Farsi-Farânse* [The Dictionary of Philosophical and Gnostic Terms, Persian-French]. Tehrān: Farhang-e Moʻāṣer.
Corbin, Henry. 1969. "La philosophie islamique, des origines à la mort d'Averroës." In *Histoire de la philosophie, tome I. 1048–1197*, edited by Yvon Belaval. Paris: Éditions Gallimard.
Corbin, Henry. 1974. "La philosophie islamique depuis la mort d'Averroës jusqu'à nos jours." In *Histoire de la philosophie, tome III. 1065–1188*, edited by Yvon Belaval. Paris: Éditions Gallimard.

Bibliography

Corbin, Henry. 1990. *Corps spirituel et terre céleste: De l'Iran mazdéen à l'Iran shï'ite*. Paris: Buchet-Chastel.
Corbin, Henry. 1991. *En Islam iranien. Aspects spirituels et philosophiques*. 4 tomes, Collection Tel (n° 189). Paris: Gallimard.
Cordonnier, Jean Louis. 1995. *Traduction et culture*. Paris: Didier.
Crystal, David. 2003. *A Dictionary of Linguistics and Phonetics*. 5th ed. Oxford: Blackwell.
Derrida, Jacques. 1985. *Difference in Translation*, "Les tours de Babel". Éditions Joseph Graham. Ithaca, NY: Cornell University Press.
Dugin, Alexander. 2018. *Ethnos and Society*. London: Arktos.
Dugin, Alexander. 2019. *Ethnosociology: The Foundations*. London: Arktos.
During, Jean. 1988. *Musique et extase, l'audition mystique dans la tradition soufie*. Paris: Albin Michel.
During, Jean. 1989. *Musique et mystique dans les traditions de l'Iran*. Paris: Institut français de recherche en Iran, Leuven: Éditions Peeters.
During, Jean, and Zia Mirabdolbaghi. 1991. *The Art of Persian Music, Lessons from Master Dariush Safvat*. Translated from French and Persian by Manuchehr Anvar. Washington, DC: Mage Publishers.
Eco, Umberto. 1968. *La struttura assente*. Milano: Bompiani.
Eco, Umberto. 1976. *A Theory of Semiotics*. Bloomington: Indiana University Press.
Eco, Umberto. 1984. *Semiotics and the Philosophy of Language*. London: Macmillan.
Elwell-Sutton, Laurence Paul. 1976. *The Persian Metres*. Cambridge: Cambridge University Press.
Ernst, Carl W. 1985. *Words of Ecstasy in Sufism*. Albany: Suny.
Even-Zohar, Itmar. 1990. *Polysystem Studies*. Tel Aviv: Porter Institute for Poetics and Semiotics, Tel Aviv University.
Even-Zohar, Itmar, and Gideon Toury, eds. 1981. *Translation Theory and Intercultural Relations*. Tel Aviv: Porter Institute for Poetics and Semiotics, Tel Aviv University.
Farhat, Hormoz. 2004. *The Dastgah Concept in Persian Music*. Cambridge Studies in Ethnomusicology. Cambridge: Cambridge University Press.
Farshidvar, Khosrow. 1387 [2008]. *Tārix-e moxtaṣar-e zabān-e fārsi: az āghāz tā konun* [A Brief History of the Persian Language from the Beginning Until Now]. Tehrān: Zavvār.
Folkart, Barbara. 1991. *Le conflit des énonciations: traduction et discours rapporté*. Montréal: Balzac.
Garcin de Tassy, Joseph. [1873] 1970. *Rhétorique et prosodie des langues de l'orient musulman; et spécialement de l'arabe, du persan, du turc et de l'hindoustani fondé sur, et en partie traduit de l'ouvrage persan du 18e siècle, intitulé Ḥâdayïq ul-Bâlagat, les jardins de l'éloquence par Mîr Schams Udâin Faqûir*. Amsterdam: Philo Press.
Genette, Gérard. 1982. *Palimpsestes: La littérature au second degré*. Paris: Éditions du Seuil.
Genette, Gérard. 1987. *Seuils*. Paris: Éditions du Seuil.
Gentzler, Edwin. 2001. *Contemporary Translation Theories*. Clevedon, UK: Multilingual Matters.
Goethe, Johann Wolfgang von. 1994. *West-östlicher Divan*. Edited by Hendrik Birus. 2 vols. Collected Works, III/1–2. Frankfurt am Main: Deutscher Klassiker Verlag.
Greimas, Julien Algirdas, and Joseph Courtes. [1979] 1982. *Semiotics and Language: An Analytical Dictionary*. Translated by Larry Crist et al. Bloomington: Indiana University Press.
Greimas, Julien Algirdas, and Joseph Courtes. [1979] 1993. *Sémiotique: Dictionnaire raisonné de la théorie du langage*. Paris: Hachette Supérieur.

Guénon, René. 1973. *Aperçus sur l'ésotérisme islamique et le taoïsme*. Paris: Gallimard.
Guillemin-Flescher, Jacqueline. 1981. *Syntaxe comparée du français et de l'anglais. Problèmes de traduction*. Paris: Ophrys.
Haugerud, Joan. 1977. *The Word for Us: The Gospels of John and Mark, Epistles to the Romans and the Galatians, Restated in Inclusive Language*. Seattle: Coalition on Women and Religion.
Hjelmslev, Louis. [1943] 1961. *Prolegomena to a Theory of Language*. Translated by J. Francis Whitfield. Madison: University of Wisconsin Press.
Hodgson, Marshall G. S. 1977. *The Venture of Islam, Volume 2: The Expansion of Islam in the Middle Periods*. Chicago: University of Chicago Press.
Holmes, James Stratton. [1988] 2004. "The Name and Nature of Translation Studies." In *The Translation Studies Reader*, edited by Lawrence Venuti, 180–192. London: Routledge.
Homāyi, Jalāleddin. 1367 [1988]. *Funun-e balāghat va ṣanā'āt-e adabi* [Rhetoric Techniques and Literary Devices]. Tehrān: Nashr-e Namā.
Huang, Eva, and David Pollard. 2009. "The Chinese Tradition." In *Routledge Encyclopedia of Translation Studies*, edited by Mona Baker et al., 369–378. London: Routledge.
Huart, Clément. 1897 *Konia, la ville des derviches tourneurs: souvenirs d'un voyage en Asie mineure*. Paris: Ernest Leroux.
Hugo, Victor. 1864. *William Shakespeare*. Paris: A. Lacroix, Verboeckhoven et Cie, Éditeurs.
Ibraheem, Meerza Mohammad. 1841. *A Grammar of the Persian Language: To Which Are Subjoined Several Dialogues: With an Alphabetical List of the English and Persian Terms of Grammar: And an Appendix, on the Use of Arabic Words*. London: W.H. Allen.
Jakobson, Roman. [1960] 1964. "Linguistics and Poetics." In *Style in Language*, edited by Thomas Sebeok, 350–377. Cambridge, MA: M.I.T. Press.
Jakobson, Roman. 1971. *Selected Writings II. Word and Language*. The Hague: Mouton.
Jerome, Saint, William Henry Fremantle, George Lewis, and William Gibson Martley. 1989. *St. Jerome: Letters and Select Works*. Grand Rapids, MI: Eerdmans Pub. Co.
Johansen, Svend. 1949. "La notion de signe dans la glossématique et dans l'esthétique." In *Recherches structurales*, 288–303. Copenhagen: Travaux du cercle linguistique de Copenhague 5.
Jones, Sir William. [1771] 1826. *A Grammar of the Persian Language*. London: Fb&c Limited.
Kazzāzi, Mir-Jalāleddin. 1368 [1989]. *Zibāyishenāsi-e Sokhan-e Parsi* [Aesthetics of Persian Discourse]. 3 vol. Tehrān: Nashr-e Markaz.
Keshavarz, Fatemeh. [1998] 2004. *Reading Mystical Lyric: The Case of Jalal al-Din Rumi*. Columbia, SC: University of South Carolina Press.
Ladmiral, Jean René. 2014. *Sourcier ou cibliste*. Paris: Les Belles Lettres.
Lambton, Ann Katharine Swynford. 1953. *Persian Grammar*. Cambridge: Cambridge University Press.
Lazard, Gilbert. 1994. *L'actance*. Paris: Presses universitaires de France.
Lazard, Gilbert.1995. *La formation de la langue persane*. Paris: Peeters.
Lazard, Gilbert. 2006. *Grammaire du persan contemporain*. Avec la collaboration de Yann Richard, Rokhsareh Hechmati, et Pollet Samvelian. Téhéran: Institut français de recherche en Iran.
Lefevere, André. 1992. *Translation, Rewriting, and the Manipulation of the Literary Frame*. London: Routledge.
Lewis, Frankin D. 2007. *Rumi Past and Present, East and West: The Life, Teachings, and Poetry of Jalal al-Din Rumi*. 2nd ed. Oxford: Oneworld.

Lewisohn, Leonard. 1989. "Shabistari's Garden of Mysteries: The Aesthetics and Hermeneutics of Sufi Poetry." In *Temenos: A Review Devoted to the Arts of the Imagination*. Tenemos. No. 10, pp. 177–207.
Lewisohn, Leonard. 1995. *Beyond Faith and Infidelity: The Sufi Poetry and Teachings of Maḥmūd Shabistarī*. Richmond, Surrey: Curzon Press.
Lewisohn, Leonard. 1997. "The Sacred Music of Islam: *Samāʿ* The Persian Sufi Tradition." *British Journal of Ethnomusicology* 6: 1–33.
Lewisohn, Leonard, ed. 2014. *The Philosophy of Ecstasy: Rumi and the Sufi Tradition*. Bloomington, IN: World Wisdom.
Mace, John. 2003. *Persian Grammar: For Reference and Revision*. London: Routledge.
Martinet, André. 1962. *A Functional View of Language*. Oxford: Clarendon Press.
Martinet, André. 1965. *La linguistique synchronique*. Paris: Presses universitaires de France.
Martinet, André. [1960] 1980. *Éléments de linguistique générale*. Nouvelle édition remaniée et mise à jour. Paris: Armand Colin.
Massignon, Louis. [1975] 2010. *La passion de Husayn ibn Mansûr Hallâj*. 4 tomes. Paris: Gallimard.
Meier, Fritz von. 1989. *Bahāʾ-i Walad: Grundzüge seines Lebens und seiner Mystik*. Leiden: E.J. Brill.
Meschonnic, Henri. 1970a. *Les Cinq Rouleaux*. Paris: Gallimard.
Meschonnic, Henri. 1970b. *Pour la poétique I*. Paris: Gallimard.
Meschonnic, Henri. 1973. *Pour la poétique II. Epistémologie de l'écriture. Poétique de la traduction*. Paris: Gallimard.
Meschonnic, Henri. 1978. *Pour la poétique V*. Paris: Gallimard.
Meschonnic, Henri. 1999. *Poétique du traduire*. Paris: Verdier.
Meschonnic, Henri, and Gérard Dessons. 1998. *Traité du rythme: Des vers et des proses*. Paris: Dunod.
Miller, Lloyd Clifton. 1999. *Music and Song in Persia: The Art of Āvāz*. Salt Lake City: University of Utah Press.
Millerman, Michael. 2021. "The Ethnosociological and Existential Dimensions of Alexander Dugin's Populism." *Katehon*. Online publication. https://katehon.com/en/article/ethnosociological-and-existential-dimensions-alexander-dugins-populism
Mounin Georges. 1976. *Les problèmes théoriques de la traduction*. Paris: Gallimard.
Mounin Georges. 1994. *Les Belles infidèles*. Paris: Cahiers du Sud, 1955, Lille, Presses Universitaires de Lille.
Munday, Jeremy. 2012. *Introducing Translation Studies*. 4th ed. London: Routledge.
Nida, Eugene. 1964. *Toward a Science of Translating: With Special Reference to Principles and Procedures Involved in Bible Translating*. Leiden: Brill.
Nida, Eugene. 1975. *Language, Structure and Translation*. Stanford, CA: Stanford University Press.
Nida, Eugene, and Charles Taber. 1969. *The Theory and Practice of Translation*. Leiden: Brill.
Nöth, Winfried. 1990. *Handbook of Semiotics*. Bloomington, IN: Indiana University Press.
Palmer, Edward Henry. 1867. *Oriental Mysticism. A Treatise on the Sufiistic and Unitarian Theosophy of the Persians*. London: Bell and Daldy.
Peirce, Charles Sanders. 1931–1958. *The Collected Papers of Charles Sanders Peirce*. Vols. I–VI, ed. Charles Hartshorne and Paul Weiss (1931–1935). Vols. VII–VIII, ed. Arthur W. Burks (1958). Cambridge, MA: Harvard University Press.

Pergnier, Maurice. 1993. *Les fondements sociolinguistiques de la traduction*. Lille: Presses universitaires de Lille.
Petitot, Jean. 1985. *Morphogenèse du Sens*. Préface par René Thom. Paris: PUF.
Petitot, Jean. 2021. "Forme." In *Encyclopædia Universalis*. Online Versions consulted on December 2, 2021. www.universalis.fr/encyclopedie/forme/
Pezeshki, Nastaran. 1388 [2009]. *Hamāhangihā ye vājegāni e 'arabi va fārsi dar she'r-e Masnavi; bā takye bar janbehā-ye musiqāy-e Masnavi va Ghazaliāt-e Shams* [The Coordination of Arabic and Persian in *Masnavi*]. Tehran: Āzādmehr.
Pinson, Jean-Claude. 1995. *Habiter en poète: essai sur la poésie contemporaine*. Seyssel: Champ Vallon.
Porter, Sir James. 1768. *Observations on the Religion, Law, Government, and Manners of the Turks*. London: J. Nourse, Bookseller to His Majesty.
Prandi, Michèle. 1992. *Grammaire philosophique des tropes*. Paris: Minuit.
Propp, Vladimir. [1926] 1968. *Morphology of the Folktale*. Translated by Laurence Scott. 2nd revised ed. Austin: University of Texas.
Rastier, François. 2017. "Cassirer et la création du structuralisme." *Texto! Textes et cultures* XXII, n°4.
Ricœur, Paul. 1975. *Métaphore vive*. Paris: Seuil.
Ricœur, Paul. 1986. *Du texte à l'action*. Paris: Seuil.
Ricœur, Paul. 2004. *Sur la traduction*. Paris: Bayard.
Royāyi, Yaddollah. 2007. "Oẓv-e jensi dar she'r" [Sexual Orgn in Poetry]. In *Kanduk*. http://kandouk.blogspot.com/2007/02/blog-post.html.
Ṣafā, Ẓabiḥollah. 2535/1355 [1976]. *Seyri dar tārix-e zabānhā va adab-e irāni* [A Review of Iranian Languages and Literatures]. Tehrān: Showrā-ye Farhang va Honar, Markaz-e Moṭāle'āt va hamāhangi-e Farhangi.
Safavi, Seyed Ghahreman, and Simon Weightman. 2009. *Rumi's Mystical Design: Reading the Mathnawi, Book One*. Albany: State University of New York Press.
Said, W. Edward. 1979. *Orientalism*. New York: Vintage Books Random House.
Saussure, Ferdinand de. (1916) 1995. *Cours de linguistique générale*, Édition critique préparée par Tullio de Mauro, coll. "Grande bibliothèque Payot". Paris: Payot.
Schimmel, Annemarie. "Sufism." *Encyclopedia Britannica*, November 20, 2019. www.britannica.com/topic/Sufism.
Schimmel, Annemarie. 1993. *Triumphal Sun: A Study of the Works of Jalaloddin Rumi*. Albany: State University of New York Press.
Schimmel, Annemarie. 2011. *Mystical Dimensions of Islam*. With a new foreword by Carl W. Ernst. Chapel Hill: University of North Carolina Press.
Schleiermacher, Friedrich. [1813] 2012. "On the Different Methods of Translating." Translated by Susan Bernofsky in Lawrence Venuti, ed. *The Translation Studies Reader*. London: Routledge, 43–63.
Sedaghat, Amir. 2015. *Le soufisme de Roumi reçu et perçu dans les mondes anglophone et francophone: étude des traductions anglaises et françaises*. Littératures. Université Sorbonne Paris Cité. https://tel.archives-ouvertes.fr/tel-01579400.
Sedaghat, Amir. 2020a. "Rūmī's Verse at the Crossroads of Language and Music." *Mawlana Rumi Review* 9, no. 1–2 (2018): 91–128.
Sedaghat, Amir. 2020b. "Roumi traduit, Roumi réécrit: enjeux politiques d'une réception." *TTR: Traduction et adaptation: un mariage de raison* 33, no. 1: 99–129.
Sedaghat, Amir. 2021. "Semiotic hybridization in Persian poetry and Iranian music." *Semiotica* 2021, no. 241: 275–310.

294 Bibliography

Shafi'i-Kadkani, Moḥammad-Reẓā. 1350 [1971]. *Ṣovar-e khiyāl dar she'r-e pārsi* [The Forms of Imagination in Persian Poetry]. Tehrān: Entesharāt-e Nil.
Shafi'i-Kadkani, Moḥammad-Reẓā. 1368 [1989]. *Musiqi-ye she'r* [Music of Poetry]. Tehrān: Entesharāt-e Khāvarān.
Shafi'i-Kadkani, Moḥammad-Reẓā, ed. 1387 [2008]. *Ghazaliyyāt-e Shams-e Tabrizi*. Tehrān: Soxan.
Shamisā, Sirus. 1363 [1984]. *Seyr-e robā'i dar she'r-e fārsi* [The Evolution of Quatrain in Persian Poetry]. Tehrān: Āshtiyāni.
Shamisā, Sirus. 1380 [2001]. *Sabkshenāsi-ye she'r* [Versification and Poetic Genres]. 9th ed. Tehrān: Ferdows.
Shamisā, Sirus. 1383 [2004]. *'Arūẓ va qāfiye* [Rhythm and rhyme]. 14th ed. Tehrān: Dāneshgāh-e Payām-e nur.
Shayegan, Daryush. 1979. *Les relations de l'hindouisme et du soufisme: d'après le Majma' al-Bahrayn de Dārā Shokûh*. Paris: Éditions de la différence.
Simon, Sherry. 1996. *Gender in Translation: Cultural Identity and the Politics of Transmission*. New York: Routledge.
Snell-Hornby, Mary. 1998. *Translation Studies: An Integrated Approach*. Amsterdam: John Benjamins.
Sørensen, Hans. 1955. *Studier i Baudelaires poesi*. Copenhaguen: Festskrift udgivet af Kebenhavns Universitet.
Steiner, George. 1975. *After Babel, Aspects of Language and Translation*. London: Oxford University Press.
Tafazoli, Hamid. 2001. "Goethe, Johann Wolfgang von." *Encyclopedia Iranica* XI, Fasc. 1: 40–43.
Theisen, Finn. 1982. *A Manual of Classical Persian Prosody: With Chapters on Urdu, Karakhanidic and Ottoman Prosody*. Wiesbaden: Harrassowitz Verlag.
Toury, Gideon. 1995. *Descriptive Translation Studies and Beyond*. Amsterdam and Philadelphia: John Benjamins.
Vaziri, Mostafa. 2015. *Rumi and Shams' Silent Rebellion: Parallels with Vedanta, Buddhism and Shaivism*. London: Palgrave Macmillan.
Venuti, Lawrence. 1998. *The Scandals of Translation*. London: Routledge.
Venuti, Lawrence, ed. [1995] 2008. *The Translator's Invisibility: A History of Translation*. London: Routledge.
Venuti, Lawrence, ed. [2000] 2012. *The Translation Studies Reader*. London: Routledge.
Venuti, Lawrence. 2013. *Translation Changes Everything: Theory and Practice*. London: Routledge.
Vinay, Jean-Paul, and Darbelnet. 1995. *Comparative Stylistics of French and English. A Methodology for Translation*. Translated and edited by Juan C. Sager and M.-J. Hamel. Amsterdam and Philadelphia: John Benjamins.
Von Flotow, Luise. 1997. *Translation and Gender: Translating in the "Era of Feminism"*. Manchester: St. Jerome.
Von Flotow, Luise. 2000. "Women, Bibles, Ideologies." *TTR: Traduction, Terminologie, Rédaction* 13, n° 1: 9–20.
Von Flotow, Luise et al. 2011. *Translating Women*. Ottawa: University of Ottawa Press.
Wellhausen, Julius. 1894. *Israelitische und jüdische Geschichte*. Vol. 2. Berlin: Druck und Verlag von Georg Reimer.
Wittgenstein, Ludwig. 1922. *Tractatus Logico-Philosophicus*. London: Kegan Paul, Rench, Trubner & CO.

Xānlari, Parviz Nātel. 1345 [1966]. *Vazn-e she'r-e fārsi* [Metre of Persian Poetry]. Tehrān: Bonyād-e Farhang-e Irān.

Xānlari, Parviz Nātel. 1366 [1987]. *Tārix-e zabān-e Fārsi* [The History of the Persian Language]. Tehrān: Nashr-e now.

Yarshater, Ehsan. 1974. "Affinities between Persian Poetry and Music." In *Studies in Art and Literature of the Near East*, edited by P. Chelowski. New York: New York University Press.

Zarrinkub, 'Abdolḥoseyn. 1369 [1990]. *Josteju dar Taṣavvof-e Iran* [Searching in Iranian Sufism]. Tehrān: Amir Kabir.

Zonis, Ella. 1973. *Classical Persian Music; an Introduction*. Cambridge, MA: Harvard University Press.

Appendices

Appendix I
Rumi's Life

Table I Rumi's Life

Year	Major Events
c. 1148 (1152?)	Bahā'oddin Valad (1148–1231), Rumi's father, was born in Balkh: he is among the notables of the clergy of this region, a jurist, and above all a Sufi master.
1180	Shamseddin-e Tabrizi was born in Tabriz in Azerbaijan.
1207	Rumi was born in Balkh or Vakhsh.
1219	Bahā'oddin Valad leaves Khorāsan with his family following a dispute with the local political authority.
1221	Mongol invasion of Iran by Khwārazm-Shahs begins.
c. 1221–1226	Rumi's family settle in the Konya region of the sultanate of Rum, at the invitation of the local princes, where a madrasa is built for Bahā'e Valad who will be its dean.
1231	Bahā'oddin Valad passes away.
	Resumption of the functions (teaching) of the father by Rumi, after a few years of preparation under the direction of the latter as well as that of Borhānoddin Mohaqqeq.
1232–1237	Rumi left for Syria to continue his religious and mystical training. The madrasa is left in the care of Borhānoddin Mohaqqeq.
1244	Arrival of Shams in Konya and Rumi's spiritual revolution.
	Beginning of a deep spiritual relationship that illuminates Rumi forever.
	Rumi began to write poetry, in particular ghazals grouped together in the *Divān-e Shams-e Tabrizi*.
1246	Shams having left Konya, Rumi stops composing poems. He resumes the composition after receiving words from Shams.
1247	Shams is back in Konya. Continuation of the poetic activity of Rumi.
c. 1247–1248	Shams is gone for good. Theses of an assassination by jealous disciples find an echo.
	Rumi sets out to find him several times, in vain.
	Salāheddin Zarkūb succeeds Shams as Rumi's spiritual companion and inspiration.
1258	Fall of the Abbasid caliphate by the Mongols, Baghdad sack.
c. 1264	Rumi begins writing the first *Book* of *Masnavi*.
1273	Rumi dies in Konya.
	Sultān Valad, his son, succeeds him at the head of the brotherhood of disciples, thus founding the famous Sufi order of Mevlevis.

Appendix II
Rumi Translations

Table 1 Chronology of English Translations

Translator	Year	Title and Place	Source[1]
Sir William Jones	1791	Prelude of *Masnavi* in *Asiatic Society*, December 1791	*Masnavi*
James W. Redhouse	1881	*The Mesnevī (usually known as the Mesnevīyi sherīf, or holy Mesnevī) of Mevlānā (our Lord) Jelālu-d-Dīn, Muhammed, er-Rūmī*, London	*Masnavi*
Edward Henry Whinfield	1887	*Masnavi i ma'navi: The Spiritual Couplets of Mauláná Jalálu-'d-Dín Muhammed i Rúmí*, London	*Masnavi*
	1898	*Selected Poems From the Dīvāni Shamsi Tabrīz*, London	*Ghazals*
Reynold Alleyne Nicholson	1926	*The Mathnawí of Jalálu'ddín Rúmí, Vol. I–VI*	*Masnavi*
	1926	*Tales of mystic meaning: being selections from the Mathnawī of Jalāl-ud-Dīn Rūmī, Translated with an introduction by R. A. Nicolson.* London: Oneworld Publications Ltd.	*Masnavi*
	1931	*Rûmî: Poet and Mystic*	*Masnavi*
	1950	*A Rumi Anthology: Rumi: Poet and Mystic Tales of Mystic Meaning*	Mixed
William Hastie	1903	*The Festival of Spring From the Diván of Jeláleddin: Rendered in English Gazels After Rückert's Versions*, Glasgow	*Divan*
C. E. Wilson	1910	*The Masnavī, by Jalālu 'd-Dīn Rūmī. Book II*, London	*Masnavi*
Arthur John Arberry	1949	*The Ruba'iyat, of Jalāl al-Dīn Rūmī, select translations into English verse.* London: Emery Walker.	*Robā'is*
	1961	*Tales from the Masnavi*, London	*Masnavi*
	1963	*More Tales from the Masnavi*, London	*Masnavi*
	1968	*Mystical Poems of Rumi*, London	*Divan*
	1979	*Mystical poems of Rumi: second selection, poems 201–400*, London	*Divan*
	1995	*Discourses of Rumi*, London	*Fihe mā fih*

Translator	Year	Title and Place	Source[1]
Colin Garbett	1956	*Sun of Tabriz: A Lyrical Introduction to Higher Metaphysics*, Cape Town	Divan
William Chittick	1984	*The Sufi Path of Love: The Spiritual Teachings of Rumi*, Albany (New York)	Mixed
	2004	*Me and Rumi, The Autobiography of Shams-I Tabrizi*, Louisville (Kentucky)	*Maqālāt* (by Shams)
Andrew Harvey	1988	*Love's Fire*, London	Mixed
	1989	*Speaking Flame*, Ithaca (New York)	
	1996	*Love's Glory: Re-creations of Rumi*, Berkeley (California)	*Robā'i*
	1997	*How Could the Soul Not Take Flight: For Double Choir*, London	*Masnavi*
	1999	*Teachings of Rumi*, Boston	
	2002	*The Way of Passion: A Celebration of Rumi*, New York	Mixed
	2004	*Light Upon Light, Inspirations from Rumi*, New York	
Coleman Barks John Moyne	1988	*This Longing: Poetry, Teaching Stories and Letters of Rumi*, Boston	*Masnavi/ Maktubāt*
	1994	*Say I Am You: Poetry Interspersed With Stories of Rumi and Shams*, Athens, (Georgia)	
	1998	*Lion of the Heart*, London	Mixed
	1998	*Heartwood: Meditations on Southern Oaks*, New York	
	1998	*Whoever Brought Me Here Will Have to Take Me Home*, London	Mixed
	1999	*Open Secret: Versions of Rumi*, Boston	*Robā'is*
	2001	*Unseen Rain: Quatrains of Rumi*, Boston	Mixed
	2001	*The Soul of Rumi*, Boston	Mixed
	2004	*The Essence of Rumi, New Expanded Edition*, New York	*Ma'aref*
	2005	*The Drowned Book: Ecstatic and Earthy Reflections of Bahauddin, the Father of Rumi*, New York	
Colman Barks	1990	*Delicious Laughter: Rambunctious Teaching Stories from the Mathnawi of Jelaluddin Rumi*, Athens	*Masnavi*
	1995	*The Essential Rumi*, NY	
	2003	*Rumi: The Book of Love: Poems of Ecstasy and Longing*, San Francisco	Mixed
	2007	*Rumi: Bridge to the Soul: Journeys into the Music and Silence of the Heart*, San Francisco	Divan
	2010	*Rumi: The Big Red Book: The Great Masterpiece Celebrating Mystical Love and Friendship*, New York	Mixed
	2014	*Soul Fury: Rumi and Shams Tabriz on Friendship*, New York	*Maqālāt*

Translator	Year	Title and Place	Source[1]
James Cowan	1992	*Where Two Oceans Meet: A Selection of Odes From the Divan of Shems of Tabriz*, Shaftsburry	Divan
	1997	*Rumi's Divan of Shems of Tabriz: Selected Odes*, Shaftsburry	Divan
Shahram Shiva Jonathan Star	1992	*A Garden Beyond Paradise: The Mystical Poetry of Rumi*, New York	Divan
Nevit Oguz Ergin	1992	*Crazy As We Are: Selected Rubais from Divan-Kebir*, Prescott (Arizona)	Robāʿis
	1993	*Magnificent One: Selected New Verses from Divan-I Kebir*, Burdett (New York)	Divan
	1997	*A Rose Garden: Selections from Meter I of Divan-I Kebir of Rumi*, Royal Oak (Michigan)	Divan
	2007	*Divan-i Kebir*, Complete English Translation, 22 vol., Royal Oak (Michigan)	Divan
Erkan Turkmen	1992	*The Essence of Rumi's Masnevi*, Konya	Mixed
	1996	*A Bouquet of Rumi's Versified Poems*, Konya	
Madan Gopal Gupta	1993	*Maulana Rum's Masnawi Translation and Commentary*, Agra, New Delhi	Masnavi
Wheeler McIntosh Thackston	1994	*Signs of the Unseen: The Discourses of Jalaluddin Rumi*, Putney (Vermont)	Fihe mā fih
Nader Khalili	1994	*Rumi, Fountain of Fire*, Hesperia (California)	Ghazals
	2001	*Rumi, Dancing the Flame*, Hesperia (California)	Robāʿis
	2020	*The Spiritual Poems of Rumi*, New York	
	2020	*The Love Poems of Rumi*, New York	
	2020	*The Friendship Poems of Rumi*, New York	
Shahram Shiva	1995	*Rending the Veil: Literal and Poetic Translations of Rumi*, Chino Valley (Arizona)	Robāʿis
	1999	*Hush, Don't Say Anything to God: Passionate Poems of Rumi*, Fremont (California)	
	2000	*Rumi – Thief of Sleep: 180 Quatrains from the Persian*, Prescott (Arizona)	
Annemarie Schimmel	1996	*Look! This Is Love*, Boston	Mixed
Krisha Khosla	1996	*Rumi Speaks Through Sufi Tales*, Chicago	Masnavi
Muriel Maufroy	1997	*Breathing Truth, Quotations from Jalaluddin Rumi*, London	Mixed
Deepak Chopra Fereydoun Kia	1998	*The Love Poems of Rumi*, Edinburgh	Mixed

Translator	Year	Title and Place	Source[1]
Kabir Edmund Helminski	**1998**	*The Rumi Collection an Anthology of Translations of Mevlāna Jalāluddin Rumi*, Boston	Mixed
	2000	*Love Is a Stranger: Selected Lyric Poetry*, Boston	
	2001	*The Pocket Rumi Reader*, Boston	
	2010	*Love's Ripening: Rumi on the Heart's Journey*, Boston and London	
	2011	*The Rumi Daybook*, Boston	
	2011	*The Knowing Heart: A Sufi Path of Transformation*, Boston	
Kabir Edmund Helminski Camille Adams Helminski	**2000**	*Jewels of Remembrance: A Daybook of Spiritual Guidance Containing 365 Selections from the Wisdom of Mevlana Jalaluddin*, Boston	Mixed
Franklin D. Lewis	**2000**	*Rumi Past and Present, East and West: The Life, Teachings, and Poetry of Jalal al-Din Rumi*, Oxford	Mixed
	2008	*Swallowing the Sun*, Oxford	
	2009	*Mystical Poems of Rumi*, Chicago	
Reza Saberi	2000	*A thousand years of Persian rubáiyát: an anthology of quatrains from the tenth to the twentieth century along with the original Persian*. Bethesda, MD: Ibex Publishers	Robā'is
Maryam Mafi Azima Melita Kolin	**2001**	*Hidden Music*, London	Robā'is
	2012	*Rumi's Little Book of Life: The Garden of the Soul, the Heart, and the Spirit*, Newburyport (Massachusetts)	
	2014	*Rumi, Day by Day*, Newburyport (Massachusetts)	
	2014	*Rumi's Little Book of Love: 150 Poems That Speak to the Heart*, San Antonio (Texas)	
Arthur Scholey	**2002**	*The Paragon Parrot: And Other Inspirational Tales of Wisdom*, London	Masnavi
Timothy Freke	**2003**	*Rumi Wisdom: Daily Teachings from the Great Sufi Master*, New York	?
Zara Houshmand	**2003**	*Rumi's Rubaiyat*	Robā'is
	2020	http://iranian.com/Arts/rumi.html *Moon and Sun*	
Robert Bly	**1981**	*Night and Sleep*, Somerville (Massachusetts)	?
	2004	*The Winged Energy of Delight: Selected Translations*, New York	?
Jawid Mojaddedi	**2004**	*The Masnavi, Book One*, Oxford	Masnavi
	2007	*Book Two*	Masnavi
	2013	*Book Three*	
	2017	*Book Four*	
	2020	*Book Five*	

Translator	Year	Title and Place	Source[1]
Iraj Anvar	2005	Divan-I Shams-I Tabriz: Forty-Eight Ghazals, The Hague	Divan
	2008	Shams-e Parandeh (Shams the Bird): Forty-Eight Ghazals from the Divan of Shams of Tabriz, Maharashtra (India)	Divan
	2008	Say Nothing: Poems of Jalal al-Din Rumi in Persian and English (English and Farsi Edition), Sandpoint (Idaho)	Divan
Alan Williams	2006	The First Book of the Masnavi-ye Ma'navi, New York	Masnavi
	2020	The Masnavi of Rumi, Book One and Two	
Harun Yildiz	2007	Selections from Mathnawi of Rūmī, Konya	Masnavi
Nevit Oguz Ergin	2006	The Forbidden Rumi, Rochester (Vermont)	Robā'is
Will Johnson	2007	The Rubais of Rumi: Insane With Love, Rochester (Vermont)	Ghazals
Jonathan Star	2008	Rumi: In the Arms of the Beloved, New York	Mixed
Camille Helminski Refik Algan	2008	Rumi's Sun: The Teachings of Shams of Tabriz, Sandpoint (Idaho)	Divan
Ali Fuat Bilkan	2008	Tales from Rumi, Somerset (New Jersey)	Masnavi
A. G. Rawan Farhadi Ibrahim G. Gamard	2008	The Quatrains of Rūmī: Ruba'iyat- Jalaluddin Muhammad Balkhī-Rūmī, San Rafael (California)	Robā'is
Nevit Oguz Ergin Colman Barks	2009	Tales of a Modern Sufi: The Invisible Fence of Reality and Other Stories, Rochester (Vermont)	Masnavi
Philip Dunn Manuela M. Dunn	2010	The Illustrated Rumi: A Treasury of Wisdom from the Poet of the Soul, New York	Masnavi
Farrukh Dhondy	2011	Rumi: A New Translation, New York	?
	2013	Rumi: A New Translation of Selected Poems, New York	
Daniel Ladinsky	2012	The Purity of Desire: 100 Poems of Rumi, New York	Divan
Rasoul Shams	2012	Rumi: The Art of Loving, Salt Lake City (Utah)	?
Edwin Solahuddin	2013	A Spiritual Journey to the Land of Love: 40 Love Poems of Jalaluddin Rumi, Kindle Edition	?
Negar Niazi John G. Oster	2013	Rumi's Fables, North Charleston (South Carolina)	Masnavi
Evren Sener	2013	Tales from Masnavi of Rumi, North Charleston (South Carolina)	Masnavi

Translator	Year	Title and Place	Source[1]
Homa A. Garemani	2014	*Rumi's Banquet of Love*, North Charleston (South Carolina)	?
Anthony A. Lee Amin Banani	2014	*RUMI – 53 Secrets from the Tavern of Love: Poems from the Rubiayat of Mevlana Rumi*, Ashland (Oregon)	Robā'is

Table II Chronology of Translations: French

Translator	Year	Title	Source
Jacques van Wallenbourg	1799	*Traduction de Masnavi*, lost in fire, Istanbul	*Masnavi*
F. Baudry	1857	"Moïse et le Chevrier", *Magasin Pittoresque*	*Masnavi*
Henri Massé	1949	*Anthologie Persane*	*Masnavi Divan*
Assaf Hālet Tchelebi	1950	*Roubā'yāt*	*Divan: Robā'is*
Pierre Robin	1955	14 Qazals in *Les Cahiers du Sud n°4, Août 1955*	*Divan: Ghazals*
Henri Massé	1964	In *Anthologie de la poésie persane* by Zabihollah Safa	*Masnavi Divan*
Eva de Vitray-Meyerovitch and Djamchid Mortazavi	**1973** 1976 1987 1990 1990	*Odes mystiques (Dîvān-e Shams-e Tabrîzî)* *Le Livre du dedans (Fîhi-mā-fîhi)* *Rubāi'yāt (extraits)* *Mathnawî: la quête de l'absolu* *Lettres*	*Ghazals* *Fihe-mā-fih* *Robā'is* *Masnavi* *Maktubāt*
Ahmed Kudsi Erguner et Pierre Maniez	1988	*Le Mesnevi, 150 contes soufis*, Paris	*Masnavi*
Skalmowski Wojciech	1991	*Sept ghazals de Rumi* in Orientalia Lovaniensia Periodica, vol. 22	*Ghazals*
Mahin Tadjadod, Nahal Tajadod and J. C. Carrière	1993 2020	*Le livre de Chams de Tabriz* *Cette lumière est mon désir: Le Livre de Shams de Tabrîz*	*Ghazals*
Christian Jambet	1999	*Soleil du réel: poèmes d'amour mystique*	*Ghazals*
Lila Ibrahim-Ouali Bahman Namvar-Motlag	2001	*Sagesses et malices de la Perse, contes du "Masnavi"*	*Masnavi*
Rachid Koraichi	2002	*Rûmî: Le Miroir Infini*	Mixed
Juliet Mabey	2003	*Rûmî: la sagesse des derviches tourneurs*	Mixed
Marjan Foulavand	2005	*Le marchand et le perroquet*	*Masnavi*
Leili Anvar	2011	*Rûmî, La religion de l'amour*	Mixed

Table III Chronology of Translations: German

Translator	Year	Title	Source
Joseph von Hammer-Purgstall	1818	*Geschichte der schönen Redekünste Persiens*	Ghazals
August Graf von. Platen	1821	*Ghaselen*	Ghazals
Friedrich Rückert	1822	*Östliche Rosen*	Ghazals
	1838	*Mytische Ghaselen nach Dschelaleddin Rumi der Perser*	
Vincenz von Rosenzweig	1838	*Gedichte des Sams aus Täbris: Eine Auswahl*	Ghazals
Gerog Rosen	1849	*Mesnewi oder Doppelverse des Scheich Mewlana Dschelal-ed-din Rumi, aus dem Persischen übertragen von Georg Rosen*	Masnavi
Annemarie Schimmel	**1978**	*Rumi: Ich bin Wind und du bist Feuer.*	Divan
	1986	*Leben und Werk des großen Mystikers*	Mixed
	1988	*Aus dem Diwan*	
	1993	*Von Allem und vom Einen Sieh! Das ist Liebe: Gedichte: Rumi*	
Johann Christoph Bürgel	1992	*Dschalaluddin Rumi: Traumbild des Herzens – Hundert Vierzeiler*	Robā'is
Uto von Melzer	1994	*Nie ist wer liebt allein: Mystische Liebeslieder aus dem Diwan-i Šams*	Rosenzweig's translation of Ghazals
	1999	*Mondenschöner, schlafe nicht: Ruba'iyat – 102 Mystische Vierzeiler*	Robā'is
Reza Maschajechi	**2004**	*Liebesmystik: Gedichte aus dem Diwan*	Divan
	2010	*Das Lied der Flöte, Zweisprachige Ausgabe der 51 Verse des Inhaltsverzeichnisses des Mathnawi, mit Rezitation*	Masnavi
Herbert Hopfgartner	2007	*Horch mit dem Ohr der Seele den zahllosen Tönen. Musikalische Notizen über den Mystiker Dschelaleddin Rumi*	Mixed (?) Musical version
Ali Ghazanfari	2009	*Ǧalāl-ad-Dīn Rūmī: Gipfel der Liebe. Ausgewählte Vierzeiler von Rumi*	Robā'is
Christoph Engen	**2009**	*Die Musik, die wir sind*	Mixed
	2015	*Durchwachte Nacht*	
	2015	*Das Eine Lied*	
Leviculus	2018	*Rumi 33 Perlen aus dem Ozean der Liebe: Gedichte*	?
Otto Höschle	2020	*Masnawi – Gesamtausgabe in zwei Bänden*	Masnavi: Complete translation of

Table IV Chronology of Translations: Italian

Translator	Year	Title	Source
Alessandro Bausani	1980	*Poesie mistiche*	Mixed
Leonardo Vittorio Arena	1993	*Il canto del derviscio. Parabole della sapienza sufi*	*Masnavi*: from English sources
Massimo Jevolella and Barbara Brevi	1995	*Racconti sufi*	*Masnavi* From French versions
Sergio Foti	1995	*L'Essenza del Reale. Fîhi mā fîhi (C'è quel che c'è)*	*Fihe mā fih*
Giorgio Fiorentini	**2000** 2015	*L'amore è uno straniero Divan (Divan-e Sams-e Tabrizi)*	Helminski's English version *Ghazals*
Gianpaolo Fiorentini	2000	*L'amore è uno straniero poesie scelte*	*Divan*: from Helminski's English version
Gabriele Mandel Khàn and Cerati Mandel	2006	*Mathnawì. Il poema del misticismo universal* in 6 volumes	*Masnavi*: Complete translation from English and/or French versions
R. Schenardi	2013	*Il libro delle profondità interiori*	*Fihe mā fih*
Stefano Pellò	2020	*Settecento sipari del cuore*	?

Table V Chronology of Translations: Spanish

Translator	Year	Title	Source
Alberto Menzano	1997	*Poemas Sufíes*	Mixed
Vandita Martin Fernandez	2005	*Un jardín más allá del paraíso, poemas de amor de Rumi*	From Jonathan Star's English version
Michel Random	2006	*Rumi. El conocimiento y el secreto*	Mixed
Clara Janés and Ahmad Taheri	**2006** 2015	*El corazon del fuego: poemas sufíes Rubayat*	Mixed *Robā'is*
Mahmud Piruz and José María Bermejo	2010	*Luz del Alma: Selección de poemas de Rumi*	Mixed
Alfonso Colodrón	2011	*En Brazos Del Amado*	From Jonathan Star's English version
Esteve Serra Arus	2015	*Cuentos Del Mathnawi*	*Masnavi*

Appendix II

Table VI Chronology of Translations: Russian

Translator	Year	Title	Source
Collective work (?)	1974	Irano-tadzhikskaja pojezija	Anthology
Naum Grebnev	1986	Pojema o skrytom smysle: Izbrannye pritchi	Masnavi
	2005	Persidskaja klassika pory rascveta	Anthology of mixed sources
	2005	Istiny: izrechenija persidskih i tadzhikskih narodov	
Kh. G. Korogly	1991	Klassicheskaja vostochnaja pojezija: Antologija/Sost	Anthology of mixed sources
M. Stepanyants	1995	Rumi v russkih perevodah Chittik U. V poiskah skrytogo smysla. Duhovnoe uchenie	From William Chittick's version
Collective work Edited by A. A. Khismatulina	2007–2012	Masnavi-ji Ma'navi "Pojema o skrytom smysle". V shesti daftarah (prozaicheskij perevod)	First complete translation of Masnavi
D.V. Shchedrovitsky and M. Oklik	2009	Doroga prevrashhenij: sufijskie pritchi	?

Note

1 It is hard to determine the source of certain contemporary translations. In these tables, we use *ghazals* or *robā'is* to refer to these poetic forms in the *Divan*. The term *Divan* refers to a mixture of both forms as the source of the target text. The question mark means the absence of clear evidence.

Index

adaptation 4, 19, 26, 44, 47, 102, 190, 191, 219, 227, 251, 252
Aflāki, Shamsoddin Ahmad 18, 20, 26
Amir-Moezzi, Mohammad-Ali 25, 26
annexationist 24, 232, 263
Anvar, Leili 20, 25, 146, 149, 151, 179, 213, 222, 238, 240, 257, 260
Arberry, A. J. 21, 37, 47, 51, 57, 103, 106, 109, 110, 111, 119, 120, 121, 130, 148, 149, 163, 165, 168, 169, 173, 175, 189, 190, 206, 212, 214, 222, 223, 224, 225, 226, 228, 229, 232, 233, 234, 236, 237, 240, 254, 257, 259, 273
'aruż 124, 125, 128, 129, 130, 143, 150
asymptote 266, 273
āvāzi 124, 133, 134, 135, 136, 140, 150

Bahā'e Valad 16, 26
Barks, Coleman 21, 103, 105, 114, 120, 147, 169, 175, 191, 212, 222, 224, 225, 226, 228, 230, 234, 240, 254, 255, 256, 257, 263, 268
Benveniste, Émile 23, 27, 30, 50, 60, 63, 74, 80, 81, 83, 117, 121, 135, 136, 137, 138, 139, 151, 180, 214, 249
Berman, Antoine 1, 5, 49, 58, 59, 60, 88, 90, 91, 93, 95, 106, 111, 121, 212, 215, 216, 220, 225, 226, 230, 242, 245, 246, 247, 248, 250, 253, 254, 255, 258, 261, 262, 267, 268, 273, 275
beyt 18, 21, 125, 126, 127, 129, 130, 143, 148, 175
Bourdieu, Pierre 218, 230, 239, 240
Browne, Edward 12, 13, 14, 21, 27, 57, 60, 119
Bühler, Karl 81, 82, 121, 180

Chittick, William 21, 25, 213, 222, 226, 229, 260, 268
chronemic 128, 131, 139, 150
Cicero, Marcus Tullius 3, 27, 248
clarification 38, 41, 254, 274, 275
coherence 170, 184, 187, 188, 189, 190, 194, 232
connotation 7, 30, 51, 53, 75, 81, 89, 90, 106, 138, 174, 261
content-form 67, 69, 75, 77, 78, 80, 271
content-substance 67, 77, 80, 89
Corbin, Henry 7, 8, 10, 13, 24, 25, 27, 141, 150, 151, 178, 206, 213, 229

deformation/deforming 38, 80, 110, 153, 191, 212, 213, 224, 237, 242, 254, 255, 256, 258, 275, 276, 277
Dilthey, Wilhelm 258
discoursive form 3, 50, 55, 63, 75, 78, 79, 80, 81, 84, 107, 108, 112, 114, 123, 147, 153, 162, 164, 167, 171, 172, 178, 182, 195, 198, 202, 205, 221, 247, 255, 260
discoursivization 63, 71, 72, 73, 74, 77, 78, 79, 80, 84, 85, 87, 167, 180, 189, 210
During, Jean 15, 133, 150, 151
dynamic equivalence 3, 32, 47, 62, 91, 93, 167, 248, 262, 263, 264, 274

esoteric 7, 9, 16, 17, 24, 25, 182, 212, 272
ethnocentric 226, 232, 233, 236, 243, 245, 246, 261, 262
exegesis 9, 12, 17, 39, 174, 177, 259
exoteric 9, 14, 17, 182
expression-form 67, 69, 77
expression-substance 67, 69, 71, 77

field of indication 180, 181, 182, 183, 186, 191, 196, 197, 199, 201, 202, 204, 205, 211, 237, 255
field of interpretation 181, 182, 183, 191, 196, 199, 202, 205, 229, 238, 255, 256, 257, 258, 259, 267
figure of speech 60, 91, 93, 106, 153, 154, 156, 158, 161, 162, 165, 166, 169, 173, 175, 187, 194, 195
Folkart, Barbara 37, 60, 78, 79, 80, 87, 88, 118, 120, 121, 137, 151, 247, 249, 261, 262, 264, 267, 268
foreignizing 49, 51, 90, 91, 215, 247, 248, 250, 251, 258, 261, 262, 264, 273, 274, 276, 277
formal equivalence 5, 30, 32, 33, 41, 44, 57, 62, 252, 264, 266
Forūzūnfar, Badiʻozzamān 17
functional theory 70, 81, 117

Genette, Gérard 230, 255, 256, 268
Goethe, Johann Wolfgang von 4, 19, 26, 28, 219, 223, 229
Greimas, Algirdas Julien 51, 52, 58, 59, 60, 65, 68, 70, 71, 72, 73, 76, 78, 89, 90, 121, 175, 176

Hegel, Georg Wilhelm Friedrich 106, 178
Heidegger, Martin 31, 179
Helminski, Kabir Edmund 21, 22
hermeneutics 2, 180, 207, 247, 258, 265, 273, 275
Hjelmslev, Louis 59, 65, 66, 67, 68, 69, 70, 71, 73, 74, 77, 78, 79, 84, 89, 117, 118, 121, 139, 151, 209, 267
Hölderlin, Friedrich 1, 178, 246
Homāyi, Jalāleddin 125, 126, 127, 151, 154, 156, 174, 175, 176, 193, 197, 212, 214
Humbolt 4
hybridity 123, 139, 144, 188
hyperbole 91, 154, 160, 193, 200, 203, 212

icon 65, 209
imitation 4, 219, 224, 225, 251
impoverishment 8, 102, 107, 192, 254
index 65, 180, 181, 182, 205, 209
indexical 180, 181, 183, 199, 200
infradiscoursive 79, 80, 84, 88, 90, 96, 111, 114, 123, 147, 154, 155, 156, 158, 167, 169, 170, 174, 211, 243, 247, 249, 262, 271
Islamization/Islamizing 224

Jakobson, Roman 5, 23, 27, 30, 31, 32, 38, 57, 60, 62, 65, 74, 78, 80, 81, 82, 83, 84, 90, 91, 121, 122, 128, 136, 138, 151, 197, 214, 217, 243, 272, 278
Jambet, Christian 20, 44, 222

Lefevere, André 126, 151, 230, 231, 232, 236, 240
Lewis, Franklin D. 2, 18, 19, 20, 21, 25, 26, 27, 44, 45, 54, 103, 106, 108, 114, 130, 142, 145, 146, 148, 149, 151, 159, 160, 163, 165, 166, 167, 171, 191, 192, 195, 222, 225, 226, 229, 234, 236, 241, 259, 273
Lewisohn, Leonard 25, 150, 151, 178, 199, 206, 207, 213, 214
lexeme 51, 52, 53, 59, 67, 91, 118
literalist 7, 12, 51, 91, 190, 239, 243, 249, 254, 262, 273, 274
live metaphor 119, 175, 213, 270, 274

Meschonnic, Henri 5, 138, 139, 150, 151, 156, 175, 176, 215, 225, 230, 240, 242, 243, 244, 245, 247, 248, 249, 261, 262, 267, 268, 271, 272
meṣraʻ 125, 126, 129, 130, 131
metaphor 17, 25, 51, 65, 91, 93, 95, 105, 119, 134, 149, 154, 158, 160, 161, 162, 164, 175, 195, 196, 197, 198, 199, 201, 202, 204, 206, 207, 208, 209, 210, 211, 212, 242, 248
metasemia/metasemic 51, 162, 180, 181, 182, 196, 206, 209
metasemic displacement 91
meter 18, 26, 111, 124, 125, 126, 127, 128, 129, 130, 131, 132, 133, 134, 136, 138, 141, 146, 148, 150, 156, 157, 159, 160, 168, 212
Mojaddedi, Jawid 21, 41, 101, 102, 103, 106, 110, 114, 147, 159, 166, 167, 204, 213, 222, 226, 234, 240, 259
morpheme 54, 59, 75, 77, 100, 102, 107, 109, 118
music 2, 23, 36, 73, 117, 118, 123, 124, 125, 130, 132, 133, 134, 135, 136, 137, 139, 140, 142, 143, 144, 147, 152, 156, 158, 159, 227, 256, 270, 275

narratology 63
Nicholson, Raymond A. 13, 14, 17, 20, 21, 25, 27, 34, 35, 41, 49, 54, 55, 56, 58, 93, 102, 106, 109, 110, 111, 112, 115, 117, 120, 130, 146, 147, 148, 149, 161, 167, 170, 171, 175, 189, 190, 195, 202, 204,

Index 311

212, 213, 222, 223, 224, 225, 226, 228, 229, 232, 233, 234, 236, 240, 241, 254, 256, 257, 259, 260, 273
Nida, Eugene 5, 30, 32, 33, 62, 78, 167, 220, 241, 242, 247, 248, 262, 264, 268, 269

paronymy 54, 108, 153, 161
patronage 231, 233
Peirce, Charles Sanders 29, 30, 64, 65, 78, 84, 85, 122, 180, 209
poetics 60, 82, 121, 123, 124, 125, 126, 127, 128, 129, 130, 131, 132, 133, 134, 135, 136, 137, 138, 139, 140, 141, 142, 143, 144, 145, 146, 147, 148, 149, 150, 151, 152, 187, 240, 243
poetology/poetological 231
polysystem 6, 78, 110, 111, 117, 118, 126, 138, 155, 167, 216, 217, 218, 219, 220, 221, 222, 223, 224, 225, 226, 227, 228, 229, 230, 231, 232, 234, 235, 236, 238, 239, 242, 244, 245, 254, 261, 267, 276
popularizing 21, 22, 91, 189, 211, 224, 225, 226, 232, 234, 276
practical translation 87
prediscoursive 78, 79, 88, 107, 144, 177, 202
prosody 18, 124, 128, 130, 133, 138, 140, 142, 144, 147, 149, 150, 167, 170, 175, 178, 207, 274

ratio difficilis 84, 85, 86, 87, 88, 89, 95, 100, 106, 107, 114, 153, 179, 196, 209, 210, 247, 262, 270, 271, 275
rationalization 254
rediscoursivization 63, 78, 80, 84, 87, 90
referential function 37, 42, 87, 180
rhetoric 5, 46, 47, 55, 63, 86, 100, 110, 112, 116, 117, 125, 153, 154, 155, 157, 161, 162, 164, 166, 169, 170, 174, 175, 180, 184, 191, 192, 196, 197, 207, 212, 215, 270
rhyme 18, 111, 123, 124, 125, 126, 127, 129, 130, 131, 132, 134, 136, 137, 142, 143, 144, 146, 147, 148, 149, 153, 156, 159, 167, 168, 169, 170, 174, 194, 212, 255, 264, 274
rhythm 30, 63, 95, 105, 123, 124, 130, 132, 133, 134, 135, 136, 137, 138, 139, 142, 143, 144, 147, 148, 149, 150, 153, 156, 167, 175, 178, 212, 232, 243, 244, 255, 264, 272, 274, 275

Ricœur, Paul 119, 144, 159, 175, 209, 210, 212, 213, 214, 258, 269, 272, 273, 278
romanticizing 225

samāʿ, 2, 22, 54, 133, 141, 142, 143, 150, 170, 178
Saussure, Ferdinand de 29, 63, 64, 65, 66, 67, 70, 80, 122
Schimmel, Annemarie 7, 13, 19, 21, 25, 28, 45, 61, 133, 150, 151, 191, 206, 222, 225, 226, 255, 268, 269
Schleiermacher, Friedrich 1, 4, 246, 248, 250
second degree 140, 238, 255
semiotic function 83, 180
semiotics 3, 23, 29, 62, 63, 64, 65, 66, 69, 70, 81, 118, 135, 144, 159, 169, 247, 267, 277
semiotization/semiotize 31, 67, 71, 119, 141, 177, 179, 210, 260, 261, 264
Shafiʿi Kadkani, Mohammad Reza 124, 130, 134, 142, 143, 156, 200, 212
Shamisā, Sirus 98, 99, 100, 107, 119, 122, 211, 214
sociolect 77, 92, 112
sociolinguistic 6, 51, 76, 77, 90, 111
source-oriented 78, 118, 233, 242, 245, 247, 249
structural semantics 51, 68, 73, 175
sufiolect 201, 275
symbol 51, 65, 82, 161, 175, 180, 183, 203, 209, 210, 212

target-oriented 78, 216, 242, 243, 245, 247, 248, 249, 253, 263, 268
transitive translation 87
trope 89, 106, 153, 161, 180, 181, 197, 199, 209

Venuti, Lawrence 4, 5, 23, 27, 28, 227, 230, 239, 240, 241, 247, 250, 251, 252, 253, 255, 264, 265, 266, 267, 269
Vitray-Meyerovitch, Eva de 20, 22, 25, 41, 44, 54, 117, 149, 160, 190, 213, 222, 224, 225, 234, 254, 257, 260

Williams, Alan 21, 37, 41, 103, 106, 147, 148, 149, 159, 167, 187, 188, 214, 222, 224, 226, 234, 254, 259

Yarshater, Ehsan 123, 124, 152, 159

Zarrinkub, Abdolḥossein 13, 28, 60, 61

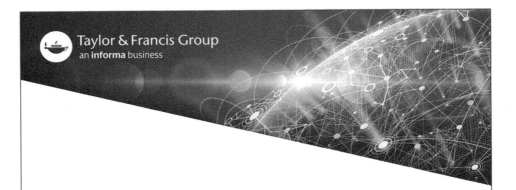